# Marriage and Same-Sex Unions

## *A Debate*

Edited by Lynn D. Wardle,
Mark Strasser, William C. Duncan,
and David Orgon Coolidge

Westport, Connecticut
London

**Library of Congress Cataloging-in-Publication Data**

Marriage and same-sex unions : a debate / edited by Lynn D. Wardle . . . [et al.].
   p.  cm.
   Includes bibliographical references and index.
   ISBN 0–275–97653–X (alk.  paper)
   1.  Same-sex marriage—United States.  2.  Gay couples—Legal status, laws, etc.—United
States.  3.  Lesbian couples—Legal status, laws, etc.—United States.  I. Wardle, Lynn D.
   HQ1034.U5M37  2003
   306.84'8'0973—dc21      2002031266

British Library Cataloguing in Publication Data is available.

Library of Congress Catalog Card Number: 2002031266
ISBN: 0–275-97653–X

First published in 2003

Praeger Publishers, 88 Post Road West, Westport, CT 06881
An imprint of Greenwood Publishing Group, Inc.
www.praeger.com

Printed in the United States of America

The paper used in this book complies with the
Permanent Paper Standard issued by the National
Information Standards Organization (Z39.48–1984).

10 9 8 7 6 5 4 3 2 1

**Copyright Acknowledgments**

The editors and publisher gratefully acknowledge permission for use of the following material:

Article by Evan Wolfson "All Together Now: A Blueprint for Winning the Freedom to Marry."
Reprinted from *The Advocate*, September 11, 2001. Copyright 2001 by Evan Wolfson. All
rights reserved.

Chapter "State Interests in Marriage" from *The Challenge of Same-Sex Marriage* by Mark
Strasser. Westport, CT: Praeger, 1991. Used by permission of Greenwood Publishing Group.

When the idea of this book began, one of its important supporters and enthusiastic co-editors was David Coolidge, Director of the Marriage Law Project at The Catholic University of America. David was indispensable in identifying and bringing together contributors and in making decisions regarding critical conceptual and organizational issues. Unfortunately, before any of the chapter manuscripts were received, David was diagnosed with a debilitating brain tumor which took his life within a few months (in March 2002) at the age of 45. In recognition of his foundational contribution to this book and, more importantly, of his commitment to reasoned and civil dialogue about marriage and same-sex unions, this book is dedicated to the memory of our friend and colleague David Orgon Coolidge.

# Contents

# Preface

Future historians studying American legal, social, and political developments at the turn of the millennium will likely identify the debate over proposals to legalize same-sex marriage or same-sex domestic partnership as one of the defining domestic policy issues of the era. Marriage implicates extremely important state and individual interests and has an exalted status, both because of what it symbolizes and because of the important benefits to which individuals having that status are entitled. The centrality of the institution of marriage for social organization has been recognized at least since the time of Aristotle, who advised that the first responsibility of wise lawmakers is to establish the rules regulating marriage. Thus it is not surprising that the proposal to legalize same-sex marriage or marriage-equivalent domestic partnerships or civil unions is and will continue to be the subject of widespread and heated public discussion.

While a great deal has been written about the legal policy issues in the escalating debate over the legal recognition of same-sex unions in the United States, there has unfortunately been very little dialogue and exchange between participants. This book is a modest attempt to open that dialogue and to exemplify the high quality of thoughtful discussion and debate that is possible.

The structure of this anthology involves a pairing of authors addressing a particular topic, one from a perspective in favor of state recognition of same-sex relationships and one from a perspective in favor of limiting state recognition to those relationships that have been traditionally recognized as marriages. Each chapter includes two main essays (one by each of the paired authors) and a response to each essay by the paired author. (In one chapter, the responding essays are by other authors.) This structure helps bring clarity to the topics under discussion, because the essayists have the opportunity not only to present their own theses but to critique an alternative perspective and thereby emphasize how their own views differ from those of the individuals with whom they have been paired. For consistency, the essay advocating the legalization of same-sex unions is presented first in every chapter, and that author has the last word also in replying to the essay of the author advocating exclusive marriage status for male-female unions.

The material is organized into four major parts, moving from historical and general social perspectives to the legal and specific. It begins, in part I, with three sets of paired essays concerning general historical and social perspectives on the legalization of same-sex unions. Evan Wolfson and Maggie Gallagher set the debate in terms of contemporary history and social order. Mark Strasser and John Witte, Jr., continue the dialogue by reviewing the lessons of tradition versus public policy. Arthur S. Leonard and Lynne Marie Kohm focus on marriage policy in their paired essays. Part II offers perspectives from legal and political philosophy regarding the issue of legalizing same-sex unions. Stephen Macedo and Robert P. George reprise their celebrated *Georgetown Law Journal* articles assessing and critiquing natural-law perspectives on marriage and same-sex unions; the responses to those classics are provided by Lynn D. Wardle and Mark Strasser. Carlos A. Ball and Teresa Stanton Collett provide contrasting views on the public advantages of legalizing same-sex unions versus the public interest in restricting marriage to potential childbearing unions. William N. Eskridge, Jr., distilling his new book, articulates equality arguments for legalizing same-sex marriage, while Lynn D. Wardle responds with a critique of the substitution of generic "relationships" for marriages in public policy. Part III turns to specific constitutional doctrines. Andrew Koppelman argues that prohibiting same-sex marriage constitutes impermissible discrimination, while Richard G. Wilkins makes the case why legal preference for heterosexual marriage has been and still is constitutional. David B. Cruz argues that the First Amendment mandates legal recognition of same-sex unions, while Richard F. Duncan distinguishes laws restricting marriage to male-female couples from laws restricting the rights of gays that have been ruled impermissible. Three pairs of essays discussing specific issues of state constitutional law and international law complete the anthology in part IV. Greg Johnson celebrates the advantages of Vermont's civil-unions statute, while William C. Duncan criticizes the interpretation of state constitutional law mandating legalization of same-sex unions. Barbara J. Cox and Patrick J. Borchers present different analyses regarding whether state choice-of-law rules necessitate interjurisdictional recognition of same-sex unions. Finally, James D. Wilets and Robert John Araujo, S.J. provide competing interpretations of whether international law requires or encourages legalization of same-sex unions.

This anthology reflects the wide range of issues implicated in the debate over marriage and same-sex unions. Questions related to jurisprudence, political theory, history, constitutional doctrine, international law, public policy, and family law are addressed in an effort to clarify the significant legal issues raised by the possibility of (re)defining marriage to include same-sex couples or of creating a quasi-marital status (generally called "domestic partnership") extending some legal recognition and marital benefits to same-sex couples.

The authors of the essays and responses in this collection have expertise in a variety of legal and nonlegal academic disciplines and include many of the most knowledgeable and widely respected scholars who have expressed opinions on opposite sides of the same-sex marriage issues. Yet the contributions to this anthology have been written for a general audience of educated readers, not just for experts in the law or in any other discipline. The goal has been to educate the thoughtful general public in the competing arguments and perspectives implicated in the social policy controversy.

The image of the current marriage controversy that is conveyed in this anthology is one of stark division and strong disagreement on many matters, but it is also a picture of willingness to continue a debate of high intellectual and civic quality, with good faith and good will, in the belief that a well-informed citizenry will support the most just and enlightened resolution to the public policy issues implicated. As the initiators and editors of this anthology, we hope that the debate that has begun in this work will continue in other settings with the same quality, good will, openness to dialogue, and mutual respect that characterize these written exchanges.

# Part I

# Marriage and Same-Sex Unions in Comparative, Historical, and Family Policy Perspectives

# Chapter 1

Essay One

# *All Together Now*

## Evan Wolfson

We can win the freedom to marry. Possibly within five years. This bold declaration, which I hope becomes a rallying cry, raises many questions— not the least of which are: Why marriage and why now? Who's "we"? How do we do it? And, five years?

Before I tackle those questions, though, let's savor the possibilities: We can seize the terms of the debate, tell our diverse stories, engage the nongay persuadable public, enlist allies, work the courts and the legislatures in several states, and achieve a legal breakthrough within five years. I'm talking about not just any legal breakthrough but an actual change in the law of at least one state, ending discrimination in civil marriage and permitting same-sex couples to lawfully wed. This won't just be a change in the law either; it will be a change in society. For if we do it right, the struggle to win the freedom to marry will bring much more along the way. It is not just the attainment but the engagement that will move us furthest and fastest.

But first, let me tackle those questions.

## WHY MARRIAGE AND WHY NOW?

Marriage is many things in our society. It is an important choice that belongs to couples in love. In fact, many people consider their choice of partner the most important choice they ever make. Civil marriage is also a legal gateway to a vast array of protections, responsibilities, and benefits (most of which cannot be replicated in any other way). These include access to health care and medical decision making for your partner and your children; parenting and immigration rights; inheritance, taxation, Social Security, and other government benefits; rules for ending a relationship while protecting both parties; and the simple ability to pool resources to buy or transfer property without adverse tax treatment.

After passing the federal antimarriage law marketed as the "Defense of Marriage Act" in 1996, the government cataloged more than 1,049 ways in which married people are accorded special status under law. Add in the state-level protections and the intangible and tangible privileges marriage brings in private life, and that makes more than 1,049 ways in which lesbians and gay couples are ripped off.

Marriage is a known commodity, permitting couples to travel without playing "now you're legally next of kin; now you're legally not." It is a social statement, describing and defining one's relationships and place in society. It is also a personal statement of commitment that receives public support and can help achieve common aspirations for stability and structure in life. It has spiritual significance for many of us and familial significance for nearly all of us.

Finally, marriage is the vocabulary in which nongay people talk of love, family, dedication, self-sacrifice, and stages of life. It is the vocabulary of love, equality, and inclusion. While recognizing that marriage should not be the sole criterion for benefits and support, nor the only family form worthy of respect, the vast majority of lesbians and gay men want the freedom to marry for the same mix of reasons as nongay people.

In the past several years we have turned an idea virtually no one talked about into a reality waiting to happen. A 1999 NBC News/Wall Street Journal poll reported that two-thirds of all Americans have come to believe that gay people will win the freedom to marry. And we know that if they believe it will happen, on some level they are learning to live with it—the positive precondition to our achieving it. This extraordinary new receptivity comes only eight years after the Hawaii Supreme Court first launched this national discussion.

We can call the first chapter of our ongoing freedom-to-marry movement the "Hawaii/Vermont" chapter. Its successes were enormous. Through court cases in both states we showed that there is no good reason for sex discrimination in civil marriage, just as there was no good reason for race discrimination in civil marriage a generation ago.

We also redefined the national debate over lesbian and gay inclusion, fostering recognition that marriage is central to any discussion about lesbian and gay equality. This was dramatically demonstrated by last year's vice presidential debate between Dick Cheney and Joe Lieberman, both of whom answered a question about gay love by talking about their evolving (and increasingly supportive) positions on marriage.

The Hawaii/Vermont chapter moved the center of our country to the "all but marriage" position. Whereas before the marriage debate, the nongay majority did not support any kind of partner recognition for same-sex couples, now we see majority support for health benefits, inheritance, and other kinds of recognition of our family relationships. That is a product of talking about our lives in the vocabulary of full equality and a happy consequence of asking nongay people to hear our stories.

In June 2000 an Associated Press poll put opposition to our freedom to marry at only 51%; the latest Gallup Poll puts it at 52%. A recent survey shows college freshmen strongly supporting our freedom to marry as well. My latest favorite poll, however, came in New York magazine early this year. It reported that 58% of nongay New Yorkers support civil marriage for gay people, and that 92%(!) of gay people agree.

All of this is occurring, of course, against a backdrop of international advances. It has been only 12 years since Denmark became the first country to create "gay marriage" (not marriage itself but a parallel marital status for same-sex couples). In 2001 the Netherlands became the first to dispense with separate and unequal formulas and allow same-sex couples to lawfully wed. Other European nations, and possibly the European Union as a whole, will certainly follow suit in the years to come. Meanwhile, Canada—which already has recognized same-sex couples' legal entitlement to "all but marriage"— is also in the midst of a campaign aimed at securing the freedom to marry.

Finally, the Hawaii/Vermont chapter brought us "gay marriage"— though not yet marriage itself—here at home. With the passage of the civil union law, Vermont created a parallel nonmarriage marital status for same-sex couples, upon which we can build.

It is worth remembering that we didn't get civil unions by asking for civil unions. We got this separate and unequal status by pressing for the freedom to marry. In Vermont local activists, New England's Gay and Lesbian Advocates and Defenders, and our allies mounted a campaign of public outreach, enlisting clergy, speaking at county fairs, and then folding in litigation—groundwork that led to victory through sustained engagement. With these successes as our new starting point, it's time for us to open the next chapter in our movement.

## WHAT ABOUT ASKING FOR LESS?

Civil unions are a tremendous step forward, but they are not good enough. They do not provide equal benefits and they leave couples and those who deal with them exposed to legal uncertainty. What we want is not separate and unequal "gay marriage" but marriage itself, the full range of choices and protections available to our nongay sisters and brothers. We do ourselves no favor when we enter this civil rights discussion bargaining against ourselves.

The attempt not to talk about marriage, to have a discussion without using the *m* word, increasingly fails. The fierce (and ongoing) right-wing backlash against civil unions in Vermont (and the right wing's use of marriage and civil unions as a club against us in campaigns in other states) shows that we do not gain much ground by calling it something else or running away from the debate. Our opponents are against us no matter what we seek. When we fight merely not to be beaten up in the streets, they are against us. If we were asking for oxygen, they would be against us. Our opponents will redefine everything we seek as "a slippery slope to gay marriage" and attack us with equal ferocity, no matter what.

If we are going to have to face opposition and work to engage the middle no matter what we strive for, why not ask for all we deserve? Remember, it is no coincidence that the two states in which we have the most expansive protections and recognition for gay people are the two in which we framed the discussion in terms of full equality.

## WHO'S "WE," AND WHAT IS THE NEW APPROACH?

It is time for a peacetime campaign to win the freedom to marry. We cannot win equality by focusing just on one court case or the next legislative battle—or by lurching from crisis to crisis. Rather, like every other successful civil rights movement, we must see our struggle as long-term and must set affirmative goals, marshal sustained strategies and concerted efforts, and enlist new allies and new resources.

More than ever, then, "we" means key organizations in key battleground states working in partnership; a national resource center doing what is best done centrally; talented and dedicated individuals who bring new resources and new focus to the table; existing and new national groups prioritizing real work on marriage; and most critically, nongay allies.

Clearly we can—and must—motivate nongay allies to become vocal advocates. Fortunately, we have good models for doing so. For instance, we can examine and replicate how the parents of students creating gay-straight alliances—or the parents, funders, and others who have taken action against Boy Scouts discrimination—have defined their relation to our civil rights and created a public responsibility and role for themselves.

Since there is no marriage without engagement, we must make enhanced efforts to have our allies speak out in a variety of forums—everything from advertorials to interfaith dialogues to TV talk shows such as *Oprah* and *Larry King Live*—describing to other nongay Americans why it's important for them to support the freedom to marry for gay and lesbian couples.

We also can enlist diverse allies among other constituencies (religious, labor, child welfare, youth, seniors, business, etc.) and seek ways to work together with overlapping communities such as women and people of color. For example, we can find common ground through joint projects to deal with problems we all face with immigration discrimination or access to health care.

Imagine, for example, a collaboration between the National Center for Lesbian Rights and La Raza or the Japanese American Citizens League, in which each group agreed to send collective information on immigration concerns to its mailing lists and then cohost a program that included gay concerns, spokespeople, and stories.

The good news here is that nongay people live in the world of marriage, and in many cases they will be more responsive to our call to join this work. As the growing list of signatories on the Marriage Resolution (www. lambdalegal.org) attests, many of them have already. We must give nongay opinion leaders at the national level as well as local clergy or organizations the impetus and framework for engaging the public on our freedom to marry.

## HOW DO WE DO IT?

Our opponents have announced yet another antigay campaign—an effort to promote a federal constitutional amendment to permanently exclude lesbians and gay men from all family protections, including marriage. Outrageous as this latest assault is, there are lessons we can learn from them: the power of a campaign over time, the importance of framing the terms of the debate, the need to present diverse and compelling stories and allies, the ability to make attainable what at one time seemed radical. The good news here is that their attack offers us an occasion to take our case to the people. We should not shy away.

I envision a sustained effort to win the freedom to marry, centering on focused work to attain a legal breakthrough in one or more states, together with sophisticated national work to create a climate of receptivity. The elements of this sustained effort would be

- serious multimethodology, multiyear freedom-to-marry efforts under way in the most promising breakthrough states. The partners in these efforts would strategically mount litigation or legislative measures to end discrimination in civil marriage, but the specific vehicles would take place within the context of our undertaking enhanced public education and outreach work.
- development of a clear and sophisticated understanding of what demographics we need to reach in order to firm up our 30%–35% base and soften up and move the 15%–20% of the public who are movable.
- deployment of resources, trainings, messages, messengers, and vehicles to help nongay and gay partners in different states and constituencies communicate transformative information and enlist additional nongay support.

For example, we need to communicate resonant portrayals that show how the exclusion of gay people from marriage has a real and detrimental impact on children, families, and society; how withholding marriage does injustice and cruel harm to lesbian and gay seniors; how the United States is lagging behind other countries; how separate and unequal treatment is wrong; and why the government should not interfere with same-sex couples who choose to marry and share fully and equally in the rights, responsibilities, and commitment of civil marriage.

Let's relate the stories of seniors and how they are denied the social safety net that comes with marriage. Let's talk about the California schoolteacher who died after 30 wonderful years teaching kids, leaving her partner unable to share her pension or Social Security death benefits—or even remain in the home they shared. Or we can discuss how, if the teacher had survived and sought to move with her partner into an assisted-living facility, they might have found themselves forbidden to live together.

Marriage discrimination wreaks real harms—kids teased because they don't have a "real family," a nonbiological parent told he or she cannot pick up an ailing child at the school because of not being legally related, couples unable to transfer income or property between them.

Let's trace the experiences—good and bad—of the 2,000-plus couples that have joined in civil union in Vermont. Let's pick up on reports such as the 1999 Stanford University study that showed how denying marriage to same-sex couples hurts kids. Let's describe the cruel sundering of binational couples, the partners turned away at hospitals, the callous dismissal of a lifetime of love in cases such as Sharon Smith's claim for wrongful death when her partner was killed in a horrible dog mauling. Let's also convey the strengths and vibrancy of many gay and lesbian couples such as my former clients Richard and Ron, who just celebrated their 31st anniversary, or my friends Jamie and Mark, who gathered friends and family from around the country to celebrate their wedding in a lovely church ceremony. Let's make sure that America hears the voice of Jamie's father, describing his growth in acceptance and wish that society could now do the same. Our job is to develop and deploy a strategic mix of messages that tell the diverse and real stories of our lives and love in a vocabulary of equality that reaches the middle.

## WHY FIVE YEARS?

Obviously no one can promise this breakthrough on any specific timetable, so of course I mean that this is doable within five years, but the victory may happen later . . . or sooner. We had victory within our reach in Hawaii years ago, only to see it blocked there because of our failure to act swiftly and strongly enough. But our opponents know the importance of sticking with the fight, and so must we. We must be prepared to ride the ups and downs. Our leaders and national organizations need to understand the lessons of the previous marriage battles as well as the lessons we should have learned from the battles over the military, federal civil rights legislation, and the Boy Scouts. Among those lessons: We cannot expect to win equality in one short burst of attention or one wartime campaign alone. Rather, we must lay the groundwork and not just try to cherry-pick the easy wins or "flavor of the month" issues.

Another lesson is that it is a mistake to define our cultural engagement and the work of our civil rights movement by what seems currently realistic or attainable in the legislatures (or the courts). For one thing, our ability to predict is often limited. I have seen us win battle after battle in state legislatures, even when our lobbyists and some of our groups said it couldn't be done; likewise, courts sometimes surprise us. More broadly, the larger work we must do (the multimethodology peacetime campaign) should not be reduced to the bills. We do the groundwork in order to build up ammo and allies for eventual legislative battles, and in order to create the climate of receptivity to prepare and embolden the courts. Our job, of course, is not to make it easy for politicians or judges (even friendly ones) to do what they want; rather, it is to make it easier for politicians to do what we want— to do justice. We should not dumb-down our demand for equality, for possibilities open up not in some linear, tidy way but in spurts of creeping and leaping. Through our work and by aiming high, we make room for luck.

## WHAT DO WE WANT TO BUILD NOW?

Last year marked the end of an extraordinarily successful chapter in the history of our civil rights movement, from the attainment of "gay marriage" to the nongay response against the Boy Scouts' discrimination. Now, in this next chapter, each of us must ask what we want to create for the young gay and nongay people watching our work and finding their voice.

To me the answer is clear: Let us build not a building or a halfway house or a better ghetto but rather a movement unafraid to seek what we and all others deserve, unafraid to reach beyond itself to talk with our nongay fellow Americans. Shimmering within our reach is a legal structure of respect, inclusion, equality, and enlarged possibilities, including the freedom to marry. Let us build the new approach, partnership, tools, and entities that can reach the middle and bring it all home.

## NOTE

Reprinted with permission from the *Advocate*, September 11, 2001.

Response

# A Reality Waiting to Happen: A Response to Evan Wolfson

## Maggie Gallagher

Evan Wolfson and I agree on many important issues. The debate over gay marriage is not primarily theoretical or academic. Gay marriage is imminent: "Possibly within five years." Five years at the outside, I would say, absent a dramatic reframing of the issue in the public mind and (in particular) among elites, whose support for same-sex unions as a civil rights issue is driving legal opinion.

Like Evan Wolfson, I believe that "this won't just be a change in the law either; it will be a change in society." In the past several years, he writes, "we have turned an idea virtually no one talked about into a reality waiting to happen." "Through court cases in both states [Hawaii and Vermont] we showed that there is no good reason for sex discrimination in civil marriage, just as there was no good reason for race discrimination in civil marriage a generation ago."

Like Evan Wolfson, I have been struck by how weak and ineffective the intellectual response to the challenge of defending the inherently sexual (rather than unisex) basis of marriage has been. Struck, but not surprised. For veterans of the marriage wars over the last twenty years the relative ineffectualness of defenders of the customary order—what I have here called normal marriage—is nothing new. When in the seventies marriage began to be redefined as one of many different equally valid sexual lifestyles (both in a long line of court cases stripping marriage of much of its preferred status and in the court of public opinion), defenders of customary marriage were similarly tongue-tied and for similar reasons. It is the nature of custom to be relatively dumb—that which has always been has never before required sophisticated intellectual argument to defend. Yet while custom or norms are not always correct and are often in need of reform, the relative inarticulateness of their defenders is no true measure of the truth or social value of what they seek to defend.

To this veteran of the marriage wars, the juggernaut for same-sex marriage, redefined as a personal right that only hatred and unreason prevent from coming to fruition, looks startlingly similar to the juggernaut for the divorce culture raised by elites in the sixties and seventies. Then too preliminary social science evidence was treated as unassailable proof that reason was on the side of divorce—easy and often. Children, we were told, after a brief period of crisis, recuperated and indeed did better when parents divorced. It took twenty years of more careful, sophisticated research and a whole generation of children of divorce who could, as adults, tell their own stories to remind us that the wisdom of the ages is not always wrong: When parents do not get married or do not build decent marriages, children suffer. Children who do not live with their fathers often feel abandoned by them. Great damage was done to both culture and law in the interim, damage that we are only now beginning to address and painfully seeking ways to undo.

While keeping mind and heart open to the stories of individual distress that Evan Wolfson tells us he plans to bring center stage, Americans of good heart and good will should not forget the far larger story of distress engraved in the hearts of millions of fatherless American children. Gay marriage requires us to embrace precisely the ideas that we need to abandon to redress this terrible toll of suffering. In a society that understands marriage as a key institution tying fathers to children and bringing mothers and fathers together in sexual unions where children are celebrated, not hindrances to adult satisfaction, decent adults of all sexual orientations will think twice or three times before placing same-sex unions at the forefront of our marriage agenda in law or public policy.

Evan Wolfson's response begs precisely the key question: is marriage just another word for a private, intimate relationship, in which case, as he says, anyone's same-sex marriage will have no impact at all on anyone else's marriage because there is enough marriage to go around? Or is marriage a normative social institution, having as its raison d'être precisely to prefer, support, and encourage a certain kind of sexual union—long lasting, child centered, faithful—precisely because this kind of sexual union plays a unique role in the protection of children and the reproduction of society?

Same-sex marriage interrupts the communicative, channeling, and signaling function of marriage law: to instruct young lovers and remind the wider society of two key ideas: (1) children need mothers and fathers, and (2) societies need babies to survive and prosper. Decouple marriage law from its basic grounding—the people who make the baby are supposed to care for the baby and each other too—and you have gutted its major purpose and usefulness.

A clearer example of what happens to family law when the relationships model of marriage is adopted could not be found than the Canadian law report Wolfson cites, "Beyond Conjugality," which argues that grounding family law in kinship obligation or conjugal relations is just too restrictive. The purpose of the law should be to regulate adult close personal relationships in the interests of equality and autonomy. Why these are the key values, or why the law has an important role in regulating them, as opposed to any other set of values, is unargued and perhaps unarguable. Certainly, in this intellectual framework, the role of the law in promoting and protecting the family as a unit with an important and coherent purpose dissipates. We are left with adults who have all kinds of intimacy needs the law is somehow supposed to acknowledge or sustain.

The family as a system is grounded not in equality and autonomy but in dependence and obligation: in the production, rearing, and nurturing of the next generation. Marriage is the means by which societies do their best to secure fathers for children and to encourage lovers to make babies in the best possible circumstances. Reshaping family law to affirm the intimate choices of adults, whatever they are, is precisely the opposite of the direction we need to move to effectively confront the really big crisis we are facing: the epidemic of fatherlessness and the ongoing depopulation of societies that adopt postmodern family systems.

When the law institutionalizes same-sex marriage, it affirms that children do not need mothers and fathers, and that marriage has nothing to do with babies. In a society in which millions of children now suffer from poverty and trauma caused by widespread fatherlessness, this is a potentially dangerous and callous message for legal elites to send.

Essay Two

# Normal Marriage: Two Views
## Maggie Gallagher

What is marriage for?[1]

Every known human society has some form of marriage. In every advanced society, marriage exists as a public, legal act and not merely a private romantic or religious rite. Why?

Advocates of same-sex unions have done us the favor of pushing the intellectual debate over marriage to the deepest questions. Before we can decide whether sex is irrelevant (or how it is relevant) to the public purposes of marriage, we have to decide what those public purposes are. Why does the state get involved in the intimate lives of its citizens?

There are two views at play in the public square, marriage as a public bond and sexual institution or marriage as a private emotional relationship. They are not mutually exclusive, in the sense that most Americans today draw their understanding of marriage from both streams. But ultimately these two competing visions of what marriage is for lead the law in dramatically opposing directions.

## THE RELATIONSHIP VIEW

Here is one view: Marriage is an essentially private, intimate, emotional relationship created by two people for their own personal reasons to enhance their own personal well-being. Marriage is created by the couple for the couple.

It is wrong and discriminatory, as well as counterproductive, therefore, for the state to privilege certain kinds of intimate relations over others. Marriage has a legal form but no specific content. Each person has the right to socially express his or her own inner vision of family, sexuality, and intimacy on an equal basis.

Sometimes this argument is made in its strongest possible form. As Rutgers law professor Drucilla Cornell put it, "The state should have no right to privilege or impose one form of family structure or sexuality over another. This would mean that some adults could choose *consensual* polygamy. Mormon men could have more than one wife. Four women who worship the mother goddess could also recognize and form a unity and call their relationship a marriage. There would be no state-enforced single relationship— not monogamy, heterosexuality, polygamy, or polyandry. . . . [Legislating] love and [conscripting] men is a sign of the fear of, not a solution to, the crisis of families. Intimate associations are different undertakings. They always have been so. The freedom to form families opens up the possibility of people creating their own families in the way most suitable to them."[2]

More often, it is tempered with an acknowledgment that the state does have a potential interest in regulating intimate relations, including marriage, but it is limited to the protection of existing dependents. To the extent that marriage protects the weak (children), the state may prefer marriage. But it makes no sense in this view for the state to deny the benefits of marriage to any two people, especially any two people with children. The only goods of marriage that the state confers are a small number of practical advantages in inheritance, Social Security, and health insurance law. There is no rational reason, therefore, to withhold these benefits from any couple who wishes to claim them on behalf of themselves or (especially) their dependents. When it comes to same-sex unions, these advocates typically rely on social science to uphold their claim that there is no rational reason why marriage should be understood as an inherently sexual (rather than unisex) institution.

More recent reviews of this body of literature call these claims into question. Due to problems in sample selection and size, study design, and other technical flaws, the current body of social science literature on gay parenting cannot tell us whether or not there are any important differences between children raised by their own two married mothers and fathers and children raised by two same-sex parents. Social science evidence, as it now stands, certainly does not refute the idea that children do better raised by their own two married mothers and fathers.[3]

Finally, even more commonly, this view of marriage as primarily an emotional good created by the private couple leads to calls (and in countries outside the United States to judicial rulings and legislation) to abolish any distinction between cohabitation and marriage, or between what some call formal and informal unions. In the summer of 2000, writing in *Family Law Quarterly*, Harry D. Krause put it this way:

[A]n irrational, sentimental cocoon . . . has clouded logical discussion and intelligent debate. . . . Today's sexual and associational lifestyles differ so much that the state should not continue to deal with them as though they were one: the old role-divided, procreative marriage of history. That marriage may not yet be history, but it should be seen for what it has become: one lifestyle choice among many.

A pragmatic, rational approach would ask what social functions of a particular association justify extending what social benefits and privileges. Marriage, *qua* marriage, would not be the one event that brings into play a whole panoply of legal consequences. Instead, legal benefits and obligations would be tailored according to the realities—speak social value—of the parties' relationship.

With regard to tax laws that treat married and cohabiting couples differently, he concludes: "The rational answer seems clear: Married and unmarried couples who are in the same *factual* positions should be treated alike."[4]

What difference does the fact of marriage make? None, because marriage is just a word for a relationship actually created by and for the couple. I looked in vain for a footnote, but of course there was none. A distinguished legal scholar in a major journal simply assumed that the idea that cohabitation and marriage are functional equivalents was self-evident, once the cocoon of sentiment was stripped away by a hardheaded rationalist like himself—so deeply ingrained in certain circles has the idea become that marriage is no more than a piece of paper that delivers certain legal benefits, and that is all.[5]

It is important to note that these contesting views of marriage have implications that cannot be confined to the same-sex-marriage debate. Are single-parent families a sign of distress or an example of expanding personal choice? Should opposite-sex cohabitors be viewed as the functional equivalent of married couples? Is it fair for the tax code to tax married couples more—or less? Is divorce a unilateral right of the individual?

In the larger sweep of history, despite significant countercurrents,[6] this view of marriage as emotional intimacy is gaining dramatic ground. In this sense, same-sex marriage is not an outlandish deviation; it is the logical result of the rather popular contemporary view of marriage as a personal right of the individual, created by the individual, for purposes that the individual alone defines. When two individuals who happen to have desires and tastes for each other coincide for a lifetime, that is beautiful. If not, it just is not anybody else's business.

Of course, if this is what marriage is for, many things about the state's traditional regulation of marriage become difficult to understand. It is difficult to understand in this scheme why the state would be involved in marriage at all, or why marriage must be confined to the couple, or why, even at the most basic level, the word *marriage* requires intimacy at all. If fairness is the issue, why can a worker give his health insurance benefits only to someone he or she is sleeping with? Why do you have to live together? Why can't business partners declare their relationship a marriage and save on the insurance premiums?

Drucilla Cornell is correct, but she does not see far enough. If marriage is just another word for an intimate union, then the state has no legitimate reason to insist that it even be intimate unless the couple, or the quadruplets, want it so. For the individual to be truly free to make unconstrained intimate choices, marriage itself must be deconstructed.

What about the children? There the state will, as Cornell puts it, separate the parenting alliance from the sexual alliance. Adults will still have obligations to children, but they will be severed from their newly unfettered intimate adult lives. What then is the source of adult obligation to specific children? There are only two possible answers: biology and contract.

Advocates of the alternative have diligently pushed the idea that contract, not biology, creates parental obligations, in part because it is the only possible way for same-sex couples to have children together. The old stubborn reality that the people who make the baby are its parents must be shoved aside to accommodate an infinite diversity of adult choice. The people who thought up the baby are its real parents. So, for example, a surrogate mother is not a mother—the baby she carries is not hers because she did not intend for it to be hers. The mind is more important than the body, especially to people with Ph.D.s.

Of course, this latter view coincides with one important reality. It is easy to make a baby, hard to love and protect and provide for children to adulthood. One important goal of state regulation of intimacy has been to ensure that children have what they need. Advocates of family diversity tell us that it is therefore cruel to deprive any actual child of whatever benefit can be milked from the state by having the law prefer any family form. If the adults have decided to be parents, the state should applaud and enforce this decision, no matter how or who or even how many. So a *New York Times* story in 2000 applauded the growing legal acceptance of gay families, like those Joseph DeFillipis and his partner, David Koteles, are in the process of making. "[T]he men entered into an arrangement to conceive a child with a lesbian couple and to raise him or her jointly . . . The arrangement could lead to a tangle of legal questions should the foursome pull in different directions." But "DeFillipis and his three prospective co-parents have not been to a lawyer. . . . Instead for the last two years, they have discussed every conceivable area of dispute, including religion, geography and finances."[7] Two parents are good, four parents are better, in this view.

But its advocates, narrowly focused as they are on the urgent desires of a small number of adults to make their unorthodox family dreams come true, ignore the implications of this argument for vast numbers of children. Even today, most children are created by acts of the body, not the will. The best data indicate that about half of all pregnancies are unintended (including about a fifth of marital births and 58 percent of unwed births). Close to half of all women will experience an unintended pregnancy.[8] Sex makes babies, sometimes on purpose, but frequently not. The womb also has its reasons, which reason knows not.

If it is choice and contract that create parental obligations, why do these mothers have any obligations for the creatures of their bodies? Why are they not legal strangers to their own babies unless they voluntarily choose to contract obligations? On a less theoretical plane, why are we hounding poor men for child support, for babies for which they never contracted? Why would any man ever feel an obligation to take care of—or even marry—the mother of the children his body created? If it is adult choice that creates parental obligation, we are imposing a monstrous injustice on some of the least privileged men in this society, as well as some of the better-off.

I interviewed a man recently—an army officer—who wanted to divorce his wife because she had become pregnant. They had an agreement, he thought, never to have children. He felt utterly betrayed. Was he justified?

Once we sever, conceptually, the sexual alliance and the parenting alliance, we sever children from their uncontested claim on their parents'—especially their fathers'—care and protection. It is the fathers who disappear, because while fathers and mothers are equally beloved and important to their children, fatherhood and motherhood are not equally natural or inevitable. Far more than mothers, reliable fathers are cultural creations, products of specific ideals, norms, rituals, and mating and parenting practices. Today, after thirty years of sexual revolution, only 60 percent of American children now live with their own two married parents.[9] Of the remaining 40 percent, the overwhelming majority live with their single or remarried mothers.[10]

A vast body of social science evidence shows that children who are not raised by their own married mother and father are at increased risk[11] for just about every negative outcome social scientists know how to measure: including physical illness, mental illness, school failure, child abuse, substance abuse, early unwed pregnancy, and criminal misconduct.[12] There is no evidence from the social sciences (including the literature on gay parenting) that credibly disrupts the assumption that a child does better raised by his or her own married mother and father.[13] But even if better research showed that individual same-sex couples do a good job with their individual children, the institutionalization of same-sex unions as marriages still threatens the well-being of other children and the public purposes (or, to lapse into legal terminology, the state's interest) in marriage.

Good fathers are made, not born. When family and sexual norms are weakened, it is generally children's access to fathers, not mothers, that is at risk. When we tell adults that parenting obligations are created by free choices of adults that the law only sanctions after the fact, the well-being of children is put at risk.

Two questions are raised by the prospect of unisex marriage: (1) Can a society or culture reliably make men into good fathers while at the same time affirming in its governing family law that children do not need mothers and fathers, and that it is choice, not biology, that creates family obligations? (2) Can a society that adopts the set of ideas and ideals driving the post-modern family even survive? I think that the answer to both these questions is, demonstrably, no.

## MARRIAGE AS A UNIVERSAL HUMAN INSTITUTION

What is the alternate view of marriage? Some might call it traditional, but this is really not the right term, in the sense that this broad view of marriage is not the product of some specific tradition—custom, religion, or culture. The specific contours of our own inherited marriage tradition, deeply rooted in Judeo-Christian culture, which include reciprocal pledges of lifelong monogamy and fidelity, are, of course, not universal. Defending these particular contours is a task for another day.

But what every known human society calls marriage shares certain basic, recognizable features, including most especially the privileging of the reproductive couple, in order to protect both the interests of children and the interests of the society. Marriage is everywhere the word we use to describe a public sexual union between a man and a woman that creates rights and obligations between the couple and any children the union may produce.[14] Marriage as a public tie obligates not only fathers, but fathers' kin to recognize the children of this union. Marriage is in every society the sexual union where childbearing and raising are not only tolerated but applauded and encouraged. Marriage is the way in which every society attempts to channel the erotic energies of men and women into a relatively narrow, but highly fruitful channel, to give every child the father his or her heart desires. Above all, normal marriage is normative. The society defines for its young what the relationship is and what purposes it serves. Successful societies do this not only because children need fathers, but also because societies need babies. It is a truism, frequently forgotten by large complex societies, that only societies that reproduce survive.

In the context of the contemporary Western family system, this point is not as academic as most people think. In addition to the direct pain and suffering caused by family breakdown (driven by the idea that children do not need families consisting of mothers and fathers, and that the sexual desires and freedoms of adults are more important than family norms), the evidence of reproductive dysfunction in all societies that adopt these post-modern family ideas is, at this point, overwhelming. For two generations every Western, industrialized nation has had subreplacement birthrates. In America, the crisis is still many generations off because our birthrates are closer to replacement and our social tolerance of immigration is higher. But many European nations are on the road to dying out, absent dramatic changes in reproductive patterns. By the year 2050, Italy's population is projected to decline by more than a quarter. The political, economic, and cultural implications of European depopulation are likely to be profound.[15]

Normal marriage is normative. Marriage does not merely reflect individual desire; it shapes and channels it. Marriage as a social institution communicates that a certain kind of sexual union is, in fact, our shared ideal: one where a man and a woman join not only their bodies, but their hearts and their bank accounts, in a context where children are welcome. Of course, not everybody wants or achieves this social ideal. In important ways marriage regulates the relationships and sexual conduct even of people who are not married and may never even get married. Its social and legal prominence informs young lovers about the end toward which they aspire, the outward meaning of their most urgent, personal impulses. It signals to cohabitors the limitations of their own and/or their partners' commitment.

Marriage, as a universal human idea, does not require the ruthless or puritanical suppression of alternatives. It is consistent with a variety of attitudes toward alternate forms of sexual expression, from stigma to acceptance. What it is not consistent with is a legal regime such as that suggested by the Vermont court: that there is no rational relation between the law of marriage and procreation.[16] Because some infertile people marry, and assisted reproductive technology is more common now, the court argued, marriage in Vermont now has nothing to do with its great universal anthropological imperative: family making in a way that encourages ties between fathers, mothers, and their children—and the successful reproduction of society.[17]

Marriage as a universal human institution is, as I have said, consistent with a variety of attitudes toward alternative intimate and sexual relations, from stigma to tolerance. But if we lose the idea that marriage is about, at some basic level, the reproduction of children and society, if our law rejects the presumption that children need mothers and fathers, and that marriage is the way in which we do our best to get them for children, then we cannot expect private tastes and opinions alone to sustain the marriage idea.

That is what same-sex marriage puts at risk. For what benefit? Responsible adults of all sexual orientations who care about children and society should be especially cautious about radical revisions of marriage law, given the extremely small number of couples on whose behalf we contemplate overturning normative marriage. The latest Census Bureau figures report that only about 0.5 percent of all households consist of same-sex couples. Most of these are likely to be gay or lesbian.[18] But many of them, like many opposite-sex cohabitors, are likely uninterested in marriage.

Could we use registered domestic partners to get an idea how many same-sex couples are being denied matrimony by current law? In August 2001, I called the domestic partnership registries of the ten largest U.S. cities that

have domestic partner registries. In these ten cities, same-sex registered domestic partners account for about 0.1 percent of the population.[19]

How many domestic partners depend on one another for health benefits—another crude proxy for denial of marriage rights? I tried to obtain
such data from the ten largest corporations that offer domestic partnership
benefits: General Motors, Ford Motor Company, Citigroup, Enron Corporation, IBM, AT&T, Verizon Communications, Philip Morris, J.P. Morgan Chase and Company, and Bank of America Corporation. However, only
one of these ten companies, General Motors, was willing to release the data:
Out of a total of 1,330,000 employees, exactly 166 workers (or just over
0.01 percent) chose to extend their health insurance to a same-sex partner.

This is not surprising. No definitive research on the gay and lesbian population exists, but the majority of gay and lesbian individuals are likely not
living with partners. Many who do live in sexual partnership may refuse
financial responsibility for each other (just like many opposite-sex cohabitors). Even where same-sex couples do wish a financial union, most partners
are likely working and maintaining their own insurance benefits.

Similarly, we suspect that the number of children who might benefit from,
say, health insurance through same-sex marriage is quite small. Why? First,
only 0.5 percent of households consist of same-sex couples. Only a minority
of these have children from the union, through adoption or donor insemination. If the child is either the natural or adopted child of the parents, he
or she is likely covered by the working parent's health insurance anyway.
Finally, while married people's income is pooled for tax and welfare purposes, that of domestic partners (especially same-sex partners) is typically
not. This means that unmarried partners are eligible for social insurance
benefits unavailable to most married couples. So unlike married couples, if
one parent in a domestic partnership drops out of the work force to care
for a baby, he or she will likely qualify for Medicaid and other means-tested
medical and financial benefits reserved for low-income and single parents.

The demand for same-sex-marriage benefits is not likely based on filling
a huge unmet need for practical benefits. Children or adults are not being
deprived of health care en masse because law and social policies favor married couples over unrelated cohabitors. Instead, the drive for same-sex marriage appears to be a largely symbolic cultural issue; the goal (or at any rate
the main effect) is not filling a need for health insurance or other practical
benefits, but making a powerful social statement: Same-sex unions are the
functional equivalent of marriage, traditionally understood, and should be
treated as such by law and public policy.

Is this a statement the law ought to make? Is it true? When it comes to
child well-being, we could not begin to say that current social science research justifies this statement. To come to this conclusion, research following a nationally representative sample of children of same-sex couples over
time, comparing children of same-sex couples to children living with their

own mothers and fathers, with adequate controls for other background variables, would be necessary. This research has, as yet, not even been attempted. Meanwhile, a large body of social science evidence confirms the advantages of the intact mother-father family over alternate family forms, including other two-parent homes, such as remarriages.

Surely there can be no legal right to ask the law to, in essence, lie—to endorse unequivocally what we do not yet know to be true: that same-sex unions are the functional equivalents of marriages when it comes to child rearing. Nor should the law of marriage focus only on the well-being of individual children of individual unions, but on the broader social impact that legal presumptions of marriage and parenthood have on the conduct of all parents, and therefore all children. When the law assumes and promulgates the idea that either mothers or fathers are dispensable, and that marriage is an essentially private matter whose form is determined by private adult desires, marriage in general and children in particular will inevitably suffer.

Marriage is an institution in crisis. Close to half of new marriages end in divorce. A third of our children are born out of wedlock. The majority of children, at current estimates, will experience a fatherless or motherless household. Making substantial new progress in actually reversing the trend toward family fragmentation requires that law and society reject the deepest presumptions driving the movement toward gay marriage: the ideas that marriage is essentially a private choice created by and for the couple, that children do just fine in whatever family forms their parents choose to create, and that babies are irrelevant to the public purposes of marriage.

People who wish to legislate same-sex unions do so in the name of high ideals: fairness, justice, compassion. I do not doubt their sincerity. But I do not share their own high estimate of their actions. To take the already troubled institution most responsible for the protection of children and the continuation of society and to gut its most basic presumption in the name of furthering adult interests in sexual liberty seems to me morally and socially cavalier.

## NOTES

1. I express my gratitude to E.J. Graff for posing the question so clearly. See E.J. Graff, 1999, *What Is Marriage For?* (Boston: Beacon Press).

2. Drucilla Cornell, 1998, "Fatherhood and Its Discontents: Men, Patriarchy, and Freedom," in Cynthia R. Daniels (ed.), *Lost Fathers: The Politics of Fatherlessness in America* (New York: St. Martin's Press): 199.

3. Most of these same-sex-parenting studies actually compare children of single heterosexual mothers to children of lesbian mothers. They may be relevant to other legal questions, such as custody, but they do not show that same-sex unions are the functional equivalent of mother-father unions. In addition, they are plagued by nu-

merous technical deficiencies that make it inappropriate to use these results as a guide to public policy. See Robert Lerner and Althea K. Nagai, 2000, *Out of Nothing Comes Nothing: Homosexual and Heterosexual Marriage Not Shown to Be Equivalent for Raising Children*, paper presented at the Revitalizing the Institution of Marriage for the 21st Century conference, Brigham Young University, Provo, UT, March. For a critique of Lerner and Nagai, see Judith Stacey and Timothy J. Biblarz, 2001, "(How) Does the Sexual Orientation of Parents Matter?" *American Sociological Review* 66 (April): 159–183. Stacey and Biblarz, however, largely ignore the technical flaws pointed to by Lerner and Nagai and focus instead on possible advantages of same-sex parenting in encouraging gender androgyny and sexual freedom. However, if Lerner and Nagai are correct, these studies are inadequate (due to sample and design flaws) to support *any* conclusion. For the clearest and best technical critique of existing social science literature on same-sex parenting, see the sworn affadavit of University of Virginia sociologist Steven Lowell Nock, requested by the attorney general of Canada, filed in *Halpern (et. al.) v. Attorney General of Canada and Eagle Canada, Inc.* (Court file no. 684/2000).

4. Harry D. Krause, 2000, "Marriage for the New Millennium: Heterosexual, Same Sex—or Not at All?" *Family Law Quarterly* 34(2): 271, 272, 300.

5. In fact, social science evidence indicates that cohabitation in this country does not produce outcomes similar to those of marriage, in terms of the benefits it provides to children and adults. In general, cohabitors resemble singles more than married people, and children of cohabiting parents resemble children of single mothers rather than children from intact marriages. This reflects in part selection effects. For an overview, see Linda J. Waite and Maggie Gallagher, 2000, *The Case for Marriage: Why Married People Are Happier, Healthier, and Better Off Financially* (New York: Doubleday).

6. See, for example, *The Marriage Movement: A Statement of Principles*, 2000 (New York: Institute for American Values), available at www.marriagemovement.org.

7. John Leland, 2000, "O.K. You're Gay. So? Where's My Grandchild?" *New York Times* (December 21): F1. See also accompanying story, John Leland, 2000, "State Laws Vary, but a Broad Trend Is Clear," *New York Times* (December 21): F4.

8. Stanley K. Henshaw, 1998, "Unintended Pregnancy in the United States," *Family Planning Perspectives* 30(1): 24–29.

9. Sharon Vandivere, Kristen Anderson Moore, and Martha Zaslow, 2001, *Children's Family Environments: Findings from the National Survey of America's Families* (Washington, DC: Urban Institute). The data on the proportion of children living with their own two married parents are from unpublished analyses provided to David Blankenhorn.

10. In 1997, 23 percent of family households were headed by a female single parent, while 5 percent were headed by a male single parent. U.S. Bureau of the Census, 1998, *Statistical Abstract of the United States: 1998*, 118th ed. (Washington, DC: U.S. Govt. Printing Office), p. 68.

11. The literature on this point now stretches into literally thousands of studies. For some important recent summaries, see Paul R. Amato and Alan Booth, 1997, *A Generation at Risk: Growing Up in an Era of Family Upheaval* (Cambridge, MA:

Harvard University Press); Sara McLanahan and Gary D. Sandefur, 1994, *Growing Up with a Single Parent: What Hurts, What Helps* (Cambridge, MA: Harvard University Press); *The Marriage Movement: A Statement of Principles*, 2000 (New York: Institute for American Values), available at www.marriagemovement.org; and Linda J. Waite and Maggie Gallagher, 2000, *The Case for Marriage: Why Married People Are Happier, Healthier, and Better Off Financially* (New York: Doubleday).

12. For a review of the evidence see Linda J. Waite and Maggie Gallagher, 2000, *The Case for Marriage: Why Married People Are Happier, Healthier, and Better Off Financially* (New York: Doubleday); Norval Glenn et. al., 2002, *Why Marriage Matters: 21 Conclusions from the Social Sciences* (New York: Institute for American Values).

13. See note 3.

14. But what of recent claims that same-sex marriages are in fact not anthropologically uncommon? Mostly these involved reinterpreting other sorts of social ties as marriage, as John Boswell did when he speculated that blood-brother ceremonies blessed by the church in medieval Europe were the equivalent of contemporary same-sex unions. John Boswell, *Same-Sex Unions in Premodern Europe* (New York: Villard Books, 1994). [For a critique of Boswell's assertion that early Christian and medieval church attitudes to same-sex relationships were either affirming or not entirely negative, see David F. Greenberg, 1988, *The Construction of Homosexuality* (Chicago: University of Chicago Press).] When same-sex relations were institutionalized in small tribal societies, it was often for the purpose of sustaining marriage systems. Men who had to wait for their betrothed wife to mature sexually before marrying, for example, were often expected to engage in sexual relationships with their future wife's older brother to cement kinship ties. Homosexual relations between unmarried juveniles were often encouraged as an alternative to potentially disruptive, procreative sex with unmarried girls. Many tribal societies engage in ritual homosexuality for the purpose of strengthening male bonds. All members are expected to marry upon reaching sexual and social maturity, however. The handful of small tribal civilizations (such as those that practiced, the Native American custom of *berdache*) that allowed men to marry men required one partner to adopt a female social role. In polygamous societies, such marriages would not have affected the birthrate (which is determined by births per woman) and may have encouraged child survival by gaining the labor of two adult men for the polygamous family group. See David F. Greenberg, *The Construction of Homosexuality*, pp. 26–73.

15. See, for example, *Replacement Migration: Is It a Solution to Declining and Ageing Populations?* 2000 (New York: Population Division of the Department of Economic and Social Affairs, United Nations, March 17).

16. *Baker v. State*, 744 A.2d. 864 (Vt. 1999).

17. The state does not require fertility tests for marriage, but historically it has imposed a sexual performance requirement on men for marriage. For example, male impotence has always been a ground for annulling a marriage, and not, one supposes, because the state viewed itself as having an interest in furthering the sexual gratification of women.

18. Census respondents who indicated that a same-sex adult was their unmarried partner or spouse were categorized as same-sex couples, since roommate or boarder

was available to individuals who did not have a romantic relationship. "Households Headed by Gays Rose in the '90s, Data Shows," 2001, *New York Times*, August 21: A17.

19. Maggie Gallagher, forthcoming. *Why Supporting Marriage Makes Business Sense.*

Response

# Enough Marriage to Share: A Response to Maggie Gallagher

**Evan Wolfson**

I am always struck when opponents of marriage equality—who spend a good chunk of their time urging people to get married and advocating special rights for those who do—then turn around and argue that gay people alone should not be allowed to marry. Their position that marriage is good for everyone except lesbians and gay men was captured well in T.H. White's sardonic formulation, "Everything not forbidden is compulsory."[1]

Maggie Gallagher, for example, together with coauthor Linda J. Waite, wrote a whole book titled *The Case for Marriage: Why Married People Are Happier, Healthier, and Better Off Financially*. Neither there nor here does she explain why gay people should not want and deserve to be happier, healthier, and financially secure, too.

To me, this is puzzling. It is not difficult to find real-life stories of gay parents and their kids, not difficult to hear about the harms and joys we experience, like any other human beings, with families and life's ups and downs.[2] Lambda Legal Defense and Education Fund's Web site, for example, details the experiences of couples such as Ivonne and Jeanette (a couple with two children who were threatened with eviction from their housing project because they are not married), Fred and Tim (who lost custody of their kids because they are not married), Ronnie and Elaine (denied health benefits and leave from work because they are not married), and others.

Why would someone sincerely concerned with the well-being of people, including children, defend discriminatory exclusion from an institution that might bring these couples and these children support and protection in life? How does it help the children being raised by gay parents to deprive these children of the protections and support that would come to their families with marriage?

Actually, as courts in Hawaii and Vermont, among others, have found, perpetuating the denial of civil marriage does not help these kids—or anyone—at all.[3] The unanimous Vermont Supreme Court concluded, "If anything, the exclusion of same-sex couples from the legal protections incident to marriage exposes their children to the precise risks that the State argues the marriage laws are designed to secure against."[4] Even if Gallagher were correct that one family configuration is "the best," the argument for discrimination fails. As an authoritative 1999 report out of Stanford University conclusively demonstrated, it simply makes no sense to say, "We care about children," and then punish some kids for having the "wrong parents" by denying their families the benefits of marriage.[5]

Moreover, contrary to her claim, there is no evidence to support the offensive proposition that only one size of family must fit all. Most studies—including ones that Gallagher relies on—reflect the common sense that what counts is not the family structure, but the quality of dedication, commitment, self-sacrifice, and love in the household. For example, the American Psychological Association surveyed the abundant and uncontroverted research and concluded that

[n]ot a single study has found children of gay or lesbian parents to be disadvantaged in any significant respect relative to children of heterosexual parents. Indeed, the evidence to date suggests that home environments provided by gay and lesbian parents are as likely as those provided by heterosexual parents to support and enable children's psychosocial growth.[6]

As the highly respected American Academy of Pediatrics affirmed in February 2002, there is simply no evidence, scientific or otherwise, to suggest that gay parents are any less fit, or that their children are any less happy, healthy, and well adjusted.[7]

In fact, much of what preoccupies Gallagher—deficiencies in parenting, divorce and failures of existing marriages, "radical fatherless[ness]" and "making men good fathers," polygamy (!), society's "need [for] babies" in order to survive—does not have any logical connection to depriving gay people of the commitment, responsibilities, and support that come with marriage. Fencing gay people out of marriage does nothing to help nongay people treat their spouses better, or behave more responsibly, or spend more time with their kids. While I agree with Gallagher that we should not "ask the law to, in essence, lie," isn't it a lie to say that committed gay couples taking on the responsibilities of civil marriage threaten this most resilient of social institutions—when nongay convicted murderers, deadbeat dads, and, for that matter, even game-show contestants on *Who Wants to Marry a Millionaire?* who never met before are all free to marry at will?[8]

Given Gallagher's emphasis on married mothers and fathers, isn't having the law pretend that there is only one family model that works (let alone exists) a lie? Isn't it a lie to claim to be caring about the kids (Gallagher cites the importance of giving kids an "uncontested claim on their parents") and then deny marriage licenses to their parents if they happen to be gay? Isn't it a lie to use kids as the excuse to deny gay people the precious freedom to marry when we grant marriage licenses to senior citizens and those who do not wish to procreate, as well as childless couples such as Bob and Elizabeth Dole, Pat and Shelley Buchanan, or even George and Martha Washington? Isn't it a lie not to recognize that people have many reasons for wanting to marry?[9]

The denial of marriage to same-sex couples helps no one. But what it does do, as the title of Gallagher's book underscores, is harm lesbians and gay men, our children, and those who care about us. Gay youth are sent a message of inferiority and exclusion; often before they even know that they are gay, they can sense that their difference means that they will be excluded from an important part of life. Gay couples are deprived of important protections and support (as necessary for lesbian and gay human beings as for nongays); if these things matter for nongay lives, why are they trivial when gay people seek them? Moreover, our nongay parents, siblings, nieces and nephews, grandparents, and friends suffer, too, when we are treated unequally and are cast outside the law's protection. What good parent does not want the same opportunities, joys, and shelter for all his or her children, gay or nongay? The law should help support families and enlarge people's possibilities, not tear them apart or put barriers in their way.

Beyond that, the discriminatory restriction on marriage injures the American commitment to equality for all and respect for each person's pursuit of happiness. As California's Supreme Court noted in striking down discrimination in marriage, the "essence of the right to marry [is] the freedom to join in marriage with the person of one's choice. . . . Human beings are bereft of worth and dignity by a doctrine that would make them as interchangeable as trains."[10]

Our opponents sometimes seem to imply that there is something sinister about these American values of equal treatment and respect for individuals' choices. They truck in the usual gloom-and-doom that opponents of equality have always invoked to hold back such "radical" changes as women's advancement, interracial marriage, divorce, and contraception.[11] But their quarrel really ought not to be with gay people (who, after all, are seeking to take part in the responsibilities and commitment of marriage Gallagher extols), or with the Vermont Supreme Court (which stuck with the facts and found that "legal protection and security for [gay people's] avowed commitment to an intimate and lasting human relationship is simply, when all is said and done, a recognition of our common humanity").[12] Rather, our opponents' real quarrel is with modernity, pluralism, the separation of church and state, the U.S. Supreme Court, and our federal Constitution.

To read Gallagher's essay, one would not know that for decades the law of the land (America, that is, unlike, perhaps, more theocratic or women-subordinating societies) has been to recognize that marriage is not just about procreation—indeed, is not necessarily about procreation at all. Many people, of course, choose to have children within the context of marriage, and commentators are free to urge them to do so. Raising kids within marriage is precisely what many gay people are seeking to do, amid fierce (and unhelpful) right-wing attacks on their families.

But the law, the courts, and the Constitution have also long recognized that people marry for reasons other than procreation. The "important attributes of marriage," as Justice Sandra Day O'Connor wrote in one unanimous case, are its "expressions of emotional support and public commitment"; its "spiritual significance" for many; the sexual fulfillment it may entail; and its role as a "precondition to the receipt of government benefits . . . and other, less tangible benefits."[13] That same year, well before the Hawaii Supreme Court required the government to show a reason for excluding gay couples from marriage, a leading family law treatise observed that the American institution of marriage had changed "from the days when it was an economic producing unit of society with responsibilities for child rearing and training, to the present, when its chief functions seem to be furnishing opportunities for affection, companionship, and sexual satisfaction."[14]

As Judge Kevin Chang held in the historic 1996 Hawaii trial decision finding no valid reason for denying same-sex couples the freedom to marry:

In Hawaii, and elsewhere, people marry for a variety of reasons, including . . . (1) having or raising children; (2) stability and commitment; (3) emotional closeness; (4) intimacy and monogamy; (5) the establishment of a framework for a long-term relationship; (6) personal significance; (7) legal and economic protections, benefits and obligations.[15]

"Gay men and lesbian women," the judge found, "share this same mix of reasons for wanting to be able to marry."[16] Nothing in Gallagher's pile of data, the meaningful as well as the dubious, refutes this central and basic point.

As former President Gerald Ford declared in October 2001 when asked about lesbian and gay families and marriage, "I think they ought to be treated equally. Period." Asked whether gay couples should get the same Social Security, tax, and other federal benefits as married couples, the Republican replied, "I don't see why they shouldn't. I think that's a proper goal."[17] Civil rights hero John Lewis, now a congressman from Georgia, decried attacks on gay people's freedom to marry, noting that the exclusion "denies gay men and women the right to liberty and the pursuit of happiness." Said Congressman Lewis:

Marriage is a basic human right. You cannot tell people they cannot fall in love. Dr. Martin Luther King, Jr. used to say when people talked about interracial marriage and I quote, "Races do not fall in love and get married. Individuals fall in love and get married." . . . Mr. Chairman, I have known racism. I have known bigotry. This bill [the proposed federal antimarriage law of 1996, adding an overlay of federal discrimination against same-sex couples] stinks of the same fear, hatred and intolerance. It should not be called the Defense of Marriage Act. It should be called the defense of mean-spirited bigots act.[18]

Following September 11, 2001, Republican Governor George Pataki of New York, noting that no one asked the firefighters entering the World Trade Center whether they were gay or whom they loved, issued an executive order requiring the state Crime Victims Compensation Board to treat surviving same-sex partners as equivalent to spouses.

More than thirty-five years ago, the Supreme Court rejected claims that allowing contraception would lead to the demise of society.[19] In its opinion, the Court also took a stand against those who sought to hijack other people's freedom to marry as a vehicle for imposing their own personal or parochial agendas. In America, under our Constitution, the Court held:

Marriage is a coming together for better or for worse, hopefully enduring, and intimate to the degree of being sacred. *It is an association that promotes a way of life, not causes*; a harmony in living, not political faiths; a bilateral loyalty, *not* commercial or *social projects*.[20]

Whether she is sincere or not, it is wrong for Gallagher to deny gay people the freedom to marry in order to promote her views on how people should conduct their own affairs or behave in their own marriages or lives, or in order to somehow chasten nongay people into being better parents or partners.

Not only is such burdening, scapegoating, and exclusion of gay people wrong, it also is counterproductive, even in terms of Gallagher's own professed agenda of supporting kids, promoting family responsibility, and building strong communities. As one expert testified in the Hawaii case—the fullest examination of the evidence on both sides of the debate over ending sex discrimination in marriage:

I think that marriage is really a high state of hope and effort for people. I think when we deny it to people we say that—that there's some other location for love and raising children and that we're not as concerned about these kids' welfare or in some ways we don't think it would be good for them to be in a married home. It's not that those children don't exist, it's not that those families don't exist, they do. [M]ost Americans believe in marriage strongly. I believe by taking other people into the fold and asking that they behave as responsible to their children to give them support to have both rituals to enter into their relationships and legal complications by exiting them, that we shore up how important we think marriage is. . . . I think it in no way undermines [marriage] and I think it strengthens it by our insistence about how important it is and why we hope this will be available for all families.[21]

By contrast, our opponents seem to believe that more can be gained by attacking gay people's families than by welcoming them, as if marriage were strengthened by who is kept out rather than by how we all treat one another and whether we all are held to a standard of care and caring.

I part company with these attackers, for I believe that marriage, like our country, is strongest when we invite, challenge, and support diverse individuals to be free, equal, and contributing parts of the whole. Equality is not a zero-sum game; the history of our country, our American faith, is that we can work to include everyone, treasure choice, respect difference, support the pursuit of happiness, and all be better off.[22]

In 2001, 2,000 same-sex couples got legally married in the Netherlands, our NATO ally and the United States' oldest, constant friend; the sky did not fall.[23] If marriage is, as Gallagher argues, good for individuals, communities, children, and our country, then surely it would be good for gay people, too.[24] It would also be good for the nation we are part of to welcome us across the threshold instead of barring the door.

## NOTES

1. T.H. White, *The Once and Future King* (White recounts the precept of an ant society that subordinated individuals' lives, loves, and aspirations to the agenda of the state).

2. See, e.g., *Denying Access to Marriage Harms Families*, http://www.lambdalegal.org/cgi-bin/iowa/documents/record?record=873; *The Plaintiff Couples*, http://www.glad.org.

3. *Baehr v. Mike* (trial); *Baker v. State* (Vt. S.Ct).

4. *Baker*, cite.

5. Michael S. Wald, *Same-Sex Couples: Marriage, Families, and Children* (Stanford University, 1999), http://www.law.stanford.edu/faculty/wald/summary.shtml.

6. *Lesbian and Gay Parenting: A Resource for Psychologists* (American Psychological Association, 1995), p. 8. Gallagher takes social science data suggesting that kids do better with two involved parents (and the financial and emotional resources they can bring) and transmutes that into an argument that this means "[their] own married mother and father," a conclusion that matches her agenda but for which there is no support. Indeed, several of the experts she cites on that very point (her note 10) have in fact filed friend-of-the-court briefs in support of gay people's freedom to marry. See, for example, Brief of Amici Curiae Andrew J. Cherlin, Frank F.

Furstenberg, Jr., Sara S. McLanahan, Gary D. Sandefur, and Lawrence L. Wu, in support of Plaintiff Couples, *Baehr v. Miike*, Haw. Sup. Ct., June 2, 1997 ("optimal outcomes for children would be *furthered* by allowing same-sex couples to marry and raise their children with State encouragement and support").

7. "Children deserve to know that their relationships with both of their parents are stable and legally recognized. This applies to all children, whether their parents are of the same or opposite sex. The American Academy of Pediatrics recognizes that a considerable body of professional literature provides evidence that children with parents who are homosexual can have the same advantages and the same expectations for health, adjustment, and development as can children whose parents are heterosexual." "Technical Report: Coparent or Second-Parent Adoptions by Same-Sex Parents," *Pediatrics* (Feb. 2002), pp. 339–340, http://www.aap.org/policy/020008.html; APA, *ibid*.

8. One of Gallagher's arguments seems to be that there are so few gay couples that it is not worth ending the sex restriction in marriage. While the exact number of gay people, let alone same-sex couples, is unknown, the 2000 census showed gay people present in nearly every county of the country and a significant number of same-sex couples, despite its serious undercounting. D'Vera Cohn, "Count of Gay Couples Up 300%," *Washington Post*, Aug. 22, 2001, p. A3. Even more tellingly, the most authoritative comparison of married nongay, cohabiting nongay, lesbian, and gay couples concluded that " '[c]ouplehood,' either as a reality or an aspiration, is as strong among gay people as it is among heterosexuals." Blumstein and Schwartz, *American Couples: Money, Work, Sex* (New York: William Morrow, 1983), p. 45. Putting aside the question of numbers (as if the injury were not severe to each couple, no matter how many or how few), it is hard to see how allowing what Gallagher believes is such an ostensibly small group of families to partake of the protections of marriage threatens civilization's collapse.

9. The state has always licensed marriages between elderly, sterile, and even impotent parties. Indeed, a refusal to allow the elderly or infertile to marry would almost certainly be unconstitutional, and Gallagher does not seem to advocate such a restriction for these nonprocreating couples. The only people upon whom our opponents seek to impose a "procreation" requirement are same-sex couples.

10. *Perez v. Lippold*, 198 P.2d 17, 19 (Cal. 1948) (because of the different-race restriction, a person "find[s] himself barred by law from marrying the person of his choice and that person to him may be irreplaceable").

11. One court, for example, upheld restrictions on different-race marriage on the grounds that it was "unnatural," saying that it would lead to children who are "generally sickly, and effeminate . . . and inferior in physical development and strength." *Scott v. Georgia*, 39 Ga. 321, 323 (1869). Dire claims such as Ms Gallagher's about the consequences of allowing gay people to marry were also made, for example, about contraception. See Evan Wolfson, "Crossing the Threshold: Equal Marriage Rights for Lesbians and Gay Men," 21 *N.Y.U. Rev. of Law & Soc. Change* 567, 610 n. 190 (1994) (e.g., one commentator declared, "Japanese birth control devices in the homes of America can be more destructive than Japanese bombers over Pearl Harbor"). For an appalling and yet sometimes amusing recital of such "jeremiads," see E.J. Graff, *What Is Marriage For?* (Boston: Beacon Press, 1999).

12. *Baker v. Vermont.*

13. *Turner v. Safley*, 482 U.S. 78, 95–96 (1997) (even convicted felons have a

constitutionally protected interest in their freedom to marry, even though they may not be able to enjoy all these enumerated attributes). The Court pointedly did not cite procreation as even one of the bases for the freedom to marry.

14. Homer H. Clark, Jr., *The Law of Domestic Relations in the United States*, 2d. ed. 1987, vol. 1, p. 74.

15. *Baehr v. Miike*, Finding of Fact 138.

16. *Id.*

17. Deb Price, "Gerald Ford: Treat Gay Couples Equally," *Detroit News*, Oct. 29, 2001.

18. Congressman John Lewis, U.S. House of Representatives, July 11, 1996.

19. Wolfson, "Crossing the Threshold," 610 n. 190.

20. *Griswold v. Connecticut*, 381 U.S. 479, 486 (1965) (emphasis added).

21. *Baehr v. Miike*, Finding of Fact 87 (testimony of Dr. Pepper Schwartz), 191 Civ. 1394 (Haw. Civ. Ct., Dec. 3, 1996), 23 Fam. L. Rep. (BNA) 2001 (Dec. 6 1996).

22. *United States v. Virginia*, 518 U.S. 515 (1996) ("A prime part of the history of our Constitution . . . is the story of the extension of constitutional rights and protections to people once ignored or excluded").

23. Associated Press, "Dutch Gay Marriage Stats Released," Dec. 12, 2001. The Dutch government reported that same-sex couples' marriages comprised 3.6 percent of all new marriages between the ending of marriage discrimination on April 1 and September 30, 2001. In Denmark, where "gay marriage" has been in existence for more than a decade, opponents are unable to cite any adverse consequences and, indeed, "acknowledge their concerns may have been overblown." L. Ingrassia, "Danes Don't Debate Morality of Same-Sex Marriage; Even Opponents Say '89 Law Brought No Social Ill," *Wall Street Journal*, June 8, 1994.

24. This was the conclusion of the official report from the Canadian government's Law Commission, which after years of study recently called on Parliament and provincial governments to eliminate discriminatory restrictions on civil marriage and allow same-sex couples the full and equal freedom to marry. Law Commission of Canada, "Beyond Conjugality" http://www.lcc.gc.ca/en/themes/pr/cpra/report.html#004e (Dec. 21, 2001).

# Chapter 2

Essay One

# *The State Interests in Recognizing Same-Sex Marriage*

## Mark Strasser

Recognition of same-sex marriage would serve a variety of state interests. Indeed, many of the reasons that are thought to establish why the state should promote different-sex marriage also establish with equal or greater force why the state should promote same-sex marriage. Nonetheless, in part because of a misunderstanding of which state interests are served by marriage or why those interests would also be served by recognizing same-sex marriage, in part because of a desire not to accept that same-sex marriages are as valuable as different-sex marriages, and in part for other reasons, no state yet permits same-sex couples to marry.

The failure to afford same-sex marriages legal recognition imposes significant costs on the state. Not only does the state suffer opportunity costs in lost productivity, for example, but it also incurs other costs as well. When the state proclaims that certain ideals and principles are very important but then adopts practices that contradict those ideals and principles, the state's commitment to those goals in particular and its credibility in general are undermined. Further, precisely because this is a rule-bound society, the kinds of decisions that permit the state to refuse to recognize same-sex marriages or to accord partnership benefits will necessarily impact the rights that other couples and families will enjoy. Thus not only does the state not receive the specific benefits that might have come from the promotion of marriage for same-sex couples, but the state incurs other costs that, while less obvious, are nonetheless real and must be considered in any analysis of the public policy considerations regarding the recognition of same-sex unions.

Marriage promotes stability for adults and children and helps them all lead happier and more productive lives.[1] The state benefits when individuals are happier and more productive, and these benefits accrue whether or not the couple happens to have children. Thus, claims to the contrary notwithstanding, state interests are promoted by recognizing same-sex marriage even apart from the issue of children.

Consider the claim that the state would not benefit by recognizing same-sex marriage because, after all, same-sex couples do not have children to raise. A moment's reflection reveals why this argument is unpersuasive. Just as state interests are promoted when different-sex individuals marry even if these individuals will not or perhaps cannot have children, state interests would also be promoted were same-sex couples to marry, even were it clear that these couples would never have or raise children.

Traditionally, courts have focused on children when they have analyzed the state interests implicated in marriage. For example, in *Adams v. Howerton*, the court implied that *the* state interest in marriage involved providing a setting for the production and raising of children.[2] Realizing that many different-sex couples marry without the intention or willingness to have children, the court implied that such couples were permitted to marry only because of the difficulties entailed in finding out whether a particular couple could or would have children. Yet two individuals who volunteered that they had no interest in having or raising children could not be barred from marrying on that account. Thus the difficulties in discovering the relevant information cannot plausibly explain why individuals who cannot or will not have children will nonetheless be allowed to marry.

It is simply inaccurate to claim that states limit marriage to those who will or might have children. Indeed, several states permit first cousins to marry only if they cannot have children together, either because at least one is beyond childbearing or child-begetting years or because at least one cannot have children for some other reason. Were the sole state interest promoted by marriage related to couples producing children through their union, states would never make the inability to procreate a condition for marriage.

Whether or not a couple has children, the state has a financial interest in promoting marriage because, for example, the marital partners will provide for each other, should the need arise, so that the state would not need to do so. Whether or not a couple has children, the state has an interest in facilitating its members' being happier and more productive because the general good is thereby promoted. Whether or not a couple has children, the state has an interest in promoting marriage if public health benefits might thereby be achieved, and the promotion of marriage might reduce the incidence of sexually transmitted diseases.

It might be argued that permitting same-sex couples to marry would not solve the difficulty posed by sexually transmitted diseases. That is correct but irrelevant. While not all married same-sex couples would be monogamous, just as not all married different-sex couples are monogamous, the relevant question is whether the recognition of such unions might increase the number of individuals who either did not have multiple sexual partners or who engaged in less risky sexual practices. A reduction in, even if not an elimination of, the incidence of sexually transmitted diseases would be a societal benefit that might be promoted through the recognition of same-sex unions.

Given the number of different-sex couples whose marriages end in divorce, it is reasonable to expect that there would be same-sex divorces were the state to recognize same-sex marriages. Yet the state also has an interest in assuring that the dissolution of relationships is orderly, that there is a fair division of assets upon such dissolutions, and, if possible, that the state will not be forced to expend public funds in supporting one or both of the parties after such dissolutions. These interests would be promoted were the state to recognize same-sex unions.

Certainly, marriage and monogamy are not for everyone. No one should be forced to marry. Further, this essay is not, for example, calling for the reinstitution of laws prohibiting fornication. Rather, this essay is merely suggesting that the state and the individuals themselves would benefit if individuals were given the option to marry their same-sex partners.

A separate question beyond the scope of this essay is whether the state should afford individuals a variety of legal options so that, for example, the state would offer the possibility of legal recognition of marriages, domestic partnerships, reciprocal-beneficiary status, and so on and would accord the parties different obligations and benefits depending upon which of the arrangements had been chosen. Presumably, one status would be best for one kind of couple, and a different status would be best for another. Assuming that the costs associated with offering a menu of options would not be too onerous, the state's legally recognizing several different types of relationships might in fact better meet the needs of its citizens. Nonetheless, the costs and benefits of offering a menu will not be discussed here, since the focus here is merely on establishing that same-sex couples should be offered the same kinds of options as are different-sex couples.

The point here is not to underestimate the importance of the state's interest in providing a setting for the production and raising of the next generation. Indeed, that interest, which is often trumpeted as one of the most important reasons that marriage should be promoted by the state, militates in favor of recognizing same-sex unions. Regrettably, while courts have recognized that providing a home for the next generation implicates an important state interest, they have refused to recognize that this provides an additional reason that same-sex couples should be allowed to marry.

Consider the *Adams* court's suggestion that "it seems beyond dispute that the state has a compelling interest in encouraging and fostering procreation of the race and providing status and stability to the environment in which children are raised."[3] Believing that there was "no real alternative to some overbreadth in achieving this goal,"[4] the court understood that the state would have to permit some individuals to marry who either would not or could not have children. Basically, the court suggested that because of the difficulties in figuring who might or would have children, the state will be more likely to achieve its goal of providing a stable and healthy environment in which children might be raised by permitting some to marry who will not have children than, for example, by having more restrictive marriage laws and thereby preventing the marriage of individuals who actually had or might have children. Ironically, the court offered this analysis regarding the necessity of having "overbroad" marriage statutes to justify precluding same-sex couples from marrying, notwithstanding that it actually militated in favor of recognizing such unions.

Precisely because same-sex couples both have and raise children, the court's analysis provided support for the recognition of same-sex marriages, both for same-sex couples with children and for same-sex couples who had no intention of either having or raising children. Thus, according to the rationale offered by the court, same-sex couples who will not raise children should be allowed to marry precisely because some same-sex couples do raise children, and there is no alternative to having some overbreadth if the state's goal of affording couples with children the stability afforded by marital status is to be achieved. Nonetheless, the court paradoxically recognized the overwhelming importance of providing a setting for children to be raised and then accepted a position that would mean that certain individuals with children to raise could not get married and that certain individuals without children could get married. If this kind of reasoning and result does not undermine respect for the courts, it is not clear what would.

Suppose that same-sex couples were not producing children, for example, by making use of artificial insemination or surrogacy. They still might be raising children who had been born into a previous marriage or who had been adopted. Since the state has a compelling interest in "providing status and stability to the environment in which the children are raised," the state still would have a compelling interest in recognizing same-sex marriage, even were same-sex couples not procreating but only helping to raise the children that others had brought into this world. Given the gay and lesbian baby boom, however, the state's compelling interest in promoting the welfare of children cannot plausibly be used to justify a state policy prohibiting same-sex partners from marrying and instead strongly supports the state's recognizing such unions.

Same-sex marriage opponents sometimes imply that the interests of the state in the creation and care of the next generation can only be served when children are produced through the union of the married couple. Yet state policies belie this claim, as is clear when one considers policies concerning adoption, foster care, and the like. Indeed, given current demographics concerning the surprisingly small percentage of children who live with both of their biological parents, it is at the very least surprising that such an argument would be offered. The state has a compelling interest in assuring that children will be in homes in which they might thrive, whether the child is biologically related to both of the parents, one of the parents, or neither of the parents.

Commentators debate whether same-sex parents are sufficiently good parents. Yet there is no evidence that children will not thrive when raised by same-sex parents and, indeed, some evidence that children may be better off in certain ways when they are raised by same-sex parents than when they are raised by different-sex parents. For example, even though children raised by same-sex parents are no more likely to self-identify as gay or lesbian than are children raised by different-sex parents, such children are nonetheless more likely to be more open to others who are gay or lesbian than are children who are raised by different-sex parents. Claims to the contrary notwithstanding, this would be an advantage rather than a disadvantage both for the child and for the state, since the state has an interest in promoting tolerance rather than bigotry.

The claim here is not that there is unanimity with respect to what optimal parents or children are like. For example, some believe that girls should only aspire to take on societal roles traditionally assigned to women, whereas others believe that girls should also aspire to take on roles traditionally assigned to men. One's belief about the appropriate aspirations of women might influence one's evaluation of whether children do well when raised by same-sex couples, since there is some evidence that girls raised in such families are more open to taking on nontraditional roles.

Suppose, however, that we leave aside these disagreements about whether children should be raised to be tolerant of lesbian, gay, bisexual, and transgendered people or whether children should only aspire to take on traditional roles. Even if all could agree about what the optimal marriages, parents, and children were like, it is quite clear that we would never as a society say that only optimal parents may raise children or that only those who would have "optimal" marriages would be permitted to marry. Yet this kind of optimality argument is used to "justify" precluding same-sex adults from marrying or raising children, notwithstanding that (1) such an argument is not used in a variety of other contexts in which the claim of non-optimality might be made with much more plausibility, and (2) there is no agreement regarding the criteria for the optimality of marriages, parents, and children.

Suppose that it could be established that children raised by certain different-sex couples were more likely to have certain problems, for example, to have antisocial or bigoted attitudes. Would it really be claimed that such individuals should not be allowed to be parents? Or suppose that it could be established that certain marriages were likely to be less optimal because children would not (or would) be born into the marriage or because married couples making that little (or that much) money were less likely to have successful marriages. Would it really be claimed that these adults should not be allowed to marry? That these rationales are used to "justify" refusing to recognize same-sex marriages but would never be used to justify refusing to permit a variety of other marriages suggests that these rationales are pretexts for refusing to recognize same-sex marriages.

If both individuals and society will benefit from permitting same-sex couples to marry, what justifies the prohibition? Many same-sex-marriage opponents claim that they are trying to "save the family." Yet it is hardly credible to claim, for example, that fewer different-sex couples will marry or that more different-sex couples will divorce if same-sex marriages are legally recognized. Same-sex marriage opponents likely mean something very different when they talk about how refusing to allow same-sex couples to marry will somehow save the family.

Some same-sex marriage opponents are willing to make their objections to such unions explicit. They argue that same-sex couples and families must not be viewed as the equal of different-sex couples and families, and that homosexuality must not be viewed as the equal of heterosexuality.[5] They further argue that because legal recognition of such unions and families might induce people to view same-sex relationships and families as on a par with different-sex relationships and families and might induce people to view individuals with a same-sex orientation as on a par with individuals with a different-sex orientation, such legal recognition must not be accorded.

While such honesty is commendable, the attitudes are not. A state that is committed to tolerance and egalitarianism should not be trying to promote the view that gay, lesbian, bisexual, and transgendered individuals are inferior. Indeed, in *Romer v. Evans*, the U.S. Supreme Court struck down a state constitutional amendment precisely because it was designed to promote the illegitimate state goal of making lesbians, gays, and bisexuals unequal to everyone else.[6]

Suppose that an individual believed that interracial or interreligious marriages were not the equal of intraracial or intrareligious marriages. One question, of course, would be whether such a belief was correct or, instead, was the product of intolerant attitudes. A separate question, however, would be whether such a belief should have any legal implications even were it true. Thus, even if there were some non-question-begging way to establish that the former unions were somehow not as good as the latter, much more would have to be shown to establish that the state would be justified in prohibiting such unions. Presumably, it would not suffice to say, for example, that such unions should not be legally recognized so that individuals would not be misled into believing that such unions were the equal of intraracial or intrareligious unions. Indeed, same-sex-marriage opponents have a difficult time in establishing why their arguments, if accepted, would not justify a whole host of marital exclusions.

Consider, for example, the attempt by some commentators to distinguish between laws prohibiting interracial marriage and laws prohibiting same-sex marriage. They argue that the former are based on immutable racial classifications, whereas the latter are based on the regulation of sexual behavior.[7] They further argue that this difference explains why the state is permitted to preclude the latter but not the former.

There are at least two difficulties with this argument. First, there is some question whether sexual orientation is itself an immutable classification, and thus it might be argued that if the interracial ban is impermissible because it is based on an immutable classification, then the same-sex-marriage ban is impermissible for the same reason. Second, whether or not sexual orientation is unchangeable once it is established before birth or early in childhood, these commentators have mischaracterized the laws that banned interracial marriage. Indeed, once these laws have been accurately characterized, the argument of these commentators could, if accepted, be used to justify a state's prohibiting interracial couples from marrying, claims to the contrary notwithstanding.

In *Loving v. Virginia*, the U.S. Supreme Court struck down Virginia's antimiscegenation law as a violation of the Fourteenth Amendment's Equal Protection Clause.[8] Suppose, however, that the distinction between immutable classifications and sexual behaviors was accepted by the Court as valid and, further, was accepted by the Court as relevant in deciding whether a state's marital restriction was permitted by the Constitution. When the state of Virginia was supporting its interracial-marriage prohibition, it might have claimed that it was not basing its law on an immutable classification but was merely trying to regulate sexual behavior, that is, to prevent interracial coupling. Thus, just as same-sex-marriage opponents might claim that regardless of whether sexual orientation is immutable, the state is permitted to regulate certain "behaviors" and thus is permitted to prohibit same-sex marriage, the interracial-marriage opponent might claim that regardless of whether race is immutable, the state is permitted to regulate certain "behaviors" and thus is permitted to prohibit interracial marriage. Were states free to regulate marriage as they see fit under the guise of regulating sexual behavior, then states would not be precluded from prohibiting interracial or interreligious marriage as long as they were clever enough to say that they were merely trying to prevent certain types of interracial or interreligious behavior. Yet states are precluded from prohibiting such marriages, claimed interest in preventing such behaviors notwithstanding.

The argument here is not that states are precluded from enacting any marital regulations whatsoever. As the Supreme Court has recognized, "[R]easonable regulations that do not significantly interfere with decisions to enter into the marital relationship may legitimately be imposed."[9] Yet the Court has also made clear that when a "statutory classification significantly interferes with the exercise of a fundamental right [like the right to marry], it cannot be upheld unless it is supported by sufficiently important state interests and is closely tailored to effectuate only those interests."[10] The question at hand is which legitimate state interests are promoted by prohibiting same-sex couples from marrying. If the answer is that such a prohibition is permissible to save the family and prevent it from being "sullied," then a variety of prohibitions would seem justifiable as long as the prohibited unions were viewed by the electorate in a particular jurisdiction as demeaning the institution of marriage.

Some same-sex-marriage opponents suggest that such prohibitions are permissible because they promote morality. Such a justification is as unpersuasive as is the "preventing of sullying." Were states permitted to prohibit unions as long as they could claim that such a prohibition "promoted morality," then states would have wide discretion with respect to which marriages might be banned.

One might reject that such a rationale would justify states' precluding interracial and interreligious marriages because, after all, such unions are morally permissible even if some individuals sincerely believe them morally offensive. Yet the same point might be made about same-sex unions, namely, that they are not immoral notwithstanding that some individuals sincerely believe that they are.

Same-sex-marriage opponents might rightly point out that some religions condemn such relationships, although they would be wrong to claim that all religions do. As Justice Harry Blackmun suggested in his dissent in *Bowers v. Hardwick* about a related issue, however, "That certain, but by no means all, religious groups condemn [same-sex relations] gives the State no license to impose their judgments on the entire citizenry. The legitimacy of secular legislation depends instead on whether the State can advance some justification for its law beyond its conformity to religious doctrine."[11]

Just as it cannot be claimed that same-sex marriages are universally recognized to offend religious principles, it simply cannot be claimed that same-sex marriages are universally recognized to offend morality. Presumably, same-sex-marriage opponents would claim that universal moral condemnation is not necessary. Rather, they might argue that it should suffice if the local populace finds such relationships immoral. Yet permitting the local populace to determine which marriages are morally offensive and thus subject to prohibition would put many unions at risk. In addition to marriages of individuals of different races or religions, numerous other marriages might be thought morally offensive and thus subject to prohibition, for example, marriages of adults of different generations or marriages of individuals who could not have children or, perhaps, who could not have sexual relations.

The argument here is not that morality is relative and that "anything goes." One can recognize that same-sex relations are morally permissible without also endorsing murder and theft.[12] It is not as if recognizing the moral permissibility of same-sex relations would entail that one would have to recognize the moral permissibility of every practice, no matter how harmful.[13]

Indeed, commentators may not realize the implications of their own position if they argue that morality is of a piece, so that if one part of it is rejected (e.g., if one rejects that same-sex relations are immoral), then all of it will be rejected.[14] To see the weakness of such a position, one need only consider that morality was cited as the justification for prohibiting interracial marriage. First, it should be clear that rejection of the immorality of interracial marriage did not suddenly cause society to disintegrate. Second, many now recognize that such a justification was using morality to mask prejudice. When morality is used in this way, not only is the particular claim rejected, for example, that interracial marriages are immoral, but confidence in other moral claims might also be diminished. So, too, when the promotion or preservation of morality is championed as the justification for denying lesbian, gay, bisexual, and transgendered individuals the fundamental right to marry and raise a family, much is lost, since our moral system itself becomes tainted.

When specious arguments are offered and accepted to justify same-sex-marriage bans when such rationales would never be accepted in other contexts, the rights of all individuals are endangered. Not only are the particular benefits that might have been accrued by recognizing same-sex unions lost, but the rule of law, the belief in morality, and the commitment to tolerance and egalitarianism are also thereby undermined. Such a price is simply too dear to pay.

## NOTES

1. Much of this piece comes from MARK STRASSER, THE CHALLENGE OF SAME-SEX MARRIAGE: FEDERALIST PRINCIPLES AND CONSTITUTIONAL PROTECTIONS, ch. 1 (1999).

2. Adams v. Howerton, 486 F. Supp. 1119 (C.D. Cal. 1980), aff'd, 673 F.2d 1036 (9th Cir.), cert. denied, 458 U.S. 1111 (1982).

3. Id. at 1124.

4. Id.

5. See, for example, Richard F. Duncan, From Loving to Romer: Homosexual Marriage and Moral Discernment, 12 BYU J. PUB. L. 239, 239 (1998) (discussing "those who seek to use the courts to accomplish a radical and dangerous agenda—the reordering of marriage to reflect the alleged equal goodness of homosexuality and heterosexuality").

6. 517 U.S. 620 (1996).

7. See, for example, Lynn D. Wardle, A Critical Analysis of Constitutional Claims for Same-Sex Marriage, 1996 BYU L. REV. 1, 82 (1996).

8. 388 U.S. 1, 11 (1967). The Court also suggested that the statute violated the amendment's substantive due process guarantees. See id. at 12.

9. See Zablocki v. Redhail, 434 U.S. 374, 386 (1978).

10. *Id.*

11. *See* Bowers v. Hardwick, 478 U.S. 186, 211 (1986) (Blackmun, J., dissenting).

12. *See id.* at 212 (Blackmun, J., dissenting).

13. Harry Jaffa does not seem to appreciate this. *See* Harry V. Jaffa, *"Our Ancient Faith": A Reply to Professor Anastaplo*, in ORIGINAL INTENT AND THE FRAMERS OF THE CONSTITUTION 369, 383 (1994) (suggesting that "if sodomy is not unnatural, then nothing is unnatural. And if nothing is unnatural, then nothing—including slavery and genocide—is unjust").

14. For such a suggestion, see Patrick Devlin, *The Enforcement of Morals*, in THE PHILOSOPHY OF LAW: CLASSIC AND CONTEMPORARY READINGS WITH COMMENTARY 338, 341 (Frederick Schauer & Walter Sinnott-Armstrong eds. 1996) ("There is disintegration when no common morality is observed and history shows that the loosening of moral bonds is often the first stage [of] disintegration, so that society is justified in taking the same steps to preserve its moral code as it does to preserve its government and other essential institutions").

Response

# *Reply to Professor Mark Strasser*
## John Witte, Jr.

"If a thing has been practiced for two hundred years by common consent, it will need a strong case for the Fourteenth Amendment to affect it," Oliver Wendell Holmes, Jr., once wrote.[1] If a thing has been practiced for two thousand years by common consent, surely the case to change it needs to be very strong indeed.

Professor Mark Strasser's principal case is that the state will benefit from changing its marriage laws to include same-sex unions. Citizens will be happier and more productive. Children will be open and more tolerant. Laws will be fairer and more credible. Fundamental rights will be more properly and generously vindicated. Arguments from religion and morality no longer should inform marital policies in a democratic society dedicated to the nonestablishment of religion. Arguments from nature and custom are mere cloaks for prejudice and discrimination, as traditional miscegenation laws make clear. Just lift the ban on same-sex marriages, Professor Strasser concludes, and all will be well. Heterosexuals can have their marriages, homosexuals can have theirs. Only old-fashioned folks like my wife's husband could object.

Some of this argument strikes home. Professor Strasser and I agree that same-sex couples can and do afford each other some of the same benefits that heterosexual couples afford each other: of mutual caring and sharing, of coinsurance and cooperation, of domestic efficiency and proficiency, of sexual comfort and constraint. But, to my mind, this is an argument that same-sex couples should enjoy equal rights of association, not necessarily equal rights to marriage. We also agree that religious communities may have their own lore and law of marriage for their voluntary members, which may or may not be consistent with that of the state. But the question is whether a state law of marriage that happens to be consistent with some religious teachings on marriage automatically constitutes an "establishment of religion" in violation of the First Amendment. Professor Strasser evidently thinks so. I think not.[2]

Some of Professor Strasser's argument is conjectured. It is too early to assert that children raised by same-sex parents will be more "open," "tolerant," and "egalitarian" than their peers raised by heterosexual parents. Even if there is a gay and lesbian "baby boom" afoot, there has not been a long-enough experience with enough children in same-sex households to offer reliable longitudinal and comparative studies. The current anecdotal evidence that I have seen of the relative sociability and toleration of these two sets of children is decidedly mixed. It is also too glib to say that equal marriage rights for traditional and same-sex couples will enhance collective happiness and productivity of citizens to the benefit of the state. Right now, the issue of same-sex practices and marriages is tearing families, schools, clubs, churches, and other communities apart in states throughout the land—Hawaii and Vermont notably included. Granting equal rights of marriage to both same-sex and heterosexual couples will provide no panacea. Granting such rights precipitously, without full democratic ventilation and experimentation, will only exacerbate the current turmoil, if the cultural fallout from *Roe v. Wade* is any indication.

Some of Professor Strasser's argument proves too much. If social expediency and individual happiness are taken as dispositive criteria for reforming marriage laws, then arguments against incestuous, adolescent, and polygamous marriages must also fall aside. This is not to say that if one breaks one traditional moral string, the whole moral fabric of a society unravels. It is rather to say that there is no basis in such an argument for rejecting sincere claims by a brother and sister, by an adolescent couple, or by Jack, Jill, Jane, and Jennifer who wish to be married and can demonstrate that their lives would be happier and more productive if they were. Similarly, if elimination of discrimination is the heart of the argument, then sincere claims by incestuous, polygamous, and adolescent couples can again have no effective rejoinder. Professor Strasser equates distinction with discrimination in arguing against marriage as an exclusively heterosexual, monogamous union between two unrelated fit adults. If one accepts his argument about the unfairness of the distinction between heterosexuals and homosexuals, why stop there? Why not regard all the other distinctions as forms of discriminations as well? Why not argue against the institution of marriage altogether and thus remove all discriminatory line drawing? Professor Strasser's stated answer of careful statutory draftsmanship only papers over this problem.

Some of Professor Strasser's argument proves too little. The notion that arguments for traditional marriage are morally loaded "pretexts" for religious prejudice while arguments for same-sex marriage are morally neutral protests for constitutional equality is hardly self-evident. Both sets of arguments have strong moral premises and prescriptions, and both sets of moral claims can find anchorage within and beyond various religious traditions. The hard question for the law is whether and how to choose between and among these competing moral claims. The notion that current arguments against same-sex marriages are as "specious" as earlier arguments against interracial marriage begs questions over which Professor Strasser passes too easily—whether homosexuality, like race, is an immutable characteristic, and whether marriage is only a simple contract between two adults or intrinsically part of an association in which children are potentially or actually present.

As a Protestant dedicated to the mandate of *semper reformanda*, I am not so averse to reforming traditional marriage laws as Professor Strasser suggests. Traditionalists like me need constantly to be reminded of the maxim of Jaroslav Pelikan that "tradition is the living faith of the dead; traditionalism is the dead faith of the living."[3] Wooden antiquarianism, a dogmatic indifference to our changing sexual and marital norms and habits, will not do. But modernists, like Professor Strasser, need to heed the instruction of Harold Berman that "we must walk into the future with an eye on the past."[4] Chronological snobbery, a calculated disregard for the wisdom of the past, also will not do.

For nearly two thousand years, the Western legal tradition reserved the legal category of marriage to monogamous, heterosexual couples who had reached the age of consent, who had the physical capacity to join together in one flesh, and whose joining served the goods and goals of procreation, companionship, and stability at once. Marriage was a form of adhesion contract, to be accepted or rejected in toto, but not individually renegotiated. Marriage was the proper place for the enjoyment of sexual activities. Those who practiced sex elsewhere, with self or others, were subject to various moral and criminal sanctions. This was not just Christian doctrine. Hebrew jurists and prophets, Greek Platonists and Aristotelians, Roman moralists and jurists, church fathers and councils, high medieval Catholics, early modern Protestants, and eighteenth- and nineteenth-century Enlightenment philosophers all accepted this core understanding of the form and function of sex and marriage and defended it with all manner of theological, philosophical, political, and social arguments.

In the face of such a long and venerable tradition, we would be wise to exercise some humility before declaring our current arguments ineluctable and some patience before rushing to radical legal change. The tradition of Western marriage has been and will be amenable to change. Same-sex couples have already gained much freedom and acceptance in recent decades through the abolition of traditional fornication and sodomy laws and the formulation of new rights of association and sexual privacy. With patient and persistent argumentation and experimentation, more legal change might well come. But we have just begun the serious discussion, and many local communities have just begun their social experiments with gay and lesbian life. There are many open questions that the natural and social sciences are now exploring in earnest—whether homosexuality is an immutable norm, habit, and character, whether children raised in gay and lesbian households are indeed as well or better off, and whether alternative forms of conception (artificial insemination, surrogacy, cloning, and others) will ultimately make the procreative potential and capacity of same-sex and heterosexual coupling any different.

While this discussion and experimentation are pending, I am much more comfortable with the "menu of options" on which Professor Strasser touches in his essay: "legal recognition of [traditional] marriage, [alternative] domestic partnerships, reciprocal-beneficiary status," and more that "would accord the parties different obligations and benefits depending upon which of the arrangements had been chosen." For now, that strikes me as a more "open, egalitarian, and tolerant" course than marshalling all who seek sexual union to accept one single legal category of legal marriage.

## NOTES

1. *Jackman v. Rosenbaum*, 260 U.S. 22, 31 (1922).

2. See my *Religion and the American Constitutional Experiment* (Boulder, CO: Westview Press, 2000), 149ff., 231ff.

3. Jaroslav Pelikan, *The Vindication of Tradition* (New Haven: Yale University Press, 1984), 65.

4. Harold J. Berman, *Law and Revolution: The Formation of the Western Legal Tradition* (Cambridge, MA: Harvard University Press, 1983), v, vii.

Essay Two

# The Tradition of Traditional Marriage
## John Witte, Jr.

The logical case for same-sex marriage seems nearly ineluctable today. In the course of the past three decades, American state laws have effectively reduced marriage to a terminal sexual contract between consenting adults. Prenuptial and separation contracts allow parties to define their own rights and duties within the marital estate and thereafter. Implied marital contracts are imputed to long-standing lovers. Unilateral no-fault divorce statutes have reduced marital dissolution to a formality. Lump-sum marital property exchanges provide many divorcing parties with a clean break to marry anew. Criminal prosecutions for fornication, adultery, polygamy, and other classic sexual crimes have largely fallen aside. Free speech laws protect all manner of sexual expression, short of obscenity. Privacy laws protect all manner of sexual conduct, short of exploitation of children or abuse of others. Given such generous freedoms of marriage and sexuality, many states will be hard pressed to resist the next logical step to legalize same-sex marriages.

"A page of history is worth a volume of logic," however, Oliver Wendell Holmes, Jr., reminds us.[1] Western history provides very little support for extending the legal category of marriage to include same-sex unions. For nearly two millennia, the Western legal tradition defined marriage as a heterosexual, monogamous union, designed for the procreation and nurture of children, the mutual help and companionship of husband and wife, and the mutual protection of both parties from sexual sin and instability. This definition of marriage has been woven deeply into the fabric of Western canon law, civil law, and common law and is still reflected today in thousands of discrete American state and federal laws. To be sure, the Western legal tradition has radically transformed many aspects of the law and lore of marriage in the course of the past two millennia. In a few isolated cases, Western rulers may have accorded individual same-sex couples some measure of marital status. But for all this radical change and equitable tinkering, the Western legal tradition has not extended the legal category of marriage to include same-sex unions. Indeed, until very recently, most Western nations criminalized the acts of sodomy and buggery that are endemic to such unions.

History alone, of course, is not reason enough to maintain traditional marriage laws. But history must be an essential part of any serious arguments for the maintenance of traditional marriage. And the enduring traditional arguments about the origin, nature, and purpose of marriage must be the starting point for any serious debate about the propriety of legalizing same-sex marriages. Law is, after all, both a steward of our traditions and a totem of our ideals. Especially when it touches on so tender and vital a topic as marriage, we should amend and emend traditional legal teachings only with ample trepidation, only with long explanation, and only with full ventilation of what is at stake on both sides of the debate. Neither brittle historicism nor brutal dogmatism can be enough to defend traditional marital teachings. But neither fashionable casuistry nor political expediency can be enough to defeat them.

This volume of cleverly juxtaposed perspectives by scholars of multiple professions and confessions is precisely the kind of candid conversation that is currently needed to address the legal status of same-sex unions. I am happy to join the conversation by offering herein a quick tour of some of the main texts that have informed our Western legal understandings of traditional marriage and a quick distillation of some of their enduring teachings on the origin, nature, and purpose of marriage.[2]

## CLASSICAL SOURCES

The writings of some classical Greek and Roman philosophers were touchstones for later Western ideals of marriage as a natural union of husband and wife, contracted for the sake of procreation, companionship, and protection. Particularly influential and enduring were Aristotle's insights that marriage is a "natural union of a husband and wife"; that marriage is at once "useful," "pleasant," and "moral" in its own right; that it provides efficient pooling and division of specialized labor and resources within the household; and that it serves both for the fulfillment and happiness of spouses and for the procreation and nurture of children. "[E]very state is composed of households," Aristotle wrote famously. Every household, in turn, is composed of "a union or pairing of those who cannot exist without one another. A male and female must unite for the reproduction of the species—not from deliberate intention, but from the natural impulse . . . to leave behind something of the same nature as themselves."[3]

Sundry Roman moralists described marriage as a "sacred and enduring union" of the persons, properties, and pursuits of husband and wife in the service of marital affection and friendship, mutual caring and protection, and mutual procreation and education of children. Cicero (106–43 B.C.E.), for example, the leading jurist and moralist of his day, called marriage a "natural sharing" of the person and property of husband and wife that served for the procreation of children, for companionship, and ultimately for the broader cultivation of dutiful affection, kindness, liberality, goodwill, and courtesy.[4] Musonius Rufus (b. ca. 30 C.E.), an influential Roman moralist, described marriage in robust companionate terms:

The husband and wife . . . should come together for the purpose of making a life in common and of procreating children, and furthermore of regarding all things in common between them, and nothing peculiar or private to one or the other, not even their own bodies. The birth of a human being which results from such a union is to be sure something marvelous, but it is not yet enough for the relation of husband and wife, inasmuch as, quite apart from marriage, it could result from any other sexual union, just as in the case of animals. But in marriage there must be above all perfect companionship and mutual love of husband and wife, both in health and in sickness and under all conditions, since it was with desire for this as well as for having children that both entered upon marriage.[5]

The Graeco-Roman historian and moralist Plutarch (46–120 C.E.) described marriage as "a union for life between a man and a woman for the delights of love and the getting of children." "In the case of lawful wives, physical union is the beginning of friendship, a sharing as it were, in great mysteries. The pleasure [of sexual intercourse] is short, but the respect and kindness and mutual affection and loyalty that daily spring from it . . . [render] such a [marital] union a 'friendship.' " Again: "No mutual pleasures are greater, no mutual services more constant, no form of affection is more enviable and estimable for its sheer beauty than when man and wife in harmony of mind keep house together."[6] Plutarch also wrote extensively about the natural affinity and affection of parents, especially mothers, to their children, and the importance of both mother and father cooperating in the upbringing, discipline, and education of children.

Some of these views about marriage entered classical Roman law well before the Christian conversion of the Roman emperor and empire in the fourth century C.E. For example, two mid-third-century legal texts defined marriage as a "union of a man and a woman, and a partnership for all life [*consortium omnis vitae*], involving divine as well as human law."[7] "[T]he marriage tie, or matrimony, is the union of a man and a woman entailing the obligation to live in inseparable communion."[8] Other second- and third-century texts of Roman law emphasized that marriage was a "sacred and enduring" union, voluntarily contracted for the sake of "marital affection" and the propagation of offspring.[9]

To be sure, these classical moral and legal formulations of marriage were

in the context of a larger classical literature that sometimes condoned and
even celebrated homosexuality and other sexual conduct outside of monogamous heterosexual marriage. But even before the Christian conversion of
the Roman Empire, it was rare indeed for Roman law and Graeco-Roman
literature to stretch the formal legal category of marriage beyond heterosexual unions.

## EARLY CHRISTIAN FORMULATIONS

Building in part on this Graeco-Roman tradition, the early Christian
Church treated marriage as a monogamous heterosexual union created and
ordered by God. Already in Paradise, God had brought the first man and
the first woman together and had commanded them to "[b]e fruitful and
multiply and replenish the earth."[10] God had created them as social creatures, naturally inclined and attracted to each other, and physically capable
of joining together sexually as "one flesh" for the sake of procreation.[11] God
had commanded them to love, help, and nurture each other and to inculcate
in each other and in their children the love of God, neighbor, and self.
These duties and qualities of marriage continued after the fall into sin. After
the fall, however, marriages also became a remedy for lust, a balm to in-
continence. Rather than allowing sinful persons to burn with lust, God provided the remedy of marriage in order for parties to direct their natural
drives and passions to the service and love of the spouse, the child, and the
broader community.

Upon this common foundation about the created and natural order of
marriage, Christian writers designed various formulas to define the goods
and goals of marriage. The most famous and enduring formulation came
from St. Augustine (354–430), the bishop of Hippo. Marriage has three
inherent goods, Augustine wrote: children (*proles*), faith (*fides*), and stability
(*sacramentum*). As a created, natural means of procreation, Christian marriage rendered sexual intercourse licit. As a contract of fidelity, marriage gave
husband and wife an equal power over the other's body, an equal right to
demand that the other spouse avoid adultery, and an equal claim to the
"service, in a certain measure, of sustaining each other's weakness, for the
avoidance of illicit intercourse." As a "certain sacramental bond," marriage
was a source and symbol of permanent union between Christians.
"[M]arriage bears a kind of sacred bond," Augustine wrote; "it can be dissolved in no way except by the death of one of the parties."[12] Children,
faith, and stability: These were the three inherent goods of marriage, in
Augustine's view. They were the reason that the institution of marriage was
good. They were why participation in marriage was good. They were the
goods that a person could hope and expect to realize upon marrying.

## CATHOLIC FORMULATIONS

While such views came to intermittent expression in later Roman and Germanic law and theology in the first millennium C.E., they came to full elaboration in the course of the Papal Revolution of ca. 1075–1300. In this era, the church developed a systematic theology of marriage that remains at the heart of Catholic teaching to this day. In this same era, the church also developed a comprehensive canon law of marriage that dominated the Western legal tradition for many centuries thereafter.

One of the most enduring theological statements on marriage came from the Dominican friar Thomas Aquinas (1225–1274), who systematized some two centuries of high medieval legal and theological thought about marriage. Marriage is at once a natural, contractual, and sacramental union, Aquinas argued, anchored respectively by the Augustinian goods of procreation, faith, and stability.

First, marriage is a natural institution devoted to the good of procreation (*proles*). Men and women are naturally inclined to come together for the sake of having children, and natural law teaches that the licit means of doing so is through marriage. Procreation, however, means more than just conceiving children. It also means rearing and educating them for spiritual and temporal living. The good of procreation cannot be achieved in this fuller sense simply through the licit union of husband and wife in sexual intercourse. It also requires maintenance of a faithful, stable, and permanent union of husband and wife for the sake of their children.

Second, marriage is a contractual association, devoted to the good of faith (*fides*). Marital faith is not a spiritual faith, but a faith of justice, Aquinas argued. It means keeping faith, being faithful, holding faithfully to one's promises made in the contract of marriage. Marital faith requires, as Augustine had said, forgoing sexual intercourse with another and honoring the connubial debt (that is, yielding to the reasonable sexual advances of one's spouse). But marital faith also involves, as Aristotle and the Roman moralists had said, the commitment to be indissolubly united with one's spouse in body and mind, to be willing to share fully and equally in the person, property, lineage, and reputation of one's spouse. It is to be and bear with each other in youth and in old age, in sickness and in health, in prosperity and adversity. Marital faith, in this richer understanding, is a good in itself, Aquinas insisted. It need not necessarily be expected or intended for the procreation of children; indeed, a marriage promise need not even be consummated to be valid and binding. If it is consummated faithfully, sexual intercourse is a good act in itself, even if procreation is a natural impossibility.

Third, marriage is a sacramental institution, devoted to the good of stability. The union of body, soul, and mind in the marital estate symbolizes the union of Christ with the church. This was an image drawn directly from a lengthy passage in Ephesians 5:22–32, where St. Paul analogizes the church as a bride and Christ as a bridegroom—an explicit heterosexual image, akin to several references in the Hebrew Bible that analogize Yahweh's relationship with his chosen people of Israel as one of a husband to a wife.[13] Just as the bond between Christ and the church is eternal and binding, Thomas argued, so the bond between husband and wife must be enduring and indissoluble.

The medieval Catholic Church built upon this theological foundation a comprehensive canon law of sex, marriage, and family life that was enforced by a hierarchy of church courts throughout Western Christendom. From the twelfth century to the sixteenth century, the church's canon law of marriage was the marriage law of the West. A civil law or common law of marriage, where it existed, was usually supplemental and subordinate.

Consistent with the natural perspective on marriage, the canon law punished contraception, abortion, infanticide, and child abuse as violations of the created marital functions of propagation and child rearing. It also proscribed unnatural relations, such as homosexuality, incest, and polygamy, and unnatural acts such as sodomy, bestiality, and buggery as being contrary to the very nature of marriage. Consistent with the contractual perspective, the canon law ensured voluntary unions by dissolving marriages formed through mistake, duress, fraud, or coercion. It granted husband and wife alike equal rights to enforce conjugal debts and emphasized the importance of mutual love among the couple and their children. Consistent with the sacramental perspective, the church protected the sanctity and sanctifying purpose of marriage by declaring valid marital bonds to be indissoluble and by dissolving invalid unions between Christians and non-Christians or between parties related by various improper legal, spiritual, blood, or familial ties.

## PROTESTANT FORMULATIONS

The Protestant Reformation, inaugurated in 1517 by the German reformer Martin Luther (1483–1546), brought fundamental change to the theology and law of Western marriage even while it retained the traditional notion of marriage as a heterosexual, monogamous union created and governed by God. In the view of most early Protestants, God had created and ordered marriage for (1) the mutual love and support of husband and wife; (2) the mutual procreation and nurture of children; and (3) the mutual protection of both spouses from sexual sin. This formula of marital goods overlapped with the Augustinian formula of faith, children, and sacramentality, but amended it in critical ways that led to important changes in marriage law and to a dramatic shift of marital jurisdiction from the church to the state.

Like Augustine and medieval Catholics, Protestants emphasized the good of marital faithfulness (*fides*). But they cast this good in increasingly overt terms of marital love, affection, friendship, and companionship. Also, like Augustine, Protestants emphasized the good of procreating children (*proles*). But they amended this good with the familiar medieval gloss that procreation included the Christian nurture and education of children.

Unlike Augustine and medieval Catholics, however, the early Protestant reformers emphasized protection from sexual sin as a good in itself, not just a function of *fides*. Since the fall into sin, they argued, humankind had become totally depraved. Lust had pervaded the conscience of every person. Participation in marriage had thus become an absolute necessity, except for those with the very rare gift of continence. Without marriage, a person's distorted sexuality became a force capable of overthrowing the most devout conscience. A person was enticed by nature to prostitution, masturbation, homosexuality, and all manner of other sexual sins.

This understanding of the protective good of marriage undergirded the reformers' bitter attack on the traditional canon law rules of mandatory celibacy. To require celibacy of clerics, monks, and nuns, the reformers believed, was beyond the authority of the church and ultimately a source of great sin. Celibacy was for God to give, not for the church to require. Mandatory celibacy, the reformers taught, was hardly a prerequisite to true service of God. Instead, it led too easily to concubinage, prostitution, and homosexuality among the celibate—offenses that the reformers condemned and punished with special earnest.

Also unlike Augustine and medieval Catholics, Protestants gave no place to the marital good of *sacramentum*—either in the Augustinian sense of symbolic stability or in the medieval Catholic sense of a permanent channel of sanctifying grace. For most early Protestants, marriage was neither a sacrament of the church on the order of baptism or the Eucharist nor a permanent union dissoluble only upon the death of one of the parties. To be sure, Protestants, like Catholics, believed that marriages should be stable and presumptively indissoluble, but this presumption could be overcome if one of the other marital goods was frustrated.

Because they rejected the sacramentality of marriage, Protestants introduced divorce in the modern sense with a right to remarry, at least for the innocent party. If there was a breach of marital love by one of the parties (by reason of adultery, desertion, or cruelty), the marriage was broken. The innocent spouse who could not forgive this breach could sue for divorce and remarry. If there was a failure of procreation (by reason of sterility, incapacity, or disease discovered shortly after the wedding), the marriage was also broken. Those spouses who could not reconcile themselves to this condition could seek an annulment, and at least the healthy spouse could marry another. If there was a failure of protection from sin (by reason of frigidity, separation, or cruelty), the marriage was again broken, entitling the parties to divorce and remarriage.

Because they rejected the sacramentality of marriage, Protestants also emphasized various psychological, social, and political goods of this civil institution. Lutherans and Calvinists emphasized that marriage had civil and spiritual "uses" in this life. On the one hand, they argued, marriage had general civil uses for all persons, regardless of their faith. Marriage deterred vice by furnishing preferred options to prostitution, promiscuity, pornography, and other forms of sexual pathos. Marriage cultivated virtue by offering love, care, and nurture to its members and holding out a model of charity, education, and sacrifice to the broader community. Marriage enhanced the life of a man and a woman by providing them with a community of caring and sharing, of stability and support, of nurture and welfare. Marriage enhanced the life of the child by providing it with a chrysalis of nurture and love, with a highly individualized form of socialization and education. On the other hand, marriage had specific spiritual uses for believers—ways of sustaining and strengthening them in the Christian faith. The love of wife and husband was among the strongest symbols Christians could experience of Yahweh's love for the elect, of Christ's love for the church. The sacrifices one made for spouse and child could be among the best expressions of Christian charity and agape.

Other Protestants emphasized that marriage was one of the three estates of the earthly kingdom, along with the church and the state, that God had appointed for the governance of the earthly kingdom. Anglicans stressed further that marriage at once served and symbolized the commonwealth (literally the "common good") of the couple, the children, the church, and the state. "A household is as it were a little commonwealth," Robert Cleaver wrote in 1598, "by the good government whereof, God's glory may be advanced, the commonwealth which stands of several families, benefited, and all that live in that family, may receive much comfort and commodity."[14] William Gouge premised his massive 800-page household manual of 1622 on the same belief that "the family is a seminary of the Church and the Commonwealth" and is indeed in its own right "a little church, and a little commonwealth, whereby a trial may be made of such as are fit for any place of authority, or subjection in Church or commonwealth."[15]

Because they rejected the sacramentality of marriage, Protestants shifted principal marital jurisdiction from the church to the state, but in devising the new civil and common law of marriage, Protestants adopted a good deal of the traditional canon law of marriage. Thus traditional canon law prohibitions against unnatural sexual relations and acts and against infringements of the procreative functions of marriage remained in effect. Canon law procedures treating wife and child abuse, paternal delinquency, child custody, and the like continued. Canon law impediments that protected free consent, that implemented biblical prohibitions against marriage of relatives, and that governed the relations of husband and wife and parent and child within the household were largely retained. Such time-tested canon law rules and procedures were as consistent with Protestant theology as with Catholic theology and were transplanted directly into the new state laws of marriage of Protestant Europe.

The new Protestant theology of marriage, however, also yielded critical changes in this new civil law of marriage in Protestant lands. In particular, these laws rejected traditional laws that forbade clerical and monastic marriage and that permitted vows of chastity to annul vows of marriage. They also severely truncated the law of impediments to marriage and, as previously noted, introduced divorce in the modern sense, on grounds of adultery, desertion, cruelty, or frigidity, with a subsequent right to remarry, at least for the innocent party.

## EARLY AMERICAN FORMULATIONS

These European models of marriage were transmitted across the Atlantic to America during the great waves of colonization in the seventeenth and eighteenth centuries and the great waves of immigration in the nineteenth and early twentieth centuries. They provided much of the theological foundation for the American law of marriage until the mid-twentieth century.

Catholic models of marriage, while not prominent in early America, came to direct application in parts of colonial Maryland, Delaware, and the Carolinas and more prominently in the colonial American South and Southwest. They spread with alacrity across America with the new waves of Irish, Spanish, Portuguese, and Italian immigrants in the later nineteenth century and the aggressive work of Catholic missionaries on the frontier.

Protestant models of marriage were much more influential in shaping American marriage legal culture in the colonies and the early Republic. Like American Catholics, American Protestants accepted many of the traditional Christian norms of sex and marriage, including the traditional insistence on marriage as a heterosexual, monogamous union and the traditional prohibition on sodomy, buggery, polygamy, and other sexual crimes. Unlike Catholics, however, Protestants rejected sacramental views of marriage and ecclesiastical jurisdiction over marital formation, maintenance, and dissolution. They encouraged ministers to be married. They permitted religious intermarriage. They truncated the law of impediments. They allowed for divorce on proof of fault. They encouraged remarriage of those divorced or widowed.

A common "Protestant temperament" attended much of the American legal understanding of marriage.[16] Most American common-law authorities accepted Protestant social models of marriage that placed special emphasis on the personal felicity, social utility, and moral civility of this institution. Joseph Story, for example, wrote famously that marriage is "more than a mere contract." He elaborated this sentiment in 1834, arguing that marriage might be best viewed as a balance of natural, social, and spiritual contracts:

Marriage is treated by all civilized societies as a peculiar and favored contract. It is in its origin a contract of natural law. . . . It is the parent, and not the child of society the source of civility and a sort of seminary of the republic. In civil society it becomes a civil contract, regulated and prescribed by law, and endowed with civil consequences. In most civilized countries, acting under a sense of the force of sacred obligations, it has had the sanctions of religion superadded. It then becomes a religious, as well as a natural and civil contract. . . . it is a great mistake to suppose that because it is the one, therefore it may not be the other.[17]

Chancellor James Kent wrote about the spiritual and social utility of the marriage contract:

The primary and most important of the domestic relations is that of husband and wife. It has its foundations in nature, and is the only lawful relation by which Providence has permitted the continuance of the human race. In every age it has had a propitious influence on the moral improvement and happiness of mankind. It is one of the chief foundations of social order. We may justly place to the credit of the institution of marriage a great share of the blessings which flow from the refinement of manners, the education of children, the sense of justice, and cultivation of the liberal arts.[18]

W.C. Rodgers opened his oft-reprinted treatise on the law of domestic relations with a veritable homily on marriage:

In a sense it is a consummation of the Divine Command to "multiply and replenish the earth." It is the state of existence ordained by the Creator, who has fashioned man and woman expressly for the society and enjoyment incident to mutual companionship. This Divine plan is supported and promoted by natural instinct, as it were, on the part of both for the society of each other. It is the highest state of existence, . . . the only stable substructure of our social, civil, and religious institutions. Religion, government, morals, progress, enlightened learning, and domestic happiness must all fall into most certain and inevitable decay when the married state ceases to be recognized or respected. Accordingly, we have in this state of man and woman the most essential foundation of religion, social purity, and domestic happiness.[19]

Similarly, the U.S. Supreme Court spoke repeatedly of monogamous, heterosexual marriage as "more than a mere contract," "a sacred obligation," "the foundation of the family and society without which there would be neither civilization nor progress."[20] In *Murphy v. Ramsey* (1885), Justice Bradley declared for the Court:

For, certainly, no legislation can be supposed more wholesome and necessary in the founding of a free, self-governing commonwealth . . . than that which seeks to establish it on the basis of the idea of the family, as consisting in and springing from the union for life of one man and one woman in the holy estate of matrimony; the sure foundation of all that is stable and noble in our civilizations, the best guarantee of that reverent morality which is the source of all beneficent progress in social and political improvement.[21]

## CONCLUSION

Already in the centuries before Christ and before the Christianization of the West, classical Greek and Roman writers taught that marriage is a natural institution to which most men and women are naturally inclined; that marriage is a useful, pleasant, moral, and even sacred institution; that it provides an efficient pooling of property and division of labor and resources within the household; that it provides mutual care, protection, and compensation to couples; that it serves both for the fulfillment, companionship, and happiness of spouses and for the procreation, nurture, and education of children.

The Roman Catholic tradition, building on Augustine and Aquinas, wove these classical insights into the famous theory that marriage has three inherent goods: (1) *fides*—a faithfulness and friendship between husband and wife that goes beyond that demanded of any other temporal relationship; (2) *proles*—children, who are to be nurtured and educated to perpetuate the human species and to transmit and live out the proper norms and habits of spiritual and temporal life; and (3) *sacramentum*—an enduring expression of Christ's love for his church, an indissoluble channel of God's grace to sanctify the couple, their children, and the broader community.

The Protestant tradition emphasized not only the intrinsic goods but also the instrumental goals of marriage. Marriage was created by God to foster love, to deter sin, and to produce children. If one or more of these created marital goals was permanently frustrated, those parties who could not reconcile themselves to this condition could seek divorce and remarry. Protestants emphasized further that marriage has "uses" in this life, such as deterring vice, cultivating virtue, and enhancing the life of a man and a woman and of the child. Such views echoed loudly in the theological and legal literature of the American colonies and the early Republic.

For all of its theological and philosophical diversity, therefore, the West has had a long and thick overlapping consensus that marriage is good, does good, and has goods both for the couple and for the children. Many writers have recognized the natural teleology and utility of marriage: (1) the natural drive on the part of most adults toward the institution of marriage because of the inherent goods of individual survival, flourishing, happiness, and even perfectibility that it provides and (2) the natural capacity on the part of most adults to engage in the expected performance of marriage—the unique combination of sexual, physical, economic, emotional, charitable, moral, and spiritual performances that become marriage. Obviously, there are ample exceptions to this natural norm of marriage that the tradition has long recognized. Some are called to celibacy or to the single or widowed life. Some lack the physical capacity or emotional temperament to engage in marriage. Some who get married should not be married and need to be removed from the institution through annulment or divorce. But the Western tradition teaches that the general inclination and instruction of nature, of the human body, of the human psyche, of the human heart, are for marriage.

The second core insight of the Western tradition is that marriage is good not only for the couple and their children, but also for the broader civic communities of which they are a part. The ancient Greeks and Roman Stoics called marriage variously the foundation of republic and the private font of public virtue. The church fathers called marital and familial love "the seedbed of the city," "the force that welds society together." Catholics called the family "a domestic church," "a kind of school of deeper humanity." Protestants called the household a "little church," a "little state," a "little seminary," a "little commonwealth." American jurists and theologians taught that marriage is both private and public, individual and social, temporal and transcendent in quality—a natural if not a spiritual estate, a useful if not an essential association, a pillar if not the foundation of civil society. At the core of all these metaphors is a perennial Western ideal that stable marriages and families are essential to the survival, flourishing, and happiness of the greater commonwealths of church, state, and civil society. A breakdown of marriage and the family will eventually have devastating consequences on these larger social institutions.

To bring to light these historical teachings on marriage models is neither to wax nostalgic about a prior golden age of the Western marriage nor to write pedantic about arcane antiquities with no modern utility. These are the teachings that have shaped the Western legal tradition of marriage—for better and for worse. These are the teachings that have to be dealt with—critically, constructively, and comprehensively—to renegotiate the forms and forums of contemporary marriage.

## NOTES

1. *New York Trust Co. v. Eisner*, 265 U.S. 345, 349 (1921).

2. This essay is excerpted in part from my article "The Goods and Goals of Marriage," 76 *Notre Dame Law Review* 1009–1076 (2001), and my books *From Sacrament to Contract: Marriage, Religion, and Law in the Western Tradition* (1997) and *Law and Protestantism: The Legal Teachings of the Lutheran Reformation* (2002), ch. 6, which include detailed citations to the sources and secondary literature.

3. *The Politics of Aristotle*, I.1.1, I.2.2, I.2.9 (Ernest Barker, trans. 1962); *The Ethics of Aristotle*, VIII.12 (trans. J.A.K. Thomson repr. ed. 1965).

4. Cicero, *De Finibus*, III. 23.65 (H. Rackham trans. 1983).

5. Musonius Rufus, fragments 12, 13A, 15, reprinted and translated in Cora E. Lutz, ed., *Musonius Rufus: The Roman Socrates* 89 (1947).

6. Plutarch, "The Dialogue of Love," in 4 *Plutarch's Moralia*, secs. 769–770 (Edwin L. Miner et al. trans., T.E. Page et al. eds., 1961).

7. *The Digest of Justinian*, 23.2.1 (Theodor Mommsen & Paul Krueger trans., Alan Watson ed., 1985).

8. Justinian, *Institutes*, 1.9.1 (T. Lambert Mears trans. 1994).

9. *The Digest of Justinian*, 24.1.32; 25.1.3; bk. 35.1.15; *Institutes*, 1.10.

10. Genesis 1:28.

11. Genesis 2:24; Matthew 19:5; Mark 10:7–8; Ephesians 5:31.

12. "The Good of Marriage," in *St. Augustine: Treatises on Marriage and Other Subjects* 17, 31–32 (R.J. Deferrari ed. 1955).

13. See Ezekiel 16; Hosea 2; Malachi 2.

14. Robert Cleaver, *A Godly Forme of Householde Gouernment* 1 (1598).

15. William Gouge, *Of Domesticall Duties: Eight Treatises* 27 (1622).

16. Philip Greven, *The Protestant Temperament: Patterns of Child-Rearing, Religious Experience, and the Self in Early America* (1977).

17. Joseph Story, *Commentaries on the Conflict of Laws, Foreign and Domestic, in Regard to Contracts, Rights, and Remedies* 100 (1834).

18. James Kent, *Commentaries on American Law* 76 (12th ed. 1896).

19. W.C. Rodgers, *A Treatise on the Law of Domestic Relations* 2 (1891).

20. *Maynard v. Hill*, 125 U.S. 190, 210–11 (1888); *Reynolds v. United States*, 98 U.S. 145, 165 (1879); *Murphy v. Ramsey*, 114 U.S. 15, 45 (1885); *Davis v. Beason*, 133 U.S. 333, 341–342 (1890).

21. *Murphy v. Ramsey*, 45.

Response

# The Logical Case for Same-Sex Marriage: A Response to Professor John Witte, Jr.

## Mark Strasser

Professor Witte rightly states that the "logical case for same-sex marriage seems nearly ineluctable today," although not for the reasons he suggests. Rather, it is because the same benefits will accrue to the state, the individuals themselves, and their children, whether the couple is composed of individuals of the same sex or, instead, of different sexes.

While countries have only recently started affording legal recognition to same-sex unions, Western history provides ample support for legally recognizing such unions if one considers the nature and purposes of marriage, Professor Witte's claims to the contrary notwithstanding. For example, Aristotle rightly suggests that marriage is (or can be) useful, pleasant, and moral and can benefit both the spouses themselves and any children that they might be raising. That insight supports rather than undermines the wisdom of legally recognizing same-sex unions. Those commentators who extol marriage as an institution embodying marital affection and friendship and mutual caring and protection, or as providing a setting for the production and raising of children, are thereby providing reasons to support the appropriateness of marriage for same-sex couples.

The inherent goods of marriage described by Augustine—children, faith, and stability—can be enjoyed by different-sex and by same-sex couples. Of course, Professor Witte would suggest that same-sex couples cannot partake of these goods because their sexual relations cannot be "natural." Thus, even if same-sex couples are faithful, willing to share in mind and body, and mutually loving and supportive, this does not matter—they cannot partake of a "real" marriage.

Suppose that we accept Professor Witte's invitation to consider a page of history but choose to go back about forty years instead of hundreds or thousands of years. We would have been told (at least in certain parts of the United States) that interracial marriages were "unnatural" and against God's will and thus were not appropriately recognized by the state. Yet the U.S. Supreme Court wisely rejected such arguments.[1] Interracial couples must be permitted to marry, both because society is benefited by such marriages and, more importantly, because marriage involves "vital personal rights essential to the orderly pursuit of happiness."[2] To justify forbidding such unions, the state would have to establish that their recognition would harm compelling state interests. The mere fact that some individuals have religious scruples against such unions and sincerely believe such unions unnatural simply does not suffice as a justification.

Professor Witte emphasizes the importance of married individuals reproducing through their union and even quotes Aristotle to suggest that married couples should not be motivated to have sexual relations by the conscious desire to have children. Professor Witte's view seems to discount the lives of many different-sex (much less same-sex) couples who for whatever reason either have great difficulty in conceiving or simply cannot conceive. Suppose that we were to adopt the implicit view offered by Professor Witte and only permit those to marry who (1) can and will have children through their union and (2) do not need to plan their sexual activity in light of when they would thereby be most likely to be able to procreate. Such a view would require our radically changing our current marriage laws in a way that would harm both society and the individuals themselves who had thereby been precluded from marrying.

Consider the argument often touted as to why marriage is important, namely, to provide a setting in which children can be raised. Yet children will be benefited by being brought up in a stable and nurturing home even if they are not biologically related to both of the individuals raising them, for example, because the children were adopted or because they were a product of a previous marriage. Concern for the next generation militates in favor of affording legal recognition to couples (seeking that recognition) who are raising children, whether or not the children are biologically related to both adults and whether or not the adults are of different sexes. Indeed, the Vermont Supreme Court recognized that the state interest in promoting the welfare of children militated in favor of rather than against recognizing same-sex unions.[3] Other state supreme courts have recognized that children are at a disadvantage when their same-sex parents are precluded by law from marrying,[4] which helps explain why some states have been willing to recognize second-parent adoptions.[5]

Some commentators fear that if same-sex unions are recognized, then all unions must be recognized, including incestuous and polygamous unions. Yet the same argument was offered to establish that interracial unions should not be recognized, and the recognition of interracial unions did not invalidate all marriage prohibitions.

Marital restrictions must be examined to make sure that they are suffi-ciently narrowly tailored and promote sufficiently important state interests. When that test has been met, the marital restrictions may remain. When that test has not been met, however, these restrictions should be abolished.

Professor Witte is correct that some religions do not recognize same-sex unions, although one would be wrong to infer that all religions refuse to endorse such unions. Yet the fact that some but not all religions refuse to recognize such unions is hardly a reason for the state to refuse to recognize such unions. At issue here is not whether religions should be forced to recognize such unions, but merely whether the state should recognize them because of the benefits that would thereby accrue to society, the individuals themselves, and any children that they might be raising.[6]

Elsewhere, Professor Witte attempts to establish that marriage offers a variety of benefits to individuals whether or not they have children.[7] His argument there helps establish that many couples have ample reason to marry. Regrettably, in this volume, Professor Witte adopts a different tack. When he writes that given the "generous freedoms of marriage and sexu-ality" afforded by the states, it will be hard to "resist the next logical step to legalize same-sex marriage," he implies that society has now changed so radically that marriage has lost its meaning and value, and that it is only for this reason that the state should recognize same-sex unions. Such a view does little to support the value of marriage for either same-sex or different-sex couples.

One of the most ironic results of the concerted effort by same-sex-marriage opponents to "defend" or "save" marriage is that they implicitly if not explicitly suggest that marriage loses its value if it is something to which same-sex couples have access, as if the sole value of marriage lies in its being something that a certain class of individuals has been precluded from enjoying. Yet the best way to save or defend marriage is not to imply that its only value lies in who can be precluded from enjoying it but, instead, to tout its actual benefits. Were more commentators to do that, it seems likely that society, individuals, and their children would all derive the ben-efits that would be afforded were marriage not viewed as one of the best tools to promote division and hatred and instead as an institution that can serve the needs and desires of many kinds of families and of society as a whole.

## NOTES

1. *See* Loving v. Virginia, 388 U.S. 1 (1967).
2. *See id.* at 12.
3. *See* Baker v. State, 744 A.2d 864, 882 (Vt. 1999) ("If anything, the exclusion of same-sex couples from the legal protections incident to marriage exposes their children to the precise risks that the State argues the marriage laws are designed to secure against").

4. *See* Adoption of Tammy, 619 N.E.2d 315, 320 (Mass. 1993) (outlining some of the financial costs to the child); In re Jacob, 660 N.E.2d 397, 399 (N.Y. 1995) (same). The state of Vermont recognized second-parent adoptions even before it recognized civil unions. See Adoptions of B.L.V.B. & E.L.V.B., 628 A.2d 1271 (Vt. 1993).

5. A second-parent adoption involves an adoption of a child by the parent's significant other when the adults are not married. Likened to a stepparent adoption, this adoption permits each of two unmarried adults who are living together to be the legal parent of the same child.

6. Of course, those religions that do recognize same-sex unions should certainly be permitted to continue to do so. Cf., for example, HAW. STAT. 572-1.6 (Cum. Supp. 2000) ("Nothing in this chapter shall be construed to render unlawful, or otherwise affirmatively punishable at law, the solemnization of same-sex relationships by religious organizations; provided that nothing in this section shall be construed to confer any of the benefits, burdens, or obligations of marriage under the laws of Hawaii").

7. See John Witte, Jr., *The Goods and Goals of Marriage*, 76 NOTRE DAME L. REV. 1019 (2001).

# Chapter 3

Essay One

# On Legal Recognition for Same-Sex Partners

## Arthur S. Leonard

Over the past twenty years, same-sex couples have achieved a startling degree of legal and social recognition for our relationships.[1] Hundreds of private-sector employers, including my own, have elected either voluntarily or through collective bargaining to recognize same-sex partners of their sexual-minority employees for purposes of various employment policies, ranging from bereavement leave to family discounts on products to health insurance and survivors' benefits.[2] In the public sector, many municipal governments and a handful of state governments have formally adopted such recognition policies for employee benefits by ordinance or statute, executive order, or collective bargaining agreement. Beginning in 1989 with *Braschi v. Stahl Associates Co.*,[3] courts have begun to recognize claims that same-sex partners should be considered at least family members, if not spouses, and the highest courts of two states, Hawaii and Vermont, have accepted arguments that same-sex couples may have valid claims to access the rights and responsibilities of legal marriage.[4] Under the pressure of the Vermont ruling, that state's legislature enacted a Civil Union Act that creates a quasi-marital status open to same-sex couples.[5] Similar recognition has come in a host of decisions concerning child custody and visitation where the same-sex partners of biological and/or legal parents sought to play a continuing role in the lives of children they had been helping to raise after a relationship with the parent had terminated.[6]

Is this a good thing for society or a bad thing? Is public policy well served or poorly served by these developments? Assuming that there is a certain momentum built up behind legal recognition for same-sex partners, is this cause for celebration, indifference, or alarm?

I believe that legal recognition for same-sex couples is a good thing. Expanding legal marriage would be the most straightforward way to extend recognition, but I consider more limited legal recognition in specific contexts to be desirable as well, and thus I regard state laws such as the Hawaii Reciprocal Beneficiaries Act or the Vermont Civil Union Act to be significant advances, not defeats. I also recognize that the emotional and symbolic significance of marriage for nongay people may prove a significant political barrier to the kind of full marriage rights that have been granted to same-sex partners in the Netherlands and Belgium, the only countries to have done this at the time of writing.[7] I further acknowledge that there are some within sexual-minority communities who have argued strongly that sexual minorities should not be seeking the right to marry because of the history of marriage as a patriarchal, confining institution inimical to human freedom and happiness; even those who make such arguments, however, tend to support more limited, specific forms of legal recognition for same-sex relationships on pragmatic grounds (such as, for example, allowing committed partners to adopt each other's children). I will begin with the factual assumptions on which I base my arguments, followed by my reasons for believing that public policy is well served by continuing and expanding the current trend in U.S. law toward such recognition.

## FACTUAL ASSUMPTIONS

My argument rests on several factual assumptions. These assumptions are not all based on empirical evidence derived from scientific research, although some of them may gain credence from the results that have been announced by scientific and historical researchers in recent years. They arise from my own experiences and observations as an active member of the sexual-minority community in New York City for almost a quarter of a century, during which I have known hundreds of individuals through organizational and community ties, especially in the legal community and the Jewish community, and have heard about the life experiences of many.[8]

Human sexual orientation is a multifactorial phenomenon with a physical basis. It is not subject to conscious choice and is relatively immutable for the overwhelming majority of individuals. There may be an inherited genetic component to it, for which recent scientific research provides suggestive evidence without conclusive proof, but I doubt that there is anything so simplistic as a "gay gene" that makes somebody "homosexual" or "bisexual."[9] How somebody expresses his or her sexuality is a matter of choice; that choice is bounded by biological and psychological factors, and whatever "change" may be induced by means of psychotherapy, shock treatments, lobotomy, or economic incentives is behavioral change that is unlikely to reflect any significant change in underlying orientation.

Despite the questionable nature of the statistics Dr. Alfred Kinsey and his associates published on the proportion of the adult population that have same-sex desires or engage in same-sex activity, Kinsey's reports on male and female sexuality contained important insights on the nature of human sexuality.[10] No subsequent study has disproved Kinsey's conclusion that human sexuality exists along a continuum in which a small percentage of the population has an exclusively same-sex orientation, a very large percentage of the population (probably exceeding a majority) has an exclusively opposite-sex orientation, and that a minority is arrayed somewhere between these poles, the "bisexuals" who can feel an erotic attraction at various times and places to members of either sex. As with anything complex, sexuality does not fit neatly into a bipolar analysis, making questions about how many "homosexuals" there are essentially unanswerable.

In light of these beliefs, I would find unpersuasive arguments that the state must adopt particular family law policies in order to influence the number of people who are "homosexual" or "bisexual," because I doubt that government policies have any significant impact on these numbers. I accept as intuitively valid Judge Richard Posner's contention that government policies can affect which people exercise choice (whether consciously or otherwise) and thus may affect, at the margins, how some people decide to lead what might be called a "gay lifestyle."[11] Thus, for example, a ban on military service by openly gay people undoubtedly influences the number of people in the military who are willing to be open about their sexual orientation, may affect the number of people who enlist, and may affect where and when military members engage in same-sex activity. Such a ban may even induce some same-sexers in the military to engage in opposite-sex activity to maintain a pretense of heterosexuality. But it surely has no effect on the proportion of military personnel who have a same-sex orientation, apart from its deterrent effect against enlistment by those who have realized, prior to the age of enlistment, that they have a same-sex orientation. (Unfortunately, at the age of military enlistment, some people have not yet figured this out about themselves, as the stories about gays in the military well illustrate.) By the same token, a criminal ban on sodomy between consenting adults may have some effect on the amount of same-sex activity between consenting adults but is unlikely to affect anybody's sexual orientation.

I also assume some things about children and sexuality. Among the many factors in the multifactorial stew that contribute to determining sexual orientation are environmental factors, but the sort of crude role-model theories used by some courts to justify discrimination against gay people in custody or adoption cases are quite implausible in default of proof that the sexual orientation or partnered relationship of a child's parents either will determine the child's sexual orientation or endanger the child's ability to develop a healthy gender identity.[12] It seems intuitively true that a child raised in a same-sex household may be less judgmental about gender roles and sexuality and thus may be more open to sexual experimentation or a nonstereotypical view of gender roles than a child raised in a traditional, heterosexual two-parent household,[13] but there is no evidence that such children ultimately differ in their sexual orientation or gender identity from other children. There is no evidence for the deterministic view that children are "fated" at birth to be "gay" or "straight," based either on genetics or the sexual orientation or genders of the child's parents, or that a child adopted by a gay adult will inevitably grow up to be gay or will have difficulty adapting to society's overall view of gender identity and gender roles.

Some small percentage of all children will turn out to have a same-sex orientation, and some subset of these, of indeterminate size, will accept that orientation as identity-defining and live their lives accordingly. Growing up in a family headed by a same-sex couple or a gay individual, or growing up knowing such people as neighbors, teachers, ministers or rabbis, or other adult figures in a child's life, may make it easier for a child who discovers his or her own same-sex orientation to deal with the challenges of that discovery.

Even if government policy with respect to same-sex partners might have some marginal effect on individual sexual orientation, one would have to ask whether any legitimate government interest in asserting such an influence would justify disadvantaging and undermining the relationships of all those who would not be influenced. This, of course, raises further the question whether government has any legitimate interest in whether any particular individual is heterosexual, homosexual, or somewhere in between or selects a partner of the same or the opposite sex with whom to bond and live as a partner.[14]

I proceed based on assumptions about the nature and history of marriage itself. Recent scholarship has documented that marriage is a socially constructed phenomenon that has varied widely between different cultures and at different times.[15] The picture of marriage obtained from the Old Testament, for example, includes polygamy and concubinage and lacks the enormous array of specific legal rights and responsibilities carried by a twenty-first-century American marriage. Professor John Boswell demonstrated the existence of ceremonies within Roman Catholic monastic communities marking communal recognition of same-sex relationships in premodern Europe.[16] As donor insemination is a recent phenomenon, it is not surprising that the legally recognized marital institution in Anglo-American legal culture, to the extent that its derivation has relied on child rearing and transmission of property to legal heirs, has been an opposite-sex institution, but it is an institution that has evolved in substantial ways through our recorded history. The legal framework of contemporary marriage in the United States is far removed from the framework that existed at the foundation of the Republic in terms of the relative status of the parties under the law, the degree of formality necessary to their social recognition as spouses, and the legal rights and obligations of the marital couple and of its constituent individuals. Any argument that the marital institution must be frozen into the mold of a particular time period, regardless of advances in knowledge, changes in social attitudes, and the actual ways that people are choosing to live their lives, is doomed by the verdict of history, especially in light of the significant numbers of children who are being raised by unmarried couples and single people. Privileging opposite-sex couples to advance society's interest in child rearing as a policy choice is startlingly underinclusive and unduly dismissive of the vital interests of thousands of children being raised by same-sex couples and single parents.

## PUBLIC POLICY ISSUES

Reflecting about how government policies affect individual lives raises fundamental questions about the government's appropriate role in the realm of family law, and most particularly about the boundaries of legitimate government concern regarding individual choice in the selection of a domestic partner. In the United States, our Constitution enshrines protection for individual liberty, expressly in the Due Process Clauses[17] and implicitly in the many provisions that were found by Justice William O. Douglas in *Griswold v. Connecticut* to provide the foundation for a constitutional right to privacy in sexual matters.[18] The same sorts of due process and privacy concerns were subsequently found by the Supreme Court to exclude the government from interfering with individual choice in the selection of a marital partner in *Loving v. Virginia*,[19] and by at least a plurality of the Court to exclude the government from dictating the intimate associations of individuals, even beyond the choice of marital partners, in *Roberts v. United States Jaycees*.[20] These and other privacy and due process cases suggest that the legitimate role of government in dictating or influencing individual choice in family relationships is quite limited. Maintaining a policy of denial of legal recognition for same-sex couples as part of a public strategy to affect the choice of life partners is illegitimate in the U.S. constitutional framework. The government has legitimate interests in signaling the public through positive law that stable family units are favored, but does that interest extend to dictating personal choice in the formation of such units?

What, then, are the legitimate concerns of government when it comes to recognizing family relationships? Public health is one legitimate concern. Government is entitled to adopt policies calculated to benefit the overall health of the population, even if it may be limited in imposing regulations against the will of individuals where such regulations are entirely paternalistic. For example, the government can require that children attending school be inoculated against contagious conditions in order to protect other children, teachers, staff, and their families, even though such a regulation abridges individual liberty.[21] A government interest in public health supports legal recognition for same-sex couples. Persons living in relationships tend on average to be healthier and more productive than persons who live alone.[22] Healthier people place fewer demands on the health care system and present less risk for the spread of contagious conditions. Legal recognition that includes entitlement to insurance coverage routinely extended by many employers, both public and private, to employees' legal spouses and children benefits public health by making a dent in the societal problem of uninsured individuals.[23] Uninsured individuals are less likely to have access to routine physical examinations, preventive care, or prompt treatment for illness. This affects both their own health and public health, for untreated individuals with contagious conditions can spread these conditions, and individuals who lack coverage for preventive care are more likely to burden the health care system. Better individual health contributes to national prosperity by minimizing the loss of productive time due to illness and premature withdrawal from the workforce.

Another legitimate ground for public policy is promotion of the general welfare of society, economic and social. Government has a legitimate concern to maintain public order, promote peaceful relations, and take steps to enhance productivity and economic prosperity. All of these concerns are undercut by the unequal legal status of same-sex partners. A policy that recognizes functional family units contributes to public order, regardless of whether they are same-sex or opposite-sex family units.

Legal recognition of same-sex couples would have the effect over time of "normalizing" such relationships, reducing the social tensions that arise when members of different groups see each other as "abnormal" or "foreign." Those who argue that the gay rights movement is out to transform society by getting people to view gay people as "normal" are completely correct. Every minority group wants to be seen as "normal" and to be accorded equal opportunity and treatment in society. As sexual minorities come to be viewed as "normal," there will be a decline in bias-related violence, discrimination, and general societal hostility toward them. It is hard to understand how a decline in violence, discrimination, and generalized hostility toward a particular social group could be anything other than a desirable public policy goal, unless one is arguing in favor of discrimination for the purpose of maintaining a social hierarchy.

Many of the privileges and entitlements government presently confers on legally recognized families are calculated to enhance prosperity by making family life economically efficient, by assisting families in providing a well-supported, nurturing environment to raise children, and by assisting families in surmounting the emotional and economic devastation inflicted by the serious injury or death of a contributing family member. All of these reasons apply to same-sex families. Failure to recognize same-sex families, to the extent that it withholds important incentives toward stability, undercuts an important public policy concern.

Perhaps the most frequently cited issue in the debate over legal recognition of same-sex families deals with children, and here the debate is all too often based on incorrect assumptions about the existing situation. Many same-sex couples are raising children or have raised children, and many of these children are genetically related to at least one of the adults who are raising them. Although present reproductive technology does not allow a same-sex couple to conceive a child directly through sexual intercourse, this is irrelevant to the debate over legal recognition. Many people discover their same-sex orientation while they are engaged in heterosexual marriages that produced children; although their heterosexual marriages end, they continue to be parents and as such are entitled to a continued parental role unless they are shown to be unfit for that purpose. Many lesbian couples have children through donor insemination, with or without the assistance of a physician, using either known donors (sometimes gay men of their acquaintance, or a male relative of the coparent so that the child will be genetically related to both mothers) or anonymous donors.[24] Some gay men have been able to have children through arrangements with women who are willing to be inseminated with their sperm or donor sperm.[25] Both lesbians and gay men have adopted children, a practice that is lawful in every state except Florida (where the legislature passed a ban on adoption by "homosexuals" in the wake of Anita Bryant's "Save our Children" campaign of 1977).[26]

These potential means of having children are not just hypothetical; indeed, during the 1990s there was a "baby boom" in the sexual-minority community, reflected in the growing body of court decisions dealing with custody and visitation disputes arising between former same-sex partners. Some significant portion of the approximately 600,000 self-identified households headed by same-sex adult partners counted in the 2000 U.S. census probably include children. Those who oppose extending legal recognition to same-sex partners based on the argument that the purpose of legal marriage is to provide an optimum environment for raising children are thus missing the point. Same-sex partners are raising children right now, even though they have no legal recognition for their partnerships in all but a few states. If public policy is concerned with optimizing conditions for child rearing, it should be concerned with how the failure to extend legal recognition penalizes children being raised in such households. If legal recognition contributes to stability for a household, and children benefit from a stable household, then legal recognition benefits children. If eligibility for insurance is beneficial to children, and legal recognition would lead to an increase in the number of children who are eligible for coverage based on a same-sex coparent's employment benefits, legal recognition benefits children. If legal recognition means that two persons rather than one person will have legal responsibility for the care and well-being of a child, then a child's welfare is enhanced by extending such legal recognition.[27]

Of course, all these asserted benefits would be heavily countered by evidence that children who are raised in same-sex households are significantly disadvantaged compared to children raised by opposite-sex couples in ways attributable to factors other than the existing lack of legal recognition for their parents. Are children psychologically harmed by being raised in same-sex households? Are they more likely to exhibit gender-role confusion because only one gender is represented among their parents? So far, the most extended consideration of this issue in a forum where opposite sides had equal opportunity to provide expert testimony was the Hawaii same-sex-marriage trial, in which the state defended its exclusion of same-sex couples from legal marriage primarily through an argument that same-sex households were inferior to opposite-sex households for raising children. After hearing the testimony of eight experts, four for each side, and reviewing the documentary evidence they submitted, the judge concluded that the state had not made its case, and that failure to extend legal recognition to same-sex couples was harmful to the children they were raising.[28] This is consistent with the rapidly expanding literature of published studies about parental sexual orientation and child development. Although many of the studies have methodological flaws, and some may be biased by the political predilections of researchers in favor of or opposed to gay people raising children, the overwhelming trend of the studies is consistent with the Hawaii court's conclusions.[29]

There is an even simpler argument to be made: that lesbians and gay men are raising children in the hundreds and thousands, under circumstances where the state would have no purpose (and no benefit) in interfering because it would be utterly incapable of providing these children with a better environment than they are experiencing, which means that children will continue to be raised in same-sex households, regardless of whether the state extends legal recognition to the relationship of their parents. The relevant public policy question is whether the current refusal to recognize their parents' relationships disadvantages these children or enhances their welfare. Those who argue that same-sex couples should not enjoy legal recognition because children are best raised in the context of traditional heterosexual households are actually arguing that society should privilege the children who are being raised in traditional households by assuring that children being raised in nontraditional households are legally disadvantaged.

Much of the opposition to legal recognition is framed in terms of the necessity to "protect" traditional marriage and "defend" it from being undermined in some way by its being expanded to include couples who have heretofore been excluded, in order to preserve the traditional "way of life." This argument is frequently accompanied by the assertion that the institution of marriage, and all the benefits and protections it accrues both from government and private actors, has been constructed to provide a nurturing environment in which to procreate and raise children and would be inappropriately applied to a coupling that is inherently unable to procreate. (The argument ignores the thousands of same-sex couples who are raising children, as well as the millions of childless married couples.) The argument is frequently accompanied by assertions, derived from religious traditions, that the marital construct found in the Bible or the basic scriptures of nonbiblical faiths evidence God's plan for humanity from which the state may not depart, or by philosophical assertions based on natural-law ideas that because people come in two genders, male and female, there is a natural or divine plan that would be upset by recognizing same-sex couples because a person can only find natural fulfillment coupled with a person of the opposite sex.[30]

I question these arguments' relevance to the question of whether civil society should extend legal rights and responsibilities of marriage to same-sex couples. They assume that government has a paternalistic right and duty to impose misery and deprivation on those who do not elect to conform to a particular model of family life, because the traditional majority believes that only their religiously or philosophically derived historical model is socially beneficial, and that individuals may not be trusted to decide for themselves what mode of living will give them fulfillment and satisfaction. Proceeding as I do from the conviction that sexual orientation is determined by the time an individual reaches puberty, and that emotional and psychological fulfillment through heterosexual marriage is not likely for the overwhelming majority of those whose sexual orientation is not heterosexual, I find these arguments unconvincing. They state, in effect, that my partner and I are to be deprived of the vast array of federal, state, and local legal benefits and responsibilities of marriage or equivalent legal recognition because some heterosexuals argue that true happiness can only be achieved through the mechanism that allegedly works for them: heterosexual marriage. But a foundational idea of American democracy is that each individual is endowed by her or his Creator with inalienable rights to life, liberty, and the pursuit of happiness,[31] and our constitutional tradition has been developed to protect minorities from being required to embrace the views of majorities in the areas of choice of marital partners and intimate associates.

John Finnis may argue that my relationship with my partner of twenty-two years is incomplete because we cannot make babies by having sex with each other, but how is his argument relevant to social policy in a nation dedicated to the proposition of individual liberty and protection of the pursuit of happiness?[32] Would the government be justified in denying him the right to marry a postmenopausal woman because their sexual congress could only be fruitless? Within the context of a constitutional order in which the government is largely precluded from interfering in the choice of intimate associates, from compelling pregnant women to bear children, or from mandating sterilization for eugenic purposes, who is he (or his like) to argue that the state should condemn me to unequal treatment in order to fulfill his philosophical ideal in matters of family life? How is the divine plan enhanced by ensuring that children being raised by same-sex partners may not benefit from health insurance benefits to which they would be entitled were their parents married? How does allowing a surviving same-sex partner to sue for wrongful death detract from the sanctity of another couple's opposite-sex marriage? Whence this bizarre mania with "defending marriage" from a portion of society that desires not to knock the institution down but to expand it to include them?

At bottom, however, proponents and opponents of legal recognition for same-sex relationships frequently appear to be arguing right past each other. The proponents are asking, quite pragmatically, for the law to catch up with the social reality, contending that the institution is constantly evolving and should continue to evolve to reflect the reality of same-sex couples, many of whom are raising children. History supports this argument, as does an evolving constitutional tradition in which respect for personal autonomy and choice in matters of home and the family have reflected the diversity of cultures and beliefs that characterize twenty-first-century America.

## NOTES

The author acknowledges a New York Law School faculty research grant underwriting his summer writing projects for 2001, including this essay.

1. I use "our" purposely, because my same-sex partner and I have been living together for more than twenty-two years, sharing a mortgage, a home, and a family life, and on an individual basis I resent the unequal treatment our relationship receives under the law.

2. I use the term "sexual minority" in this essay to refer to persons whose sexual orientation is homosexual or bisexual.

3. 74 N.Y.2d 201, 543 N.E.2d 49, 544 N.Y.S.2d 784 (N.Y. 1989) (holding that same-sex partners in a committed relationship should be treated as family members for purposes of rent-control regulation blocking eviction of surviving family members in a residence when the tenant dies).

4. Baehr v. Lewin, 852 P.2d 44 (Haw. May 5, 1993) (same-sex couples may state a sex-discrimination claim in challenging denial of a marriage license under the state constitutional ban on sex-discrimination); Baker v. State of Vermont, 744 A.2d 864 (Vt. Dec. 20, 1999) (same-sex couples are entitled to equal access to rights and responsibilities of marriage, pursuant to the state constitutional equal benefits clause).

5. An Act Relating to Civil Unions, 2000 Vermont Statutes No. 91 (Apr. 26, 2000).

6. See, e.g., V.C. v. M.J.B., 748 A.2d 539 (N.J. Sup. Ct.), cert. denied, 531 U.S. 926 (2000) (recognizing a lesbian coparent as a "de facto" parent for legal purposes of visitation and custody, citing and relying on a prior decision by the Minnesota Supreme Court).

7. Act on the Opening Up of Marriage; Act of December 21, 2000, amending Book 1 of the Civil Code of the Netherlands, effective April 1, 2001, upon royal assent given on March 20, 2001; Joris van Poppel, Belgian Gays: Children First, Then Marriage, Algemeen Dagblad (January 30, 2003). An accompanying statute also opens up adoption so that married same-sex couples can adopt children on the same basis as married opposite-sex couples.

8. I was the founding president of New York City's lesbian and gay legal organization, now known as the Lesbian and Gay Law Association of Greater New York,

as well as the founding cochair of the New York City Association of the Bar Special Committee on Lesbians and Gay Men in the Legal Profession and a founding member of the National Lesbian and Gay Law Association. I have been a frequent speaker at legal conferences and programs presented by all three of these organizations. Since 1977, I have been a member of Congregation Beth Simchat Torah, the world's largest lesbian and gay Jewish congregation, having served on various committees (including the Rabbi Search Committee and the board of directors) and having led services small and large (ranging in size up to 2,500 people at Yom Kippur in the Jacob Javits Convention Center). These organizational involvements have brought me into contact with thousands of other lesbians and gay men. My impressions about gay people are not based on a small, homogeneous sample. I know gay conservative Republicans who thought that the Supreme Court's decision in Boy Scouts of America v. Dale, 530 U.S. 640, 120 S.Ct. 2446 (2000), was correctly made and gay radicals who argue that marriage is a conservative patriarchal institution that gay people should not be interested in joining.

9. For some recent research on the etiology of human sexual orientation, see, for example, D. McFadden and E.G. Pasanen, Spontaneous Otoacoustic Emissions in Heterosexuals, Homosexuals, and Bisexuals, J. Acoust. Soc. Am., 105(4): 2403–2413 (Apr. 1999); S.M. Stonski Huwiler and G. Remafedi, Adolescent Homosexuality, Adv. Pediatr., 45:107–44 (1998); and G. Sanders and M. Wright, Sexual Orientation Differences in Cerebral Asymmetry and in the Performance of Sexually Dimorphic Cognitive and Motor Tasks, Arch. Sex. Behav., 26(5):463–480 (Oct. 1997). The search for biological or genetic explanations for human sexual orientation has been criticized on both ideological and scientific grounds. See, e.g., W. Byne and E. Stein, Ethical Implications of Scientific Research on the Causes of Sexual Orientation, Health Care Anal., 5(2):146–148 (June 1997).

10. A. Kinsey et al., Sexual Behavior in the Human Male (1948); A. Kinsey et al., Sexual Behavior in the Human Female (1953).

11. Richard Posner, Sex and Reason (1992). There are, of course, many different "gay lifestyles," including settled, middle-class suburban soccer moms raising children—two soccer moms in one household. Opponents of equal rights for gay people tend to fixate on scantily clad sexual libertines "flaunting" their flesh on floats at gay pride marches, who represent a tiny segment of the sexual-minority population, whose rights must be protected, but who are hardly representative of the "gay lifestyle."

12. E.g., Lofton v. Kearney, 157 F. Supp. 2d 1372 (S.D. Fla. 2001) (suggesting that children adopted and raised by gay parents will suffer from gender confusion due to lack of heterosexual role models, citing no credible empirical evidence whatsoever).

13. See Judith Stacey and Timothy J. Biblarz, (How) Does the Sexual Orientation of Parents Matter?, 66 Am. Sociological Rev. 159 (Apr. 2001).

14. The Supreme Court has long since accepted the proposition that the government has no legitimate interest, consistent with due process and equal protection, in an individual's choice of a marital partner where the race of the partners is concerned, and the Court has intimated that government's legitimate interest ends at the point of intimate associational choices. See Loving v. Virginia, 388 U.S. 1 (1967); Roberts v. United States Jaycees, 468 U.S. 609 (1984).

15. William N. Eskridge, Jr., The Case for Same-Sex Marriage (1996).

16. John Boswell, Same-Sex Unions in PreModern Europe (1994).

17. "No State shall make or enforce any law which shall abridge the privileges or immunities of citizens of the United States; nor shall any State deprive any person of life, liberty, or property, without due process of law." U.S. Const., amendment XIV. "No person shall be . . . deprived of life, liberty, or property, without due process of law." U.S. Const., amendment V.

18. 381 U.S. 479 (1965). Further, in Eisenstadt v. Baird, 405 U.S. 438 (1972), the Court held that equal protection would be offended by depriving unmarried individuals of the same privacy that had been recognized in Griswold for married individuals.

19. 388 U.S. 1 (1967).

20. 468 U.S. 609 (1984).

21. See Jacobson v. Massachusetts, 197 U.S. 11 (1905) (public health concerns held to justify a state law requiring mandatory vaccination against serious contagious diseases).

22. For detailed documentation of the physical, psychological, and economic advantages enjoyed by married persons, see Linda J. Waite and Maggie Gallagher, The Case for Marriage: Why Married People Are Happier, Healthier, and Better Off Financially (2000).

23. This justification disappears, of course, in a society that acknowledges the importance of adequate health care by providing universal coverage.

24. For example, consider the factual background in Thomas S. v. Robin Y., 599 N.Y.S.2d 377 (N.Y. Fam. Ct. 1993), rev'd, 618 N.Y.S.2d 356 (N.Y.A.D. 1 Dept. 1994) (a lesbian couple had children with sperm donated by gay men).

25. For example, consider the factual background of Decker v. Decker, 2001 Westlaw 1167475 (Ohio App. 3rd Dist. 2001) (unpublished opinion) (a gay man and his sister agreed that she would bear a child using donor sperm to be raised by him and his male partner).

26. F.S.A. § 63.042(3). See Brendan Farrington, Ex-Legislator Regrets Her Vote Banning Gay Adoption in '77, Orlando Sentinel, Sept. 8, 2001 (former Florida legislator Elaine Bloom). The plaintiffs' attempt to introduce evidence of the atmosphere in which the Florida statute was passed in a recent constitutional challenge was rebuffed by the trial judge, who found the legislature's motivation to be irrelevant to the rational-basis review of the statute the court decreed to be appropriate for an equal protection challenge to sexual-orientation discrimination. Lofton v. Kearney, 157 F. Supp. 2d 1372 (S.D. Fla. 2001). A similar statute passed by the New Hampshire legislature in hysterical reaction to a media frenzy over the placement of two young boys with a gay male couple as foster parents in the Boston area was repealed a generation later after the state passed a law banning sexual-orientation discrimination.

27. A similar point was made by the New York County Surrogate Court in Adoption of Evan, 583 N.Y.S.2d 997 (Surr. Ct N.Y. Co. 1992), in which the court decided in a matter of first impression to approve a same-sex coparent adoption petition, emphasizing the psychological and economic benefit to the child of being legally related to both of the women who were raising him. The New York Court of Appeals subsequently approved adoptions by same-sex coparents in Matter of Jacob, 86 N.Y.2d 651 (N.Y. 1995).

28. Baehr v. Miike, 1996 WL 694235 (Haw. Cir. Ct. 1st Cir. Dec. 3, 1996)

(Hawaii's prohibition against same-sex marriages violates the state constitution's equal protection clause).

29. For a wide-ranging overview of the topic by a pair of avowedly heterosexual researchers, see Judith Stacey and Timothy J. Biblarz, (How) Does the Sexual Orientation of Parents Matter?, 66 Amer. Sociological Rev. 159 (Apr. 2001). This article includes an extensive bibliography of published studies and articles on the topic.

30. One could flippantly respond to these arguments by challenging the simplistic logic that presumes to derive the divine plan for family life from the "fact" of sexual dimorphism, especially in a world where we now know about intersexuals, transgendered persons, and the extraordinary variations on sexual dimorphism found throughout the animal kingdom, of which we are biologically a part. Of course, many of those making these arguments would stoutly reject the notion that we are part of the animal kingdom.

31. Declaration of Independence (1776).

32. John Finnis, The Good of Marriage and the Morality of Sexual Relations: Some Philosophical and Historical Observations, 42 Am. J. Juris. 97 (1997).

# Response

# *Reply to Arthur S. Leonard*
## Lynne Marie Kohm

An appropriate response to Professor Leonard's remarks ought to contain some strong statements as to the mutual respect existent between us. While attempting to be academically realistic (if such a state of being is at all possible), we are both pragmatists and idealists at heart. That is, each of us is completely idealistic about our philosophy supporting our view and contemporaneously as practical and realistic as we can be. My appreciation and respect for Professor Leonard is all the greater. Indeed, we even agree on some things.[1] His candor and honesty in the goals of the gay movement are refreshingly disarming, eliciting my sympathies for the negative treatment he has endured as a result of his personal position.

There are four points that need to be made in response to his work. These involve philosophic basis for law, assumptions and assertions therefrom, parenting and benefits to children, and concepts about liberty interests.

First, the fundamental flaws inherent in law based on existentialism are answered with an ontology and design basis for law. Existentialism speaks of one's personal experience, and that as independent of natural laws that exist free of and separate from any experience. Ontology investigates the structure of reality as a whole.[2] Ontology applied to marriage, and therefore to the family, not only claims and promotes, but also proves that marriage (and the begetting of children) is by design.[3] Regardless of individual experience to the contrary, the design of one man and one woman in marriage is the design of ultimate reality, and any notion of the family structure evolving away from that design is by nature flawed.

Second, assumptions and assertions based on existentialism do not prove legal truth; they merely validate one's experiences. Assertions based on ontological design, however, do indeed provide a factual basis for legal truth.

Form rather than matter is the bestower of identity, and the design of any-thing demonstrates the virtue of that thing by its nature. Applying this the-ory to anything means that that thing has a design, a basic nature by design that gives that thing its virtue and attributes. Therefore, marriage has an original design, no matter how that design has been mutated or made to evolve.[4] It is that basic nature from which flows the design of marriage between one man and one woman, being therefore the foundation for a family. Thus a family, by virtue of its nature and origin, is of original, unique, and authentic design and provides a factual (or a real rather than experi-ential) basis for legal truth, and thus for basic American family law. This is precisely why marriage between a man and a woman by design, as the basic human institution, is afforded protection by our government or any gov-ernment. Marriage is not a socially constructed phenomenon at all (despite recent scholarship), but indeed existed before even the most basic form of government, proving again its original design, preexistent to law, which thereafter resulted logically in legal protection as a matter of course. This leads directly to the next significant point of this discussion.

Children benefit from this basic design. Children benefit not just from a stable household, but from a household that is stable because it follows the original design. Children benefit not from having two parents, but rather from having a father and a mother that lovingly care for and protect them simultaneously—and this precisely states the unfixable and fundamental flaw with gay parenting. Gay parenting is the intentional deprivation of a parent to a child. Gay parenting denies a child either a father or a mother. Such a deviation from the original design tends to inherently provide its own de-mise.

Finally, the distinction must be made between a request for government action and intervention and constitutional protection of the freedom from government intervention. A request for government intervention in creating a new status of marriage, as is being purported in this debate, is the inverse of, and therefore directly opposed to, the freedom from government inter-vention in one's liberty interests. These concepts and strategies have been tried in the end-of-life decision-making debate. Any fundamental right to die was proved to be without any liberty interest as not deeply rooted in the history and legal traditions of our nation[5] and not subjecting (or con-demning) one to unequal treatment, because those requesting government intervention to obtain liberty are directly in contradiction to those wishing to preserve freedom from government intervention in matters of autonomy and choice.[6] The same-sex-partnership debate is equally analogous to the end-of-life decision-making debate in that there is no historical legal basis for a liberty interest in same-sex partnership (and therefore not in same-sex marriage). There is also no subjection to unequal protection when individ-uals who are not similarly situated with respect to basic requirements for entry into marriage are treated differently. Governments that uphold the original design of marriage (which are all governments in the past, present, and, I suggest, the future as well) have no paternalistic right or duty to impose misery and deprivation on those who elect not to conform to a particular model of family life. Rather, such governments are merely following the order of the original design, imposing nothing on anyone, but upholding that which has already evidenced goodness and preexistent truth.

Marriage between a man and a woman is by original ontological design and therefore does not evolve. It does not evolve culturally, and it does not evolve legally. Marriage and the ensuing marital act are protected by law and legal tradition not because of culture, but because of original design. This original design may seem inimical to human freedom to those who wish that it would more quickly evolve, but that human freedom is precisely the ultimate benefit and result that flows from the original design. Political barriers may seem significant, but they swiftly fade to nothing in comparison to the strength of original design.

## NOTES

1. I, too, "find unpersuasive arguments that the state must adopt particular family law policies in order to influence the number of people who are 'homosexual' or 'bisexual.' " Law does not make the people under it; the people make the law under which they live.

2. John H. Kok, *Patterns of the Western Mind*, 1997, p. 4. See also Edward Pols, *Radical Realism: Direct Knowing in Science and Philosophy*, 1992, p. 8 (stating that ontology is that body of "theory that gives us (indirect) knowledge of the extra-theoretically real"); Jean Paul Sartre, *Being and Nothingness: An Essay on Phenomenological Ontology*, 1956, p. 632; and Jonathan Barnes, ed., *The Cambridge Companion to Aristotle*, 1995, p. 73 (stating that "Aristotle not infrequently observes that this or that philosophical theory goes wrong because it fails to take note of a crucial homonymy," and that this sameness or crucial homonymy is that of having an original design or having its nature by virtue of design).

3. See Sheldon M. Cohen, *Aristotle on Nature and Incomplete Substance*, 1996, p. 100.

4. Vast and sweeping assertions about conscious choice are unfounded assumptions in that sexuality is always a conscious choice by human nature, which is then based in experience, but such experience placed in the context of the reality of original design puts in perspective any underlying orientation as merely a blanket on the original form.

5. See Washington v. Glucksberg, 521 U.S. 702 (1997) (unanimous decision).

6. See Vacco v. Quill, 521 U.S. 793 (1997) (unanimous decision).

## Essay Two

# *Marriage by Design*

## Lynne Marie Kohm

In pursuit of an anthology on the marriage relationship, it is essential to review historical rules and underpinnings of family law, particularly in light of the effects of the seemingly shifting state of those laws in current events. When principles that have been the state of affairs of law and culture for all of recorded history are called into question, an honest, fair, and open discussion is necessary for the further procession of progress in human civilization. That is exactly what this chapter intends to do with the nonconstitutional policy concerns surrounding this critical issue.

The first section of this essay begins with documenting and explaining the design of marriage first from a historical perspective, which necessarily includes an overview of the religious history. Religious principles were the primary overseer of marriage until the modern to postmodern period. Second, because marriage is the basis of the family, the design of the family will then be discussed thoroughly. Because the family is founded in the marriage relationship, family laws have arisen and been implemented since the common-law era, many of which have survived to this day. The third section brings together the integration of marriage, the family, and the law in an explanative manner, making the argument from design the most viable and authentic explanation for the current form of marriage.

But more than these principles needs to be addressed in any complete anthology. The effects of these principles, as well as the effect of diverting from these principles, demonstrate the authority of the original design. These effects appear in case law, in regulatory schemes, and in statutory rules and changes and manifest themselves in our culture and ultimately in our civilization.

This essay addresses the vital significance of the original design of marriage

as a relationship between one man and one woman for a lifetime, thus forming the basis for the common family. It ought to challenge our complete
knowledge beyond each person's individual existentialism to a broader plain
of insight.

## THE HISTORICAL DESIGN OF MARRIAGE

Marriage was not invented, codified, or planned by human government.
Rather, human government gave the stamp of approval to a design already
manifested, honored, maintained, and flourishing. Any civil government that
ratified marriage as an institution did so only after organized religion had
established a methodology for upholding the marriage concept as a good
to be promoted in human civilization.

Marriage has been historically defined by the church as "a natural association, a contractual unit [prescribing] for couples a lifelong relation of
love, service, and devotion, to each other and proscribed unwarranted
breach of relaxation of their connubial parental duties.[1] As the temporal and
human union of body, soul, and mind within the marital estate, marriage
symbolized the eternal union between Christ and his church, bringing sanctifying grace to the couple, the church, and the community at large.

Theology is not out of place in a discussion of the value of an original
design of marriage. On the contrary, it is a useful guide for ages and centuries of experience and knowledge, for many ideas about God that seem
like new ones today are simply the same ones that real theologians tried
centuries ago and rejected.[2] Our desire in this anthology is not to regress
and forget history, but to use it as a guide in wise decision making in our
law and culture today. This is absolutely necessary for any discussion on
marriage.

Church history filled with classic and timeless theology does indeed shed
light on the bases for the principles of marriage and for the intact marriage
as the basis of the unitary family. Historic time-honored truths ought to be
summoned for usefulness in legal analysis to illuminate our understanding
of matters basic to human relationships. Patristic and biblical teachings reveal that the law and theology of marriage were important concerns of the
Judeo-Christian church and of many Eastern traditions from the very beginning. This is reflected in the fact that the teachings of Moses, Christ, and
St. Paul have directed millennia of law and theology on marriage. These
also set out the first principles of marriage.

Augustine's writings reveal some of these first principles, namely, the natural, spiritual, contractual, and social perspectives on marriage as a creation
of God, with its own inherited goods. The transformation of marriage law
in Lutheran Germany after the Protestant Reformation required civil authorities to divest the Roman Catholic Church of its jurisdiction over marriage. The Reformation called for new civil marriage laws that were

consonant with God's word but required that the church (and thus the reformers themselves) advise the civil authors on what God's word commands. Both the magistrates' seizure of jurisdiction over marriage and the reformers' active development of new marriage law were thus seen as divine tasks.[3]

Theology faculties and law faculties of the new Protestant German universities became the child of agents for the reform of marriage law in the early years of the Reformation. Lutheran theologians throughout evangelical Germany, several themselves trained in law, joined with university jurists to debate detailed questions of marriage also raised by Scripture, Roman law, canon law, and local custom. This theology and law of marriage developed by evangelical Lutherans provided a paradigm for Protestants that led to the Calvinist tradition of marriage as covenant. This in turn provided a distinctive law and theology of marriage that would come to dominate a good deal of the Protestant world in subsequent centuries. Calvin's critique of the canon law produced publications and statutory regulations that became civil law and set out the church's new role in the family life and law of the community. The law set out the outer boundaries and defined the middle line of this theology, defining the core doctrines of marriage.

These outer boundaries were set out in minimum requirements for entry into marriage. Anyone desiring to enter into the matrimonial bond must be mentally competent to do so with mutual consent from his or her future partner. Each must be unrelated by consanguinity or affinity. Each must be of proper age to consent to such a venture, with an understanding that this was so for the lifetime of each partner, or at least one at a time. Each must also be of a different sex from the other, one male and one female.[4] These basic requirements for entry into the holy and legal union of marriage were considered naturally inherent, yet simultaneously flexible to consistently accommodate an emerging Western epistemology of reasonableness.

From the Reformation concept of marriage to the commonwealth concept of marriage in the Anglican tradition, the way was neatly paved for marriage as a contractual concept in the Enlightenment tradition. The church and canon law history of the model of marriage is more than artifacts of ancient cultures. Indeed, until recently these were the laws in much of the West, particularly in England and America.[5] "With ample variations, English and American law generally defined marriage as a permanent monogamous union between a fit man and a fit woman of the age of consent, designed for mutual love and support, and for mutual procreation and protection."[6]

Mosaic law forbade marriage of blood and family relatives, as well as sex between people of the same gender and bestiality. Singled out for harsh criticisms by the early Roman Catholic Church were Roman practices of temple harlotry, transvestitism, and homosexuality, among others.[7] The push for such recognition in the United States, in fact, has caused a countermovement. In 1996, Congress established a federal definition of marriage as between a man and a woman, and to date thirty-one states have adopted similar norms. Legislation is pending in many other states. Activists realize that this debate must continue to take place not only in the courts of law, but in the culture-shaping churches and synagogues of America. Marriage law activists understand that law still works with religion in forming or re-forming basic principles for marriage and the family.

The debate in contemporary mainline churches is interesting. The two largest denominations in America, the Southern Baptist Convention (SBC) and the Roman Catholic Church, firmly oppose any endorsement of homosexual unions. The Presbyterian Church of America has hotly debated sanctioning same-sex unions. The Episcopal Church and the Anglican Church have equally echoed these sentiments to permit and encourage homosexual marriage ceremonies.

Most religious scholars agree at least on the source for the discussion, the Holy Scriptures, because marriage is discussed throughout the Bible with significant honor attached to it. From Genesis to Hebrews, marriage is discussed with utmost dignity and in a manner that implicitly and inherently reflects the complementarity of a man and a woman in a holy union for a lifetime.[8]

Biblical marriage rituals go back to the wedding of Isaac and Rebecca in Genesis. The Hebrew idea of "two becoming one flesh" as the marriage of a man and a woman runs from Genesis to Christ and the Apostle Paul. The Catholic Church made marriage a divine and holy "sacrament" in the year 1139 and likened its permanence to Christ and his church-as-bride, much as the Hebrews likened Israel to being the wife of Yahweh. The Protestant Reformation dropped the "sacramental" view of marriage, and in 1529 Martin Luther declared it a civil contract sanctioned by public vows before God and the church. The reformer John Calvin emphasized the "covenant" between man and woman.

Attempts to reshape the marriage tradition for homosexuals have raised the church debate on several fronts. These include the Bible's prohibitions on same-sex genital relations, the claim that the church honored "unions" in the past, and new discussions in science about the cause of homosexuality.

Among the change agents surrounding the family, the homosexual discussion is taking on marriage and the original design of the family through both theology and the law. While same-sex unions offer fuel for enlarging the debate over marriage to other forms of sexuality, particularly transgendered and multipartner notions of sexual relationships, marital status has never been afforded these partnerships in any church or lawful jurisdiction.

In light of the long history of heterosexual marriage, many believe that the homosexual debate will serve to render the heterosexual marriage not all the more fragile and outdated, but rather all the more stable, in light of analysis of the circumstances as a whole. The debate over same-sex unions discussed in the context of marriage causes the issues involved to come into sharper focus, revealing the deep and profound basis for marriage between a man and a woman founded on the complementarity of male and female. This theological and legal history of marriage has driven the rich development of Western family law as well.

## THE HISTORICAL DESIGN OF THE FAMILY

The family is essentially the smallest and most intimate form of government. Its historical design is founded in the marriage relationship and thus depends wholly thereupon. Marriage was viewed not as a system of encumbrance, but as a system of strength and authority. As the institution of marriage socially gained strength, it was further judicially clarified and defined as the "voluntary union of a man and a woman to the exclusion of all others." Marriage has always been, and remains now, one of the most important relationships in any culture, causing every society to be based conceptually upon this unit and on the institutionalization of this unit.[9]

The family is one of nature's masterpieces. It would be hard to conceive a system of instincts more nicely adjusted, where the constituents should represent or support one another better. . . . [T]here are insuperable difficulties in proposing any substitute for the family. In the first place, all society at present rests on this institution, so that we cannot easily discern which of our habits and sentiments are parcels of it, and which are attached to it adventitiously and have an independent basis. A reformer hewing so near to the tree's root never knows how much he may be felling. Possibly his own ideal would lose its secret support if what it condemns had wholly disappeared. For instance, it is conceivable that a communist, abolishing the family in order to make opportunities equal and remove the more cruel injustices of fortune, might be drying up that milk of human kindness which had fed his own enthusiasm; for the foundlings which he decreed were to people the earth might at once disown all socialism and prove a brood of inhuman egoists. Or, as not wholly contemptible theories have maintained, it might happen that if fathers were relieved of care for their children and children of all paternal suasion, human virtue would lose its two chief stays. . . .

Nevertheless, no suggested substitute for the family is in the least satisfactory. Those forms of free love or facile divorce to which radical opinion and practice incline in these days tend to transform the family without abolishing it. The family in a barbarous age remains sacrosanct and traditional; nothing in its law, manners, or ritual is open to amendment. The unhappiness which may consequently overtake individuals is hushed up or positively blamed, with no thought of tinkering with the holy institutions which are its cause.[10]

Placed on display in this essay are millennia of legal and ecclesiastical ordinances supporting marriage as the foundation for the family. Quite recent U.S. history is important, but cultural changes and the rapid growth of nontraditional families do not hinder the original family design from its authenticity. Nor does the use of societal substitutes prohibit the Supreme Court from recognizing the policy basis behind thousands of years of rules that have worked for the best interests of the parties involved in a family. Rather, this debate strengthens the meaning of marriage under the historical and original design. There remains, certainly, a deeply felt need to be sensitive to nontraditional families and the difficulties that those individuals in broken, rather than intact, families must endure.

"Nevertheless, it seems unlikely that the majority of state legislatures will abolish these 'anachronistic' marriage requirements in the foreseeable future. And even if the parties were able to contract privately free from all state regulation of marriage, what legal protection would be afforded to prevent the possible exploitation of one contracting party by the other contracting party?"[11] Furthermore, a plethora of individuals today still choose (traditional) marriage, even when our culture accepts many types of people groupings and living arrangements. "Notwithstanding these developments, a majority of Americans still marry in the traditional way and continue to regard marriage as the most important relationship in their lives."[12]

## MARRIAGE AS THE BASIS OF FAMILY MANIFESTED IN FAMILY LAW

Family law as we know it today is based on what we have been describing in the historical family. One of the most important factors for the staying power of the intact (or traditional) family is the protection of children.[13] Resting on the necessity of marriage and the family as a unit, our culture continues to use the historical, traditional family as the normative model, based on the original design. The significance of the intact family ought not to be quickly discarded or underestimated. An intact family would be defined as one man and one woman who have been married to each other while conceiving and raising their children. Contemporary scholars have also referred to this as the traditional family or the marital family.[14] Although fast becoming a novelty in American life, "[l]asting marriage is the goal and, even as the divorce statistics increase, remains the norm."[15] The emphasis on individual rights has produced "a body of family law that protects only the autonomous self and thereby fails to nurture the relationships between individuals that constitute families."[16]

In light of these trends, a particular Supreme Court family law decision sets itself apart and signals the impact of the marital family. *Michael H. v. Gerald D.* is a parental rights and visitation case testing California's presumption of legitimacy that was heard by the U.S. Supreme Court.[17] *Michael H.* reflects the key to reconcile design and culture. The fast-paced lifestyle of the marriage between an international model and an oil executive was the focus of this case in which a daughter was born to the marriage, but

DNA evidence showed that the child was likely the product of the model's relationship with a neighbor. Based on the importance of the unitary family, as the court termed it, the Supreme Court ruled that a third party was prohibited from asserting individual rights to a child born within an intact family. Our culture, twisted as it is between types and frequencies of relationships, determined personally (via the marriage remaining intact between the husband and wife) and judicially (by the Supreme Court) that marriage, even a shaky one at times, is the foundation of the family for the best interests of children and for legal order. Although the facts of *Michael H.* are certainly not a glowing tribute to the wonder of family life, the legal principles used to arrive at the conclusion were historically consistent. Our anomalous culture, however, has indeed had to deal with the effects of twisting the original design of marriage and of eroding marriage as the foundation for the family.

## THE EFFECTS OF TWISTING THE ORIGINAL DESIGN OF MARRIAGE

Empirical evidence is the substantiation or verification of our experience with some thing, or some principle, or the violation of that principle. It is not about fairness, equality, or even justice. It is simply the data as it has demonstrated itself in the lives of real people. This is indeed what tests and makes manifest the design theory.

The 2000 census of the United States reveals the following changes. For the first time in the country's history, nuclear families dropped below 25 percent of households, and same-sex couples increased in two states, Vermont and Delaware.[18] Even though some same-sex partnerships may try to build their own families, there will still be myriad children coming into not only heterosexual blended families, but same-sex blended families and all sorts of additional familylike situations that do not reflect the original design of the family based on marriage. "This means that about half of all children growing up in America today will spend at least part of their childhood in single-parent homes. Imagine a world where most children will have several "moms" and "dads," perhaps six or eight "grandparents," and dozens of half siblings. Little boys and girls will be shuffled to and fro in an ever-changing pattern of living arrangements. It does not take a child psychologist to realize that this type of environment will be, and already is, devastating to children.[19] Furthermore, studies that claim that same-sex parenting makes no difference in the life of a child have been determined to have no scientific, empirical, social science, psychological, or policy basis whatsoever.[20]

For these reasons we see many sides entering into this battle. For those who see this authentic and time-honored design, the horizon is clear. Mar-

riage must be protected legally to foster cultural influence and even to protect religious liberty and moral freedom.[21]

## CONCLUSION

A principled understanding of marriage and family is necessary to make
good legal and policy decisions. These principles are not based on libertarian
or egalitarian views, but rather on the original design, what some have
termed traditionalism. These traditions, however, are not merely habits.
They are truths based on authentic designs that have been originally established and proved right and true over time. Although our entertainment
culture may be looking for the next new relationship, marriage is reaffirmed
in a culture that is suffering from its empirical evidence of departing from
the design. Though our culture may be less inclined to look to the law to
uphold marriage and the family, the law is based on the original design for
the best of mankind's civilization.

The state's role in marriage promotes marriage-based families. But the law does not
merely promote. It also permits and it prohibits. Promotion and prohibition set the
positive and negative limits of the legal order. Permission is what is left alone by law
and or handled by private contractual means. . . . Promotion is a way in which the
law endorses marriage. Because marriage is a unique social institution formed by the
union of one man and one woman, the law sets parameters for who can marry. Within
those parameters, all individuals must be treated equally. The state properly structures
the legal dimension of marriage in terms of status, rights, duties, and, as appropriate,
additional benefits to reward or strengthen marriage. . . . This explains why supporters of marriage strongly oppose creating a status parallel to marriage. Such a public
status would thereby endorse non-marital sexual relationships and lower the public
esteem of marriage. This also explains why supporters of marriage strongly oppose
public school curricula that equate same-sex relationships with marriage.[22]

In pursuit of an anthology on the marriage relationship, historical rules
and underpinnings of family law are essential to a thorough analysis of the
current legal events. These principles that have been described have been
the state of affairs of law and culture for all of recorded history. They are
authentic and they are pragmatic. An honest perspective does not toss this
time-tested formula to the wind, and a fair and open discussion reveals the
inherent design of marriage. These principles from design will survive and
somehow even continue to flourish, particularly in light of the current debate over gender difference being necessary in marriage.

## NOTES

1. John Witte, Jr., *From Sacrament to Contract: Marriage, Religion, and Law
in the Western Tradition*, 1997, pp. 3–4. The first establishment of state intervention

into marriage probably occurred when John Calvin, an attorney and minister, worked with the reformers, bringing together both law and theology into a mix that would regulate the institution of marriage. Prior to that, however, human government for marriage was manifested in church authorities. Prior to any church authorities, the beginning of time displayed a demonstration of the natural functions of the original commands to the first man and the first woman in the Garden. See id. at 74, 96.

2. See C.S. Lewis, Walter Hooper, ed., *Reading for Meditation and Reflection*, 1992, pp. 46–47.

3. See Witte, *supra* note 1, at 16, 19, 74, 81.

4. See Harry D. Krause, Marsha Garrison, Linda D. Elrod, & J. Thomas Oldham, *Family Law*, 2000, pp. 12–42.

5. See generally Mary Ann Glendon, *State, Law, and Family: Family Law in Transition in the United States and Western Europe*, 1977. There is little to no discussion of these basic inherent minimal requirements for marriage entry in the East.

6. Witte, *supra* note 1, at 194. See generally Max Rheinstein, *Marriage Stability, Divorce, and the Law*, 1972. chs. 1–2; Milton C. Regan, Jr., *Family Law and the Pursuit of Intimacy*, ch. 1. For an English overview, see R.H. Graveson & F.R. Crane, eds., "A Century of Family Law," *Journal of Legal Education* 46 (1996): 546.

7. See Witte, *supra* note 1, at 19–20, 53.

8. Genesis 2: 24–25 clearly outlines the meaning of marriage: "For this cause a man shall leave his father and his mother, and shall cleave to his wife; and they shall become one flesh. And the man and his wife were both naked and were not ashamed." With no form of government, Church, family or law, this incident of the union of the first man and the first woman characterize the unity of the two in what later was identified as marriage. Hebrews 13: 4 states, "Let marriage be held in honor among all and let the marriage bed be undefiled." From the beginning of the Old Testament to the end of the New Testament, marriage is adhered to honorably and only encompasses a holy union of a man and a woman.

9. Peter N. Swisher, H. Anthony Miller, & William I. Weston, *Family Law: Cases, Materials, and Problems*, 1993, p. 1, citing and quoting Hyde v. Hyde, L.R. 1 P & D 130 (1866).

10. George Santayana, *Reason in Society*, 1980, pp. 35–36, 47, 50, 53–54.

11. See John DeWitt Gregory, Peter N. Swisher, & Sheryl Scheible-Wolf, *Understanding Family Law*, 1993, pp. 11, 96.

12. Homer Clark, *The Law of Domestic Relations in the United States*, 2d ed., 1987, p. 75.

13. See Leslie J. Harris & Lee E. Teitelbaum, *Family Law*, 2d ed., 2000.

14. See Marsha Garrison, "Law Making for Baby Making: An Interpretive Approach to the Determination of Legal Parentage," *Harvard Law Review* 113 (2000): 835, 883.

15. See Harry D. Krause, *Family Law*, 1993, pp. 18–19.

16. Martha Minnow, "Forming Underneath Everything That Grows: Toward a History of Family Law," *Wisconsin Law Review* (1985): 819, 894. This discussion on the tension between family rights and individual rights has resulted in an array of literature. See Roback Morse, "Family Law in Transition: From Traditional Families to Individual Liberties" in *Changing Images of the Family*, 1979, p. 327; Frances Olsen, "The Politics of Family Law," *Law and Inequality* 2 (1984): 1; and Jane

Rutherford, "Beyond Individual Privacy: A New Theory of Family Rights," *University of Florida Law Review* 39 (1987): 627, 634–640.

17. 491 U.S. 110 (1989).

18. See Eric Schmitt, "For the First Time, Nuclear Families Drop Below 25 Percent of Households," *New York Times*, May 15, 2001, A1; David Popenoe & Barbara Dafoe Whitehead, *The State of Our Unions 2000*, The National Marriage Project, Rutgers University, at http://marriage.rutgers.edu; and David Gram, "Census: Same-Sex Couples Increased," Associated Press, June 13, 2001.

19. James Dobson, *Focus on the Family Magazine*, August 2001, 2.

20. Robert Lerner & Althea Nagai, *No Basis: What the Studies Don't Tell Us About Same-Sex Parenting*, 2001.

21. A good summary of the various state battles is included in this volume in the essay authored by William C. Duncan.

22. David Orgon Coolidge, "Justice for Marriage," *Family Policy* 14 (March–April 2001): 6.

Response

# Reply to "Marriage by Design"
## Arthur S. Leonard

In her essay titled "Marriage by Design," Lynne Marie Kohm adopts an essentialist, religiously inspired view of marriage that is the polar opposite of the view I advance in my essay "On Legal Recognition for Same-Sex Partners." By her account, marriage is an institution devised by the church (which church is not specified) to symbolize the eternal union between Christ and his church. I rather doubt that the marriage of Abraham and Sarah in Genesis has anything to do with Christ and his church. Indeed, if one is inclined to accept Genesis as a historical record, some sort of community-recognized familial relationship between two adults clearly predates organized religion as such. But Genesis is the product of a particular ancient culture that is just one of many ancient world cultures, all of whose diverse descendants are now participants in the multicultural phenomenon that is modern American society.

I reject Professor Kohm's contention that a contemporary conception of the family needs to be bound by the particular theology that was intertwined with governmental authority during the period of European history when the antecedents of the current structures governing legal recognition of adult family relationships in the United States began to take shape. Societies engineer their social institutions out of a combination of historical precedents and current needs, and what worked for medieval agrarians does not necessarily work for us. Our contemporary American society was born out of a rejection of established churches and an insistence under our constitutional structure that there be a secular justification for every legal rule, reflecting an early recognition of religious and cultural diversity in a new nation whose residents were drawn from a multitude of cultural and religious heritages. Perpetuating an image of the "eternal union between Christ and his church" is thus not under any circumstances a legitimate basis in American legal policy for recognizing or refusing to recognize a particular family definition.

I concede Professor Kohm's point that the family has been a central institution in our society for many generations, but her account of history strikes me as unduly simplified in according such centrality to church-defined and sanctioned marriage as the basis for the family. Common-law marriage was routine and widespread until it was displaced by civil marriage in more recent times, and there have always been significant religious minorities who embraced marital customs that depart from those of so-called mainstream Christian churches. African American slaves in America had families without benefit of marriage (although slave masters frequently disrespected these relationships), and several generations of Mormons practiced plural marriage. Our historical record is fraught with variety, making a monolithic focus on certain Christian traditions inappropriate in the American context.

I also differ with Professor Kohm's description of recent U.S. developments. While it is true that the Hawaii Supreme Court's 1993 decision in *Baehr v. Lewin* led to a successful campaign by antigay forces to enact the Defense of Marriage Act at the federal level and laws barring recognition of same-sex marriages in a majority of the states, at the same time many American jurisdictions have moved legislatively to extend legal recognition short of marriage to same-sex partners, including the states of Hawaii, Vermont, and California and some of the nation's largest municipalities, including New York, Los Angeles, Chicago, and San Francisco. Taken together with growing judicial recognition of same-sex partners in a variety of specific legal contexts, the picture is decidedly mixed.

Also, contrary to Professor Kohm's assertion that no nation has allowed same-sex partners to marry, the Netherlands and Belgium have opened up marriage to same-sex partners, and many other countries have moved in recent years to extend legal recognition in the form of registered partnerships carrying many of the rights and responsibilities of marriage, including Denmark, Norway, Finland, Germany, France, and Canada.

The 2000 U.S. census reveals that same-sex couples live everywhere in this country, and that the number of same-sex couples has increased virtually everywhere since they were first counted in the 1990 census. Facts are facts. We are talking about thousands of couples—and singles—in this country who are systematically disadvantaged by archaic statutory schemes that fail to accord with contemporary reality.

Professor Kohm laments the "effects of twisting the original design." I despair of the effects of failing to twist it. The "original design" has long since been rendered obsolete by societal developments, and its perpetuation in domestic relations statutes relegates to second-class citizenship a growing portion of the population, not just same-sex couples. By privileging a narrow segment of American families, it perpetuates discrimination against single people, widows and widowers, unmarried domestic partners, transgendered persons, and same-sex partners—taken together, the clear majority of the population. It has helped to exacerbate the problem of lack of health insurance coverage because of its relationship to qualifying features of employee benefit plans. It has worked inhumane exclusions under zoning laws and imposed cruel hardship on binational couples under immigration laws. It has led to financial catastrophes under trust and estate laws that incorporate its assumptions.

The "original design" is a cultural relic whose continued maintenance in the United States threatens to render this country a backwater in an increasingly progressive world. As Canada, the European Union, South Africa, Australia, and New Zealand all move toward increasing recognition of same-sex partners, it is time for the United States to wake up and reconceive the legal framework governing its domestic relations to serve those legitimate functions for which governments recognize family structures.

# Part II

Issues of Jurisprudence and Political Philosophy in the Debate on Marriage and Same-Sex Unions

# Chapter 4

## Essay One

# *Homosexuality and the Conservative Mind*

### Stephen Macedo

Some of the most divisive political conflicts of our time hang at least partly on the answer to the question of whether legal discrimination against gays and lesbians has a reasoned basis. Is there a reasoned ground for the sharply different evaluations of heterosexual and homosexual intimacy embodied in the Supreme Court's privacy jurisprudence?[1] Is the government acting on mere prejudice by excluding active and open homosexuals from military service? Are there any good reasons for not allowing gays and lesbians to marry?

Some conservative academics and intellectuals have recognized the importance of trying to provide a reasoned ground for denying gays and lesbians access to such important public opportunities as marriage and military service. The most powerful and extensive arguments for the intrinsic immorality of homosexuality have issued from proponents of the "new natural law."[2] These scholars concede that discriminatory laws and public policies are often motivated by popular prejudice and unthinking hostility, which are, on their own, inadequate bases for exercising political power. John Finnis, for example, argues that "public policies must be based on reasons, not mere emotions, prejudices, and biases."[3] He also concedes, however, that "embarrassment" makes "most people more than usually inarticulate" with respect to homosexuality.[4] The new natural lawyers have tried to supply the "public" arguments and widely accessible "reasons" that are often missing from popular attacks on the morality of homosexuality.

This essay critically examines the new natural law's case against homosexuality and argues that these scholars fail to justify the legal disabilities imposed on homosexuals. I proceed by conceding a good deal to the natural lawyers. I allow, for example, that conservatives seem right to worry about teenage pregnancy, the excesses of sexual permissiveness and promiscuity, and liberationist ideals that condemn all traditional restraints indiscriminately. I agree that public moral judgment has a legitimate role to play even in the most personal aspects of our lives.[5] I admit a degree of sympathy with Germain Grisez's challenge to the libertarianism that certainly characterizes an extreme form of liberalism that came to the fore in the 1960s:

> The promoters of sexual liberation thought it would eliminate the pain of sexual frustration and make society as a whole more joyful. What has happened instead shows how wrong they were. The pain of sexual frustration is slight in comparison with the misery of abandoned women and unwanted children, of people lonely for lack of true marital intimacy, of those dying wretchedly from sexually transmitted disease. Moreover, unchastity's destructive effects on so many families impact on the wider society, whose stability depends on families. . . . Boys and girls coming to maturity without solid formation in a stable family are ill prepared to assume adult social responsibilities.[6]

I feel sure that this is not the whole truth, but it may represent an important part of the truth. Such charges at least need to be taken seriously.

Natural-law scholars nevertheless fail to justify discrimination against gays and lesbians.[7] Like some other conservatives, natural lawyers translate their opposition to promiscuity and liberationism into blanket condemnations of homosexual conduct. This is as puzzling as it is illegitimate. Such arguments are a form of moral scapegoating that is both unreasonable and unjust. Condemning all gays and lesbians on the basis of opposition to the promiscuous behavior of some gays (and many heterosexuals also) is no better than condemning all men because some men rape women. To deny basic public rights and opportunities to a whole class of people on the basis of opposition to the behavior of some within the class is fundamentally arbitrary and unjust.

My analysis is not purely negative. By making various concessions to conservatives—by allowing that promiscuity, teen pregnancy, and other matters are reasonable causes for public concern—I hope to show that acceptance of equal rights for gays and lesbians does not require that we scrap the whole of traditional morality. Indeed, by jettisoning the unreasonable and arbitrary parts of traditional morality, we may well strengthen the elements that remain.

## THE BROAD SWEEP OF NATURAL LAW SEXUAL PROHIBITIONS

At least some of the new natural lawyers—secular philosophers such as John Finnis, Germain Grisez, and Robert George, working in one part of the Catholic natural-law tradition—allow that some people are homosexual by nature. Finnis, at least, would not, moreover, deploy the criminal law against private homosexual acts. The law should, however, supervise "the *public realm or environment*," within which young and old are morally educated toward good or bad lives. Finnis argues that openly active homosexuals are "deeply hostile to the self-understanding of those members of the community who are willing to commit themselves to real marriage." The law should, therefore, deny "that homosexual conduct—a 'gay lifestyle'—is a valid, humanly acceptable choice and form of life," and it should do "whatever it *properly* can . . . to discourage such conduct."[8]

The new natural lawyers go out of their way to distinguish their position from the narrow prejudice and mere disgust that characterize much popular opposition to equal rights for gays and lesbians. They do not claim that homosexual acts are unique in being distractions from real human goods or in justly being subject to legal discouragement. The new natural lawyers strikingly treat gay and lesbian sexual activity like most forms of heterosexual activity: all sex outside of marriage and all contracepted sex, including all contracepted sex between married couples.

The new natural law's broad prohibitions against extramarital and "recreational" sexual activity (contracepted or homosexual) are based on the contention that many forms of sexual activity are like masturbation, through which individuals forgo opportunities to participate in real human goods and wrongly use the body as a mere instrument of pleasure.[9] Masturbation involves only fantasy, Finnis insists, rather than real friendship, play, knowledge, and other goods embodied in genuine intimate relations with others.[10] Germain Grisez similarly maintains that "the pleasurable sensations of sexual activity culminating in orgasm are in themselves a private and incommunicable experience."[11] Finnis and Grisez also believe that masturbation violates the good of personal integrity, for it is the use of one's body by the conscious self for the mere production of pleasure, with no connection to any real projects, goods, or other persons.[12]

The sexual act should be subordinate to the real goods that are relevant to the kind of act that it is; and those real goods are the complex of goods united in a permanent heterosexual marriage. Our understanding of proper sexuality should take its bearings from the "specific, intrinsic perfection" of relations between man and woman, which perfection is found in marriage: "for marriage realizes the potentiality of man and woman for unqualified, mutual self-giving," oriented toward not simply the "begetting and raising of children," but also the spouses' own "open-ended community" of mutual love, companionship, willing and loving cooperation, help, and comfort, all of which fulfill the spouses' marital good, even if procreation does not occur on account of infertility, sterility, or some other unchosen condition.[13] Sexual pleasure must be subordinate to these marital goods if it is to be "the experience of loving cooperation in one-flesh communion." Pleasure expe-

rienced as an intrinsic part of marriage is good, however intense it may be.[14]
As Finnis argues:

The union of the reproductive organs of husband and wife really unites them biologically (and their biological reality is part of, not merely an instrument of, their
*personal* reality); reproduction is one function and so, in respect of that function, the
spouses are indeed one reality, and their sexual union therefore can *actualize* and
allow them to *experience* their *real common good—their marriage* with two goods,
parenthood and friendship.[15]

Valuable sexual activity, therefore, must take place within a permanent
heterosexual marriage, it must involve total mutual self-giving, and it must
be open to all of the goods of marital communion, including the transmission of new life (meaning that it must not be contracepted).[16]

All nonprocreative, recreational sexual acts merely instrumentalize bodies
for mutual use and pleasure. All are equivalent to mutual masturbation:
simultaneous individual gratifications incapable of realizing any shared goods
such as friendship or love (which could be better realized in other activities),
or any "real communion of persons." This is certainly true of homosexuality,
"inasmuch as the coupling of two bodies of the same sex cannot form one
complete organism." But Grisez is quite explicit that much heterosexual
activity is of the same moral character: "such heterosexual activities—including contracepted intercourse, within or outside marriage—are morally
similar to sodomy."[17]

It may be, indeed, that the case against recreational heterosexual sex is
even stronger than that against gay sex, for the former risks the great evil
of bringing unwanted children into the world. Even when effectively contracepted, recreational heterosexual acts are (in natural-law terms) choices
to forgo the great good of new life. Gay sex is not, on the new natural-law
account, a choice against the great integrating goods of heterosexual marriage: the goods of heterosexual intimacy may not be available to those who
are gay by nature.[18]

The wrongfulness of gay sex is merely its "self-disintegrity": the failure to
act in a way that is consistent with a desire for the real goods that homosexual friends may share in common. When sex is chosen by homosexuals,
it is as a source of "subjective satisfactions" through the use and instrumentalization of each other's bodies.[19] The wrongfulness of homosexual acts
and of heterosexual fornication is that, in both instances, the coupling of
the bodies can form no single organism, and so the sexual act can have no
real point or realize any real good in common. That homosexual lovers—
or heterosexuals using contraception—think that their sexuality expresses
friendship, care, affection, and intimacy is merely illusory: these goods could
be better expressed by nonsexual acts of friendship, such as mutual helping
at home.

This natural-law teaching—the surface of which I have barely scratched—is by far the most elaborate intellectual case for distinguishing between heterosexual and homosexual activity. Unlike the almost offhanded pronouncements of some conservatives, the judgments issued by Finnis and Grisez are tied closely to a complex intellectual system. Notice, however, where this system of ideas has taken us: to the extent that the state has an interest in discouraging homosexuality on these natural-law grounds, it has an equal interest in acting against all extramarital and contracepted sex. To the extent that the state exhibits no interest in discouraging the use of contraceptives, it has evidently rejected new natural-law reasoning and must find some other grounds to justify discouraging homosexuality.[20]

Let us also recall that the very foundation of modern privacy jurisprudence—*Griswold v. Connecticut*—was laid when the Supreme Court insisted that married couples should be free to decide for themselves whether to use contraceptives.[21] The Court subsequently extended the right of privacy to the decision of unmarried couples to use contraceptives.[22] The new natural law offers no ground for drawing fundamental distinctions between the privacy rights the Court has protected and the privacy rights of homosexuals.

In these ways, the new natural law performs the vital service of revealing the gross and unreflective arbitrariness of public policies and proposals that—in the name of family values—fix their scornful attention on gays and lesbians. Nothing could be easier in the face of heterosexual promiscuity, premarital sex, teenage pregnancy, and skyrocketing divorce rates than to fasten our attention on a long-despised class of people who bear few children. The new natural law shows that on reflection, such attitudes embody a double standard of permissiveness toward straights and censoriousness toward gays who engage in acts that are essentially the same.

The new natural law has the apparent virtue of consistency. If it rejects equality for homosexuals, it poses an even greater challenge to the conventional wisdom that would single out homosexuality as singularly perverse and "unnatural." This fair-mindedness and broad sweep may also make the new natural-law politically irrelevant. It supports only very broad public actions against sexual immorality in general: against divorce, contraception, all sex outside of marriage, and homosexuality. To reject natural-law teachings on contraception, for example, is to jettison natural-law grounds for acting against homosexuality. This natural-law philosophy cannot be of help to any but those few Americans who accept its extremely broad strictures. It provides no aid and comfort to the vast majority of those who would condemn homosexual activity while accepting the availability of divorce, contraception, and premarital sex.

Those sympathetic to natural law's broadly conservative sexual teaching might reply that simply because some justifiable moral strictures have been relaxed, that is no reason to relax them all. But it is a reason (both a moral reason and a constitutional one) when a long-despised minority is arbitrarily saddled with restrictions that the majority is unwilling to impose on itself.[23] Even if one accepts natural-law judgments, therefore, considerations of fairness suggest that they should not be applied against the homosexual minority until we also apply them against the heterosexual majority.

Insuperable obstacles lie in the path of any state that would rely on natural-law grounds for selective prohibitions on homosexual conduct. There are, moreover, other problems with the natural-law position still to be considered. I have commended the new natural law's sexual teaching for its fair-mindedness and broad sweep, but this may have been premature, for the position is plagued by a major inconsistency, to which we now turn.

## THE NEW NATURAL LAW'S DOUBLE STANDARD

The new natural lawyers argue that sex within a marriage of sterile heterosexuals is not only permissible but good: "marital union itself fulfills the spouses."[24] But how can we justify this favored treatment of sterile heterosexuals given that their bodies, like those of homosexuals, can form no "single reproductive principle," no "real unity"?[25] If there is no possibility of procreation, then sterile couples are, like homosexuals, incapable of sex acts "open to procreation."

What is the point of sex in an infertile marriage? Not procreation; the partners (let us assume) know that they are infertile. If they have sex, it is for pleasure and to express their love, or friendship, or some other shared good—precisely the same reasons that committed, loving gay couples have sex. Why are these good reasons for sterile or elderly married couples but not for gay and lesbian couples? If, on the other hand, sex detracts from the real goods shared by homosexual couples, and indeed undermines their friendship, this should also be the case for infertile heterosexual couples. Sterile couples' experience of sexual intimacy should be as "private and incommunicable" as that of gays.

Of course, sterility is an unchosen condition beyond the control of sterile heterosexual couples. But the new natural lawyers allow that the same is true of homosexuality. Then again, gays and lesbians do not have the physical equipment (the "biological complementarity") such that anyone could have children by doing what they can do in bed. They can, Finnis and Grisez repeatedly tell us, only imitate or fantasize real procreative acts. Is not exactly the same thing true of sterile couples?

The new natural lawyers want to widen the circle of valuable sexuality beyond the narrowly procreative to bring in sterile and elderly couples. Sexual activity is itself part of the good of marriage, so long as sexual acts are open to new life and subordinate to "marital love":[26] we must not choose against the good of new life, and we must ensure that what predominates in our sexual relations is "loving cooperation in one-flesh communion."[27] The "one-flesh communion" of sterile couples would appear, however, to be more a matter of appearance than reality. So why should these couples be included while we exclude committed, stable, monogamous gay couples—who, no more than the sterile, choose against the good of new life and who, as much as sterile heterosexual couples, can subordinate sexual passion to love, friendship, and other "marital" goods?

This double standard gives rise to several puzzles. It is hard to know in what sense sterile heterosexual couples (who know themselves to be so) can engage in sexual acts that are "open to procreation," given that procreation for them is and is known to be just as impossible as it is for gay and lesbian couples. One would think that the crucial distinction between valuable and valueless sex in a sterile marriage is the partners' openness to goods that they can share, not to goods that they cannot share. From within the natural-law framework itself, it would seem sensible to focus on the importance for sterile partners of subordinating their passionate impulses to love, affection, mutual devotion, a self-giving desire to please the other, and so on.

Once we focus on the importance of integrating sexual activity into a larger pattern of attainable goods, sterile married couples and devoted, loving, committed homosexual partners seem to fall into the same camp. This is one way in which the apparent double standard might be dissolved. Procreation is equally unattainable by sterile and same-sex couples; other goods (mutuality, love, and the like) are attainable by both. Looked at in this way, the natural lawyers' own framework argues for equal treatment for sterile heterosexuals and homosexuals.

We could interpret Finnis's criterion of "openness to procreation" more figuratively, but this also argues for the moral similarity of homosexual and sterile heterosexual couples. We might say that gays and lesbians can have sex in a way that is "open to procreation" (albeit figuratively) and to new life. They can be, and many are, prepared to engage in the kinds of loving relations that would result in procreation were conditions different. Like sterile married couples, many would like nothing better. All we can say is that conditions would have to be more radically different in the case of gay and lesbian couples than in that of sterile married couples for new life to result from sex, but what is the moral force of that argument?

Finnis ridicules this argument. "Here," he says, "fantasy has taken leave of reality. Anal or oral intercourse, whether between spouses or males, is no more a biological union 'open to procreation' than is intercourse with a goat by a shepherd who fantasizes about breeding a faun."[28] Finnis insists once again on the importance of "biological union" and "openness to procreation." But the sterile heterosexual couple's "openness to procreation" is as much a fantasy as that of Finnis's kinky shepherd. Sterile heterosexuals have as great a chance of breeding a child as the shepherd and his goat do a faun. The shepherd and goat analogy is poor in any case, for they cannot share the goods of intelligent friendship, commitment and affection, mutual help and comfort—among moral equals—all of which can be shared by sterile heterosexual and homosexual couples (once again making these cases appear similar to each other and radically different from bestiality). The focus on procreation appears opportunistic, selected so as to allow sterile heterosexuals into the tent while keeping all homosexuals out.

Still, Finnis and Grisez seek to avoid this conclusion. Finnis insists that the sexual acts of sterile heterosexuals can actualize their "two-in-one-flesh common good" because they can, unlike homosexuals, be united biologically: fertile or sterile, heterosexual couples have the equipment that allows them to engage in the behavior that, as behavior, is "suitable for generation."[29]

Is sterile heterosexual intercourse "as behavior" suitable for generation? Andrew Koppelman observes that pointing a gun at someone and pulling the trigger is in general behavior suitable for murder, but not when the gun is unloaded.[30] Nor is this behavior suitable for murder when the gun shoots water or is made of licorice.

The National Rifle Association might have said, "Guns don't kill people, bullets kill people." Likewise, penises and vaginas do not unite biologically, sperm and eggs do (at least under the right conditions). For Finnis, however, the crucial thing is penises and vaginas, functional or not.

This gives rise to other puzzles. If the presence of nonworking equipment of the "right" sort is a crucial distinguishing feature of permissible sexual relationships, artifice might supply what nature has not. One gay male might have a partial sex-change operation, having his penis removed and a vagina installed. Does this allow a gay couple to re-create the appearance of bio-logical complementarity closely enough to have valuable sex? Or suppose that a gay male couple simply eschews oral sex, anal sex, and mutual mas-turbation in favor of intercrural sex (inserting the penis between the thighs of the partner). Would this resemble heterosexual intercourse closely enough to have "procreative significance?"[31]

In the end, it is hard to see why sex between sterile couples has any more "procreative significance" than gay or lesbian sex. These cases are distin-guished by appearances only, and matters of great moral significance should not hang on mere appearances.

The new natural law's double standard could be resolved in more ways than one. The proscriptions against homosexuality could be saved by ar-guing that involuntarily sterile heterosexual couples, including all women past menopause and their spouses, may not have sex. Elderly and otherwise sterile heterosexuals can enjoy mutual helping and friendship, but sex will distract from these goods, as with homosexuals. Public policy should do "whatever it *properly* can" to deter fornication by the elderly and sterile, including denying them the right to marry and prohibiting the promotion or facilitation of sex among the elderly (though not criminalizing sexual acts as long as they are committed in private).

There is an alternative, inclusive path to consistency that we should prefer: broadening the scope of legitimate sexuality to include committed gay couples. The new natural lawyers furnish no grounds for supposing that the goods shared by infertile and elderly couples cannot be shared by gays in committed relationships. The inclusive path would acknowledge all of this while preserving the reasonable natural-law claim that sexual activity should be channeled into committed and loving relationships, whether heterosexual or homosexual.

## THE NEW NATURAL LAW'S CRAMPED VIEW OF VALUABLE SEXUAL RELATIONS

I have already said enough to suggest that the new natural law fails to supply a reasoned public ground for discrimination against homosexuals. I have not yet touched on an even more basic problem, namely, the new natural law's extremely narrow view of valuable sexual activity as only that which is open to procreation within a permanent heterosexual marriage. According to the new natural lawyers, homosexual acts, all contracepted heterosexual acts, and all sex outside of marriage "can do no more than provide each partner with an individual gratification."[32] Homosexual sex, like heterosexual "fornication," forgoes opportunities to participate in real goods and undermines the goods that homosexual friends can share. Goodwill and affection can be expressed far more effectively by conversation, mutually beneficial help in work, and shared domestic tasks.

The new natural law seems to exaggerate greatly the subjective, self-centered character of all nonprocreative sexuality. The reductionism here is striking: "whatever the generous hopes and dreams" of "some same-sex partners" (and many heterosexuals), their sexual acts "cannot express or do more than is expressed or done if two strangers engage in such activity to give each other pleasure, or a prostitute pleasures a client to give him pleasure in return for money, or (say) a man masturbates to give himself a fantasy of more human relationships after a grueling day on the assembly line."[33] Homosexual sex or contracepted sex in marriage at best embody no more than anonymous bathhouse sex, a quick trip to a prostitute, or masturbation.

Is it plausible that there are no distinctions to be drawn here? My guess is that most committed, loving couples—whether gay or straight—are sensitive to the difference between loving sexual acts expressing a shared intimacy and mere mutual masturbation. Finnis and Grisez may not be all wrong: promiscuous, "anonymous," casual sex may tend toward the valueless character they describe. Even sexual acts within marriage may tend to become "masturbatory" if the aim is merely to heighten and intensify one's own erotic pleasure, with no thought given to mutuality, romantic self-giving, or the proper subordination of lust to love. Having said all this, and having agreed with Finnis and Grisez that a healthy sexual life requires

a measure of self-control that may be hard to achieve for many people—
especially in a culture such as ours that is heavily charged with sexuality—
it seems, nevertheless, strikingly simplistic and implausible to portray the
essential nature of every form of nonprocreative sexuality as no better than
the least valuable form.

Many will find deeply unreasonable, as well, the judgment that pleasure
is not in and of itself a good. Consider the analogy between sex and eating.
We eat and have sex not only to sustain and reproduce human life, but also
for their intrinsic pleasure. Eating is especially pleasurable when it is shared
with others (most think that the same is true of sex): social dining cements
friendships, expresses affection, and so on. But suppose eating and nourishment are severed? Is eating for the sake of mere pleasure unnatural or irrational? Is it permissible to chew sugarless gum, which gives pleasure but has
no nutritional value, as Andrew Koppelman asks, or is doing so the gastronomic equivalent of masturbation (assuming that we are not doing it to
exercise the jaw or clean the teeth)? Is it immoral?[34] Is either sexual or
gastronomic pleasure sought and achieved for its own sake immoral, or does
the immorality lie in excessive or compulsive pursuit of these pleasures (as
seems far more reasonable)?

It also has to be said that certain parts of the natural law's analytic structure are far from clear. The basic good of "self-integration" is obviously
crucial, but exactly what this means and how it is violated are not clear. It
is hardly obvious, for example, that contracepted sexual acts are a direct and
significant assault on "the basic good of self-integration," or that masturbation is wrong because it violates "the body's capacity for self-giving."[35]

For the new natural lawyers, the essential nature of sexual acts is known
by analytical inquiry, not by consequentialist calculations or by historical or
cultural investigation of actual lives. Sexual activity unconnected with the
realization of real goods (as defined by natural law) is objectively valueless.
The sexual act is essentially a conjugal act that realizes a tightly knit array
of marital goods. Chaste marital communion—open to the transmission of
new life—is not only a very fine way of expressing our sexuality (as many
might be prepared to concede), it is for Finnis and Grisez the only legitimate
way of expressing our sexuality. All else—from masturbation to contracepted
heterosexual sex, extramarital sex, and homosexuality—is a set of variations
on the same themes: acts of self-disintegrity, using the body as an instrument
of pleasure, simulating or fantasizing the conjugal act, and so on. All else is
valueless, and not only valueless, but a choice to materially damage the social
environment: "masturbation tends to make everyone's body into a sex object and predisposes masturbators to treat their sexual partners as masturbatory tools . . . Masturbation is essentially a social sin against interpersonal
communion."[36] What is true of masturbation is true of all contracepted and
homosexual acts.

To many, this philosophical approach will seem an odd way to proceed.

Many will wonder whether the level of philosophical abstraction and generality employed here is really adequate for drawing all of the distinctions that should be drawn. Sometimes even Finnis does not seem entirely sure. He says, for example, that the "essential features" of "solitary masturbation" are to be found in "casual promiscuous sexual relations, such as heterosexual fornication or adultery *often is* and homosexual activity *usually is.*"[37] "Often" and "usually" are very different from "always." "Often" and "usually" suggest a bad tendency that is not inevitable. This is far more plausible than the main line of argument, which suggests that the bad forms are found "always" and inevitably.

The valueless quality of homosexual acts is established analytically for the new natural law, but Finnis also invokes the sorts of unsupported empirical generalizations about homosexual relationships found in conservative polemics. He refers offhandedly to "the modern 'gay' ideology," which treats "sexual capacities, organs, and acts as instruments to be put to whatever suits the purposes of the individual 'selves' who have them."[38] Millions of homosexual lives are thus presumptively epitomized by a promiscuous, liberationist "gay lifestyle" that rejects all sexual restraints and value judgments.[39] These sweeping generalizations are, however, overgeneralizations. Not all gay people are promiscuous. If gay people are somewhat more likely to be promiscuous than heterosexuals, many things are likely to contribute to this. Mistakes in judgment about what makes for a good life, the pressures of life in the "closet," exclusion from the institution of marriage, and other socially contingent factors must be at least partly responsible for the tendency (to the extent that it exists) for same-sex sexual relations to be "often," "usually," or "sometimes" rather casual.[40] But the new natural lawyers know what they know on the basis of abstract philosophical analysis, so none of this matters.

In the end, Finnis relies, in part at least, on sweeping stereotypes about actual behavior. He may need these stereotypes to support the new natural law's equally sweeping moral condemnations, which have little room for complexity or ambiguity.

## HOMOSEXUALITY, MARRIAGE, AND THE FAMILY

Conservatives are right to remind us that public policy plays a legitimate role, even in a liberal regime, in favoring better over worse ways of life and promoting a healthy moral culture. Offering certain advantages to those who settle down and enter into the bonds of matrimony is one way of promoting more stable relationships and happier, healthier lives. Conservatives, however, too often ignore the liberal insistence that everyone's good counts, and that we may not rightly pursue the majority's good at the expense of the basic rights and opportunities of minorities. A modicum of fair-mindedness requires us to consider not simply whether to protect the young and reinvigorate the family, but how we should do so. That same fair-mindedness suggests that we should remember the vulnerabilities of all the young, gay as well as straight.

The reasonable core of the conservative sexual teaching is the concern with promiscuity and sexual license. There surely is something to the observation of Plato, Aristotle, and others that the relative intensity of the "animal pleasures" means that most people will tend toward overdoing rather than underdoing with respect to sex and food—at least absent efforts at self-control and a well-developed character.[41] The sexual appetite, conservatives properly remind us, is tyrannical and unruly: "a powerful, continuing motivator, not easily restrained and not naturally opposed by other emotional motives."[42] The self-control crucial to a healthy and happy life is a difficult and fragile achievement that benefits from social support. This includes a general atmosphere of restraint and reasonable modesty, as well as the inducements to stability that flow from the institution of marriage.

It is difficult to see, however, why reasonable conservative cultural concerns should translate so frequently into blanket condemnations of homosexuality. If promiscuity and sexual license are problems, why not co-opt the part of the populace most in need of bourgeois domestication, the part that poses the greatest cultural threat to the family? Leaving strategic matters aside, justice requires that we take seriously the good of all. It is not only irrational but unjust to deny homosexuals access to the social institutions intended precisely to cement and stabilize sexual relationships and thereby to foster a culture of sexual restraint.[43]

Extending marriage to gays and lesbians is a way of allowing that conservative moralists are not all wrong: promiscuous sex may well tend toward the essentially masturbatory, distracting, and valueless character that Finnis describes. As Andrew Sullivan puts it:

Society has good reason to extend legal advantages to heterosexuals who choose the formal sanction of marriage over simply living together. They make a deeper commitment to one another and to society; in exchange, society extends certain benefits to them. Marriage provides an anchor, if an arbitrary and weak one, in the chaos of sex and relationships to which we are all prone. It provides a mechanism for emotional stability, economic security, and the healthy rearing of the next generation. We rig the law in its favor not because we disparage all forms of relationship other than the nuclear family, but because we recognize that not to promote marriage would be to ask too much of human virtue.[44]

By the same token, we should offer inducements to stability evenhandedly to all whose real good can thereby be advanced: to the elderly and the sterile, to gays and lesbians, and not only to fertile heterosexuals for whom sex can be procreative.

Conservatives vehemently resist the extension of marriage to homosexuals.

Hadley Arkes, in a response to Sullivan, doubts that marriage would mate-rially affect the behavior of gay males, but he offers no evidence for his view.[45] He also argues that traditional monogamous marriage is tied indis-solubly to the "natural teleology" of the body, and the fact that "only two people, no more and no fewer, can generate children."[46] Gay marriage offers such an "implausible want of resemblance" to heterosexual marriage, Arkes charges, "that it would appear almost as a mocking burlesque." This mock-ery could be avoided only if marriage were opened wider still to include polygamy and incest. With gay marriage, "all kinds of questions, once placed in merciful repose, may reasonably be opened again."[47]

Just why homosexuality, incest, and polygamy are all lumped together is unclear. Perhaps because they all depart from tradition? To simply oppose all departures from traditional marriage would be absurd and unreasonable. Interracial marriage was long proscribed, and some no doubt argued that repealing antimiscegenation statutes would reopen "all kinds of questions once placed in merciful repose." All but the most mindless traditionalist will allow that some departures from tradition are good and to be applauded. We cannot avoid distinguishing what is good and worth preserving in a tradition from what is mere prejudice.

Incest would certainly undermine many of the goods of family life: it entails a horrible and revolting form of vulnerability for children. Arkes sup-plies no reason for supposing that extending marriage to gays and lesbians would have the same effect. Arkes needs to do better than to trade on our justifiable revulsion at incest.[48]

It is difficult to see why extending marriage to gays and lesbians would weaken the institution of marriage. A high proportion of heterosexual mar-riages end in divorce. Gays and lesbians make up a very small portion of the population: the latest and perhaps soundest estimates are that only 2.8 per-cent of men and 1.4 percent of women identify themselves as homosexual or bisexual.[49] Arkes claims that few homosexuals would take advantage of the marriage option anyway. If marital instability is a problem, it is not a problem on which gays are going to have much effect. Extending marriage to gay and lesbian couples would broaden, but not necessarily dilute, soci-ety's support for marriage and long-term interpersonal commitment.

Extending marriage to gays and lesbians would do something (how much is hard to say) to curb precisely those promiscuous aspects of the gay sub-culture that conservatives find troubling. Fundamental fairness argues for including same-sex couples in this important public institution.

## CONCLUSION

The conservative academics and intellectuals whose views have been ex-amined here fail to make a reasonable case for legal discrimination against active homosexuals. Perhaps sensing the weakness of their moral arguments, conservatives fall back on stereotypes depicting all homosexuals as promiscuous, uncommitted, and irresponsible. Such overgeneralizations may provide psychological comfort, but no reasoned grounds, to those who support discriminatory treatment, including the denial of access to marriage. Rather than opposing promiscuity per se wherever it appears, conservative moralists tar an entire class of people—long despised and easily reviled—for the behavior of only some in this class and many outside it.

Richard A. Posner is on the mark in arguing that statutes criminalizing homosexual behavior "express an irrational fear and loathing of a group that has been subjected to discrimination, much like that directed against the Jews, with whom indeed homosexuals—who, like the Jews, are despised more for what they are than for what they do—were frequently bracketed in medieval persecutions."[50] Homosexuals have a difficult time even in a tolerant society, Posner argues, and statutes criminalizing homosexual acts (and, though to a lesser extent, those discriminating against homosexuals) have "a gratuitousness, an egregiousness, and a meanness" that should embarrass conservatives.[51]

Gay and lesbian citizens have made and will continue to make political and cultural progress in the United States and elsewhere. Gays and lesbians are increasingly visible on television and in other aspects of the popular culture, as well as in politics. Increasing numbers of universities and corporations are extending spousal benefits to same-sex couples. Increasing numbers of children live in same-sex households. This progress will continue, and the passage toward a more just society will be eased when thoughtful conservatives embrace more reasonable and enlightened views on homosexuality.

## NOTES

This essay is excerpted from 84 Geo. L.J. 251–300 (1995).

1. Some will regard the "gay-straight" dichotomy that I deploy here as an oversimplifying distortion of reality and as "essentializing" categories that are historically fluid. My purpose is only to use these categories in order to make coherent arguments against others who use them.

2. "Conservative" and "conservative moralist" refer here to those who argue that homosexual conduct is immoral; it should not be taken to imply that those so designated take conservative positions on other matters.

3. John Finnis, *Is Natural Law Theory Compatible with Limited Government?*, in *Natural Law, Liberalism, and Morality: Contemporary Essays* (Robert P. George, ed., Oxford: Clarendon Press, 1996).

4. Finnis, *Law, Morality, and "Sexual Orientation,"* 69 Notre Dame L. Rev. 1049 (1994).

5. See generally Robert P. George, *Making Men Moral: Civil Liberties and Public Morality* (Oxford: Clarendon Press, 1993).

6. Germain Grisez, *The Way of the Lord Jesus*, vol. 2, *Living a Christian Life* 662 (Quincy, IL: Franciscan Press, 1993).

7. My aim is to show that even those who share some conservative concerns should endorse fundamental equality of treatment for homosexuals.

8. "[A] homosexual orientation is natural only in the sense that any handicap for which an individual is not personally responsible is natural." Grisez, *The Way*, 654 n. 194. See also Finnis, *Law, Morality, and "Sexual Orientation,"* 1069–1070. Finnis allows that the Supreme Court might properly have overturned the criminal prosecution of private homosexual acts in Bowers v. Hardwick, 478 U.S. 186 (1986), but only while distinguishing such private conduct from "the advertising or marketing of homosexual services, the maintenance of places of resort for homosexual activity, or the promotion of homosexualist 'lifestyles,' " as well as homosexual marriages and the "adoption of children by homosexually active people." Finnis, *Law, Morality, and "Sexual Orientation,"* 1076.

9. See John M. Finnis, *Natural Law and Natural Rights*, 95–97 (Oxford: Clarendon Press, 1980); John M. Finnis, *Personal Integrity, Sexual Morality, and Responsible Personhood*, I Anthropos: Rivista di Studi Sulla Persona e la Famiglia 43, 45–46 (1985). This argument shows only the great loss that would come from plugging into an experience machine for life. It does not show why plugging in for half an hour several times a week would be such a great disaster. To make the experience-machine analogy helpful with respect to masturbation or pleasure more broadly, one might have to add that plugging in is addictive and so is bound to lead to excess for the majority of people.

10. Among the basic goods are life, knowledge, play, aesthetic experience, sociability or friendship, and practical reasonableness. Finnis, *Natural Law and Natural Rights*, 81–99. Basic goods are foundational reasons for action; they are self-evident, intrinsic, and incommensurable goods, known to people of ordinary experience, that can be embodied in any number of "commitments, projects and actions." *Id.* at 63–64. Our choice of projects and pursuits becomes explicable and intelligible by reference to the ways in which these choices realize basic goods.

11. Grisez, *The Way*, 637.

12. Finnis, *Personal Integrity*, 47. Grisez elaborates on the argument: "In choosing to masturbate, one does not choose to act for a goal which fulfills oneself as a unified, bodily person. The only immediate goal is satisfaction for the conscious self; and so the body, not being part of the whole for whose sake the act is done, serves only as an extrinsic instrument . . . The choice of self-disintegrity damages the basic good of self-integration. . . . The self-integration damaged by masturbation is the unity of the acting person as conscious subject and sexually functioning body. This specific aspect of self-integration, however, is precisely the aspect necessary so that the bodily union of sexual intercourse will be a communion of persons, as marital intercourse is. Therefore, masturbation damages the body's capacity for the marital act as an act of self-giving which constitutes a communion of bodily persons." *The Way*, 650.

13. Grisez, *The Way*, 569–570, 634–635.

14. *Id.* at 636–637.

15. Finnis, *Law, Morality, and "Sexual Orientation,"* 1066 (emphases added).

16. Practical reason, as the new natural lawyers conceive it, bars any action or project that represents a direct choice against any of the basic goods, as Finnis asserts:

"To choose an act which in itself simply (or primarily) damages a basic good is thereby to engage oneself willy-nilly (but directly) in an act of opposition to an incommensurable value (an aspect of human personality) which one treats as if it were an object of measurable worth that could be outweighed by commensurable objects of greater (or cumulatively greater) worth. To do this will often accord with our feelings, our generosity, our sympathy . . . But it can never be justified in reason." *Natural Law and Natural Rights*, 120. One of the basic goods that must never be chosen against is "human life in its transmission," and this is the basis of the new natural law's condemnation of contraception, abortion, and much else.

17. Grisez, *The Way*, 648–656 (claiming that nonmarital sexual acts are wrong); Finnis, *Law, Morality, and "Sexual Orientation,"* 1066–1067.

18. Grisez seems to allow all this and says that "while sodomites may not choose, as fornicators do, an illusory good instead of a real one, they do choose to use their own and each other's bodies to provide subjective satisfactions, and thus they choose self-disintegrity as masturbators do. Of course, while masturbators can be interested exclusively in the experience of sexual arousal and orgasm, sodomites also are interested in the illusion of intimacy." *The Way*, 654; see also 653.

19. *Id.* at 653–654.

20. One might reply that promiscuity is greatest in the gay male population, but if this is true, it is hard to see how it furnishes grounds for discrimination. Why punish all for the wrongs of some? Not all homosexuals are promiscuous, and not all promiscuous people are homosexual. Are there not more honorable and just means for discouraging promiscuity? So long as we refuse, moreover, to extend to gay men the inducements to stability and self-control (such as marriage) available to heterosexuals, we should regard promiscuous gay men as (at least in part) victims of fate, circumstance, and public policy rather than of a special moral depravity.

21. 381 U.S. 479 (1965).

22. See Eisenstadt v. Baird, 405 U.S. 438 (1972).

23. As John Hart Ely observes, the doctrine of "suspect classifications" means that special scrutiny should apply to those laws "that disadvantage groups we know to be the object of widespread vilification, groups we know others (specifically those who control the legislative process) might wish to injure." John Hart Ely, *Democracy and Distrust: A Theory of Judicial Review* 153 (Cambridge, MA: Harvard University Press, 1980).

24. Grisez, *The Way*, 573.

25. I have benefited greatly in this section from conversations with Andrew Koppelman.

26. Grisez, *The Way*, 636.

27. *Id.* at 637–638.

28. Finnis, *Law, Morality, and "Sexual Orientation,"* at 1066–1067.

29. *Id.*

30. This analogy is from Andrew Koppelman's excellent article *Is Marriage Inherently Heterosexual?*, 42 Am. J. Juris. 51 (1997).

31. Finnis insists that valuable sex must have not only the "generosity of acts of friendship" but also "the procreative significance." Finnis, *Law, Morality, and "Sexual Orientation,"* 20.

32. Finnis, *Law, Morality, and "Sexual Orientation,"* 1066.

33. *Id.* at 1067.

34. See Koppelman, *Is Marriage Inherently Heterosexual?* As Andrew Sabl suggested to me, suppose that a person lost his capacity to digest but not the capacity to eat, so that nutrition had to be delivered intravenously. Would it then be immoral to eat for the sake of mere pleasure, or perhaps for the sake of pleasure as well as the camaraderie of dining companions? Would it be incumbent on one in such a state to eat only a healthy, balanced diet, or would it be permissible to binge on chocolate to one's heart's content? Would it be necessary (in Sabl's words) "to go on eating beets and tofu because this would be the kind of eating which, 'as eating,' is suitable for a human being" though useless to the digestively impaired individual? Sabl rightly suggests that this "would not make rational sense (though it might provide psychological solace)." Private communication from Andrew Sabl, June 13, 1994.

35. Grisez, *The Way*, 650–651.

36. *Id.* at 664.

37. Finnis, *Personal Integrity*, 47 (emphases added).

38. Finnis, *Law, Morality, and "Sexual Orientation,"* 1070.

39. See generally Finnis, *Law, Morality, and "Sexual Orientation."*

40. Reliable figures for levels of promiscuity—about which many conservatives pronounce confidently—are hard to come by. An extensive survey of sexual practices found that the differences in the mean number of sexual partners between those with exclusively heterosexual relationships and those with at least some same-gender activity "do not appear very large." This survey also points out that to the extent that differences do exist, they may be misleading, because those who report some same-gender sexual relations also tend to be "younger, more educated, more likely to live in large cities, and generally less religious," and "all these factors are also associated with having more sex partners." Edward O. Laumann, John H. Gagnon, Robert T. Michael, and Stuart Michaels, *The Social Organization of Sexuality* 316 (Chicago: University of Chicago Press, 1994).

41. See Plato, *The Republic* 329c–d, 389e, 390c, 402e–403c, passim (Allan Bloom trans., New York: Basic Books, 1968); Aristotle, *Nicomachean Ethics*, bk. 3, at 77–82 (Martin Ostwald trans. Indianapolis: Bobbs-Merrill, 1962).

42. Grisez, *The Way*, 668.

43. David Boaz has pointed out that many conservatives express their moral outrage about contemporary sexual mores by condemning homosexuality while remaining virtually silent about the much greater and more widespread harm done to "traditional family values" and to many children by divorce and single parenting (especially teenage single parenting). He shows that conservative publications such as the *American Spectator* and the *National Review* run many more articles on homosexuality than on parenthood, teenage pregnancy, or divorce. David Boaz, *Don't Forget the Kids*, N.Y. Times, Sept. 10, 1994, at A19.

44. Andrew Sullivan, *Here Comes the Groom: A (Conservative) Case for Gay Marriage*, New Republic, Aug. 28, 1989, at 20 (arguing that gay marriage is consistent with conservative goals). For an important recent elaboration, see generally Andrew Sullivan, *Virtually Normal: An Argument About Homosexuality* (New York: Knopf, 1995).

45. Arkes says that arranging men in "sets of two or three" will do as much to tame and civilize gays as moving in with college roommates does to control the hormones of young men. The analogy is a poor one unless the roommates Arkes has

in mind are romantically linked. See Hadley Arkes, *The Closet Straight*, National Review, July 5, 1993, at 43, 43–44.

46. *Id.* at 45.

47. *Id.*

48. I leave polygamy aside. It is a somewhat harder issue than incest, but in practice it is typically part and parcel of a system of gender inequality. In any case, the question raised by gay marriage is, first and foremost, whether everyone should have the opportunity to marry one other person.

49. See generally Laumann et al., *Social Organization*; see also Tamar Lewin, *Sex in America: Faithfulness in Marriage Thrives After All*, N.Y. Times, Oct. 7, 1994, at A1, A18 (discussing Laumann et al.).

50. Richard A. Posner, *Sex and Reason* (Cambridge, MA: Harvard University Press, 1994), 346.

51. *Id.*

Response

# Image, Analysis, and the Nature of Relationships

## Lynn D. Wardle

Professor Stephen Macedo's fine essay "Homosexuality and the Conservative Mind" attacks the "powerful" arguments against same-sex marriage of what he calls "the new natural law."[1] He asserts that "denying gays and lesbians access to such important public opportunities as marriage" constitutes legal discrimination, and that the critical issue is whether there is "a reasoned ground" for such discrimination.[2] He argues that new natural-law justifications for excluding same-sex couples from marriage are based on stereotypes, not reason. However, he confuses description of the essential inherent nature and qualities of human relationships with artificial images, masks, and stereotypes that misrepresent them, and he relies on false stereotypes himself.

Professor Macedo does not dispute that there are good reasons to have grave concerns about excessive sexual permissiveness and agrees "that public moral judgment has a legitimate role to play even in the most personal aspects of our lives."[3] He claims, however, that the new natural-law arguments against same-sex marriage are inadequate for four reasons. First, he charges that natural-law arguments that distinguish the inherent nature of human marriage from homosexual relations for purposes of law are just "a form of moral scapegoating," based on an invidious "sweeping stereotype" of gays, "condemning all gays and lesbians on the basis of opposition to the promiscuous behavior of some gays."[4] This simply begs the question—what is the true, real, actual nature of homosexual relationships in general? He disputes that promiscuity or infidelity are particularly distinctive qualities of homosexual relations, any more characteristic of gay and lesbian relations than of marital relations. This is surprising because the reality of multiple partners, promiscuity, and lack of sexual fidelity in homosexual relationships is beyond serious dispute today. Some of the most definitive empirical work demonstrating that temporary liaisons, promiscuity, infidelity, and instability are defining characteristics of typical (most) gay relationships has come out of the gay community itself. For example, Bell and Weinberg reported that 28 percent of white homosexual males claimed 1,000 or more partners, while 84 percent claimed 50 or more partners during a lifetime; 550 different sexual partners was the average.[5] Another gay author has written that "among gay men a long-lasting *monogamous* relationship is almost unknown. Indeed both gay women and gay men tend to be involved in what might be called multiple relationships."[6] While there may be exceptions, public policy must face these common realities.

Until gay and lesbian relationships become marriagelike in such essential aspects as monogamy, fidelity, and the intrinsic good inherent in the nature of marital relations, it makes no sense to call them "marriages." Professor Macedo retorts by suggesting that if same-sex relationships were called marriages, they would become more marriagelike. The Kelsean flaw of that argument was illustrated by Lincoln's memorable question, how many legs would a dog have if you called a tail a leg? To the response "five," Lincoln replied no, that a dog would still only have four legs; calling a tail a leg does not make it so.[7]

Because the public policy issue concerns the nature and meaning of marriage, an examination and a comparison of the nature and essential characteristics of traditional marital relationships and of same-sex sexual relationships (not merely the subjective preference for a particular type of sexual experience) are critical. Of course, there is an important difference between the real essential nature and qualities of human relationships, such as marriage and homosexual relations, and slick Madison Avenue images or hostile caricatures of them. But Professor Macedo, even more than the new natural lawyers, seems to forget this distinction. Quite properly he criticizes unfactual myths, demeaning pejoratives, and degrading mischaracterizations of homosexual relations. Sadly, however, he promotes an undeniably misleading (rose-colored) stereotype of homosexual relationships while unjustly condemning natural-law advocates for stereotyping simply because they describe the essential qualities of marriage that same-sex couples lack.

Professor Macedo charges that the natural-law arguments are mere "scapegoating" for a second reason, because instrumental sex—which natural law condemns—is both rampant among heterosexuals (e.g., contraception, masturbation, sex out of wedlock, and so on) and very problematic (sometimes producing children out of wedlock), yet these practices are not legally proscribed, so to single out homosexual behavior for legal restriction is unfair. This is a variation of the famous "Nixon" defense used by former President Richard M. Nixon and his closest advisors during the Watergate crisis. When Nixon faced impeachment and his aides were indicted, they argued that many politicians, especially Democrats (including Presidents

Lyndon B. Johnson and John F. Kennedy) had engaged in the same or worse kinds of political espionage, sabotage, and cover-ups without prosecution, so to single out the Republican president and his assistants was unfair. The argument was unpersuasive in the Watergate scandal in 1974, and it is equally unpersuasive today when raised by advocates of same-sex marriage. Sorry, but the fact that Bill Clinton "got away" (or even if he still "gets away") with sexual infidelity does not excuse irresponsible sexual practices of others, and just because all violations of some versions of natural law are not enacted or enforced in law does not logically or morally prevent the adoption and enforcement of other principles. That is how democracy works.

Moreover, not all deviations from the natural-law ideal of sexual experience exclusively within marriage threaten social order (particularly the institution of marriage) as much as legalizing same-sex marriage or domestic partnership would. Tolerating human imperfection to the degree manifest in laws tolerating contraception, masturbation, and pornography is a far cry from legitimating a radical new conjugal institution by legalizing same-sex marriage or domestic partnership.

Third, Professor Macedo asserts that new natural lawyers are guilty of a double standard because they allow sterile heterosexuals to marry and have sexual relations, but deny marriage to, and condemn sexual relations of, same-sex couples. Thus he asserts that same-sex couples are morally indistinguishable from sterile heterosexual couples for purposes of sexual relations and marriage. He goes so far as to suggest that the procreation justification for marriage "appears opportunistic, selected so as to allow sterile heterosexuals into the tent while keeping all homosexuals out."[8] The vast conservative conspiracy that Professor Macedo has uncovered is another lapse, for the identification of procreation as a (or *the*) core purpose of marriage is thousands of years old (at least back to Aristotle) and has been endorsed by commentators who had no hostility or other motive against homosexuals.[9] More fundamentally, sexual relations between a man and a woman differ in kind from sex between two men or two women because there are profound, inherent differences between men and women that make integrative, cross-gender relations significantly and innately different from same-sex relations.[10] Among the critical inherent differences is the relative procreative potential (and importance to society) of traditional marriages and same-sex relations.[11] Homosexual sex is never procreation; male-female sex (even in sterile couples) is always potentially and at least symbolically procreative in kind.

Finally, Professor Macedo, quoting Richard Posner, plays the homophobia card, charging that laws discriminating against homosexuals have "an egregiousness, and a meanness."[12] Such pejorative accusations chill responsible public debate and are antithetical to serious scholarship. They are designed to punish those who speak out against same-sex marriage and to intimidate others from openly opposing laws barring homosexual relations and legal unions. This unfortunate slip in Professor Macedo's essay detracts from his rigorous arguments for same-sex marriage, but it shows that even the most analytical advocates of same-sex marriage may slip in to the same kinds of negative stereotyping that they find so appalling when applied to them. Thus, ironically, Professor Macedo's essay illustrates the message underlying his arguments—how easily one may slip from the analytical and accurate to false images, pejoratives, and stereotypes when discussing same-sex marriage.

## NOTES

1. Stephen Macedo, *Homosexuality and the Conservative Mind, supra* at 97.

2. *Id.*

3. *Id.*

4. *Id.*

5. Alan P. Bell & Martin S. Weinberg, Homosexualities:A Study of Diversity Among Men and Women 85, 86, 308, 312, & 336 (1978); *see also* Marshall Kirk & Hunter Madsen, After the Ball: How America Will Conquer Its Fear and Hatred of Gays in the '90s 330 (1989).

6. Dennis Altman, The Homosexualization of America, the Americanization of Homosexuality 187 (1982) (emphasis in original).

7. Bartlett, The Shorter Bartlett's Familiar Quotations 218d (1961), *cited in* Stephen A. Newman, *Baby Doe, Congress, and the States: Challenging the Federal Treatment Standard for Impaired Infants,* 15 Am. J.L. & Med. 1, 15 n.56 (1989).

8. Macedo, *supra* at 104.

9. *See* Aristotle, Politica 1334–1335 (Benjamin Jowett, transl., W.D. Ross ed. 1921).

10. Lynn D. Wardle, *A Critical Analysis of Constitutional Claims for Same-Sex Marriage,* 1996 B.Y.U.L. Rev. 1.

11. Lynn D. Wardle, *"Multiply and Replenish": Considering Same-Sex Marriage in Light of State Interests in Marital Procreation,* 24 Harv. J.L. & Pub. Pol'y 771 (2001).

12. Macedo, at 110.

# Essay Two

# *Neutrality, Equality, and "Same-Sex Marriage"*

## **Robert P. George**

It is not uncommon these days to hear people say: "I believe that true marriage is a union of one man and one woman. But I think that it is wrong—a violation of the principle of equality—for the state to base its laws on controversial moral judgments, even if I happen to share those judgments. Therefore, I support proposals to revise our law to authorize same-sex 'marriages.' " The thought here is that the state, for the sake of equality, ought to be neutral as between competing understandings of the nature and value of marriage.

Of course, the claim that the law ought to be morally neutral about marriage or anything else is itself a moral claim. As such, it is not morally neutral, nor can it rest on an appeal to moral neutrality. People who believe that the law of marriage (and/or other areas of the law) ought to be morally neutral do not assert, nor does their position presuppose, that the law ought to be neutral as between the view that the law ought to be neutral and competing moral views. It is obvious that such neutrality is logically impossible. Sophisticated proponents of moral neutrality therefore acknowledge that theirs is a controversial moral position whose truth, soundness, correctness, or, at least, reasonableness they are prepared to defend against competing moral positions. They assert, in other words, that the best understanding of political morality, at least for societies such as ours, is one that includes a requirement that the law be morally neutral with respect to marriage. Alternative understandings of political morality, insofar as they fail to recognize the principle of moral neutrality, are, they say, mistaken and ought, as such, to be rejected.

Now, to recognize that any justification offered for the requirement of moral neutrality cannot itself be morally neutral is by no means to establish the falsity of the alleged requirement of moral neutrality. My purpose in calling attention to it is not to propose an argument purporting to identify self-referential inconsistency in arguments for moral neutrality. Although I shall argue that the moral neutrality of marriage law to embrace same-sex relationships is neither desirable nor, strictly speaking, possible, I do not propose to show that there is a logical or performative inconsistency in saying that "the law (of marriage) ought to be neutral as between competing moral ideas." It is not like saying, "No statement is true." Nor is it like singing, "I am not singing." At the same time, the putative requirement of moral neutrality is neither self-evident nor self-justifying. If it is to be vindicated as a true (correct, sound, and so on) proposition of political morality, it needs to be shown to be true (and so on) by a valid argument.

It is certainly the case that implicit in our matrimonial law is a (now controversial) moral judgment: namely, the judgment that marriage is inherently heterosexual and monogamous—a union of one man and one woman. (I shall discuss the deeper grounds of that judgment later.) Of course, this is not the only possible moral judgment. In some cultures, polygyny or (far less frequently) polyandry is legally sanctioned. Some historians claim that "marriages" (or their equivalent) between two men or two women have been recognized by certain cultures in the past.[1] However that may be, influential voices in our own culture today demand the revision of matrimonial law to authorize such "marriages."

There are two ways to argue for the proposition that it is unjust for government to refuse to authorize same-sex (and, for that matter, polygamous) "marriages." The first is to deny the reasonableness, soundness, or truth of the moral judgment implicit in the proposition that marriage is a union of one man and one woman. The second is to argue that this moral judgment cannot justly serve as the basis for the public law of matrimony irrespective of its reasonableness, its soundness, or even its truth.

In this essay, I shall mainly be concerned with the second of these ways of arguing. The task I have set for myself is to persuade you that the moral neutrality to which this way of arguing appeals is, and cannot but be, illusory. To that end, however, it will be necessary for me to explain the philosophical grounds of the moral judgment that marriage is inherently heterosexual and monogamous—a union of one man and one woman—and to discuss the arguments advanced by Stephen Macedo and other critics of traditional matrimonial law in their efforts to undermine this judgment.

Despite his manifest good faith in trying to understand both the moral core of the traditional conception of marriage and the arguments advanced in its defense by Germain Grisez, John Finnis, and myself, Professor Macedo doesn't quite get it right. I should therefore begin by stating the position we defend: Marriage is a two-in-one-flesh communion of persons that is consummated and actualized by acts that are procreative in type, whether or not they are procreative in effect (or are motivated, even in part, by a desire to procreate). The bodily union of spouses in marital acts is the biological matrix of their marriage as a multilevel relationship that unites persons at the biological, emotional, dispositional, and spiritual levels of their being. Marriage, precisely as such a relationship, is naturally ordered to the good of procreation (and to the nurturing and education of children) as well as to the good of spousal unity, and these goods are tightly bound together. The distinctive unity of spouses is possible because human (like other mammalian) males and females, by mating, unite organically—they become a single reproductive principle. Although reproduction is a single act, in humans (and other mammals) the reproductive act is performed not by individual members of the species, but by a mated pair as an organic unit. The point has been explained by Germain Grisez:

Though a male and a female are complete individuals with respect to other functions—for example, nutrition, sensation, and locomotion—with respect to reproduction they are only potential parts of a mated pair, which is the complete organism capable of reproducing sexually. Even if the mated pair is sterile, intercourse, provided it is the reproductive behavior characteristic of the species, makes the copulating male and female one organism.[2]

Although not all procreative-type acts are marital, there can be no marital act that is not procreative in type.[3] Masturbatory, sodomitical, or other sexual acts that are not procreative in type cannot unite persons organically, that is, as a single reproductive principle.[4] Therefore, such acts cannot be intelligibly engaged in for the sake of marital (i.e., one-flesh, bodily) unity as such. They cannot be marital acts. Rather, persons who perform such acts must be doing so for the sake of ends or goals that are extrinsic to themselves as bodily persons: Sexual satisfaction, or (perhaps) mutual sexual satisfaction, is sought as a means of releasing tension or obtaining (and sometimes sharing) pleasure, either as an end in itself or as a means to some other end, such as expressing affection, esteem, friendliness, and the like. In any case, where one-flesh union cannot (or cannot rightly) be sought as an end in itself, sexual activity necessarily involves the instrumentalization of the bodies of those participating in such activity to extrinsic ends.

In marital acts, by contrast, the bodies of persons who unite biologically are not reduced to the status of mere instruments. Rather, the end, goal, and intelligible point of sexual union is the good of marriage itself. On this understanding, such union is not a merely instrumental good, that is, a reason for action whose intelligibility as a reason depends on other ends to which it is a means, but is rather an intrinsic good, that is, a reason for action whose intelligibility as a reason depends on no such other end. The central and justifying point of sex is not pleasure (or even the sharing of pleasure) per se, however much sexual pleasure is sought—rightly sought— as an aspect of the perfection of marital union; the point of sex, rather, is marriage itself, considered as a bodily ("one-flesh") union of persons con-summated and actualized by acts that are procreative in type. Because in marital acts sex is not instrumentalized, such acts are free of the self-alienating and disintegrating qualities of masturbatory and sodomitical sex.[5] Unlike these and other nonmarital sex acts, marital acts effect no practical dualism that volitionally and thus existentially (though, of course, not meta-physically) separates the body from the conscious and desiring aspect of the self that is understood and treated by the acting person as the true self that inhabits and uses the body as its instrument.[6] As John Finnis has observed, marital acts are truly unitive and in no way self-alienating, because the bodily or biological aspect of human beings is "part of, and not merely an instru-ment of, their *personal* reality."[7]

But, one may ask, what about procreation? On the traditional view, isn't the sexual union of spouses instrumentalized to the goal of having children? It is true that St. Augustine was an influential proponent of something like this view, and there has always been a certain following for it among Chris-tians. The strict Augustinian position was rejected, however, by the main-stream of philosophical and theological reflection from the late Middle Ages forward, and the understanding of sex and marriage that came to be em-bodied in both the canon law of the Roman Catholic Church and the civil law of matrimony does not treat marriage as a merely instrumental good. Matrimonial law has traditionally understood marriage as consummated by, and only by, the procreative-type acts of spouses; by contrast, the sterility of spouses—so long as they are capable of consummating their marriage by a procreative-type act (and thus of achieving bodily, organic unity)—has never been treated as an impediment to marriage, even where sterility is certain and even certain to be permanent (as in the case of the marriage of a woman who has been through menopause or has undergone a hysterec-tomy).[8]

According to the traditional understanding of marriage, then, it is the nature of marital acts as procreative in type that makes it possible for such acts to be unitive in the distinctively marital way. This type of unity has intrinsic, and not merely instrumental, value. Thus the unitive good of mar-riage provides a noninstrumental (and thus sufficient) reason for spouses to perform sexual acts of a type that consummates and actualizes their mar-riage. In performing marital acts, the spouses do not reduce themselves as bodily persons (or their marriage) to the status of means or instruments.

At the same time, where marriage is understood as a one-flesh union of persons, children who may be conceived in marital acts are understood not as ends that are extrinsic to marriage (either in the strict Augustinian sense or the modern liberal one), but rather as gifts that supervene on acts whose central justifying point is precisely the marital unity of the spouses.[9] Such acts have unique meaning, value, and significance, as I have already sug-gested, because they belong to the class of acts by which children come into being—what I have called "procreative-type acts." More precisely, these acts have their unique meaning, value, and significance because they belong to the only class of acts by which children can come into being, not as "products" that their parents choose to "make," but rather as perfective participants in the organic community (i.e., the family) that is established by their parents' marriage. It is thus that children are properly understood and treated—even in their conception—not as means to their parents' ends, but as ends in themselves; not as objects of the desire or will of their parents, but as subjects of justice (and inviolable human rights);[10] not as property, but as persons. It goes without saying that not all cultures have fully grasped these truths about the moral status of children. What is less frequently noticed is that our culture's grasp of these truths is connected to a basic understanding of sex and marriage that is not only fast eroding, but is now under severe assault from people who have no conscious desire to reduce children to the status of mere means, or objects, or property.

It is sometimes thought that defenders of traditional marriage law deny the possibility of something whose possibility critics of the law affirm. "Love," these critics say, "makes a family," and it is committed love that justifies homosexual sex as much as it justifies heterosexual sex. If marriage is the proper or best context for sexual love, the argument goes, then marriage should be made available to loving, committed same-sex as well as opposite-sex partners on terms of strict equality.

In fact, however, at the bottom of the debate is a possibility that defenders of traditional marriage law affirm and its critics deny, namely, the possibility of marriage as a one-flesh communion of persons. The denial of this possibility is central to any argument designed to show that the moral judgment at the heart of the traditional understanding of marriage as inherently heterosexual is unreasonable, unsound, or untrue. If procreative-type acts in fact unite spouses interpersonally, as traditional sexual morality and marriage law suppose, then such acts differ fundamentally in meaning, value, and significance from the only types of sexual acts that can be performed by same-sex partners.

Liberal sexual morality, in denying that marriage is inherently heterosexual, necessarily supposes that the value of sex must be instrumental either to procreation or to pleasure, considered, in turn, as an end in itself or as a means of expressing affection, tender feelings, and the like. Thus proponents of the liberal view, such as Professor Macedo, suppose that homosexual sex acts are morally indistinguishable from heterosexual marital intercourse whenever the motivation for marital intercourse is something other than procreation. The sexual acts of homosexual partners, that is to say, are indistinguishable in motivation, meaning, value, and significance from the marital acts of spouses who know that at least one spouse is temporarily or permanently infertile. Thus, the liberal argument goes, traditional matrimonial law sins against the principle of equality in treating sterile heterosexuals as capable of marrying while treating homosexual partners as ineligible to marry.

Thus Macedo accuses the traditional view and its defenders of a "double standard." He asks:

What is the point of sex in an infertile marriage? Not procreation: the partners (let us assume) know that they are infertile. If they have sex, it is for pleasure and to express their love, or friendship, or some other shared good. It will be for precisely the same reason that committed, loving gay couples have sex.[11]

But Macedo's allegation of a double standard—the centerpiece of his attack on traditional sexual morality—fails to tell against the traditional view because it presupposes as true precisely what the traditional view denies, namely, that the value (and thus the point) of sex in marriage can only be instrumental. On the contrary, it is a central tenet of the traditional view that the value (and point) of sex is the intrinsic good of marriage itself that is actualized in sexual acts that unite spouses biologically and thus interpersonally. The traditional view rejects the instrumentalization of sex (and thus of the bodies of sexual partners) to any extrinsic end. This does not mean that procreation and pleasure are not rightly sought in marital acts; it means merely that they are rightly sought when they are integrated with the basic good and justifying point of marital sex, namely, the one-flesh union of marriage itself.

It is necessary, therefore, for critics of traditional matrimonial law to argue that the apparent one-flesh unity that distinguishes marital acts from sodomitical acts is illusory, and that the apparent bodily communion of spouses in procreative-type acts—which, according to the traditional view, form the biological matrix of their marital relationship—is not really possible.

So Richard Posner declares that Finnis's claim that "the union of reproductive organs of husband and wife unites them biologically" is unclear in its meaning and moral relevance and cannot "distinguish . . . sterile marriage, at least when the couple *knows* that it is incapable of reproducing, from homosexual coupling."[12] Turning to my own claim that "intercourse, so long as it is the reproductive behavior characteristic of the species, unites the copulating male and female as a single organism," Posner asserts that "[i]ntercourse known by the participants to be sterile is not 'reproductive behavior,' and even reproductive intercourse does not unite the participants 'as a single organism.' "[13]

On the question of "reproductive behavior" or, better, the idea of "procreative-type" acts, it is important to see that identical behavior can cause conception or not depending entirely on whether the nonbehavioral conditions of reproduction obtain. The intrinsic, and not merely instrumental, good of marital communion gives spouses reason to fulfill the behavioral conditions of procreation even in circumstances in which they know that the nonbehavioral conditions do not obtain. This is true precisely inasmuch as fulfillment of the behavioral conditions of reproduction is interpersonally unitive. So the question is whether Posner is right to deny what Finnis, Grisez, and I affirm: namely, that procreative-type acts unite a male and female as a single organism, that is, make them "two-in-one-flesh."

It is, a plain biological fact that, as Grisez says, reproduction is a single function, yet it is carried out not by an individual male or female human being, but by a male and female as a mated pair. So, in respect of reproduction, albeit not in other respects (again, like locomotion or digestion), the mated pair is a single organism, and the partners form a single reproductive principle; they become "one flesh." So, I would ask Judge Posner, what is there not to understand?[14] The issue is not one of translating medieval Latin; it is a matter of simple biology. Of course, the question remains, is there any particular value to the biological (organic) union of spouses? One will judge the matter one way or another depending, for example, on whether one understands the biological reality of human beings, as Finnis says, as part of, rather than a mere instrument of, their personal reality. But as to the fact of biological unity, there is no room for doubt. As to its moral implications, I suspect that Posner's difficulty is simply a specific instance of his general skepticism—skepticism emphatically not shared by Macedo—regarding the possibility of noninstrumental practical reasons and reasoning. If Posner were pressed to deal with the question, he would no doubt deny that the biological reality of human beings is anything more than an instrument of ends that are themselves given by feelings, emotions, desire, or other subrational motivating factors. As I have elsewhere sought to show, the implicit operating premise of Posner's treatment of sex and other moral questions is the Humean noncognitivist understanding of practical reason as the "slave of the passions."[15] Marital communion cannot be a noninstrumental reason as far as Posner is concerned because on his account of human motivation there are no noninstrumental reasons.

Stephen Macedo, by contrast, is no Humean. Although he quotes approvingly some of Posner's speculations and stated political opinions about certain forms of morals legislation, he plainly rejects Posner's instrumentalist understanding of practical reason. Still, Macedo claims that "the 'one-flesh communion' of sterile couples would appear . . . to be more a matter of appearance than reality." Because of their sterility, he contends, such couples cannot really unite biologically: "their bodies, like those of homosexuals, can form no 'single reproductive principle,' no real unity."[16] Indeed, Macedo argues that even fertile couples who conceive children in acts of sexual intercourse do not truly unite biologically, because, he asserts, "penises and vaginas do not unite biologically, sperm and eggs do."[17]

John Finnis has aptly replied that "in this reductivist, word-legislating mood, one might declare that sperm and egg unite only physically and only their pronuclei are biologically united. But it would be more realistic to acknowledge that the whole process of copulation, involving as it does the brains of the man and woman, their nerves, blood, vaginal and other secretions, and coordinated activity is biological through and through."[18] Moreover, as Finnis points out, "the organic unity which is instantiated in an act of the reproductive kind is not, as Macedo . . . reductively imagine[s], the unity of penis and vagina. It is the unity of the persons in the intentional, consensual *act* of seminal emission/reception in the woman's reproductive tract."[19]

The unity to which Finnis refers—unity of body, sense, emotion, reason, and will—is, in my view, central to our understanding of humanness itself. Yet it is a unity of which Macedo, Posner, and others who deny the possibility of true marital communion can give no account, for this denial presupposes a dualism of "person" (as conscious and desiring self), on the one hand, and "body" (as instrument of the conscious and desiring self), on the other, that is flatly incompatible with this unity. Person/body dualism is implicit in the idea, central to Macedo's denial of the possibility of one-flesh marital union, that sodomitical acts differ from what I have described as acts of the procreative type only as a matter of the arrangement of the "plumbing." According to this idea, the genital organs of an infertile woman (and, of course, all women are infertile most of the time) or of an infertile man are not really "reproductive organs" any more than, say, mouths, rectums, tongues, or fingers are reproductive organs. Thus the intercourse of a man and a woman where at least one partner is temporarily or permanently sterile cannot really be an act of the procreative type.

But the plain fact is that the genitals of men and women are reproductive organs all of the time—even during periods of sterility. Acts that fulfill the behavioral conditions of procreation are acts of the procreative type even where the nonbehavioral conditions of procreation do not happen to obtain. Insofar as the point or object of sexual intercourse is marital union, the partners achieve the desired unity (i.e., become "two-in-one-flesh") precisely insofar as they mate, that is, fulfill the behavioral conditions of procreation, or, if you will, perform the type of act—the only type of act—upon which the gift of a child may supervene. Finnis has carefully explained this point:

Sexual acts which are marital are "of the reproductive kind" because in willing such an act one wills sexual behaviour which is (a) the very same as causes generation (intended or unintended) in every case of human *sexual* reproduction, and (b) the very same as one would will if one were intending precisely sexual reproduction as a goal of a particular marital sexual act. This kind of act is a "natural kind," in the morally relevant sense of "natural," not . . . if and only if one is intending or attempting to produce an *outcome*, viz. reproduction or procreation. Rather it is a distinct rational kind—and therefore in the morally relevant sense a natural kind—because (i) in engaging in it one is intending a *marital* act, (ii) its being of the reproductive kind is a necessary though not sufficient condition of its being marital, and (iii) marriage is a rational and natural kind of institution. One's reason for action—one's rational motive—is precisely the complex good of marriage.[20]

The dualistic presuppositions of the liberal position are fully on display in the frequent references by Macedo and other proponents of the position to sexual organs as "equipment." Neither sperm nor eggs, neither penises nor vaginas, are properly conceived in such impersonal terms. Nor are they "used" by persons considered as somehow standing over and apart from these and other aspects of their biological reality. The biological reality of persons is, rather, part of their personal reality. (Hence where a person treats his body as a subpersonal object, the practical dualism he thereby effects brings with it a certain self-alienation, a damaging of the intrinsic good of personal self-integration.) In any event, the biological union of persons—which is effected in marital acts but not in sodomitical ones—really is an interpersonal ("one-flesh") communion.

Macedo considers the possibility that defenders of the traditional understanding are right about all this: that marriage truly is a "one-flesh union" consummated and actualized by marital acts; that sodomitical and other intrinsically nonmarital sexual acts really are self-alienating and, as such, immoral; that the true conception of marriage is one according to which it is an intrinsically heterosexual (and, one might here add, monogamous) relationship. But even if the traditional understanding of marriage is the morally correct one—even if it is true—he argues, the state cannot justly recognize it as such. For if disagreements about the nature of marriage "lie in . . . difficult philosophical quarrels, about which reasonable people have long disagreed, then our differences lie in precisely the territory that John Rawls rightly marks off as inappropriate to the fashioning of our basic rights and liberties."[21] From this it follows that government must remain neutral as between conceptions of marriage as intrinsically heterosexual (and by this logic, surely, monogamous) and conceptions according to which "marriages" may be contracted not only between a man and a woman, but also between two men or two women (and, presumably, a man or a woman and multiple male and/or female "spouses," so long as no oppression is involved). Otherwise, according to Macedo, the state would "inappropriately" be "deny[ing] people fundamental aspects of equality based on reasons and arguments whose force can only be appreciated by those who accept difficult to assess [metaphysical and moral] claims."[22]

It seems to me, however, that something very much like the contrary is true. Because the true meaning, value, and significance of marriage are fairly easily grasped (even if people sometimes have difficulty living up to its moral demands) where a culture—including, critically, a legal culture—promotes and supports a sound understanding of marriage, both formally and informally, and because ideologies and practices that are hostile to a sound understanding and practice of marriage in a culture tend to undermine the institution of marriage in that culture, thus making it difficult for large numbers of people to grasp the true meaning, value, and significance of marriage, it is extremely important that government eschew attempts to be "neutral" with regard to competing conceptions of marriage and try hard to embody in its law and policy the morally soundest conception. Moreover, any effort to achieve neutrality will inevitably prove to be self-defeating. The law is a teacher, and it will teach either that marriage is an intrinsic human good that people can choose to participate in, but whose contours people cannot make and remake at will (e.g., a one-flesh communion of persons consummated and actualized by acts that are procreative in type and perfected, where all goes well, in the generation, education, and nurturing of children in a context—the family—that is uniquely suitable to their well-being), or the law will teach that marriage is a mere convention that is malleable in such a way that individuals, couples, or, indeed, groups can choose to make it whatever suits their desires, interests, subjective goals, and so on. The result, given the undeniable biases of human sexual psychology, will be the development of practices and ideologies that truly do tend to undermine the sound understanding and practice of marriage, together with the pathologies that tend to reinforce the very practices and ideologies that cause them.

Joseph Raz, though himself a liberal who does not share my views regarding homosexuality or sexual morality generally, is rightly critical of forms of liberalism, including Rawlsianism, that suppose that law and government can and should be neutral with respect to competing conceptions of morality. In this regard, he has noted that "monogamy, assuming that it is the only valuable form of marriage, cannot be practiced by an individual. It requires a culture which recognizes it, and which supports it through the public's attitude and through its formal institutions."[23] Raz does not suppose that in a culture whose law and public morality do not support monogamy, someone who happens to believe in it somehow will be unable to restrict himself to having one wife or will be required to take additional wives. His point, rather, is that even if monogamy is a key element of a sound understanding of marriage, large numbers of people will fail to understand that or why that is the case—and will therefore fail to grasp the value of monogamy and the intelligible point of practicing it—unless they are assisted by a culture that supports, formally and informally, monogamous marriage. What is true of monogamy is equally true of the other marks or aspects of a morally sound understanding of marriage. In other words, marriage is the type of good that can be participated in, or fully participated in, only by people who properly understand it and choose it with a proper understanding in mind; yet people's ability properly to understand it and thus to choose it depends upon institutions and cultural understandings that transcend individual choice.

But what about Macedo's claim that when matrimonial law deviates from neutrality by embodying the moral judgment that marriage is inherently heterosexual, it denies same-sex partners who wish to marry "fundamental aspects of equality"? Does a due regard for equality require moral neutrality? The appeal to equality is rhetorically useful to Macedo and other proponents of liberal sexual ideology, but does no real work in their argument. If the moral judgment that marriage is inherently heterosexual is false, then the reason for recognizing same-sex marriages is that such unions are as a matter of moral fact indistinguishable from marriages of the traditional type. If, however, the moral judgment that marriage is inherently heterosexual is true, then Macedo's claim that the recognition of this truth by government "denies fundamental aspects of equality" simply cannot be sustained. If, in other words, the marital acts of spouses consummate and actualize marriage as a one-flesh communion and serve thereby as the biological matrix of the relationship of marriage at all its levels, then the embodiment in law and policy of an understanding of marriage as inherently heterosexual denies no one fundamental aspects of equality.

True, persons who are exclusively homosexually oriented lack a psychological prerequisite to enter into marital relationships. But this is no fault of the law. Indeed, the law would embody a lie (and a damaging one insofar as it truly would contribute to the undermining of the sound understanding and practice of marriage in a culture) if it were to pretend that a marital relationship could be formed on the basis of, and integrated around, sodomitical or other intrinsically nonmarital (and, as such, self-alienating) sex acts.

It is certainly unjust arbitrarily to deny legal marriage to persons who are capable of performing marital acts and entering into the marital relationship. So, for example, laws forbidding interracial marriages truly were violations of equality. Contrary to the published claims of Andrew Sullivan, Andrew Koppelman, and others, however, laws that embody the judgment that marriage is intrinsically heterosexual are in no way analogous to laws against miscegenation. Laws forbidding whites to marry blacks were unjust, not because they embodied a particular moral view and thus violated the alleged requirement of moral neutrality; rather, they were unjust because they embodied an unsound (indeed a grotesquely false) moral view—one that was racist and, as such, immoral.

Macedo makes clear his opposition to "excesses of sexual permissiveness and promiscuity." He says that "the reasonable core of the conservative sexual teaching is its concern with promiscuity and sexual license." He proposes not an alteration in the meaning of marriage or an abandonment of its constitutive norms of monogamy, fidelity, and permanence of commitment, but merely an extension of the opportunity to marry to persons who have hitherto been excluded. However, it is a standing challenge to Macedo and other defenders of "same-sex marriage" to provide principled moral grounds for the norms of monogamy, fidelity, and permanence that are compatible with their rejection of the traditional conception of marriage as a one-flesh union. I do not doubt that Macedo personally disapproves of polygamy, promiscuity, open marriages, and yet grosser forms of sexual vice, such as anonymous sex and sex with animals. But there are more freethinking liberals who do not. They believe that so long as care is taken to prevent unwanted pregnancy and the transmission of disease, sexual relations between any two or more persons who (without deception) consent to enjoy an encounter together are morally innocent and even good. On the account of sexual morality Macedo offers in defending the idea of "same-sex marriage," it is simply impossible to say why these people are wrong. Certainly the essentially prudential considerations Macedo mentions in favor of sexual self-restraint are insufficient to the moral task. The question is not one of his or anyone else's subjective scruples or even prudential concerns about sexuality; it has to do, rather, with the objective logical implications of his rejection of the principles of traditional sexual morality—implications that are clear enough not only to conservatives but to rigorously consistent liberals as well. If, in fact, the rejection of the traditional conception of marriage as a one-flesh union undercuts the grounds of moral principle for upholding marriage's constitutive norms, the case for "same-sex marriage" collapses as anything more than an effort to undermine the institution of marriage "from within"—an effort that some activists in the cause of redefining "marriage" to include same-sex relationships expressly endorse in publications targeted to audiences likely to be sympathetic to their agenda.

Perhaps sensing their vulnerability on this most critical of points, promoters of what has been described as the "conservative" case for "gay marriage" sometimes fall back on stereotypes of their critics as "bigots" who foster "discrimination" against their fellow citizens and seek to deny them equality. This is unfortunate. Defenders of the traditional conception of marriage and sexual morality have stated their challenge fairly and clearly. If their opponents can meet it, let them do so.

## NOTES

This essay originally appeared in T. William Boxx and Gary M. Quinlivan, Toward the Renewal of Civilization: Political Order and Culture (Grand Rapids, Michigan: Wm. B. Eerdmans Publishing Co., 1998). It has been revised for inclusion in the present volume.

1. The late John Boswell, for example, claimed that brother/sister-making rituals found in certain early medieval Christian manuscripts were meant to give ecclesiastical recognition and approval to homosexual relationships. See John Boswell, Same-Sex Unions in Premodern Europe (New York: Villard Books, 1994). However, as Robin Darling Young has observed, "[T]he reviews [of Boswell's work] after the early burst of hopeful publicity have been notably skeptical—even from sources one would expect to be favorable" (Gay Marriage: Reimagining Church History, First Things, November 1994, at 48). Darling herself concludes that Boswell's "painfully strained

effort to recruit Christian history in support of the homosexual cause that he favors is not only a failure, but an embarrassing one." *Id.*

2. Germain Grisez, "The Christian Family as Fulfillment of Sacramental Marriage" (paper delivered to the Society of Christian Ethics Annual Conference, September 9, 1995).

3. Adulterous acts, for example, may be procreative in type (and even in effect) but are intrinsically nonmarital.

4. Securely grasping this point and noticing its significance, Hadley Arkes has remarked that " 'sexuality' refers to that part of our nature that has as its end the purpose of begetting. In comparison, the other forms of 'sexuality' may be taken as minor burlesques or even mockeries of the true thing." Arkes is not here suggesting that sexual acts, in what he calls "the strict sense of 'sexuality,' " must be motivated by a desire to procreate; rather, his point is that such acts, even where they are motivated by a desire for bodily union, must be procreative in type if such union is to be achieved. This, I believe, makes sense of what Stephen Macedo and other liberal critics of Arkes's writings on marriage and sexual morality find to be the puzzling statement that "[e]very act of genital stimulation simply cannot count as a sexual act." *See* Hadley Arkes, *Questions of Principle, Not Predictions: A Reply to Stephen Macedo*, 84 Georgetown Law Journal 323 (1995).

5. This is by no means to suggest that married couples cannot instrumentalize and thus degrade their sexual relationship. *See* Robert P. George and Gerard V. Bradley, *Marriage and the Liberal Imagination*, 84 Georgetown Law Journal 301–320 (1995), esp. at 303, n. 9. This article contains responses to various arguments advanced by Professor Macedo and others that I do not pause to address here, including arguments based on analogies between unloaded guns and the sexual organs of infertile people and between sex and eating. For additional development of the substance of the arguments presented in the article, *see* Patrick Lee and Robert P. George, *What Sex Can Be: Self-Alienation, Illusion, or One-Flesh Union*, 42 American Journal of Jurisprudence 135–157 (1997).

6. On person/body dualism, its implications for ethics, and its philosophical untenability, *see* John Finnis, Joseph M. Boyle, Jr., and Germain Grisez, Nuclear Deterrence, Morality, and Realism 304–309 (Oxford: Clarendon Press, 1987); and Patrick Lee, *Human Beings Are Animals*, in Robert P. George (ed.), Natural Law and Moral Inquiry (Georgetown University Press, 1998).

7. John Finnis, *Law, Morality, and "Sexual Orientation,"* in John Corvino (ed.), Same Sex: Debating the Ethics, Science, and Culture of Homosexuality, sec. III (Totowa, New Jersey: Rowman and Littlefield 1997).

8. *See* George and Bradley, *Marriage and the Liberal Imagination*, 307–309.

9. *See id.* at 304.

10. I am not here suggesting that traditional ethics denies that it is legitimate for people to "desire" or "want" children. I am merely explicating the sense in which children may be desired or wanted by prospective parents under a description that, consistent with the norms of traditional ethics, does not reduce them to the status of "products" to be brought into existence at their parents' will and for their ends, but rather treats them as "persons" who are to be welcomed by them as perfective participants in the organic community established by their marriage. *See* George and Bradley, *Marriage and the Liberal Imagination*, 306, n. 21. *See also* Leon Kass, *The*

*Wisdom of Repugnance: Why We Should Ban the Cloning of Humans*, New Republic, June 2, 1997, at 17–26, esp. 23–24.

11. Stephen Macedo, *Homosexuality and the Conservative Mind*, 84 Georgetown Law Journal 278 (1995).

12. Richard Posner, The Problematics of Moral and Legal Theory 77 (Cambridge, MA: Belknap Press of Harvard University Press, 1999). Apparently having in mind accusations that he had in an earlier publication unfairly quoted fragments of Finnis's argument without providing their context, Posner goes on to say: "It may seem unfair of me to quote Finnis out of context. But the context is dominated by even stranger sentences, which read as if they had been translated from medieval Latin and makes one wonder whether Finnis agrees with Aquinas that masturbation is a worse im-morality than rape" (*Id.*). This unfortunate and, indeed, unworthy sentence of Judge Posner's responds to a charge of implicit unfairness (i.e., not providing the essential context of quoted material to which one directs criticism) by manifesting explicit, indeed blatant, unfairness—and doing so in a way that has no evident purpose other than to appeal to prejudices that many of Posner's readers can be counted upon to share. (In fact, Finnis has made abundantly clear his own view that the profound injustice of rape makes it morally far worse than masturbation or other forms of unchastity not involving injustice. *See* John Finnis, Aquinas: Moral, Political, and Legal Theory 153 (Oxford: Oxford University Press, 1998). In the same place, he provides a careful and fully documented explanation of the sense in which Aquinas, while considering the unchastity involved in rape to be graver than the unchastity involved in masturbation, recognizes that rape involves serious injustice that mastur-bation does not involve.) Having thus dealt with Finnis, Posner turns his attention to the present author: "Robert George makes the same point in a more modern idiom, but I still can't make any sense of it."

13. Posner, Problematics, n. 143.

14. Germain Grisez proposes a thought experiment. Imagine a type of bodily, rational being that reproduces, not by mating, but by some act performed by indi-viduals. Imagine that for these same beings, however, locomotion or digestion is performed not by individuals, but only by complementary pairs that unite for this purpose. Would anybody acquainted with such beings have difficulty understanding that in respect of reproduction the organism performing the function is the individ-ual, while in respect of locomotion or digestion, the organism performing the func-tion is the united pair? Would anybody deny that the union effected for purposes of locomotion is an organic unity?

15. *See* Robert P. George, *Can Sex Be Reasonable?* 93 Columbia Law Review 783 (1993).

16. Macedo, *Homosexuality and the Conservative Mind*, 278.

17. *Id.* at 280.

18. Finnis, *Law, Morality, and "Sexual Orientation,"* sec. V.

19. *Id.*

20. *Id.*

21. Stephen Macedo, *Reply to Critics*, 84 Georgetown Law Journal 335 (1995).

22. *Id.* at 335.

23. Joseph Raz, The Morality of Freedom 162 (Oxford: Clarendon Press, 1986).

Response

# On Justice, Exclusion, and Equal Treatment: A Response to Professor Robert P. George

## Mark Strasser

Professor George offers an analysis of why marriage is a union of one man and one woman and then suggests that his view could justly serve as the basis for the public law of matrimony. Whether or not it could be so used, it clearly is not, at least in part because the theory is much more exclusive than it might appear to be and has implications that no state would embrace. Because his theory cannot explain or account for any state's current marriage laws, however, it cannot fairly be used to justify any state's current refusal to recognize same-sex unions.

Professor George argues that marriage is a two-in-one-flesh communion of persons that is consummated and actualized by acts that are procreative in type. He implicitly suggests that individuals who will not or cannot engage in acts that are procreative in type cannot engage in "marital acts" and thus should not be allowed to marry. (If this were not his view, then it is not clear why his theory would have any import for whether the state should recognize same-sex marriages.) Because marriage promotes such important individual and societal interests, Professor George's theory, if it were persuasive, would have important implications and thus must be examined more closely.

Professor George makes clear that an act might be procreative in type even if that act cannot result in conception and thus that sterile couples can engage in acts of a procreative type. After all, he explains elsewhere, the "difference between sterile and fertile married couples is not a difference in what they do."[1] Yet Professor George also argues that marital couples cannot engage in acts of a procreative type if one or both have been voluntarily sterilized,[2] notwithstanding that couples who have undergone voluntary sterilization "do" what fertile and naturally sterile couples do.[3]

Suppose that Professor George could offer a plausible explanation of why certain sterile couples do not "do" what other sterile couples do. His view would still have the additional difficulties that (1) no state would preclude a couple from marrying merely because they had voluntarily undergone sterilization, and (2) it is not at all clear that a state could pass a law precluding such marriages without offending the U.S. Constitution.

Professor George's theory holds that marital couples are not engaging in marital acts if they engage in sexual relations with the sole ends of (1) giving each other pleasure,[4] (2) expressing their love for each other,[5] (3) producing children,[6] or (4) any combination thereof.[7] Suppose, then, that a couple would not or perhaps could not have sexual relations for a reason other than one of those listed in 1–4. According to Professor George's theory, this couple could not engage in marital acts and, presumably, should also be precluded from marrying. Needless to say, the U.S. Constitution would never permit a state to pass a law precluding such a couple from marrying.

Professor George suggests that same-sex-marriage proponents must assert that the value and point of sex in marriage can only be instrumental, but that is false. A same-sex-marriage proponent might (but need not) claim that the value and point of sex in marriage is the good of marriage itself, although that person might disagree with Professor George about the correct specification of the content of that good. A different same-sex-marriage proponent might assert that the value and point of sex in marriage is its symbolism and communication of love, fidelity, and commitment. Yet another could assert that there is no one value and point of sex or marriage. In any event, few if any theorists would support the state's deciding who can marry based on whether those individuals have the "proper" understanding of *the* purpose of sex or marriage.

Professor George suggests that antimiscegenation laws are not analogous to laws that limit marriage to different-sex couples because, after all, the former embody an unsound moral view whereas the latter embody a sound one. Of course, supporters of antimiscegenation laws did not and do not agree with his analysis, just as he does not accept others' claims that his view is morally unsound, and his assertion that he is correct and that others are not is unlikely to convince many people.

Professor George admits that most Americans do not agree with him about the use of contraception by marital couples, and thus his theory does not seem to capture the popular view.[8] Yet even were his view more generally accepted, that would not settle the matter, since something so fundamental as whether one has the right to marry should not simply be determined by popular vote or sentiment.

Many agree with Professor George that the true meaning, value, and significance of marriage are fairly easily grasped, although they instead analyze marriage in terms of love and commitment or, perhaps, of providing a setting for the raising of the young. Either of these latter analyses would *support* the state's recognizing same-sex marriage.

Professor George suggests that if the moral judgment that marriage is inherently heterosexual is false, then the reason for recognizing same-sex marriage is that such unions are as a matter of moral fact indistinguishable from marriages of the traditional type. While many same-sex-marriage proponents accept the falsity of the moral judgment that marriage is inherently heterosexual and the truth of the moral judgment that same-sex unions are as a matter of moral fact indistinguishable from marriages of the more traditional type, the argument for the legal recognition of same-sex unions is often not based on these moral truths for a very pragmatic reason. Just as it is difficult to convince someone that something has intrinsic goodness when that person is committed to another view,[9] it is also difficult to convince someone of the truth of a particular moral judgment when that person is firmly committed to a different position. How, for example, would one convince individuals of the falsity of their moral judgments that marriage can only be between individuals of the same race or only between individuals who can produce a child through their union?

It is not argued here that there are no moral truths, but merely that it is notoriously difficult to change the minds of people who are firmly committed to opposing views and at best unhelpful to simply assert that one has captured moral truth and that the state should reflect that "truth" in its laws. As a separate point, it should be noted that the rhetorical strategy of claiming to have moral truth on one's side was used to support antimiscegenation laws. History has repeatedly shown that claims to moral truth are sometimes misused to deny others' fundamental rights. Professor George too cavalierly dismisses discussions of antimiscegenation laws and thus misses some of the lessons suggested by their former existence.

Suppose that one brackets whether Professor George has presented an internally consistent system or whether he can offer more than a bare assertion that his moral view is correct. It is quite clear that the state does not prevent all those unable to engage in "marital acts" from marrying, and it is hard to understand why fundamental aspects of equality and fairness would not be denied were Professor George's theory used to deny same-sex couples but not other "unqualified" couples the right to marry.

It is not claimed here that equality and fairness would be respected if only all "unqualified" couples were denied the right to marry. Indiscriminate imposition of an unfair burden does not somehow make that imposition fair or just.

Marriage promotes very important interests of individuals and the state, whether or not those unions are made up of individuals of different sexes and whether or not those individuals can engage in marital acts, and such an important right should not be denied for the kinds of reasons offered by Professor George. Even had Professor George offered a consistent theory that, for example, had not relied on mysterious notions of procreative-type acts or what "do" means, he still would not have offered a justification for preventing those who cannot engage in what he calls "marital acts" from enjoying something as fundamental as the right to marry, much less a justification for the selective use of his theory to deny such a fundamental right.

## NOTES

Some of the discussion contained here can be found in a more extended analysis of Professor George's view in Mark Strasser, *Marital Acts, Morality, and the Right to Privacy*, 30 N.M. L. Rev. 43–67 (2000).

1. *See* Patrick Lee & Robert P. George, *What Sex Can Be: Self-Alienation, Illusion, or One-Flesh Union*, 42 Am. J. Juris. 135, 150 (1997).

2. *See* Robert P. George & Gerard V. Bradley, *Marriage and the Liberal Imagination*, 84 Geo. L.J. 301, 310 n. 30 ("Nobody, we believe, performs a reproductive-type act when he or she deliberately thwarts that act's reproductive potential).")

3. *Cf.* Lee & George, *What Sex Can Be*, 42 Am. J. Juris. at 150.

4. *See id.* at 138.

5. *See id.* at 142.

6. *See* George & Bradley, *Marriage and the Liberal Imagination*, 84 Geo. L.J. at 304.

7. *See id.* at 305 ("We reject the proposition that sex can legitimately be instrumentalized, that is, treated as a mere means to any extrinsic end, including procreation).")

8. *See id.* at 319.

9. Professor George discusses the difficulty in establishing which things have intrinsic value and which do not. *See id.* at 306.

# Chapter 5

Essay One

# Marriage, Same-Gender Relationships, and Human Needs and Capabilities

## Carlos A. Ball

There are certain basic needs that are constitutive of our humanity. There are certain needs, in other words, that must be satisfied if we are to lead lives that are recognizably human. Basic needs include the need for nourishment, shelter, and periodic rest. The need for companionship and affiliation with other humans is also a basic need. So is the need for sexual satisfaction. As the philosopher Martha Nussbaum notes, "sexual need and desire are features of more or less every human life. It is . . . a most important basis for the recognition of others different from ourselves as human beings."[1]

Human beings, however, are not only needy creatures; they are also *capable* ones. If basic needs must be satisfied in order to lead a life that is recognizably human, basic capabilities must be exercised in order to lead a *full* human life. While needs are mostly about what can be done for individuals, capabilities are about what individuals can do or accomplish.[2] For Nussbaum, basic capabilities that are constitutive of our humanity include being able to use the five senses; to imagine, think, and reason; to love and take care of others; to control one's body and protect it against abuse by others; to live for and with others and to engage in various forms of familial and social interactions; and to laugh, play, and enjoy recreational activities.[3]

It is impossible to satisfy basic human needs and exercise basic human capabilities in isolation from others. Unless we are Robinson Crusoe (and even he relied on the assistance of his loyal sidekick Friday), it is our interactions with others, as well as our dependencies on others, that allow us to lead lives that are fully human. Even the most basic needs, such as those for food and shelter, are difficult to satisfy without the assistance of others. Other needs and capabilities, such as the need to be loved and cared for by others and the capability to love and care for others, by their very nature require affiliations with fellow human beings. This is why a discussion of important needs and capabilities inevitably raises questions of moral and political philosophy: What obligations do individuals and societies have for the creation of conditions that make it possible for individuals to satisfy those needs and exercise those capabilities that are constitutive of their full humanity? Which rights should be deemed fundamental because they emanate directly from our status as human beings with certain basic needs and capabilities?

It should come as no surprise, therefore, that basic needs and capabilities are implicated in many of our societal debates over gay rights. Whether we are assessing the scope of the right to engage in sexual intimacy without interference by the state or deciding whether the state should recognize and support gay and lesbian relationships and families, we are in effect determining the societal conditions under which those who are attracted to others of the same gender are allowed and encouraged to meet basic human needs and exercise basic human capabilities associated with physical and emotional intimacy. If we believe that lesbians and gay men share commonalities with all other human beings that make their basic needs and capabilities as morally relevant as those of heterosexuals, then we must be sensitive to the ways in which public policies allow or impede the satisfaction of those needs and the exercise of those capabilities.

Those of us who argue in favor of gay rights positions contend that the ability of lesbians and gay men to create relationships around sex, love, loyalty, respect, and commitment is constitutive of their humanity and personhood. The needs and capabilities for physical and emotional intimacy that lesbians and gay men share with all others are constitutive elements of their humanity. It is impossible, therefore, to separate their identity as human beings from those basic needs and capabilities. It is for this reason that efforts to distinguish between lesbians and gay men as persons on the one hand and their needs and capabilities associated with physical and emotional intimacy on the other are morally problematic.[4] Lesbians and gay men, like everyone else, pursue and express their humanity in part through their intimate relationships, including sexual ones. Lesbians and gay men need and are capable of participating in intimate sexual relationships because they too are human. It is no more possible to separate their needs and capabilities for physical and emotional intimacy from their moral personhood and their identity as human beings than it is to do so for heterosexuals. To attempt to do so is to quite literally dehumanize lesbians and gay men because it is an effort to strip them of a meaningful and enriching sexuality that helps define them as human beings. If we morally strip lesbians and gay men of their same-gender sexuality and thus deny that they have needs and capabilities for meaningful physical and emotional intimacy along with everyone else, we fail to recognize them as full human beings.

We as a society should reject any effort to place a group of individuals outside of the human community, even if it is for the "limited" purpose of justifying our failure to recognize the value and importance of their physically and emotionally intimate lives. We should remind ourselves that the greatest injustices committed in our nation's history have been the result of perceiving some of our fellow citizens as less than full human beings. "To guard against this," as Robin West notes, "we should assume, and insist, and re-affirm, that those whose lives are affected by our actions are fundamentally, essentially and in material, emotional and biological ways *like us*, and act accordingly."[5]

It was only when women were viewed as fully human (including as having the capability to reason and to make intelligent decisions about their lives and their futures) that society granted them the right to vote as well as the opportunity to seek happiness and fulfillment outside as well as inside the home. It was only when African Americans were viewed as fully human that society granted them meaningful access to the most basic civil rights. As Raimond Gaita notes, "[o]nly when one's humanity is fully visible will one be treated as someone who can intelligibly press claims to equal access to goods and opportunities."[6] Our society is slowly coming to the realization that lesbians and gay men, too, are fully human, and that their need for and capability to provide love and affection within a sexually intimate relationship merits *moral* respect.

It is important to keep all of this in mind when determining the meaning of marriage in our society and whether the state has an obligation to recognize and support committed same-gender relationships. As mentioned earlier, most of the basic needs and capabilities that are constitutive of our humanity involve interactions with and dependencies on others. This is especially true of those needs and capabilities associated with sexual intimacy. If we view these needs and capabilities narrowly—for example, simply in terms of our needs to satisfy sexual urges and our capabilities to satisfy the sexual urges of others—then it can be argued that a society meets its obligations to promote and protect basic human needs and capabilities associated with sexual intimacy by simply giving individuals the necessary freedom to connect with potential sexual partners. One can imagine that a perfectly libertarian state, where any consensual sexual relationship is tolerated but where no relationship is recognized or privileged over any other, would satisfy that minimum moral threshold. When we speak of human needs and capabilities associated with sexual intimacy, however, we mean more than just the satisfaction of sexual urges. Since the need to be cared for by others and the capability to care for others often accompany sexual intimacy, there is more at stake for individuals than simply having opportunities for sexual satisfaction.

There are, of course, many different kinds of caring relationships that contain within them a sexual component. These include, but are not limited to, relationships where the primary focus is the physical intimacy and where the caring for the other as an emotional matter is of secondary importance; relationships where the opposite is the case, namely, where the primary focus is the caring for or friendship with the other, with physical intimacy being of secondary importance; and relationships where the emotional and physical intimacy are not easily separable and where the giving and receiving of sexual pleasure go hand in hand with emotional mutuality and commitment. It is this latter category of relationships that is of particular interest to us here because it is their participants, experience tells us, who are most likely to seek societal recognition of and support for their relationships.

The ability to connect physical intimacy with emotional intimacy (whether in its limited or expansive forms) is one of the distinctive characteristics that make us human. Only humans are able to construct their lives around the unique and powerful emotional intimacy that can accompany physical intimacy. The ability to combine both kinds of intimacies allows human beings to explore their full potential to love and care for another human being.

Human relationships do not exist in a social or cultural vacuum. As Joseph Raz notes, "[m]arriage, friendships, parenthood," among other relationships, "are all molded and patterned by the common culture which determines to a very considerable degree the bounds of possible options available to individuals."[7] It is society, through its norms, policies, and practices, that provides the support and conditions that can turn what might otherwise be fleeting sexual encounters or short-term relationships into meaningful, rewarding, and long-lasting relationships. The principal way through which our society seeks to provide the necessary support and conditions that make the formation and maintenance of sexually intimate long-term relationships more likely is through the institution of companionate marriage. It is primarily through that institution that our society encourages us to construct our lives around the love for and commitment to another human being in order to meet the needs and provide for the well-being (emotional, physical, and material) of ourselves and of that other. Through the institution of marriage, in other words, society encourages us to be less egoistic, to live for another person at the same time that we live for ourselves.[8]

One of the truly magical characteristics of love is that it allows for an expansion of the self. When a person loves another, she begins to see that other as an extension of herself. The object of love does not prioritize the welfare of the subject over her own as much as she sees it as an extension of her welfare.[9] While this kind of deep affection and commitment can, of course, exist outside of a socially recognized relationship such as the marital one, commitment "may be more comfortably sustained and reciprocating love more easily offered where personal feelings are reinforced and expectations are coordinated by social institutions."[10] Public recognition of relationships also makes it clear that there is an identifiable individual (a "spouse" or a "parent," for example) whose responsibility it is to care for the well-being of another. That public recognition, when it is accompanied by social support and encouragement, makes it more likely that the relevant responsibilities will be met. The structure that marriage provides and the obligations that it requires, then, can strengthen and make more durable the affectional components of sexual intimacy that are characterized by on-going commitment and mutuality. The socially recognized marital relationship can provide the structure through which the well-being of another becomes inextricably linked to the well-being of the self as "the boundary between self and other becomes blurred."[11] By creating and promoting an institution such as companionate marriage, our society encourages (though, of course, by no means guarantees) the kind of self-expansion that most frequently takes place in committed sexually intimate relationships. This is the potentially enduring value of a relationship such as the marital one: it potentially allows for self-definition and self-expansion through love and commitment for another human being in a relationship whose very purpose is to provide for the satisfaction and exercise of physical and emotional needs and capabilities in the context of long-term reciprocity and mutuality.

The Vermont Supreme Court in *Baker v. State* was thinking along these lines when it ruled on the constitutionality, under the state constitution's Common Benefits Clause, of the state's ban against same-sex marriage.[12] Marriage, the court argued, "is a singularly human relationship," and "the essential aspect of the [plaintiffs'] claim is simply and fundamentally for inclusion in the family of state-sanctioned human relations."[13] The court cited the U.S. Supreme Court's opinion in *Dred Scott v. Sandford* (the nineteenth-century case that held that African Americans were not citizens eligible for constitutional protections) to argue that "[t]he past provides many instances where the law refused to see a human being when it should have."[14] A refusal to recognize committed same-gender relationships through which many lesbians and gay men meet their human needs and exercise their human capabilities associated with physical and emotional intimacy is similarly a failure to recognize their full humanity. It tells lesbians and gay men that their needs and capabilities associated with physical and emotional intimacy are less worthy and less valuable simply because they involve someone else of the same gender. The court could not countenance such a view of lesbians and gay men because the principle of equality as enshrined in the Vermont Constitution required it to view them as full human beings. As the court noted, "[t]he extension of the Common Benefits Clause to acknowledge plaintiffs as Vermonters who seek nothing more, nor less, than legal protection and security for their avowed commitment to an intimate and lasting human relationship is simply, when all is said and done, a recognition of our *common humanity*."[15]

The state of Vermont, in defending its ban against same-sex marriage, relied primarily on the "government's interest in furthering the link between procreation and child rearing."[16] With the large number of lesbians and gay men who are becoming parents, however, this argument is becoming increasingly nonsensical. As the court pointed out, "[i]f anything, the exclusion of same-sex couples from the legal protections incident to marriage exposes *their* children to the precise risks that the state argues the marriage laws are designed to secure against."[17] If the goal is to provide stability, continuity, and support for children, then the state has an interest in promoting stability, continuity, and support for the relationship of the parents (whether legal or de facto), even if they are of the same gender.

The egalitarian principles enshrined in Vermont's Common Benefits Clause, which led the Vermont court to require equal treatment for gay and lesbian couples, can be found in every state constitution as well as in the Equal Protection Clause of the federal Constitution. There is arguably no more important bulwark against oppression in our constitutional system than the idea that groups of individuals should not be excluded from the rights, benefits, and protections afforded by the law based on claims that they lack the necessary attributes of human beings. When lesbians and gay men are told that they (as a group) lack the capability to create meaningful, enduring, and valuable relationships or that they (as a group) lack the attributes required to be good and caring parents of their children, they are in effect being told that they lack crucial constitutive characteristics of what it means to be human. Although individuals are free to hold such views of lesbians and gay men, our constitutional values prohibit the state from basing exclusionary public policies on them.

An attempt to exclude lesbians and gay men from the rest of the community was precisely what was at issue in *Romer v. Evans*.[18] In that case, the gay and lesbian plaintiffs successfully challenged a Colorado constitutional amendment that prohibited the enactment of discrimination protection under state and local laws on the basis of sexual orientation. Colorado argued that the constitutional amendment was simply the denial of "special rights" for lesbians and gay men.[19] The U.S. Supreme Court rejected that argument, noting that the amendment was not about special rights but about "special disabilit[ies] [imposed] upon [lesbians and gay men] alone."[20] The majority noted that a century before, Justice John Marshall Harlan, in his dissent in *Plessy v. Ferguson*, "admonished this Court that the Constitution 'neither knows nor tolerates classes among citizens.' "[21] The legal protections that the Colorado constitutional amendment prohibited, the *Romer* Court added, "are protections taken for granted by most people either because they already have them or do not need them; these are protections against exclusion from an almost limitless number of endeavors that constitute ordinary civic life in a free society."[22] The Colorado constitutional amendment was inconsistent with the idea that we all share basic commonalities as persons and that the community cannot exclude a particular group of persons from the basic protections of the law. The amendment, the Court concluded, was "a classification of persons undertaken for its own sake, something the Equal Protection Clause does not permit."[23]

In their defense that they are not violating egalitarian values that are deeply embedded in our laws and traditions, conservative opponents of gay rights argue that there truly is something different about same-gender sexual intimacy that justifies the exclusion of lesbians and gay men from institutions such as marriage and parenting. They argue, as John Finnis and Robert George have done, that same-gender sexual intimacy is by definition non-reproductive in nature and that it therefore entails an improper use of human bodies in the instrumental pursuit of sexual pleasure,[24] or, as Roger Scruton has done, that it is inherently narcissistic,[25] or, as Lynn Wardle has done, that it is potentially harmful to children.[26] In reality, the conservative argument holds, gay and lesbian sexual intimacy is inherently hedonistic, dangerously narcissistic, and potentially harmful, and it is these characteristics that justify the unequal treatment by society of same-gender intimate relationships. This line of reasoning is typical of arguments that have sought to place historically marginalized individuals (be they African Americans, women, or lesbians and gay men) outside of privileged social institutions and their corresponding rights and benefits. "Because they are not part of our community of equals," the reasoning holds, "they can be treated differently in spite of apparent similarities, and because they can be so treated, it must then be the case that appearances to the contrary notwithstanding, they actually do not share in precisely those universal shared traits that make us human and that mandate *our*, as opposed to their, equal treatment."[27] As many conservatives see it, then, when lesbians and gay men say that they love and are committed to their same-gender partners, or, for that matter, that they are capable of providing their children with a care that is both loving and healthy, it may appear as if they are doing nothing more than expressing their humanity, but what they are really doing is dressing up their abnormal and harmful behavior in the trappings of marital and parental responsibility. It is in this way that lesbians and gay men are denied the opportunity to share in those institutions (such as marriage and parenthood) that are meant, in part, to provide and account for the needs and capabilities of individuals to share their physical and emotional intimate lives with others.

It is, of course, possible for some individuals to meet their human needs and exercise their human capabilities associated with physical and emotional intimacy in such a morally objectionable way that the community would be entitled to treat them differently without violating our egalitarian values as codified in our federal and state constitutions. An obvious example is someone who uses force or coercion as a way to satisfy his needs for sexual intimacy and who can therefore be deprived of his liberty as a result. But even this obvious example is quite telling because the Supreme Court held in *Turner v. Safley* that convicted criminals have a constitutional right to marry, even while they are incarcerated.[28] It should strike reasonable people as unjust that our society allows murderers, rapists, and child molesters the right to marry *even while they are being punished for their crimes* but withholds that right from lesbians and gay men. As a result of *Turner*, we acknowledge (as we should) that even after someone commits a horrible crime of violence against another, there still remains a recognizable human being with certain needs and capabilities that would make it unjust for society to withhold from that person the right to marry. Not so with lesbians and gay men, however. Their kind of physical intimacy is apparently so perverse, so abnormal, so inconsistent with acceptable human standards of sexual intimacy that they can be denied access to the social institution of marriage and to the myriad of rights and benefits that accompany it. I do not believe that such an exclusionary policy is consistent with our egalitarian constitutional values grounded on the respect that we owe each other as human beings.

It should be noted that it is precisely because we are dealing with basic human needs and capabilities that the issue of same-sex marriage is a proper one for the courts. A familiar refrain heard among opponents of same-sex marriage is that it is the people through their legislatures who should decide whether lesbians and gay men are entitled to marry. As the Supreme Court has recognized when dealing with heterosexual plaintiffs who are challenging marriage restrictions imposed by legislatures, however, marriage raises questions about our fundamental rights to autonomy and equality, questions that should not be left to majoritarian will alone.[29] It is entirely consistent with our constitutional tradition for courts to involve themselves in disputed issues when there are allegations made that particular social policies improperly exclude and marginalize entire segments of the society.

Now that the Vermont legislature has sought to address the violation of the state constitution's Common Benefits Clause through the creation of civil unions, the interesting question arises whether these unions are sufficient to remedy the fundamental unfairness of denying state recognition of committed gay and lesbian relationships. The debate over the recognition of these relationships has so far implicated the meaning of marriage because, as mentioned earlier, that is the principal institution through which our society encourages us to construct our lives around love and commitment for another human being in order to meet the needs and provide for the well-being of ourselves and of that other. The struggle has so far been over marriage because that is the way that our society, through its laws and norms, has encouraged and fostered commitment and mutuality in sexually intimate relationships. But it does not have to be the *only* way. There must be social institutions and policies that provide for the meeting of basic needs and the exercise of basic capabilities associated with physical and emotional intimacy, but those institutions and policies can take different forms.

I think that it is still too early to answer the question of whether civil unions are an acceptable alternative to marriage because we do not yet know what the meaning and impact of civil unions will be in our society. On the one hand, there are some who argue that civil unions are inadequate because there remains a two-tiered system whereby society continues to exclude lesbians and gay men from the most privileged form of socially recognized intimate relationships, namely, the marital one.[30] On the other hand, there are some who argue that civil unions are an appealing way for lesbians and gay men to enjoy the same legal benefits that heterosexual married couples enjoy while retaining the egalitarianism and distinctiveness of gay relationships.[31] In my opinion, if civil unions end up providing the structure, security, and permanence for committed same-gender intimate relationships without stigmatizing or demeaning those relationships, then civil unions will be an acceptable alternative. Time will tell.

Whether we are discussing same-sex marriage or civil unions (or, for that matter, parenting by lesbians and gay men), my sense is that opponents of gay rights know that theirs is, in the long run, a losing effort. Conservatives sometimes blame this on what they see as the general decay in societal moral standards or, as Justice Antonin Scalia insinuated in his bitter dissent in *Romer v. Evans*, on the political influence of a supposedly well-heeled minority.[32] But it seems to me that there is something much more fundamental and important going on, namely, a gradual recognition by growing sectors of society that the love and commitment for their partners and families that lesbians and gay men feel, express, and realize are not any different from the love and commitment that heterosexuals feel, express, and realize for their partners and families. A growing understanding that lesbians and gay men share in essential commonalities associated with physical and emotional intimacy enjoyed by all human beings accounts, I believe, for a significant part of the progress that the gay rights movement has made in only one generation and for the progress that is still to come. Perhaps conservative opponents of gay rights can find some solace in the fact that when our society concludes for good that human needs and capabilities associated with physical and emotional intimacy are more important criteria in determining the meaning of the institution of marriage than the gender of the spouses, we will be able to focus on those issues that merited our attention all along (and that conservatives avowedly seek to promote), namely, love, respect, commitment, and loyalty in human relationships and what society can and should do to foment these values.

## NOTES

1. Martha C. Nussbaum, *Human Functioning and Social Justice: In Defense of Aristotelian Essentialism*, 20 POL. TH. 202, 217–218 (1992). My thinking on human needs and capabilities has been greatly influenced by Nussbaum's numerous writings on moral and political philosophy. Some of these writings are helpfully summarized in MARTHA C. NUSSBAUM, WOMEN AND HUMAN DEVELOPMENT: THE CAPABILI-

TIES APPROACH 34–101 (2000). I discuss some of the issues raised in this essay at greater length in chapter 3 of my book THE MORALITY OF GAY RIGHTS: AN EXPLORATION IN POLITICAL PHILOSOPHY (2003).

2. See AMARTYA SEN, RESOURCES, VALUES, AND DEVELOPMENT 514 (1984).

3. NUSSBAUM, WOMEN AND HUMAN DEVELOPMENT, *supra* note 1, at 78–80.

4. This is the position taken by the Catholic Church when it seeks to distinguish between lesbians and gay men, who as persons are worthy of respect and compassion, and same-gender sexual acts, which are deemed to be "intrinsically disordered and in no case to be approved of." *See* "Some Considerations Concerning the Response to Legislative Proposals on the Non-Discrimination of Homosexual Persons" (July 23, 1992). The complete text of this Vatican statement can be found in VOICES OF HOPE: A COLLECTION OF POSITIVE CATHOLIC WRITINGS ON GAY AND LESBIAN ISSUES 229 (Jeannine Gramick and Robert Nugent eds. 1995).

5. Robin West, *Is The Rule of Law Cosmopolitan?*, 19 QUINNIPIAC L. REV. 259, 276 (2000) (emphasis in original).

6. RAIMOND GAITA, A COMMON HUMANITY: THINKING ABOUT LOVE AND TRUTH AND JUSTICE xvi (2000).

7. Joseph Raz, *Liberalism, Skepticism, and Democracy*, 74 IOWA L. REV. 761, 783 (1989).

8. The understanding of marriage that I present here is an admittedly normative and idealized one. The descriptive reality of marriage for many women differs from this understanding, given that gender roles within marriage have undermined rather than promoted the needs and capabilities of countless women. As I argue in my book *The Morality of Gay Rights*, a normative and to some extent aspirational understanding of marriage is not inconsistent with a forceful critique of the patriarchal practices that have been traditionally and improperly promoted and defended through the institution of marriage. *See* Ball, The Morality of Gay Rights, *supra* note 1 at 112–15, 126–29.

9. *See generally* Arthur Aron & Elaine N. Aron, LOVE AND THE EXPANSION OF SELF: UNDERSTANDING ATTRACTION AND SATISFACTION (1986).

10. Carl E. Schneider, *The Law and the Stability of Marriage: The Family as a Social Institution*, in PROMISES TO KEEP: DECLINE AND RENEWAL OF MARRIAGE IN AMERICA 187, 190 (David Popenoe et al. eds., 1996).

11. MILTON C. REGAN, JR., ALONE TOGETHER: LAW AND THE MEANINGS OF MARRIAGE 12 (1999).

12. 744 A.2d 864 (Vt. 1999).

13. *Id.* at 889.

14. *Id.* at 889, citing Dred Scott v. Sandford, 60 U.S. (10 How.) 393 (1856).

15. *Baker*, 744 A.2d at 889 (emphasis added).

16. *Id.* at 881.

17. *Id.* at 882.

18. 517 U.S. 620 (1996).

19. *Id.* at 626.

20. *Id.* at 631.

21. *Id.* at 623, quoting Plessy v. Ferguson, 163 U.S. 537, 559 (1896) (Harlan, J., dissenting).

22. *Romer*, 517 U.S. at 631.

23. *Id.* at 635.

24. *See* John M. Finnis, *Law, Morality, and "Sexual Orientation,"* 69 NOTRE DAME L. REV. 1049, 1067–1070 (1994); Patrick Lee & Robert P. George, *What Sex Can Be: Self-Alienation, Illusion, or One-Flesh Union,* 42 AM. J. JURIS. 135, 146–56 (1997).

25. *See* ROGER SCRUTON, SEXUAL DESIRE: A MORAL PHILOSOPHY OF THE EROTIC 310 (1986).

26. *See* Lynn D. Wardle, *The Potential Impact of Homosexual Parenting on Children,* 1997 U. ILL. L. REV. 833. Janice Pea and I respond to Professor Wardle's arguments in Carlos A. Ball and Janice Farrell Pea, *Warring with Wardle: Morality, Social Science, and Gay and Lesbian Parents,* 1998 U. ILL. L. REV. 253.

27. West, *supra* note 5, at 275 (emphasis in original).

28. 482 U.S. 78, 94–96 (1987).

29. *See* Zablocki v. Redhail, 434 U.S. 374 (1978); Loving v. Virginia, 388 U.S. 1 (1967).

30. *See* Andrew Sullivan, *State of the Union,* NEW REPUBLIC, May 8, 2000, at 18, 22.

31. *See* Greg Johnson, *Vermont Civil Unions: The New Language of Marriage,* 25 VT. L. REV. 15, 19 (2000).

32. *See Romer,* 517 U.S. at 645–646 (Scalia, J., dissenting).

Response

# The Illusory Public Benefits of Same-Sex Encounters: A Response to Professor Carlos A. Ball

## Teresa Stanton Collett

It is an axiom of the American legal system that similarly situated individuals should be treated similarly. Conversely, and equally axiomatic, is the principle that differently situated individuals may and often should be treated differently. The current debate over the state's recognition of same-sex unions will be resolved by implementing one of these principles. Thus the fundamental task of advocates on both sides of the debate is persuading the public that same-sex unions are either similar to or different from heterosexual unions.

In making his case that same-sex unions are fundamentally similar to heterosexual unions, Professor Ball relies upon the universal need for physical intimacy and sexual satisfaction, as well as the common capacity to satisfy these needs in others. He argues for state recognition of same-sex unions as marriage because they provide the structural support for the turning of "what might otherwise be fleeting sexual encounters or short-term relationships into meaningful, rewarding, and long-lasting relationships." This argument, however, ignores a fundamental difference in the nature of heterosexual and homosexual unions.

The legitimacy of my response can be illustrated by the following thought experiment. Suppose a state passed a law restricting sexual encounters between members of the same sex to partners who had entered into civil unions or some marriagelike equivalent. Assume further that the laws governing adultery and fornication were simultaneously amended to make clear that intentional contact with the genitalia of another, not his or her spouse or civil-union partner, for the purpose of sexual gratification was criminal conduct. Certainly one could expect a swift and vigorous challenge to such a law.

On what basis could the state defend its decision to restrict the sexual encounters of homosexual individuals to those who had entered into civil unions? Protection of the public health through a legal requirement of monogamy certainly constitutes a substantial, if not a compelling, state interest in light of the dramatic increase in certain sexually transmitted diseases, particularly the increase of HIV infection among men who have sex with men.[1] Yet legally enforced monogamy, while among the most certain methods of containing the spread of sexually transmitted diseases, might be questioned on the basis of whether such a statute is narrowly tailored to achieve the state's interest.[2]

In the case of legally enforced monogamy for heterosexual couples, the law can be further justified by the state's interest in reducing or eliminating extramarital or nonmarital pregnancies, as well as easing the identification of fathers once conception has occurred. Both these tasks are important to ensuring that both partners to the sexual encounter care for children resulting from their acts.[3] Yet it would be nonsensical for the state to assert these interests as a basis for restricting homosexual encounters, since conception of a child is impossible.

Professor Ball seeks to avoid this biological distinction by converting the state's interest from encouraging the conception of children only in enduring monogamous relationships to promoting stability in the relationships of those who care for children. While this second interest may be a worthy societal goal in many cases, it is unrelated to any sexual component of the relationship between care providers.

It is beyond dispute that children benefit from stable relationships with responsible caregivers. Historically, this stability has been found in the biological ties of parent and child and to a lesser extent in the other ties of blood or kinship. In contemporary society, an increasing number of caregivers are biologically unrelated to the child—stepparents, childcare providers, teachers, and others. A child's relationship with any of these people is formative and often benefits from stability, but the state does not impose continuing obligations of care or support on these individuals as a general rule.[4] Nor is such an obligation desirable. Absent radical restructuring of the law pertaining to support of biologically unrelated children, recognition of same-sex unions creates no legal benefit to children.

Professor Ball might well respond that the indirect benefit to a child of a continuous relationship with an adult who has shared a household with a biological parent is sufficiently desirable to support recognition of same-sex unions. Yet such a rule has no logical linkage to the sexual relationship of same-sex partners. Any benefits to children would attach equally to their relationship with any long-term resident of the household, be the resident a roommate, boarder, or domestic employee. The fact that the resident is the biological parent's lover is unrelated to the child's relationship with that person and forms little basis for the recognition of same-sex unions.

The second benefit relied upon by Professor Ball in his justification of same-sex marriage is the benefit to the sexual partners from stabilizing the relationship. While he fails to identify any public benefit from stabilization, I agree that long-term relationships of mutual commitment and support may benefit both the individuals involved and the broader community. Often we all profit when people are willing to undertake personal sacrifices to ensure the well-being of another. Such willingness, however, while sometimes accompanying sexual relationships, is often unrelated to and in fact devoid of any sexual relationship—as evidenced by the sacrifices family and friends make for each other on a daily basis.

Love, companionship, and mutual commitment can and do flourish in the many forms of human relationships existing independent of state involvement. The societal value of sexual relations between members of the same sex is not established by the commitment and self-sacrifice that marks the relationships of some who engage in this conduct. So, notwithstanding Professor Ball's accurate description of our common humanity, the fundamental question remains: What is the distinctive societal benefit of state recognition and stabilization of the sexual encounters of same-sex couples? No satisfactory answer has been presented at this point in our public dialogue. It remains to be seen whether one will emerge.

## NOTES

1. Centers for Disease Control and Prevention, *Tracking the Hidden Epidemics: Trends in STDs in the United States 2000*, at 4 (2000), available at www.cdc.gov/nchstp/dstd/Stats_Trends/Trends2000.pdf. "Researchers estimate that men who have sex with men (MSM) still account for 42 percent of new HIV infections annually in the United States and for 60 percent of all new HIV infections among men. Several recent studies have pointed to high, and increasing, levels of other STDs among MSM." *Id.*

2. E.g., Doe v. Duling, 603 F. Supp. 960, 967–968 (E.D. Va. 1985) (striking down a Virginia fornication and cohabitation statute as violating the plaintiffs' right to privacy), *rev'd on other grounds* 782 F.2d 1202 (4th Cir. 1986).

3. Since 1950, both men and women's poverty rates have declined. Yet during the same period, families headed by single women grew to comprise a substantial majority of those living in poverty. Many researchers attribute this to changing family structure—women choosing to have children outside of marriage or raising children alone due to divorce or abandonment. Sara S. McLanahan & Erin L. Kelley, "The Feminization of Poverty: Past and Future," *Handbook of the Sociology of Gender*, ed. Chafetz (New York: Plenum Publishing), 127–145. This theory is supported by the wide discrepancy between the 4.8 percent of poor families headed by married couples and the 27.8 percent headed by a woman. U.S. Census Bureau, *Table 17. Poverty Status of Families in 1999 by Family Type: March 2000*, available at www.census.gov/population/socdemo/gender/ppl-121/tab17.txt (visited Nov. 12, 2001).

4. For an examination of the general rule that stepparents have no duty to support children, see Laura W. Morgan, *Positive Parenting and Negative Contributions: Why Payment of Child Support Should Not Be Regarded as Dissipation of Marital Assets*, 30 N.M.L. REV. 1 (2000).

Essay Two

# Should Marriage Be Privileged? The State's Interest in Childbearing Unions

## Teresa Stanton Collett

The debate regarding same-sex unions took a new turn in 2000 with the passage of Vermont legislation granting legal status to such unions. Responding to a state supreme court order to "create a parallel licensing or registration scheme, and extend all or most of the same rights and obligations provided by the law to married partners,"[1] the legislature established a new legal relationship that it called "civil union." This relationship by statute is identical to marriage in terms of "benefits, protections and responsibilities under law."[2] By affording all legal benefits, protections, and responsibilities afforded marriage, the legislature announced the public equivalency of marriage and civil unions in Vermont.

According to the legislation, creation of the status of "civil union" is rooted in the state's "strong interest in promoting stable and lasting families, including families based upon a same-sex couple."[3] By grounding the legal status of same-sex unions in their capacity to be the bases of "families," the legislation implicitly redefines the familial relationship as one of affection rather than biology or bloodline. This is a striking departure from the traditional definition of family, which "most commonly refers to a group of persons consisting of parents and children; father, mother and their children; immediate kindred, constituting [the] fundamental unit in civilized society."[4] Rejecting biological linkage or kinship as the necessary foundation for family, the Vermont legislation appears to adopt a functional definition of marriage and, by extension, of family. "These [gay and lesbian] couples live together, participate in their communities together, and some raise children and care for family members together, just as do couples who are married under Vermont law."[5]

The legal and civil consequences of this redefinition remain to be seen, yet even at this early point several questions can be posed. The first and most obvious question, perhaps, is why it is important that the state recognize these unions and, furthermore, recognize them as comparable to unions that the state recognizes as marriages. The Vermont Supreme Court's answer was that the status of marriage afforded opposite-sex couples substantial benefits that should be shared by same-sex couples who wish to have their relationship recognized by the government. This answer, of course, assumes that whatever public interest justifies the state's recognition of marriage as the basis for a unique legal status is also found in the relationships of same-sex couples. To assess this conclusion, it is necessary to identify the state's interest in recognizing marriage of heterosexuals as a legal status and to compare that interest with the interests that may support recognition of same-sex unions. That is the task of this essay.

## THE NEED FOR STATE RECOGNITION OF MARRIAGE

While every contemporary legal system recognizes some marriage-based status, it is possible to conceive of a legal regime in which marriage is of no more concern to the state than is any other form of friendship. Assuming that the state took no official notice of friendship, it could similarly take no official notice of marriage. It seems likely that such a regime would deal with citizens exclusively as individuals or through other legally recognized forms of association such as partnerships or corporations. The relationship of the state to the individual might be similar to that experienced today, with the primary exception being the manner in which the state deals with individuals who lack the ability to receive and process information in order to make informed decisions. This inability is commonly found during childhood and during periods of illness or disability. The state and others dealing with incapacitated individuals need someone to make decisions on behalf of those individuals. Traditionally, parents and spouses have assumed this responsibility.

## ALLOCATING RESPONSIBILITY FOR THE CREATION AND CARE OF CHILDREN

For women, a presumption of decision-making authority regarding a child could still follow biological lines since the vast majority of children are conceived through an act of penile-vaginal intercourse.[6] Even in the few cases involving the use of assisted reproductive technology, the woman giving birth has provided the egg used in the conception of that child.[7] The decision-making authority of the biological father would be more attenuated simply because, absent scientific confirmation of paternity, there are no self-evident indicia of a male sexual partner's biological relationship to any particular offspring. Absent recognition of marriage or some other form of exclusive sexual partnering, any legal presumption of paternity would be unjust.

Legal responsibility for support and care of children could follow the same pattern, vesting full responsibility in the mother or requiring both biological parents to assume responsibility. However, absent a shared household, the contribution of the nonresident parent would most likely be limited to financial support. While having at least some minimal level of financial resources is widely perceived as a necessary condition for the successful raising of children, it is not a sufficient condition. Time, energy, and commitment always accompany good parenting, regardless of the material wealth of the child's household. The American experience with single parenting due to divorce and out-of-wedlock births suggests that these precious commodities are often limited in homes with only one parent present, regardless of the socioeconomic level of that parent. In a society without marriage, it would be desirable to create some legal mechanism to ensure that sexual partners who participate in the creation of a child not only assume financial responsibility for costs related to the child, but also provide a minimal level of personal interaction with the child to ensure that the child receives the emotional and psychological benefits comparable to those afforded by the traditional two-parent household of intact traditional marriages.

As an alternative to marriage as the primary setting for child rearing, utopians since the time of Plato have suggested that the community at large could raise children via the state.[8] State nurseries or childcare centers staffed by experts could care for children from birth to adulthood, ensuring their physical well-being while inculcating the values of civic virtue. Yet the lessons of the past century with Eastern European and other regimes embracing such practices suggest that the state is a poor surrogate parent and that comprehensive state education from cradle to grave is not the way to achieve a free and prosperous society.

Alternatively, the state could adopt a system of presumptive parenting that recognizes the parental rights of the biological parents when and if the parents elect to exercise those rights at birth. In cases of parental neglect or repudiation of their rights, the state would stand ready to serve as a default parent. Such a position is foreshadowed by the case law regarding the paternal rights of men who fail to interact with their infant children and by the recent passage of state statutes allowing parents to relinquish custody of infants to the state with "no questions asked" for a set period of time after birth.[9] While the cases reflect judicial attempts to ensure the well-being of children in the face of absentee fathers, and the statutes were enacted as a response to reported cases of injuries to abandoned infants, these laws set the stage for the assumption of broader duties by the state in parenting those children who are conceived by parents who reject any parental obligation beyond birth. To date, American states have viewed their primary role in the lives of children as transitory, with the goal of placing abandoned or orphaned children not in some state institution, but in the private homes of responsible and loving parents through adoption. This view, however, is not preordained and could be revised if citizens were persuaded to embrace a new position on this issue.

Assuming that we maintain our current presumption against state nurturing of children and in favor of enforcing legal responsibilities attendant to the creation of a child, in the absence of recognizing marriage as a legal status, the state would need some legal mechanism to ensure that sexual partners who participate in the creation of a child remained responsible to ensure the proper upbringing of that child. Registration of all births with identification of the woman giving birth, accompanied by compulsory paternity registration, could serve this function to some degree. This is the regime we have been pursuing in recent years for children born to unwed mothers who seek public assistance.[10] Yet, as our experience with such programs has shown, while such a system may be superior to placing all responsibility for the child with the mother, compulsory paternity registration comes at a cost. Postconception registration is often resisted by both sexes as an unwanted and unfair imposition on their freedom. Men who are unable or unwilling to provide the level of support required by state laws, yet willing to provide informal support to the mother and child, suddenly disappear. Women, who looked to the fathers of their children for nothing more than fleeting companionship or temporary relief from the responsibilities of full-time care of their infants, find that they are abandoned. While it takes a man and a woman to create a child, motherhood is more readily apparent than fatherhood, and the responsibilities of fatherhood are more easily evaded. Public recognition of marriage as a public announcement of a sexually exclusive union, with its attendant expectations that both partners will share all responsibilities related to the creation and nurturing of children, has traditionally eliminated or limited this disparity.

## MARRIAGE AS MUTUAL COMMITMENT

Even if it is accepted that the procreative potential inherent in almost every act of sexual intercourse justifies the state's recognition of marriage as a unique legal status, supporters of same-sex unions argue that this is an outdated and overly restrictive view of marriage. They claim that contemporary marriage laws recognize marriage as a legal status ordered toward companionship and mutual support rather than procreation. As evidence of this, they point to the absence of any marriage-entry requirement of procreative ability or intention. In their view, state recognition of marriages between elderly or infertile couples unable to conceive or younger couples intentionally thwarting conception through the use of various forms of contraception evidences the state's indifference to procreation as an essential purpose or activity within legally recognized marriages.

In contrast to an earlier legal regime that viewed marriage as oriented toward the creation and nurturing of children, contemporary laws view marriage as primarily a vehicle for self-fulfillment through extended mutual self-giving and support. In this view, it is the couple's willingness to publicly assume mutual obligations of support that is the primary interest advanced by state recognition of marriage. These obligations are independent of any particular sexual act and are as unique as the couples making their marriage vows. For some, the obligations include the support and care of children conceived through sexual union of the marriage partners. For others, the obligations extend to the support and care of children conceived in other unions or care for other relatives who look to one of the marital partners for support. Some find their obligations of financial support relatively light, but emotional support requires great sacrifice. Others find themselves providing extensive support for a partner facing a debilitating or terminal illness. Advocates of this "commitment model" of marriage argue that human fulfillment is most often found in intimate communities of love and commitment, and the law of marriage and family should encourage and sustain such communities, regardless of whether or not they have procreative potential.

## OBJECTIONS TO RECOGNITION OF SAME-SEX UNIONS AS EQUIVALENT TO MARRIAGE

It is possible to accept many of these arguments and still remain persuaded that state recognition of marriage should be limited to unions of one man and one woman, or that marriage should be privileged above all other unions. Underlying the commitment model of marriage is what philosophers call a perfectionist model of the state. Perfectionism is based upon an understanding that "politics and good law aspire not only to help make people safe, comfortable, and prosperous, but also to help make them virtuous."[11] Thus law is not limited to merely restraining harmful conduct. It also properly promotes good conduct. Fulfillment of one's commitment to one's partner is seen as "good conduct," and participation in intimate communities of love and commitment is seen as a means to making people safe, comfortable, and prosperous.

Several objections can be raised to the commitment model of marriage. A classical liberal following the tradition of John Stuart Mill might reject the initial perfectionist premise, arguing that the proper role of law is merely the restraint of harm. Under this view, it can be argued that legal recognition of marriage may be necessary to avoid the harm of men unjustly avoiding responsibility to assist the women they impregnate and support the children they father, but there is no comparable justification for recognition of same-sex unions.

Even assuming that the state properly promotes good conduct, many citizens object to legal recognition of same-sex unions as contrary to virtue.
To the extent that the legal creation of civil unions necessarily encompasses
recognition of a sexual component to same-sex relationships, these unions
are rejected as contrary to nature and thus contrary to human good.[12] The
morality of sexual acts between same-sex partners is deeply contested in
American society. To many, acts of anal intercourse, fellatio, or cunnilingus
are unnatural and degrading. Opponents argue that these acts treat the human body as a mere instrument for selfish pleasure and fail to express any
meaningful union of persons. To affirm relationships involving such acts
would not promote good conduct, but instead would falsely suggest an
equality of these acts with penile-vaginal intercourse, the distinctive activity
of heterosexual marriage.

Limiting legal recognition to heterosexual marriage recognizes that marriage is more than an intimate community of love and commitment. It is a
unique sexual community that leads to human flourishing through the union
of sexual difference and the potential creation of new life. One distinctive
aspect of marriage is the requirement that couples engage in penile-vaginal
intercourse. Incapacity or refusal to engage in vaginal intercourse historically
has been grounds for annulment of a marriage in all fifty states.[13] No other
legal status is dependent upon a sexual act, and no other sexual act is a legal
condition to any other form of agreement or contract. The unique connection of marital status to vaginal intercourse exists because this act is the
primary means by which married couples form families, expand kinship
groups, and extend bloodlines to the next generations. There is no comparable distinctive activity for same-sex couples.

Any objection to state recognition of same-sex sexual activity can be
avoided by crafting a definition of civil unions devoid of any expectation of
sexual contact, but such a definition would likely fail to garner much support. The need for or desirability of creating a new legal status for any two
people who live together and participate in their communities together is
questionable, yet these are the only two activities the Vermont legislature
identified as universally engaged in by same-sex couples and married couples.[14] Embracing these as the defining activities of a legal status equivalent
to marriage would render a definition that is simultaneously underinclusive
and overinclusive. Some married couples do not live together, as evidenced
by the growth of "commuter marriages" where a married couple maintain
two households, often due to diverse work locations. Others, such as roommates, cohabiting couples, and members of religious communities, live together and often participate in the community together, yet would rightly
resist any attempt to characterize their arrangements as civil unions or the
functional equivalent of marriage.

Even if the definitional problems related to same-sex unions can be overcome, equating these relationships with marriage poses another set of prob-

lems. While societal expectations regarding the responsibilities of husbands and wives have changed during the last century, there is still relatively broad consensus about sexual fidelity, sharing resources, providing mutual support, and aspiring to lifelong duration.[15] There are no similarly shared expectations regarding same-sex couples. Sexual contact with someone other than the legally recognized partner in a civil union is unlikely to result in unwitting parental responsibility for an unrelated child. It is obvious that a lesbian involved in a civil union was not impregnated by her partner, and the gay man who fathers a child can do so only through a sexual encounter with someone other than his civil-union partner. Living together and joint participation in a community offer little guidance for judges ruling on enforceability of agreements by those involved in civil unions to limit sharing of assets or obligations of mutual support. Legislators considering changes in laws governing the dissolution of marriage properly presume that these changes will impact a substantial number of households including minor children. Such an assumption regarding dissolution of civil unions is less likely to be valid. The impact of childbearing on the income-producing capacity of women should be factored into any system of allocating marital property, yet the sterile nature of same-sex unions makes childbearing within these unions a nonissue for these couples. In the absence of children, neither partner is likely to have become economically dependent by assuming primary responsibility for managing the household and attending to the needs of children. In short, if same-sex unions are to be legally recognized, that recognition should reflect the dominant experience and characteristics of these couples rather than the common experience of heterosexual couples.

The Vermont legislature asserted an interest in the stability and duration of same-sex unions, yet it is hard to understand why the state should concern itself with encouraging continuation of a civil union in the face of a request for dissolution. Statistically the couple is unlikely to have children, so there will be few third parties whose lives will be disrupted or dramatically altered by dissolution. In the absence of children, there will be no continuing ties of blood and kinship that cannot be severed by the courts. Encouraging continued participation in same-sex unions will be abhorrent to those who believe such relationships to be abnormal or immoral. Even those who believe that participation in same-sex unions may be natural to those whose sexual orientation directs them toward members of the same sex may be reluctant to endorse continued efforts to sustain a civil union when one partner wants out to pursue a relationship with a member of the opposite sex. The public dimension of any difficulties in disentangling the economic lives of a couple and the communal loss suffered by the dissolution of an extended relationship of care and concern seem no greater, and no less, than those arising from the end of a economic partnership or long-term friendship, matters largely relegated to private agreement.

## CONCLUSION

Historically the primary function of marriage has been the legitimization of children conceived within the marital union, with subsequent support, socialization, and property transmission to those children. Families comprised of parents and children often acted as a single economic unit, with interdependence among family members and independence from strangers.

Sexual restraint was understood as a necessary component of family harmony reinforced by a legal system that ensured that children conceived within marriage would receive acknowledgment and support of the husband, and children conceived outside of marriage would have little or no claim against family-accumulated wealth. Adultery was a crime, and fault-based divorce laws often gave the innocent wife a claim to lifetime support free of any continuing duty to reside with the adulterous husband.

In the last half of the twentieth century, our communal conception of marriage has changed, as has our understanding of the state's proper role in regulating sexual conduct. Required showings of fault before decrees of divorce issued were displaced by "no-fault" schemes permitting divorce upon the petition of either of the spouses.[16] Judges and legislators alike began to discard laws penalizing sexual intercourse outside of marriage.[17] Birth-control devices, initially restricted by legislatures as dangerous to public morals, were found to be constitutionally protected by the courts, first in the context of regulating births within marriage[18] and then as a means to individual fulfillment.[19] The "just-say-no" presumption of prior generations regarding unmarried sexual conduct was replaced by a "safe-sex" campaign premised partially upon a belief that singles were incapable of sexual abstinence and partially on a belief that sexual experiences were an integral part of human fulfillment. Court decisions overruled legislative judgments that certain benefits should only be extended on the basis of legitimacy,[20] and icons of popular culture presented beguiling pictures of unwed parenting.[21]

With marriage no longer presumed to be enduring, sex no longer limited to the marital bed, and children no longer understood to be the natural consequence of engaging in sexual intercourse, it should come as no surprise that skepticism greets those who argue that the state's recognition of marriage is inextricably tied to procreation and family. To many, the lessons of contemporary culture, reinforced by current laws related to marriage and sexual conduct, argue for a definition of marriage as an at-will affiliation of affection, an institution grounded in mutual self-fulfillment, with few externally imposed responsibilities, yet protected by the remnants of legal presumptions and cultural norms that afford it a unique and protected status. Childbearing is seen as an optional activity, legitimately occurring either inside or outside of marriage, with technology offering an ever-expanding array of means to obtain the "perfect child."

Given this new understanding of marriage, there seems to be little basis for refusing to officially recognize relationships between two men or two women as equally capable of leading to mutual self-fulfillment, particularly where these relationships serve as the setting for the rearing of children who were conceived in earlier heterosexual relationships or through the use of reproductive technology on who were adopted. Yet before extending legal recognition to these unions, we should stop and consider whether the lived experience of marriage comports with the minimalist conception embodied in the law and reinforced by much of popular culture. If contemporary marriage truly is primarily a means of self-fulfillment, perhaps the proper response is to dethrone marriage from its privileged position in the legal landscape and achieve equality of relationships by indifference to all. However, if marriage maintains a fuller connection with self-restraint and establishment of family in the popular imagination than is currently reflected in some laws and many movies, then perhaps the proper response is to maintain the existing definition of marriage as the union of one man and one woman and begin the more difficult work of reestablishing the formal recognition of the connection of marriage to self-giving, sexual restraint, and procreation.

## NOTES

1. Baker v. State, 744 A.2d 864, 886 (Vt. 1999).
2. 15 VT. STAT. ANN. sec. 1204(a).
3. Vt. House Bill 847, sec. 1(7).
4. BLACK'S LAW DICTIONARY 543 (5th ed. 1979).
5. Vt. House Bill 847, sec. 1(9).
6. Less than 1 percent of all births in the United States in 1999 involved the use of artificial reproductive technology, according to the most recent reports of the Centers for Disease Control on artificial reproductive technology and birth. Centers for Disease Control, 1999 Assisted Reproductive Technology Success Rates: National Summary and Fertility Clinic Reports available at www.cdc.gov/nccdphp/drh/ART99/section1.htm (visited Dec. 18, 2001) ("CDC estimates that ART accounts for approximately 0.8% of the total U.S. births").
7. Id. at sec. 3, available at www.cdc.gov/nccdphp/drh/ART99/section 3.htm#Section 4: fig. 29 ("Donor eggs were used in approximately 10% of all ART cycles carried out in 1999, or 9,066 cycles").
8. See Meyer v. Nebraska, 262 U.S. 390 (1923).

For the welfare of big Ideal Commonwealth, Plato suggested a law which should provide:
"That the wives of our guardians are to be common, and their children are to be common, and no parent is to know his own child, nor any child his parent. . . . The proper officers will take the offspring of the good parents to the pen or fold, and there they will deposit them with certain nurses who dwell in a separate quarter; but the offspring of the inferior, or of the better when they chance to be deformed, will be put away in some mysterious, unknown place, as they should be."
In order to submerge the individual and develop ideal citizens, Sparta assembled the males

at seven into barracks and entrusted their subsequent education and training to official guardians. Although such measures have been deliberately approved by men of great genius, their ideas touching the relation between individual and state were wholly different from those upon which our institutions rest; and it hardly will be affirmed that any Legislature could impose such restrictions upon the people of a state without doing violence to both letter and spirit of the Constitution.

*Id.* at 401–402.

9. For a summary of legislation related to abandoned infants, *see* National Conference of State Legislatures, *Infant Abandonment Legislation 2000–2001*, available at www.ncsl.org/programs/cyf/ABSL2001.htm (updated Nov. 7, 2001).

10. United States Dept. of Health and Human Services, *Welfare Reform: Implementing the Personal Responsibility and Work Opportunity Reconciliation Act of 1996* (Sept. 5, 2001), available at www.os.dhhs.gov/news/press/2001pres/01fswelreform.html (visited Dec. 18, 2001).

11. ROBERT P. GEORGE, MAKING MEN MORAL 20 (1993).

12. *See* Robert P. George & Gerard P. Bradley, *Marriage and the Liberal Imagination*, 84 GEO L.J. 301 (1995).

13. *See* David P. Perlmutter, Annotation, *Incapacity for Sexual Intercourse as Ground for Annulment*, 42 A.L.R.3d 589 (1974), and M.L. Cross, Annotation, *Refusal of Sexual Intercourse as Ground for Annulment*, 28 A.L.R.2d 499 (1953).

14. H. 847, sec. 1(9).

15. National Marriage Project, *The State of Our Unions 2001*, at 6–16 (2001), available at http://marriage.rutgers.edu/NMPAR2001.pdf.

16. *See* Allen M. Parker, *Reforming Divorce Reform*, 41 SANTA CLARA L. REV. 379 (2001).

17. *See* Robert E. Rodes, Jr., *On Law and Chastity*, 76 NOTRE DAME L. REV. 643 (2001).

18. Griswold v. Connecticut, 381 U.S. 479 (1965).

19. Eisenstadt v. Baird, 405 U.S. 438 (1972).

20. *E.g.*, Levy v. Louisiana, 391 U.S. 68 (1968) (the Constitution requires equal treatment of legitimate and illegitimate children in establishing a right to sue for the wrongful death of a parent).

21. Dana Calvo, *Few Now Quail at TV's Unwed Moms*, L.A. Times (Oct. 26, 2001), available at http://www.calendarlive.com/top/1,1419,L-LATimes-Search-X! ArticleDetail-45737,00.html (visited Dec. 18, 2001).

Response

# One Last Hope: A Response to Professor Teresa Stanton Collett
## Carlos A. Ball

Professor Collett in her thoughtful essay "Should Marriage Be Privileged?" raises several important issues, including the way in which a society without the institution of marriage would find it difficult (though perhaps not insurmountably so) to assign parental obligations (including but not limited to financial ones) to sexual partners in a consistent and effective manner. She also makes two principal arguments against state recognition of committed same-gender relationships. The first is that penile-vaginal intimacy in a committed relationship *matters*. The second is that the absence of children in same-gender relationships merits their differential treatment by the law. Given the focus of this anthology, I will limit my comments to these two arguments, addressing the second one first.

We cannot easily dismiss the fact that thousands of gay and lesbian couples in the United States are either currently raising children together or are planning to do so in the near future.[1] As a descriptive matter, therefore, the children/no-children distinction no longer clearly distinguishes committed straight relationships from committed gay and lesbian relationships, a problem for opponents of gay rights that is likely to become even more evident in the future. My colleague Harry Krause has suggested that the rights and obligations that we currently assign individuals based on marital status be based instead on parental status.[2] I do not believe that Professor Collett could agree to Professor Krause's proposal because parental status by itself does not give her the justification required to withhold state recognition of at least some committed same-gender relationships.

Furthermore, if the crucial distinction in the assignation of marital rights and obligations were to be whether a couple is raising children together, then it is not at all clear why the law should not treat all childless heterosexual relationships (including those that we have up until now deemed to be marital) in the same way that Professor Collett suggests we should treat childless same-gender couples, namely, one in which the community's interests are "relegated to private agreement." There are some who argue that we should leave the formation of familial associations among adults largely to enforceable private agreements, but such proposals are usually made by progressive scholars who seek to expand (rather than contract or maintain) the current definition of family as recognized by law.[3] But I take it that Professor Collett is not interested in having the definition of family *writ large* governed by intent or private agreement. What she appears to be after is a two-tiered system that keeps privileged *marital* relationships exclusively for heterosexual couples (regardless of whether they have children), while everyone else can use contract law to patch together their intimate lives as best they can. I do not believe that a tiered system that makes distinctions among different kinds of relationships is per se improper, but we need justifications for the differential treatment. Children by themselves do not provide us with a justification, given that not only are thousands of gay and lesbian couples having, adopting, and raising children, but they are also doing the latter well.[4]

Another way of distinguishing between committed straight and committed gay and lesbian relationships is by arguing that the quality of the mutuality generally found in the former is better (or more meaningful or more valuable) than in the latter. To her credit, Professor Collett does not question that real mutuality and love can exist in a same-gender relationship, as do some other academic opponents of same-sex marriage.[5] But Professor Collett does argue "that marriage is more than an intimate community of love and commitment." For Collett, marriage is also a "unique sexual community" of "sexual difference and the potential creation of new life." She adds that vaginal intercourse has always been a "distinctive aspect of marriage."

If there is one act that gay and lesbian couples do not engage in, it is penile-vaginal intercourse. If neither children nor mutuality can serve as the essential distinguishing criterion that justifies the differential treatment of same-gender relationships, the claim that penile-vaginal intercourse is distinctively valuable provides opponents of same-sex marriage with one last hope. The question then becomes whether that last hope has a normative bite to it.

For penile-vaginal intimacy to do the moral lifting that opponents of same-sex marriage require of it, we cannot view its value instrumentally. The value of that intimacy, in other words, cannot arise from its consequences, that is, from the fact that it sometimes leads to reproduction, because that would deprive sterile and elderly heterosexual married couples of its value. Professor Collett at times implies an instrumental view of the value of penile-vaginal intercourse when she defends the traditional definition of the family as one defined by biology and bloodlines. Surely, however, biology and bloodlines can no longer be dispositive in the definition of family now that our laws, and increasingly our culture, recognize adoptive families as being the equivalent of biological ones.

If the value of penile-vaginal intimacy as it relates to our understanding of marriage and family, then, is not its instrumental connection to procreation, there must be a distinctive intrinsic value associated with it. Professor Collett has argued elsewhere that the distinctive value arises from the "complementarity" of males and females.[6] Heterosexual intimacy, under this view, is enriched by the physical, experiential, and behavioral differences between men and women, while same-gender sexual intimacy is weakened by the similarities among men and among women.

The complementarity argument simultaneously diminishes marriage as an institution and spouses as individuals. The value of marriage arises (as I argue in my essay included in this anthology) from the human needs and capabilities that it seeks to promote and protect, needs and capabilities that merit moral respect regardless and independently of gender. To claim that the similarities between two men or between two women somehow disqualify them from participating in the institution of marriage is to reduce the full panoply of human complexity and diversity to a handful of socially constructed gender attributes and particular bodily organs. Differences based on gender attributes and sexual organs pale in comparison to the differences in interests, motivations, and aspirations that are characteristic of the rich diversity of human beings. In order to "save" marriage from the purported threat represented by state recognition of committed same-gender relationships, the conservatives' last hope strips individuals and marriage of much of their complexity and multifacetedness. The complementarity argument serves the purpose of trying to link the value of sexually intimate relationships to gender distinctiveness, but it presents us with an unconvincing and highly simplified conception of the human needs and capabilities associated with physical and emotional intimacy that serve as important normative foundations for the institution of companionate marriage.

I cannot disagree with Professor Collett that the law, as a descriptive matter, has traditionally required the consummation of marriage through penile-vaginal intercourse. I do not believe, however, that either she or any of the other thoughtful opponents of same-sex marriage have presented us with a convincing argument as to why that form of intimacy should be *the* dispositive normative criterion in distinguishing marital from nonmarital relationships.

## NOTES

1. *See* Steven Gray, *New Families, New Questions: Same-Sex Couples Turn to Parenthood in Growing Numbers*, Wash. Post, Apr. 12, 2001, at T10.

2. *See* Harry D. Krause, *Marriage for the New Millennium: Heterosexual, Same-Sex—or Not at All?*, 34 FAM. L.Q. 271, 298–300 (2000).

3. *See, e.g.*, Martha M. Ertman, *Marriage as a Trade: Bridging the Private/Private Distinction*, 36 HARV. CIV. RIGHTS CIV. LIB. L. REV. 79 (2001).

4. *See* Carlos A. Ball & Janice Farrell Pea, *Warring with Wardle: Morality, Social Science, and Gay and Lesbian Parents*, 1998 U. ILL. L. REV. 253.

5. *See* John M. Finnis, *Law, Morality, and "Sexual Orientation,"* 69 NOTRE DAME L. REV. 1049, 1067 (1994) (arguing that a real mutuality cannot arise from same-gender sexual intimacy and that therefore it is no different than masturbation or soliciting a prostitute); Patrick Lee & Robert P. George, *What Sex Can Be: Self-Alienation, Illusion, or One-Flesh Union*, 42 AM. J. JURIS. 135, 136 (1997) (arguing that same-gender sexual acts, like all sexual acts that are not penile-vaginal, "constitute the pursuit of a merely illusory experience").

6. *See* Teresa Stanton Collett, *Recognizing Same-Sex Marriage: Asking for the Impossible?*, 47 CATH. UNIV. L. REV. 1245, 1261–1262 (1998).

# Chapter 6

Essay One

# The Same-Sex-Marriage Debate and Three Conceptions of Equality
## William N. Eskridge, Jr.

There is nothing new about a polity's recognizing same-sex marriages,[1] but the institution has been virtually unknown to the modern West. This is about to change, as lesbian and gay activists have pressed for full marital rights in Western countries with increasing success. In 1989, Denmark created a new institution, registered partnerships, giving same-sex couples almost all the rights and duties of marriage; a number of countries (including France and Germany) have followed with similar laws.[2] In the 1990s, the highest courts in Hungary and Canada ruled that cohabitation laws cannot constitutionally discriminate against same-sex couples.[3] In 1999, the Vermont Supreme Court ruled in *Baker v. State* that discrimination against same-sex couples in allocating the benefits and obligations of marriage violates the state constitution; in the next year, the legislature created a new institution for same-sex couples, civil unions, with all the benefits and obligations of marriage. In April 2001, the Netherlands' Parliament recognized same-sex marriages. Debate has been joined.

The same-sex-marriage debate illustrates the structure and dynamics of equality discourse in the modern West. This essay will outline the doctrinal arguments for same-sex marriage as they have emerged in the constitutional jurisprudence of Canada and the United States and then suggest how the demand for same-sex marriage fits into more abstract theories of equality. The arguments against same-sex marriage operate within these larger categories as well, though. The clash of pro and con arguments around this topic reflects both the importance of equality to all kinds of groups in the modern West and the many ways that equality itself can be understood. A widely accepted lesson of the American civil rights movement that ended racial apartheid is that equality is liberatory and transformational, and this has inspired gay rights groups and their strategies. But, as this essay will show, equality is a Janus-faced principle. Under certain assumptions, the equality principle can be a rallying point for religious traditionalists who seek suppression of gay people in the social and political sphere.

## EQUALITY ARGUMENTS FOR SAME-SEX MARRIAGE IN CANADIAN AND AMERICAN CONSTITUTIONAL JURISPRUDENCE

Equality is a specific guarantee in both Canadian and American constitutional law. Section 15(1) of the Canadian Charter of Rights and Freedoms provides that "[e]very individual . . . has the right to the equal protection and equal benefit of the law without discrimination," with particular reference to race, sex, and other forms of discrimination. The Equal Protection Clause in the U.S. Constitution similarly provides that a state cannot "deny to any person within its jurisdiction the equal protection of the laws," albeit without specifying particularly invidious forms of discrimination. Denying same-sex couples the legal recognition of their unions routinely afforded different-sex couples denies these couples "equal protection" in a literal sense, but that ought not to end serious discussion of the issue. The supreme courts in both countries have developed principles limiting the discriminations that the courts will examine skeptically. Although the most obvious limiting basis is to confine serious scrutiny to the discriminatory classifications identified in section 15(1) of Canada's Charter, both courts have also closely scrutinized state laws discriminating with other classifications, or against subordinated groups, or in the provision of particularly important rights.

### State Deployment of a Suspect Classification

Canada's section 15(1) specifically protects against "discrimination based on race, national or ethnic origin, colour, religion, sex, age or mental or physical disability," and the U.S. Supreme Court has interpreted the Constitution's equal protection guarantee to give heightened scrutiny to classifications based on race, national origin, and sex. The judiciaries of each country will demand more exacting justifications from the state when it is deploying these classifications but will not be very demanding for laws deploying other, less suspicious classifications. At first glance, this structure of equal protection jurisprudence would appear unfriendly to same-sex-marriage claims, yet such claims have substantial doctrinal justification in each country.

Canada's Justice L'Heureux-Dubé maintained in 1993 that rules barring same-sex couples from state benefits routinely accorded different-sex couples are invidious discriminations based on sexual orientation, which she argued was "analogous" to the classifications listed in section 15(1).[4] That is, section 15(1) is not an exclusive list of classifications requiring heightened scrutiny, and other classifications analogous to the listed ones are to be deemed similarly suspect. Canadian governments in subsequent cases have conceded the correctness of her view, and Justice Cory's opinions for the Canadian Supreme Court in *Vriend v. Alberta*[5] and *Attorney General v. M. and H.*[6] have elaborated on the sociopolitical basis for this conclusion: Sexual orientation is like race and sex in that it is a deeply personal characteristic that has been the basis for social and political disadvantage resulting from stereotyping and prejudice. In Canadian jurisprudence, substantive discrimination based upon a section 15(1) ground or an analogous ground like sexual orientation is invalid unless it is rationally related to the aim of the law, minimally impairs the right to equal treatment, and serves an important social goal that outweighs the right.[7]

The argument for same-sex marriage in Canada therefore runs as follows: The denial of marriage licenses to same-sex couples is substantive discrimination against them because of their sexual orientation. This discrimination is analogous to those characteristics listed in section 15(1) because it is based on prejudice against lesbians, gay men, and bisexuals and reflects the historic disadvantage that group has suffered. The discrimination cannot be justified by the purpose of the legislation, because the state goal of recognizing marriage is to support the unitive features of human partnerships, a goal that is as equally applicable to lesbian and gay couples as it is to straight ones. To the extent that the state is also encouraging a good environment for child rearing through its recognition of marriage, the evidence suggests that lesbian couples (the only ones studied so far) do just as good a job as straight couples in this socially important task.[8] The traditionalist policy of procreation is not an important goal per se of modern marriage legislation, and even if it were, it would not outweigh the couples' rights.

Unlike the Canadian Supreme Court, the U.S. Supreme Court has not ruled on the status of sexual orientation as a classification, but one state court has reasoned from the national court's precedents that the same-sex-marriage bar is a sex-based discrimination requiring heightened justification. In *Loving v. Virginia*, the Supreme Court held that a state law barring different-race marriages violated the Equal Protection Clause because the state was discriminating on the basis of race, a suspect classification.[9] The Hawaii Supreme Court in *Baehr v. Lewin* held that denying a same-sex couple the marriage license that would be given to a similar but different-sex couple was discrimination on the basis of sex in the same way that denying a different-race couple a marriage license that would be given to a same-race couple would be discrimination on the basis of race.[10] In the latter case, the classification (the variable item) is the race of one partner; in the former case, the classification (the variable item) is the sex of one partner.[11] Because sex is a classification that cannot be used to confer legal disadvan-

tages unless there is good justification, the *Baehr* court remanded the case
for trial to determine whether the state could show a compelling public
interest served by the sex discrimination. The lower court held that the state
failed to make such a showing and invalidated the bar.[12] This ruling was
overridden in 1998 by a state constitutional amendment allowing the legislature to limit marriage to man-woman couples.

The sex-discrimination argument for same-sex marriage has the virtue of
identifying the precise basis for the discrimination, namely, the sex of one
partner. Lesbians are not absolutely denied the right to marry; they may
certainly marry males, as many lesbians do. Nor are gay women barred from
marrying homosexuals; unions of lesbians and gay men are recognized. Lesbians are only denied the right to marry the women of their choice, which
is, literally, a sex-based discrimination. To be sure, this argument has a trans-
vestic quality, as it seems to dress up gay rights in feminist doctrinal garb.
*Loving* might be different in the sense that the race-based discrimination
was invalid because it subserved a regime of "white supremacy," as the Court
explicitly noted. But the bar to same-sex marriages is a sex-based discrimination that subserves a regime of rigid gender roles, precisely the ideology
that the U.S. Supreme Court has identified as the problem at which its sex
discrimination jurisprudence is directed.[13]

### State Deprivation of Important Rights

In *M. and H.*, Justice Cory emphasized not only the historical prejudice
and hostility to lesbians, gay men, and bisexuals as grounds for heightened
scrutiny under section 15, but also the fact that the discrimination "restricts
access to a fundamental social institution, or affects a basic aspect of full
membership in Canadian society."[14] This is an important feature of equality
jurisprudence: the nature of the deprivation as well as the particular classification might trigger judicial monitoring. For another example, a state rule
saying that citizens who have defaulted on their child-support payments—
the prototypical "deadbeat dad"—cannot vote should be subject to serious
judicial scrutiny, not because of the classification deployed, a morally appealing criterion, but because of the importance of the right denied. This
idea has been more fully developed in American jurisprudence.

As an alternative ground for the U.S. Supreme Court's invalidation of
different-race-marriage bars, Chief Justice Warren's opinion in *Loving* invoked a "freedom to marry" that is "one of the vital personal rights essential
to the orderly pursuit of happiness by free men."[15] The Court in *Zablocki
v. Redhail* applied this holding of *Loving* to invalidate a state bar to remarriage by people with outstanding child- or spousal-support obligations. Justice Marshall's opinion ruled that no state restriction of the "freedom of
personal choice in matters of marriage and family life" can be sustained
unless the state can show that its restriction is narrowly drawn to serve a

compelling social purpose.[16] Because there was no suspicious classification in *Zablocki* comparable to the race-based classification in *Loving*, the stricter judicial scrutiny was justified solely from its restriction of the right to marry. *Zablocki* established a doctrinal structure logically applicable to other cases: A state law or practice that places a "direct legal obstacle in the path of persons desiring to get married" denies these persons the equal protection of the laws unless the state policy is "supported by sufficiently important state interests and is closely tailored to effectuate only those interests."[17] For gays and lesbians, this means that the burden of persuasion as to same-sex marriage lies with the opponents. The issue is not, Why gay marriage? but instead, Why not gay marriage?

Under American law, therefore, the state's refusal to recognize same-sex marriages would seem to be discrimination both in the allocation of a fundamental right (*Zablocki*) and on the basis of sex (*Baehr*). In light of the modern state's emphasis on the unitive goal of marriage and rejection of rigid gender roles for men and women, the constitutional requirement is that the state must justify its discrimination by showing a compelling public interest in denying same-sex couples the right to marry. This ought to be hard to accomplish, as many lesbian and gay couples desire to marry for precisely the reasons emphasized by the Supreme Court in its most recent marriage case. In *Turner v. Safley*, the Court overturned a state bar to marriages by incarcerated criminals. Justifying its extension of the right to marry to inmates, the Court ignored procreation as a goal of marriage and emphasized how inmate marriages are "expressions of emotional support and public commitment," can be exercises of "religious faith as well as an expression of personal dedication," and are tied to receipt of tangible benefits and property rights accorded to marriage in our society.[18] All of these reasons, as well as sexual consummation, are equally relevant for lesbian and gay couples, as is a reason not mentioned by the Court but contested on remand in *Baehr*: the rearing of children in a stable family environment. As the trial court found in *Baehr*, same-sex couples not only raise children, they do so comparably as well as different-sex couples do, a finding strongly supported by social science studies of children reared in such households.[19]

## State Rules Grounded in Prejudice or Animus

Although almost all adjudicated violations of the equality guarantee focus on what classification is deployed and how fundamental the deprivation is, another possible ground for heightened judicial scrutiny is why a particular group has been deprived of important rights. The why-deprived question is different from even as it is strongly related to the what-classification question. Some classifications have been shown to be unreliable ones, partly because they have historically reflected prejudice-based thinking, but also because they have historically reflected stereotype-based thinking that has too loose a connection to socioeconomic reality. Racial classifications have traditionally exemplified what social psychologists call *hot discrimination*, because they have been inspired by both emotional prejudice seeking to harm or exclude racial minorities and the cognitive biases of stereotypical thinking. Many sex-based classifications, in contrast, exemplify *cold discrimination*, for they do not harm or exclude women, but do rest on unjustified stereotypes about men as well as women.[20] The Canadian Supreme Court's "analogous-grounds" jurisprudence under section 15(1) maintains that sexual-orientation-based classifications reflect hot discrimination: they are typically driven by the prejudicial desire to harm or exclude and rest upon erroneous stereotypes about lesbians, gay men, and bisexuals.

Although the U.S. Supreme Court has not ruled on the broad issue of how to treat sexual-orientation categories generally, its decision in *Romer v. Evans* held that the state is not insulated from critical judicial scrutiny of hot discrimination simply because the state has not deployed one of the recognized suspect classifications.[21] (The same idea underlies the Court's rule that state policies having a disparate impact upon racial minorities will be subject to strict scrutiny when the policies are inspired by race-based animus.)[22] *Evans* involved a Colorado initiative that amended the states constitution to void any local or state law or policy "whereby homosexual, lesbian or bisexual orientation, conduct, practices or relationships shall constitute or otherwise be the basis of or entitle any person or class of persons to have or claim any minority status, quota preferences, protected status or claim of discrimination." The Court found the initiative invalid because "its sheer breadth is so discontinuous with the reasons offered for it that the amendment seems inexplicable by anything but animus toward the class that it affects." The Court characterized the initiative as a "status-based" law aimed at a class of citizens; such laws violate the core equal protection command that "a bare . . . desire to harm a politically unpopular group cannot constitute a legitimate government interest."[23]

*Evans* illustrates a proposition that is at the core of the equal protection guarantee. Because courts will be loath to attribute animus or prejudice to the legislative process, this proposition will not often trigger judicial invalidation of legislation, but it remains an idea that ought to inform public debate, including legislative debate, about same-sex marriage. Under this antiprejudice reading of equal protection, opponents not only have the burden of showing that same-sex couples should be excluded from the institution, but also cannot meet their burden by relying on mere popular dislike of lesbians, gay men, and bisexuals. Before turning to responses made by opponents of same-sex marriage, it is useful to put the foregoing equal protection arguments into a broader framework of theories about equality itself.

## THE SAME-SEX-MARRIAGE MOVEMENT AND THREE UNDERSTANDINGS OF EQUALITY

Arguments from precepts of equality are not limited to constitutional cases. Ultimately, the case for same-sex marriage must be made politically, for judges will not be able to force the institution upon an unwilling population. One lesson of twentieth-century civil rights movements is that courts are well situated to break political logjams and can put an issue on a state's policy agenda, but a larger political struggle is required to make progress against alleged social injustices. The social and political struggles for equality by racial minorities and women paved the way for the gay rights movement and intellectually informed that movement's understanding of what it ought to be seeking. A profound lesson of prior egalitarian movements has been that equality itself has different meanings. These multiple meanings not only help us understand the different things that are stake in the state's stance toward same-sex marriage, but also help us think more deeply and complexly about equality. The different ways of thinking about equality can inform the jurisprudence of any or all the states of the Americas.

### Formal Equality

The most common meaning of egalitarian aspiration is *formal equality*: like things and people will be treated alike. The concept is a core feature of modern political liberalism, whereby everyone in the polity will be rewarded or punished by the state based on their individual acts and performances, not on their social status or subjective considerations. A jurisprudence of formal equality weeds out classifications that reflect stereotyped or prejudice-based thinking and serve no productive social goal—and especially those that are socially divisive. For example, the state regulates the driving of cars for safety reasons. State licensing rules classify people by age, sightedness, and the ability to obtain insurance, all of which are criteria that exclude many good people, but people who arguably should not be driving. The licensing rules do not exclude people based on their eye color, left-handedness, or sexual orientation, nor could the rules discriminate along these lines, because these traits bear no rational relation to safety concerns.

Formal equality is a key component of the rule of law. The neutrality and predictability entailed in law encourage the socially marginalized to improve their lot by being productive, which helps them at the same time it helps society. Energy is directed toward creating one's own sphere of happiness (family and home) and contributing to overall wealth (the market). Laws that derogate from that goal are not only diversionary, but can be destructive, as apartheid was. This explication of formal equality helps explain why lesbian and gay people are so insistent on same-sex marriage, and why the liberal polity ought to go along. The legal obligations of civil marriage foster commitment and serve social insurance goals, and the legal benefits help the family unit flourish and protect it against undue public and private interference.[24] There is no cogent neutral reason to deny these obligations and benefits to same-sex couples. Not only would the couples potentially benefit from them, but society would, too. Consider the following analogy.

Assume that you are running a household of three children, and you set arbitrarily different ground rules as to important matters for different children. In so doing, you are being unjust and inviting family turmoil. If, for example, Tommy was allowed to learn how to drive at age fifteen so that he could obtain his driver's license promptly on his sixteenth birthday, his younger sisters Martha and Sally would expect the same treatment when they become fifteen. Denying that rule to Martha and Sally is a bad idea: you are not only sending a message to the disfavored children that you do not respect them, but you are likely spreading discord among the children and perhaps even spoiling Tommy. Extend the example. If one of the children were bisexual in her orientation and the parents were disgusted by this knowledge, would they be justified in denying that child her opportunity for a driver's license? The precept of formal equality suggests not. The presumptive equal worth of each child is inconsistent with a regime where the children are treated differently because of "who they are." Although the impulse to give vent to one's feelings through different rules is a natural human impulse, it is one mature adults are supposed to resist. The state has even greater cause to resist such impulses.

### Reparative Equality

In some situations, formal equality is not enough. Consider American apartheid. Formal equality required the state to end the rules instantiating segregation of the races and prohibiting different-race cohabitation and marriage. Some critical theorists maintain that eliminating old racial classifications is not a sufficient response and that creating affirmative policies benefiting racial minorities is also needed to repair the attitudinal and economic damage accomplished by generations of racist policies.[25] If the state has helped create prejudicial attitudes stigmatizing an entire race, the state has harmed not only the historical group, but present-day individuals in the group whose opportunities are limited by the persistence of those attitudes and by other ongoing institutional barriers.[26] Just as tort law can be justified as imposing the costs of wrongs on parties that contributed to those wrongs, so reparative social policies can be justified as imposing some of the ongoing costs of racism on the state that contributed to racist attitudes. Return to the family example. If Martha's parents traumatized her during childhood by excessive spankings, justice may not be completely served by having the parents cease spanking her. The parents may have a moral obligation to repair the psychological damage caused by their unjustified conduct, and that obligation would in turn justify benefits for Martha that are not afforded the other, less spanked children.

For political reasons, gay rights are rarely articulated in terms of reparative equality, but this idea has a role to play in the same-sex-marriage debate. By criminalizing their consensual behavior and pathologizing their relationships, the modern state has contributed not only to stereotypes of gay people as promiscuous and incapable of forming marital relationships, but has actually made it harder for gay people to live out the romantic ideals that saturate American culture.[27] To repair the ongoing damage done to gay people, the state has a responsibility to make available a supportive institution for same-sex relationships. This kind of argument can support same-sex marriage, but it can also support state creation of a different institution altogether—one that is tailored to whatever particular needs same-sex couples might have. Rather than creating registered-partnership laws that provide most but not all the legal benefits of marriage, as Denmark has done, the state might create a same-sex-union law that provides all the benefits of marriage plus additional ones. For example, the state might assure stronger procedural and maybe substantive protections for same-sex spouses when one is incapacitated or dies, because the blood family more often feels emboldened to push the spouse aside when the relationship is homosexual rather than heterosexual.

The foregoing suggestion is tentative and speculative, but the next is not. The idea of reparative equality is a useful way to understand the sex-discrimination argument for same-sex marriage. The sex-discrimination argument acquires its formal power from the facts that same-sex couples are technically discriminated against "because of [one partner's] sex" and that discrimination because of sex is considered suspect in modern liberal polities without substantial justification. The Achilles heel of the argument is that the discriminatory classification (sex) does not match up with the discriminated-against class (gays). One solution was suggested earlier: the sex discrimination in marriage imposes rigid gender roles on men and women, a policy that is the critical target of sex-discrimination jurisprudence. The idea of reparative equality deepens this response.

Feminist thinkers have observed that formal equality often has few or no good consequences for women, in part because removing open sex discriminations from current law does little and maybe nothing to ameliorate women's structural inequality.[28] For example, opening up jobs for women to seek on an equal basis with men does not satisfy the goal of equality if women are still disadvantaged by other institutions and attitudes to which the state has contributed, especially the family ideal where the woman is presumptively limited to the domestic sphere. The institution of different-sex marriage is not only part of this ideology, but it is central to it. By insisting that women can only marry men, the state is not only violating the rule of formal equality for lesbians and bisexual women, but is violating the idea of reparative equality for women generally. One way the state can start to repair the damage done to women is by opening up marriage to two women (and even to two men). Such an opening up would be both a formal and functional repudiation of the separate-spheres idea. Female-female marriages are much less likely to allocate roles based upon the traditional domestic/workplace distinction,[29] and even when they do, they violate that distinction by having the workplace role filled by a woman.[30] Although same-sex marriage is only one small part of a genuine feminist program to repair social and individual damage wrought by sexism, it is a reparative response to the reality of functional sex segregation.

### Transformative Equality

Reparative conceptions of equality are accusatory as well as corrective: the state has contributed to a wrong and now has an obligation not just to stop contributing but also to help heal the injury. Such a retrospective, duty-based understanding of equality can be contrasted with a prospective, opportunity-based understanding. A *transformative* conception maintains that equality in some circumstances offers opportunities for the modern state to rethink past practices and reconfigure institutions in ways that are better for society as a whole, and not just for the previously marginalized group. Under this conception, prior inequalities are not just discriminations that should be ended (formal equality) or wrongs that need to be corrected (reparative equality), but flaws that reveal imperfections in existing institutions and that suggest the possibility of reformed or new institutions better serving social purposes.

Transformative equality is most inspired by critical theories but is supportable under liberal premises as well. If the inequality of racial minorities and women has not just been historically pervasive but also has helped form the basis for ongoing institutions, formal equality is not meaningful and reparative equality not really possible unless the institutions are themselves transformed. Recall the dysfunctional family introduced earlier in this chapter. If upon reflection it appears that the gendered treatment of the children and the harsh punishments meted out to daughter Martha are strongly related to the family's patriarchal and authoritarian decision-making structure ("Father knows best"), a transformative conception of equality would urge that the decision-making structure itself be changed. To assure equality among the children, Father should be required to share decision-making authority with Mother, to consult with the family on important matters, and perhaps to undergo counseling to deal with his authoritarian personality disorder. Such a rehabilitation of the family will not only help Martha, but ought to benefit all the family members. The normative appeal of transformative equality is not just that it offers a thicker egalitarianism, but also that it may be instructive as to what institutional forms best serve society in general. Apartheid in the American South, for example, was not only unjust to people of color, but held back the entire region morally, socially, and economically.

Same-sex marriage is defensible as a productive transformation of the institution of marriage. Marriage, it can be argued, becomes less gendered and more explicitly unitive in its focus once same-sex unions are recognized as its exemplars rather than its antitheses. The same-sex marriage movement and its traditionalist opponents have contributed to a transformation in the options the state offers to different-sex as well as same-sex couples. Because traditionalists fervently oppose same-sex marriage, they have pushed states into compromises whereby legislatures have created new institutions for recognizing intimate relationships. Many of the new institutions, such as Denmark's registered partnerships and Vermont's civil unions, are available only for same-sex couples. Other new institutions, such as domestic partnerships recognized in many American cities, Vermont's reciprocal beneficiaries, France's *pactes civiles*, and the Netherlands' version of registered partnerships, have been open to different- as well as same-sex couples. By thwarting same-sex marriage, traditionalists have unwittingly helped advance the agenda of radical critics, who maintain that the state should create new, nonpatriarchal institutions for supporting human relationships and families.[31]

## EQUALITY ARGUMENTS AGAINST SAME-SEX MARRIAGE AND THEIR UNDERLYING CULTURAL ANXIETIES

Notwithstanding the foregoing equality-based arguments, neither judges nor legislators have rushed to require state recognition of same-sex marriages. Opposition remains intense, even among some people who are otherwise progay. Why is that? It is interesting that traditionalist opponents usually do not concede that the same-sex-marriage bar is a denial of equality or is a state discrimination (albeit justified by social policy). Indeed, some opponents argue that their position is required by the concept of equality, properly understood. The three conceptions of equality developed earlier help frame the oppositionist stance and the underlying cultural anxieties that render that stance persuasive to many people.

### The Definitional Argument (Formal Equality)

The most popular argument against same-sex marriage rests on the following syllogism: by definition, "marriage" involves procreation; procreation can only be achieved by the sexual union of a man and a woman; therefore, same-sex marriage is an oxymoron.[32] This argument is popular because it explains how formal equality need not embrace same-sex marriage. Because same-sex couples (who cannot procreate) are not similarly situated to different-sex couples (who can), they are not treated "differently" when they are denied marriage licenses. Indeed, to treat them as "married" would violate the idea of formal equality, because it would be treating dissimilar couples alike.

The definitional argument has some analytical holes. To begin with, it rests upon a premise that is factually erroneous, namely, that marriage must be procreative. When confronted with the question whether a sterile couple could marry under a natural-law conception of marriage, St. Augustine reasoned in *De Bono conjugali* that the unitive rather than the procreative goal of marriage supports their union.[33] In the modern polity, the unitive conception of marriage dominates the procreative one. Not only does the state offer sterile couples marriage licenses to seal their unions, but it would be unconstitutional for the state to refuse to do so. Indeed, the American and Canadian constitutions protect the rights of couples to avoid or terminate conception. The modern policy is that the state is neutral as to procreation: it is left up to couples and individual women to decide for themselves. Moreover, the unitive goals of civil marriage are just as applicable to same-sex as to different-sex couples. Empirical studies published in the leading refereed journals have found that same-sex couples derive satisfaction from committed relationships similar to, and for lesbians greater than, those of different-sex couples.[34] Same-sex marriage, as a unitive institution, is not an oxymoron. Indeed, same-sex unions have been culturally and legally recognized throughout human history and in America itself.[35]

Although analytically problematic, the definitional argument remains culturally potent. For one thing, such arguments are a matter of religious faith for many persons.[36] But the appeal of natural-law arguments is not limited to the religious fundamentalist, and for this reason: the longer a social or legal differentiation has been in place, the more "natural" it appears to people, and the more "loss" they feel if the differentiation is removed. This phenomenon is related to the *endowment effect*: people place a higher value on something they "own" than on the same thing they do not own; stated another way, people ask more money for an object (like a coffee cup) they own than they would be willing to pay for the same object whose ownership rests with someone else. To the extent that people have internalized differentiations as a part of their self-identities or statuses, they will be reluctant to give them up. To the extent that they consider these differentiations to be their entitlements, they will ask much more for their revocation than they would be willing to pay for them. Indeed, most people will not even see differentiations to which they are personally bonded as "discriminations" in derogation of the principle of formal equality. Like blacks and women, who confronted precisely these arguments before them, gay people must surmount a high burden of proof before mainstream society will undo what it considers long-standing discriminations.

## No-Promo-Homo Arguments (Reparative Equality)

Another kind of argument against same-sex marriage sidesteps issues of formal equality and suggests that equality for gay people needs to be balanced against inequalities that would be imposed on other people. The "no-promo-homo" argument takes the following form: For prudential reasons, the state should not penalize gay people, but neither should the state "promote" or encourage "homosexuality," which is a condition inferior to and less happy than heterosexuality; recognizing same-sex marriage would be a stamp of approval promoting not-so-good homosexuality and threatening or disrespecting good old heterosexuality; therefore, the state should not recognize same-sex marriages. This has become the primary justification against same-sex marriage among people, especially intellectuals, who support tolerance and even compassion for gay people.[37] It is the flip side of the progay argument from reparative equality: same-sex marriage will not repair the worst problem faced by lesbians and gay men, namely, their homosexuality, and threatens to instigate new harms in confused people who might be corrupted by state promotion of less desirable sexual orientations. Rather than correcting past injustices, same-sex marriage will be creating new ones.

In response to the no-promo-homo argument, it might initially be objected that when the state recognizes same-sex marriages, it purports to be and actually is supporting interpersonal commitment (marriage), not homosexuality. Mark this contrast. The state hands out marriage licenses to convicted rapists and spouse abusers to marry people who are statistically likely to be abused. Does the state thereby "promote" rape or spouse abuse? No secular moral system considers rapists and sexual abusers more worthy than people who engage in consensual intimacy with others of the same sex, yet family law gives the rapist and the abuser the benefit of marriage and, if the critics of same-sex marriage were faithful to their stated reason, a social stamp of approval as well. This paradox can be explained in part by reference to the endowment effect discussed earlier. Abusive couples have long been assured marriage licenses, and so their inclusion has come to seem unproblematic, whereas the inclusion of a long-excluded group such as same-sex couples raises status anxieties that can be expressed through rhetorical fears about promotion and stamps of approval.

The anxiety is actually much deeper. At bottom, the no-promo-homo critics of same-sex marriage are concerned about children. Adolescent sexuality is a situs of enormous anxiety in modern culture. Even tolerant parents may fear that their offspring will be gay, because of the social disadvantages and the diminished likelihood of grandchildren. Same-sex marriage has become the newest focal point for this parental concern. The fear is that if the state makes any move toward normalizing "homosexual" relationships as anything but grim, the sexually wavering adolescent will "go gay." Even worse (from this point of view), gay people will be emboldened to "recruit" adolescents to their "lifestyle," which mainstream society believes can be superficially attractive to adolescents. According to the no-promo-homo script, state recognition of same-sex marriage might repair harms to gay people at the expense of imposing "worse" harms on the young and on society itself. Corrective justice does not require a wrongdoer to repair harm to the victim by actions that impose new harms on innocent third parties. (The genuinely tolerant purveyors of the no-promo-homo argument would favor other kinds of remedies, short of same-sex marriage.)

Culturally, this is a powerful position, but it rests in part on questionable assumptions, the most questionable being those regarding the consequences of state promotion. Would state normalization of gay relationships affect adolescent sexuality? The theories that have the most support among scientists situate sexual orientation in a person's genes, prenatal or postnatal hormonal environment, or early childhood experiences.[38] All these theories suggest that there is little that the state can do to determine adolescent sexuality. No respectable scientific theory of sexuality maintains that individuals choose a sexual orientation the way they choose a car. Conduct a thought experiment. Can even parents control their children's sexuality by telling them how they should feel, by being role models, or by giving their stamp of approval only to certain feelings? Not readily. The great majority of lesbian and gay adults were themselves children in families where the role models, the parental signals, and the social reinforcements were all heterosexual. The great majority of children of lesbian families are heterosexual notwithstanding their parents' positive views about homosexuality. Parents and society influence their children's sexuality, but rarely in the ways that are planned. This is one of the great adventures in having children.

Even if the no-promo-homo argument were better grounded factually, it would be normatively questionable. The proposition that being homosexual is so much worse than being heterosexual is supported mainly by reference to conditions, such as social opprobrium, to which the state has vigorously contributed. The most minimal version of reparative equality would augur against discriminating against gay people because of social attitudes engendered by prior discrimination itself. The argument that gay people are unhappy because they cannot procreate is a canard. Many gay people have biological or adopted children, and an increasing number of same-sex, especially lesbian, couples are raising children in stable households.

Moreover, it is not clear that some (highly speculative) promotion of a certain kind of status justifies unequal treatment in state apportionment of important rights, such as the right to marry (or the right to vote, to take another example). Could the state constitutionally legislate that people with heritable disabilities cannot marry? The argument would be that marriage would directly promote disabilities that disgust many Americans by encouraging people with disabilities to produce offspring who themselves would have higher odds of such disabilities. It is not clear that such social consequences could justify denying disabled people fundamental rights. There is even less justification for denying gay people marriage rights because the no-promotion-of-homosexuality chain of causation is more indirect than the no-promotion-of-disability chain is.

## The Defense-of-Marriage Argument (Transformative Equality)

The queerest argument against same-sex marriage is that recognition would undermine marriage. When Hawaii seemed likely to recognize same-sex marriages at some point, a political coalition headed by President Clinton, Senate Majority Leader Dole, and House Speaker Gingrich secured enactment of the Defense of Marriage Act (DOMA) in 1996.[39] Their contention was that any kind of state recognition for same-sex marriage would imperil the institution of marriage, already in trouble. This kind of thinking turns the progay argument from transformative equality on its head: contrary to progay and feminist theories, admitting same-sex couples into the institution of marriage will not transform the institution in socially productive ways and may well hasten marriage's demise.[40]

Like the other arguments against same-sex marriage, this one appears analytically anemic. It is not clear how admitting enthusiastic new converts to marriage will undermine the institution for everyone. Will state recognition of the unions of lesbian couples demoralize straight couples? The defense-of-marriage argument has more than a whiff of hypocrisy. The marital infidelities of straight people like Clinton, Gingrich, and Dole have disrespected the institution of marriage, yet these three adulterers insist that it is gays who represent the deepest threats to the institution they have embarrassed. Why should gay people suffer the consequences of straights' marriage anxiety?

Once again, the phenomenon is related to the before-noted endowment effect: not only is it hard for outsiders to break into an established institution, it is doubly hard when the institution is perceived to be in decline. Furthermore—and this is critical—the reasons many perceive as causing the decline of marriage are directly related to the movement for same-sex marriage. The last generation has witnessed a liberalization of marriage law.[41] The state has moved away from the old communitarian model of marriage as a lifetime committed union for the rearing of children to a new liberal model of individuals working together as long as it suits them. State rules removing old impediments to marriage, such as race- and disease-based limits, allowing easy divorce, protecting wives against their husbands, and treating the marital partners as individuals rather than as a unit all have changed the institution in ways that traditionalists lament and cannot stop. But they can stop same-sex marriage, which serves as the proxy for the previous liberalizations. (There is an irrationality here. Marriage has been undermined by high rates of spousal abuse and divorce—not by admitting new couples to the institution. If traditionalists want to protect marriage, they should defend spouses against abuse and make divorce harder.)

Evidence that the defense-of-marriage argument is a displaced anxiety about the decline of marriage can be found in the popularity of the polygamy analogy. Opponents of same-sex marriage argue that once marriage is opened up to two persons of the same sex, it must or will then be opened up to three persons.[42] Analytically, this is a tendentious argument. The right to marry can be limited if the state has a strong justification for doing so. A fourteen-year-old girl's right to marry can be limited for standard parentalist reasons: the adolescent's decision-making capacities are not fully developed, and she is prone to poor choices, especially if they are made under the influence of an older lover. The adult man's right to have two wives can, similarly, be limited if the state can show (as I think it can) that polygamy would undermine the status of women in the family and in society. There is no similarly persuasive justification for denying a lesbian the right to marry the partner of her choice. Indeed, the reason why polygamy is problematic—women's equality trumps traditional gender roles—is also the reason why denying marriage to same-sex couples is sex disrimination.[43]

## CONCLUSION

I hope that the foregoing account has revealed that the public debate about same-sex-marriage implicates deep issues about the meaning of equality. The same-sex-marriage debate illustrates how equality can be formal, reparative, and transformative and how these different conceptions of equality can be deployed by opponents as well as proponents of social reform movements. Along these lines, the gay rights movement is replicating and sometimes deepening the political and intellectual lessons of racial civil rights and women's rights movements. But the same-sex-marriage movement has some conceptually distinctive features as well. Most obvious from my account is the idea that resistance to egalitarian demands is ultimately grounded not just in status competition or even the social-endowment effect, but in larger cultural anxieties, especially anxieties about appropriate sexuality. The sex negativity especially notable about the United States, but also characteristic of the West as a whole, is classically revealed in the same-sex-marriage debate. Fervent opposition to same-sex marriage is best explained by fears about its unpredictable and possibly catastrophic effect on adolescent sexuality, homosexuality in the public culture, and the romantic and friendship features of marriage itself. Even the supporters of same-sex marriage, such as I, emphasize the civilizing, domesticating features of the institution. The ultimate fear both sides share is that sexuality is becoming a consumer good, merely hedonic (pleasure-giving), without the deepening interpersonal features St. Augustine celebrated.

Second, equality is a discursive production rather than a legal one. What is at stake in the same-sex-marriage movement appears, superficially, to be the same entitlements for same-sex couples that different-sex couples can now receive. These entitlements can indeed be important, but they are hardly what is at stake. The debate itself is what is at stake. By grabbing the national agenda, the same-sex-marriage movement and its most fervent opponents are creating a discursive equality that is important to lesbian and gay rights: for the first time in modern Western history, lesbian and gay couples are being routinely referred to in the public sphere as "married," and an increasing array of private as well as public actors are taking their claims to benefits and duties seriously. Even if not a single American state recognizes same-sex marriages as a matter of law, a certain kind of equality will have advanced, and the continued denial of formal equality will assure a continuing constitutional agitation and ensuing public discourse concerning the topic. A turning point has been reached in the United States without the same-sex-marriage movement's winning a single vote.

Finally, equality generates new inequalities. The metaphor that has most dominated queer theory has been that of the closet, the hybrid of refuge and prison in which most gay people still discreetly reside. A powerful reason for citizen opposition to same-sex marriage, and the genuine object of the no-promo-homo argument, is fear that many more gay people and couples will come out of their closets if the state recognizes their unions as marriages. This fear is characteristically overstated; only a few thousand same-sex couples have registered as partners in the ten-year history of the Danish law. The more interesting concern about same-sex marriage is that it will generate new inequalities. By promoting same-sex couples to equality with different-sex couples, same-sex marriage as it is heavily endowed in the West may discursively devalue cohabiting relationships of all sorts and the lives of people not desiring to form long-term committed relationships.

## NOTES

1. See William N. Eskridge, Jr., *The Case for Same-Sex Marriage*, ch. 2 (1996).

2. On the 1989 Danish law and subsequent developments in Scandinavia, the Netherlands, France, Germany, Canada, and other countries, see generally Robert Wintemute & Mads Andenaes, eds., *Legal Recognition of Same-Sex Partnerships* (2001).

3. See The Attorney General v. M. and H., 171 D.L.R. (4th) 577 (Can. Sup. Ct. 1999); Decision 14/1995 on the legal equality of same-sex partnerships (Hung. Sup. Ct. Mar. 13, 1995).

4. Canada v. Mossop, [1993] S.C.R. 554, 630–631 (L'Heureux-Dubé, J., dissenting).

5. [1998] 1 S.C.R. 493, 156 D.L.R. (4th) 385 (Can. Sup. Ct. 1998).

6. 171 D.L.R. (4th) 577 (Can. Sup. Ct. 1999).

7. See Regina v. Oakes, [1986] 1 S.C.R. 102, 26 D.L.R. (4th) 200 (Can. Sup. Ct. 1986).

8. Social science studies indicate that children raised by lesbian and gay parents do not "suffer" ill effects. See generally Carlos A. Ball & Janice Farrell Pea, "Warring with Wardle: Social Science, Morality, and Gay and Lesbian Parents," 1998 *U. Ill. L. Rev.* 253 (reviewing the literature and responding to Lynn D. Wardle, "The Potential Impact of Homosexual Parenting on Children," 1997 *U. Ill. L. Rev.* 833). For a thoughtful middle view, see Judith Stacey & Timothy Biblarz, "(How) Does the Sexual Orientation of Parents Matter?," 66 *Am. Soc. Rev.* 159 (2001).

9. Loving v. Virginia 388 U.S. 1, 12 (1967).

10. Baehr v. Lewin 852 P.2d 44 (Haw. 1993).

11. See Andrew Koppelman, "Why Discrimination Against Lesbians and Gay Men Is Sex Discrimination," 69 *N.Y.U. L. Rev.* 197 (1994).

12. Baehr v. Miike, 1996 WL 694235 (Haw. Cir. Ct. Dec. 1997), vacated sub nom. Baehr v. Anderson, 994 P.2d 566 (Haw. Sup. Ct. Dec. 9, 1999).

13. See United States v. Virginia, 518 U.S. 515 (1996).

14. *M. and H.*, 171 D.L.R. (4th) at 620–621, quoting Law v. Canada, 170 D.L.R. (4th) 1, 32 (Can. Sup. Ct. 1999).

15. *Loving*, 388 U.S. at 12.

16. Zablocki v. Redhail, 434 U.S. 374, 385 (1978), quoting Cleveland Board of Education v. LaFleur, 414 U.S. 632, 639–640 (1974).

17. *Id.* at 387 n.12 & 388.

18. Turner v. Safley, 482 U.S. 78, 95 (1987).

19. See the sources in note 8612 above.

20. See, e.g., Craig v. Boren, 429 U.S. 190 (1976) (invalidating a state law allowing eighteen- to twenty-one-year-old women, but not men, to buy 2 percent beer). Note that most sex-based discriminations do harm or exclude women.

21. Romen v. Evans 517 U.S. 620 (1996).

22. See Washington v. Davis, 426 U.S. 229 (1976).

23. *Evans*, 517 U.S. at 632 and 634–635, quoting Department of Agriculture v. Moreno, 413 U.S. 528, 534 (1973).

24. See Eskridge, *Case for Same-Sex Marriage* 66–70, 215–217; David Chambers, "What If? The Legal Consequences of Marriage and the Legal Needs of Lesbian and Gay Male Couples," 95 *Mich. L. Rev.* 447 (1996).

25. See, e.g., Derrick Bell, Jr., *Race, Racism, and American Law* (3d ed. 1992); Kimberlé Crenshaw, "Race, Reform, and Retrenchment: Transformation and Legitimation in Antidiscrimination Law," 101 *Harv. L. Rev.* 1331 (1988).

26. See Owen Fiss, "Groups and the Equal Protection Clause," 5 *Phil. & Pub. Aff.* 107 (1976).

27. See generally William N. Eskridge, Jr., *Gaylaw: Challenging the Apartheid of the Closet* (1999); Andrew Koppelman, Why Gay Legal History Matters, 113 *Harv. L. Rev.* 2035 (2000) (reviewing Eskridge, *Gaylaw*).

28. See, e.g., Catharine MacKinnon, *Toward a Feminist Theory of the State* (1991) and "Reflections of Sex Equality Under Law," 100 *Yale L.J.* 1281 (1991); Deborah

Rhode, *Justice and Gender: Sex Discrimination and the Law*, chs. 6–11 (1989); Mary Becker, "Prince Charming: Abstract Equality," 1987 *Sup. Ct. Rev.* 201.

29. See Letitia A. Peplau, "Lesbian and Gay Relationships," in *Homosexuality: Research Implications for Public Policy* 177, 183 (J.C. Gonsiorek ed. 1991); M.S. Schneider, "The Relationships of Cohabiting Lesbian and Heterosexual Couples: A Comparison," 10 *Psychology of Women Q.* 234–239 (1986); *M. and H.*, 171 D.L.R. (4th) at 60–61 (Gonthier, J., dissenting).

30. See Nan D. Hunter, "Marriage, Law, and Gender: A Feminist Inquiry," 1 *Law & Sexuality* 9 (1991).

31. See Paula L. Ettelbrick, "Since When Is Marriage a Path to Liberation?," *OUTLOOK*, Autumn 1989, at 8–12; Martha A. Fineman, *The Neutered Mother, the Sexual Family, and Other Twentieth Century Tragedies* (1995).

32. Jones v. Hallahan, 501 S.W.2d 588, 589 (Ky. 1973); see G. Sidney Buchanan, "Same-Sex Marriage: The Linchpin Issue," 10 *U. Dayton L. Rev.* 541 (1985).

33. But see John M. Finnis, "Law, Morality, and 'Sexual Orientation,' " 69 *Notre Dame L. Rev.* 1049 (1994), who interprets St. Augustine's distinction to assume that the unitive and procreative purposes of marriage are interrelated; by engaging in penile-vaginal intercourse, the sterile couple is doing the best it can to follow the natural-law script.

34. See Lawrence Kurdek, "Relationship Outcomes and Their Predictors: Longitudinal Evidence from Heterosexual Married, Gay Cohabiting, and Lesbian Cohabiting Couples," 60 *J. Marr. & Fam.* 553 (1998).

35. See Eskridge, *Case for Same-Sex Marriage*, ch. 2.

36. E.g., Rev. Louis Sheldon, "Gay Marriage 'Unnatural,' " *USA Today*, Dec. 9, 1996 ("homosexual marriage is an oxymoron").

37. See Pope John Paul II, "Letter to Families" (Feb. 2, 1994), reprinted in 23 *Origins* 637 (Mar. 3, 1994); Richard A. Posner, *Sex and Reason* 311 (1992); Finnis, "Law, Morality, and 'Sexual Orientation,' " 1051–1053.

38. The various scientific theories of sexual orientation are critically discussed in Edward Stein, *The Mismeasure of Desire: The Science, Theory, and Ethics of Sexual Orientation* (1999).

39. Defense of Marriage Act, Pub. L. No. 104-199, 110 Stat. 2419 (1996).

40. See George Grant & Mark A. Horne, *Legislating Immorality: The Homosexuality Movement Comes out of the Closet* 97–99 (1993); The Ramsey Colloquium, "The Homosexual Movement," 41 *First Things* 15, 17 (1994).

41. See Jana B. Singer, "The Privatization of Family Law," 1992 *Wis. L. Rev.* 1443.

42. E.g., Hadley Arkes, "Questions of Principle, Not Predictions," 84 *Geo. L.J.* 321, 326 (1995); Charles Krauthammer, "When John and Jim Say, 'I Do': If Gay Marriages Are O.K., Then What About Polygamy? Or Incest?," *Time*, July 22, 1996, at 102.

43. See Maura I. Strassberg, "Distinctions of Form or Substance: Monogamy, Polygamy, and Same-Sex Marriage," 75 *N.C.L. Rev.* 1502 (1997).

Response

# *Beyond Equality*

## Lynn D. Wardle

In his essay "The Same-Sex-Marriage Debate and Three Conceptions of Equality," Professor William N. Eskridge, Jr., summarizes three equality arguments for same-sex marriage based in contemporary American and Canadian constitutional doctrines, articulates three theories of equality that might be furthered by legalizing same-sex marriage, and criticizes the use of these same three theories by opponents of same-sex marriage. The simple sophistication and disarming charm of his essay conceal some huge assumptions that challenge deeply rooted principles of equality, marriage, and social order.

Professor Eskridge suggests that sexual orientation should be deemed a suspect classification triggering heightened judicial scrutiny, as it is in Canada. He invokes *Loving v. Virginia*, in which the Supreme Court of the United States held that a state law barring interracial marriage violated equal protection.[1] However, the designation of race as a suspect classification reflects a constitutional consensus established by supermajoritarian enactment of the Fourteenth Amendment. No similar mandate exists for giving preference to homosexual orientation. Race is unrelated to any legitimate purpose states could have for regulating marriage, but sexual behavior is directly related to the fundamental purposes of marriage laws. As General Colin Powell put it in another setting: "Skin color is a benign non-behavioral characteristic. Sexual orientation is perhaps the most profound of human behavioral characteristics. Comparison of the two is a convenient but invalid argument."[2]

Suspect classifications like race involve immutable biological characteristics; same-sex attraction is not immutable (as the large and growing number of happily married heterosexual ex-gays and ex-lesbians attests). Allusion to claims that homosexual attraction is caused by immutable biology is unpersuasive because numerous efforts to find organic brain causes or "gay genes" have been repeatedly discredited.

Professor Eskridge argues that refusal to legalize same-sex marriage violates gays' and lesbians' basic freedom to marry. But that begs the essential question: What is marriage? If marriage refers to a special relationship between a man and a woman, it is not a violation of the right to marry for a state not to confer the status of marriage on same-sex couples. Professor Eskridge's argument that *Zablocki v. Redhail* supports the claim that same-sex marriage is a fundamental right fails because in *Zablocki* the Supreme Court emphasized that it was protecting "the decision to marry and raise the child *in a traditional family setting*."[3] In protecting the right of Redhail to marry his pregnant girlfriend, the Court also linked the constitutionally protected relationship of marriage directly with procreation, identifying marriage as "the foundation of the family and society" and "fundamental to the very existence and survival of the race."[4] Likewise, reliance on *Turner v. Safley* is misplaced.[5] The Court in *Turner* did not hold that marriage was a fundamental right because inmates could enjoy certain incidents while incarcerated; rather, it was because marriage is a fundamental right that prisoners were entitled to enjoy those incidents of marriage even though they were incarcerated.[6] The Court in *Turner* rejected a "functional-equivalence" argument similar to Professor Eskridge's when it upheld severe prison restrictions on other relationships with similar functional and emotional benefits.[7]

Professor Eskridge's assertion that laws restricting marriage to male-female couples are tainted by prejudice or animus confuses traditional morality (which underlies most contemporary and common law) with animus and prejudice. Marriage laws based upon the traditional belief that homosexual relations are not morally equivalent to male-female marriage manifest no more "animus" or "prejudice" than laws based upon traditional beliefs that murder, rape, incest, stealing, lying, and fraud are immoral. The Court's decision in *Romer v. Evans*, holding that Colorado's sweeping disenfranchisement amendment was unconstitutional, was tailored to avoid implicating marriage laws.[8] By indicating that laws discriminating against homosexual relations would be upheld if they were rationally related to any legitimate state interest, *Romer* tacitly endorsed male-female marriage, which protects compelling social interests in safe sex, responsible procreation, optimal child rearing, social order, and civic virtue and is deeply rooted in the history of America and of the world.

The legal status of marriage reflects the reality that the union of two persons of different genders creates a special relationship of unique potential strengths and inimitable potential value to society. The integration of the universe of gender differences (profound and subtle, biological and cultural, psychological and genetic) associated with sexual identity constitutes the core and essence of marriage and greatly benefits children.

Professor Eskridge argues that formal equality supports legalization of same-sex marriage. However, since the rejection of the separate-but-equal doctrine in equality law, formal equality disconnected from substantive equality has had no moral or constitutional merit. Equality does not mandate that things that are substantively different must be treated formally as if they were the same. Abraham Lincoln is said to have once asked a heckler how many legs a dog would have if you called the tail a leg. To the response "five legs," Lincoln said, "No; calling a tail a leg doesn't make it a leg."[9]

Professor Eskridge argues that same-sex marriage would further reparative gender equality, but he provides no evidence of a link between male-female marriage and invidious discrimination against women. Rather than violating equality principles, heterosexual marriage is the oldest gender-equality institution in the law. The requirement that marriage consist of both a man and a woman emphasizes the absolute equality and equal necessity of both sexes for the most fundamental unit of society. It recognizes the indispensable and equal contribution of both genders to the basic institution of our society.

Legalizing same-sex marriage would promote transformative equality, Professor Eskridge asserts. Certainly it would revolutionize the institution of marriage. That is a powerful reason for opposition to same-sex marriage. In these days when marriage has already been weakened by many social forces, what is needed is restoration and revitalization of marriage, not a mutation of it to erase what remains of its institutional integrity. If persons practicing homosexual relations are allowed to marry, why not persons practicing polygamy, incest, and other long-forbidden relationships? Must any relationship of intimacy and commitment be deemed a marriage? The concession that legalizing same-sex marriage will transform marriage undermines the equality claim, for equality is predicated upon the notion that the law should treat like things alike, and it is the difference between same-sex unions and existing marriages that would transform the institution of marriage.

Finally, Professor Eskridge admits that the "formal, reparative, and transformative . . . conceptions of equality can be deployed by opponents as well as proponents" of same-sex marriage.[10] That is a courageous admission that beyond equality are directive values. Advocates of same-sex marriage use equality to promote the substantive value of transforming society to embrace and support homosexual relationships. Opponents use equality to protect the interests of children, families, and society by preserving the integrity of the foundational institution of social order.

## NOTES

1. 388 U.S. 1 (1967).

2. Gen. Colin L. Powell, Letter to Representative Patricia Schroeder (May 8, 1992), in David F. Burrelli, Homosexuals and U.S. Military Personnel Policy, at 25–26 (1993); see also Gen. Colin Powell, Gays in the Military, Hearing of the Military Forces and Personnel Subcomm. of the House Armed Serv., Comm., Fed. News Serv., July 21, 1993, at 26.

3. 434 U.S. 374, 386 (1978) (emphasis added).

4. 434 U.S. at 384 (citing Maynard v. Hill, 125 U.S. 190, 211 (1988), and Skinner v. Oklahoma, 316 U.S. 535, 541 (1942)).

5. 482 U.S. 78 (1987).

6. 482 U.S. at 94.

7. 482 U.S. at 113–15 (Stevens, J., dissenting in part).

8. 517 U.S. 620 (1996).

9. Lynn D. Wardle, *Legal Claims for Same-Sex Marriage: Efforts to Legitimate a Retreat from Marriage by Redefining Marriage*, 39 S. Tex. L. Rev. 735 (1998).

10. William N. Eskridge, *The Same-Sex-Marriage Debate and Three Conceptions of Equality, supra*, at 182.

Essay Two

# Marriage, Relationships, Same-Sex Unions, and the Right of Intimate Association

## Lynn D. Wardle

### INTIMATE ASSOCIATIONS, RELATIONSHIPS, AND SAME-SEX UNIONS

Same-sex marriage is not likely to be legalized in any American jurisdictions in the foreseeable future. The battle over marriage has been fought, and advocates of legalizing same-sex marriage have lost, and lost convincingly, whenever the people have been allowed to vote on the issue. Statewide ballot decisions in Hawaii, Alaska, California, Nebraska, and Nevada (by votes ranging from 61 percent to 70 percent against legalizing same-sex marriage) and legislative enactments in nearly two-thirds of the states have emphatically confirmed that the overwhelming majority of Americans still strongly believe that marriage is a unique relationship that should be preserved exclusively as the union of a man and a woman.[1]

While the question of the definition of marriage has been largely settled as a matter of democratic governmental policy, at least for the time being, several critical questions remain to be decided in the ongoing public policy battle over same-sex unions, and these will occupy American lawmakers and courts for many years to come. In this essay, I will address one of these critical remaining issues: Should or must states create a new domestic institution for same-sex couples, like Danish domestic partnerships or Vermont civil unions (herein both called "domestic partnerships"), with legal status, rights, benefits, and obligations comparable to marriage? In the second part of this essay, I review the developing movement to treat all adult consensual intimate relationships as equivalent and will suggest some flaws in this movement. In the third part I rehearse some of the most appealing arguments for legalizing same-sex domestic partnership and attempt to show that these proposals are both impossible and unwise. In the fourth part I review the constitutional version of the argument that same-sex relationships must be given special governmental protection and explain briefly why the constitutional right of intimate association does not compel states to legalize same-sex domestic partnerships.

## THE MOVEMENT TO SUBSTITUTE GENERIC ADULT INTIMATE "RELATIONSHIPS" FOR "MARRIAGE"

Within the last thirty years, a new discipline, the science of close relationships, has emerged.[2]

Close relationship theorists argue that we need to bring a common theoretical and methodological approach to the study of all "sexually based primary relationships." They argue that, at the level of relational processes, alternative sexual lifestyles are not "qualitatively other from what is known as the benchmark conventional nuclear family." Close relationship theorists are convinced that the traditional nuclear family can no longer serve as a meaningful paradigm and focus for scholarly research. They maintain that current social trends are on their side. . . . According to John Scanzoni and Karen Polonko, courtship, spousal, and familial relationships can and should be "subsumed under the broader construct of close or *primary* relationships."

The "generalizing construct" for research on adult relationships should be the construct of "primary" or "close" relationships, [these scholars assert]. The main focus of close relationship research is "dyadic," or the relationship between two people. Close relationships are characterized by "strong, frequent, and diverse interdependence that lasts over a considerable period of time." . . .

One result of redefining all relationships as inherently "dyadic" is that it becomes all but impossible to see the institutional aspects of marriage. In the taxonomy of sexually based adult relationships, the presence or absence of a legally recognized bond, such as marriage, is a secondary consideration. Marriage is merely a "de jure" category, not an actual scientific reality. In addition, the family itself largely fades away as a unit of analysis. For close relationship theorists, the only way effectively to understand a family system is to break it down into bi-directional dyadic pairs: father-mother, mother-child, father-child, or brother-sister relationships.[3]

The "relationships" movement also emerged in legal writing in the 1970s. For example, Justice William Brennan's well-known dictum in *Eisenstadt v. Baird* boldly declared:

[T]he marital couple is not an independent entity with a mind and heart of its own, but an association of two individuals each with a separate intellectual and emotional makeup. If the right of privacy means anything, it is the right of the *individual*, married or single, to be free from unwarranted governmental intrusion into matters so fundamentally affecting a person as the decision whether to bear or beget a child.[4]

In a subsequent line of "privacy" cases, especially abortion cases, certain members of the Supreme Court developed this atomistic view of marriage in dicta and holdings attempting to reformulate the vision and role of marriage. In *Planned Parenthood v. Casey*, the plurality declared that the Constitution protects "the right to define one's own concept of existence, of meaning, of the universe, and of the mystery of human life."[5] Later in the same opinion, the role of marriage and homemaking was denigrated in clear terms. "Only one generation has passed since the Court observed that 'woman is still regarded as the center of home and family life,' with attendant 'special responsibilities' that precluded full and independent legal status under the Constitution. . . . These views are no longer consistent with our understanding of the family, the individual, or the Constitution."[6] While these expressions have had little impact on constitutional law outside the area of contraception and abortion regulation, they have created an alternative line of cases challenging the long-established precedents that emphasize the unique importance and value of marriage to individuals and society.[7] Of course, many legal scholars have embraced the notion that relationships are the new paradigm in lieu of the traditional marriage-based family.[8]

The movement to substitute adult personal relationships for marriage is beginning to influence legislation and proposed legislation dealing with families. For example, in May 2000 the prestigious American Law Institute approved model family law reforms entitled *Principles of the Law of Family Dissolution*, including provisions for recognition of nonmarital domestic partnerships (both heterosexual and homosexual, by both married [with extramarital paramours] and unmarried persons) and for the extension to such relationships of the same economic benefits that married spouses enjoy upon dissolution of the relationship.[9] These economic incidents of marriage are extended to same-sex and heterosexual cohabitants who "for a significant period of time share a primary residence and a life together as a couple."[10] In proving that they shared their life and residence, claimants are aided by two strong presumptions that arise after cohabitation for a minimal period.[11] Property acquired during the relationship "should be divided according to the principles set forth for the division of marital property,"[12] and "a domestic partner is entitled to [alimony] on the same basis as a spouse."[13]

Also in the millennial year, the Vermont legislature passed "An Act Relating to Civil Unions" creating a new legal status called "civil unions" with registration and benefits comparable to those of marriage.[14] Parties to "civil unions" are deemed "spouse[s]" and "family" and are included in other terms that denote the marital relationship. The statute further states that parties to civil unions "shall have all the same benefits, protections and responsibilities under law . . . as are granted to spouses in a marriage."[15] The new Vermont civil-union statute "sets out a nonexclusive list of benefits available to spouses and explicitly grants the same benefits to parties to a civil union."[16] "For example, parties to a civil union are responsible for supporting each other to the same extent that spouses are."[17]

Likewise, the Law Commission of Canada recently published a discussion paper entitled *Recognizing and Supporting Close Personal Relationships Between Adults* to consider how the Canadian Parliament could reform existing law in order to support all forms of intimate adult relationships.[18] The paper began with two very questionable assumptions: "A broad diversity of close adult personal relationships is a sign of a vibrant society. Permitting people to form relationships that matter to them and in which they can find happiness and comfort is the mark of pluralism and freedom."[19] In its conclusion, the Law Commission discussion paper features this revealing quote: "All people should be able to freely choose their intimate partners and their legal relational status without penalty from the state or without financial inducement to abandon their choices. . . . The role of the law ought to be to support any and all relationships that further valuable social goals, and to remain neutral with respect to individuals' choice of a particular family form."[20]

Thus there is a growing movement to substitute generic adult intimate relationships for "marriage" in our public law and policy. The proposal to legalize same-sex domestic partnerships and give them quasi-marital status and benefits is a logical extension of the "relationships" movement.

## WHY SAME-SEX DOMESTIC PARTNERSHIP IS AN IMPOSSIBLY BAD IDEA

At first blush, some arguments for legalizing same-sex domestic partnerships or civil unions seem very appealing. These arguments go something like this:

Like it or not, there are many same-sex couples in this country. Many of them have made the decision to fully share and integrate their lives, resources, and obligations. They are willing to assume (and often voluntarily have undertaken) legal, economic, and emotional responsibility for each other in some ways similar to married couples. They desire legal protections for their joint, intertwined lives and relationships. Yet their relationships are not legally recognized; they do not enjoy any legal status, protection, or benefits as couples. At least the economic dimensions of these relationships should be recognized.

Because of the significant socialization of economic life in America, the failure to legally recognize same-sex unions has very severe consequences. Before significant federal (and state) income taxes, welfare programs, Social Security, Medicaid, employee benefits, and pension laws mandating protections for spouses existed, the fact that the government did not recognize a couple's relationship could have comparatively minimal economic consequences. Today, however, with so many economic dimensions of our personal lives controlled and regulated by government rules, the fact that the government does not recognize a couple's relationship has much greater potential economic significance than ever before. In a semi-socialist economy, people ought not to be denied basic governmental benefits (food, shelter, and medical assistance, for example) just because their relationship is unpopular or does not conform to widely held views of personal morality.

Moreover, legalizing same-sex unions would give these relationships more stability, and that would benefit these couples and the public generally. America has a long tradition of innovation, experimentation with new forms and structures, and accommodation of the "free spirits" who want to try different paths and exercise their freedom to be different.

It is not obvious how recognition of same-sex domestic partnership would impair the institution of marriage. There is growing social acceptance of homosexual couples already, and that does not seem to have hurt marriages. The only people who might be hurt if the law recognizes same-sex domestic partnerships are the partners who voluntarily choose to enter these relationships, and they assumed the risk.

These arguments appeal to powerful principles of pluralism, tolerance, legal realism, and socioeconomic realism that are deeply ingrained in the American legal tradition, and, at first blush, they seem very attractive. They seem to support the creation of a new, nonmarital relationship—domestic partnership—with legal status and benefits that are tailored to the characteristics of same-sex relationships. The critical key is that domestic partnership must be *unique*—it must be significantly and obviously different from marriage in its legal characteristics and attributes and reflect the relationship's distinctive contribution to society. Otherwise, domestic partnership would (*a*) amount to same-sex marriage by another name, (*b*) pose a serious threat to marriage by confusing the concept and meaning of marriage, (*c*) send a false message to society concerning the qualities and characteristics of the relationships, and (*d*) result in excessive, unjust benefits disproportionate to the contributions of these relationships to society. Thus it is essential that domestic partnership be customized, limited, and unique, not just an imitation of marriage. Therein lies the fatal flaw.

While the creation of a carefully tailored, customized domestic partnership statute might be appealing intellectually, it is impossible. First, many gay advocates would be offended and oppose it because, for reasons ranging from a desire for the social validation to purely economic motives, they demand no less than benefits and status equal to those of marriage—the same benefits and status that are enjoyed by married couples. Second, activist courts would not be satisfied. As *Baker v. State* shows, if an activist court believes that it can get away with it, it will mandate full, equivalent status to that of marriage.[21] By enacting a customized, limited domestic partnership bill, the legislature would send a message of vulnerability that even the slowest activist or sympathetic judge would recognize and exploit.

Third, the creation of a customized domestic partnership would make it easier for advocates of same-sex marriage or marriage-equivalent domestic partnership to convince courts that equal protection mandates giving status and benefits fully equivalent to those of marriage to same-sex couples. The argument is simple: By enacting a narrow, customized domestic partnership law, the state has recognized the inequality of denying same-sex couples marital status and benefits; thus equality is in order; but the limited domestic partnership the legislature created is not equal to marriage; the remedy is that the state must expand the benefits and status it created to provide status and benefits to same-sex couples fully equivalent to those of marriage. The Vermont Supreme Court applied a similar "trick" analysis in *Baker v. State*, noting that by enacting (after judicial decision) a law allowing same-sex couples to adopt children, the state had effectively conceded that same-sex couples were as good (as parents) as heterosexual couples, and since child rearing is one of the key reasons for marriage, it followed (said the court) that the state had to go all the way and either legalize same-sex marriage or grant equivalent status (civil unions) to same-sex couples. If the Common Benefits Clause of the Vermont Constitution can be judicially manipulated to mandate marriage-equivalent same-sex civil unions, comparable provisions of other states' constitutions could also be so manipulated.

Fourth, defenders of traditional marriage would oppose the "camel's-nose" proposal, for they would foresee that it would lead to the creation of a marriage-equivalent status. Fifth, advocates of federalism and separation of powers, who believe that such fundamental public policy questions should be decided by democratic processes, would object to the invitation to judicial legislation. Thus the enactment of a customized, limited domestic partnership would offend nearly everyone, invite litigation, and evolve into an imitation-marriage form of domestic partnership with full benefits and status equal to marriage—the very thing a carefully tailored domestic partnership would be designed to avoid.

There are also other problems with the arguments for legalizing same-sex domestic partnerships. On close examination, the risks to the institution of marriage are simply ignored, and the argument for economic protection is based on highly debatable assumptions. While this is not obvious to those obsessed with the immediately and evident, legalizing same-sex domestic partnership would significantly devalue, weaken, and compromise the critical institution of marriage. It is just a small step from same-sex domestic partnership to same-sex marriage.[22]

Scandinavian countries have recognized same-sex domestic partnership for a dozen years and heterosexual domestic partnerships for decades. The experience of these countries suggests that legalizing domestic partnerships weakens marriage. "[T]here is evidence that the widespread substitution of cohabitation for marriage in Sweden has given that country the highest rate of family dissolution and single parenting in the developed world."[23] Moreover, the demographer William Goode suggests that after marriage is weakened in a society, it is nearly impossible to revitalize it without perhaps some traumatic and dramatic external pressure such as military conquest, economic collapse, or natural disaster of widespread proportions.[24] It is very difficult to put the genie back in the bottle. Before starting down the road to domestic partnership, we had better be very sure that it leads in a direction we want to go, for history suggests that it is a one-way street.

The assumption that same-sex unions are fungible with marriages in terms of social policy is false. The heterosexual dimensions of the relationship are at the very core of what makes "marriage" what it is and why it is so valuable to individuals and to society. The union of two persons of different genders creates something of unique potential strengths and inimitable potential value to society. It is the integration of the universe of gender differences (profound and subtle, biological and cultural, psychological and genetic) associated with sexual identity that constitutes the core and essence of marriage. In the same way that "separate but equal" was a false promise, and that racial segregation is not equivalent to racial integration, same-sex marriage is not equal to real, heterosexual marriage. Thus cross-gender uniting in marriage is not merely a matter of arbitrary definition or semantic word play; it goes to the heart of the very concept or nature of the marriage relationship itself. A union of two men or of two women is not the same as the union of a man and a woman.

The main weakness of close-relationship theory "is that it radically relativizes and privatizes every possible dimension of human relationships, rejecting any criterion for relationship success other than the self's subjective assessment of the self's needs, denying any real connection between courtship and marriage, and obliterating any meaningful distinction between marriage and other sexually close relationships."[25] It is simplistically reductionist and, in its haste to see similarities, overlooks and eliminates the essence of what makes marriage valuable for couples and for society. "Marriage is not just an inferior version of going steady, or a sexual barter, or a consumer good. Love is more than a style."[26] Marriage has an ethical and moral dimension lacking in other relationships that transfigures it into a truly unique institution.

The astounding thing about the close-relationships movement is that it has developed at a time in history when there is overwhelming evidence of the unique value and superior benefits of marriage compared to other adult intimate relationships. Married couples live longer, are healthier, report that they are happier, have lower rates of mental illness, have lower rates of substance abuse, earn more, have more (and more enjoyable) sexual intercourse, and experience less physical and emotional abuse, and their children are happier than children of unmarried adults, use drugs less, engage in less teenage sexual behavior, have fewer pregnancies and fewer children out of wedlock, do better in school, and commit fewer crimes. In fact, marriage is a boon on almost all personal and social indicia of well-being for adults and children.[27]

## THE CONSTITUTIONAL RIGHT OF INTIMATE ASSOCIATION DOES NOT PROTECT SAME-SEX RELATIONSHIPS

Some advocates of compulsory legal protection for same-sex unions invoke the "right to intimate associations." The basic argument is that the Constitution shelters an unwritten right of persons to form and maintain intimate human relationships, that the consensual relationship between adult homosexuals who are committed to each other is among the intimate human relationships protected by the constitutional right of intimate association, and that the failure to extend to same-sex couples legal status and benefits unconstitutionally infringes this fundamental right.

In an influential 1980 law review article, Professor Kenneth Karst defined "intimate association" as a "close and personal relationship with another that is in some significant way comparable to a marriage or family relationship,"[28] asserted that the right to form and maintain such associations is the real basis for the "right-to-privacy" cases, and argued that it included protection for and expression of "the values of self-identification, intimacy, and caring and commitment."[29] Professor Karst suggested that "the freedom of intimate association extends to homosexual associations."[30] Professor Milton Regan asserts that homosexual relations constitute the functional equivalent of heterosexual marriage for persons who believe themselves to be gay or lesbian, and should be given constitutional protection as a form of intimate association because homosexual relations are, for some couples, as crucial to their own identity and fulfillment as marriage is for heterosexual couples.[31]

A few courts have embraced this approach. For example, in *Brause v. Bureau of Vital Statistics*, Anchorage Superior Court Judge Peter Michalski invoked this concept when he denied the Alaska attorney general's motion to dismiss a lawsuit by same-sex couples seeking to compel the state to legalize same-sex marriage.[32] The court held that "the recognition [by the state] of one's choice of a life partner, is a fundamental right."[33]

Dicta in some Supreme Court opinions have acknowledged that the Constitution protects "choices to enter into and maintain certain intimate human relationships,"[34] characterized by "relative smallness, a high degree of selectivity in decisions to begin and maintain the affiliation, and seclusion from others in critical aspects of the relationship."[35] Dicta in some cases that do not mention a "right of intimate association" might also be cited to support the claim to special constitutional protection for same-sex domestic partnership.[36]

On closer examination, however, the claim that the fundamental right of intimate associations requires legalization of same-sex domestic partnership falls far short. To begin with, what a particular individual or couple subjectively believes to be the functional equivalent of constitutionally protected marital relationship is not a sound basis for creating new constitutional rights. Social order, as well as constitutional integrity, requires a more objective test. Moreover, this argument proves too much because there are many persons whose preferred intimate associations involve pedophilia, incest, polygamy, or bestiality, as well as same-sex relations. Surely subjective personal identity cannot be the test for this constitutional right; for some people, smoking or drinking or using drugs is as much a strongly held personal identity issue as homosexual relations are claimed to be by the most passionate advocates of same-sex marriage. The immutability considerations (at least that of biological dependency) involved with chemical dependency in tobacco, alcohol, and drug use are at least as credible as the immutability arguments for homosexual behavior.

Second, while many of the cases holding that certain family relationships are fundamental constitutional rights could be grouped comfortably under the "intimate-association" label, that does not mean that all aspects of all family relations or all long-term, meaningful, close personal or sexual associations have fundamental-right status. "The freedom of intimate association is . . . a useful organizing principle, not a machine that, once set in motion, must run to all conceivable logical conclusions"; otherwise, it would become "an invitation to moral chaos."[37]

Third, careful examination of the cases in which the Supreme Court has mentioned a possible "right of intimate association" reveals the narrowness of the kinds of associations protected by any such right. The Court has emphasized that the kinds of associations that might be protected by the "right of intimate association" involve "*traditional* personal bonds,"[38] a description that does not by any stretch of revisionist historical imagination apply to same-sex domestic partnership. Moreover, the Court has never yet sustained the claim of a "right of intimate association"; all references by the Court to such a possible right are in cases in which the Court has rejected the claim.[39]

Fourth, the doctrinal underpinnings of the claim that same-sex domestic partnership is part of a fundamental constitutional right of intimate association were obliterated in *Bowers v. Hardwick*. The Eleventh Circuit Court in that case had ruled that the Georgia sodomy statute "violated respondent's fundamental rights because his homosexual activity is *a private and intimate association* that is beyond the reach of state regulation by reason of the Ninth Amendment and the Due Process Clause of the Fourteenth Amendment."[40] However, the Supreme Court reversed the Eleventh Circuit's judgment, rejected the highly rhetorical mode of constitutional rights creation used by the appellate court, used the deeply-rooted-in-tradition-or-essential-to-ordered-liberty test instead, and emphatically repudiated the "intimate-association" claim.

Fifth, even if the *Bowers* precedent is disregarded, however, the claim to a substantive constitutional right to state-legalized same-sex domestic partnership is untenable in constitutional doctrine. For example, *Shahar v. Bow-*

*ers* involved a suit by a young lesbian attorney whose offer of employment with the Georgia attorney general's office had been withdrawn when she revealed on official employment forms that she was engaged to be married to someone of the same gender. While the Eleventh Circuit panel concluded that the plaintiff stated a proper claim for violation of a constitutionally protected right of intimate association,[41] the court clearly declined to hold that the Constitution protects the right of same-sex couples to enter into a legal relationship comparable to marriage. "Homosexual relationships have not played the same role as marital or familial relationships in the history and traditions of the Nation. Shahar's relationship with her partner is not a 'fundamental element of personal liberty' protected as an intimate association."[42]

Thus Professor Nancy J. Knauer was surely correct when she wrote: " 'Domestic partnership' does not describe a relationship based on a fundamental right, such as the right to marry or the right to freedom of intimate association."[43] The issue is not a constitutional issue, and reasonable (indeed compelling) legislative policy supports the refusal to create marriage-like same-sex domestic partnership.

## CONCLUSION

The decay of the family at the dawn of the third millennium is not merely due to a lack of morals or corruption or social weakness, but also to the rise of a whole new doctrine against the family. Today, as in some previous eras, we are "contending with a new metaphysics, a different vision of life and death on this corner of the galaxy."[44] That contest is played out most prominently today in the movement to equalize in law all adult intimate relationships, and specifically in the debate over legalization of broad, quasi-marital domestic partnership. Much more depends upon this policy dispute than may be obvious, for the institution of marriage is fundamental to the social ordering and economic functioning of society. We must not succumb to the seduction of false claims of equivalence. The legalization of broad same-sex domestic partnership is neither required by the Constitution nor in the best interests of society.

## NOTES

I am grateful to John Eskelson and James Fontano for valuable research assistance. Some of the material in this essay is excerpted from Lynn D. Wardle, *A Critical Analysis of Constitutional Claims for Same-Sex Marriage*, 1996 B.Y.U. L. Rev. 1.

1. *See generally* Marriage Law Project, *State Information*, http://marriage law.cua.edu/State_in.htm; Marriage Watch, State Information, http://www. marriagewatch.org/.

2. Dan Cere, The Experts' Story of Courtship,' 15 (Institute for American Val-

ues, 2000). Cere provides a pithy review of the "close-relationship" scholarly literature. *Id.* at 15–26.

3. *Id.* at 15–16.

4. 405 U.S. 438, 453 (1972) (Brennan, J., for plurality) (emphasis in original).

5. 505 U.S. 833, 849 (1992).

6. 505 U.S. at 897.

7. *See, e.g.*, Reynolds v. United States, 98 U.S. 145, 165 (1878) (" 'Upon [marriage] society may be said to be built, and out of its fruits spring social relations and social obligations and duties, with which government is necessarily required to deal"); Murphy v. Ramsey, 114 U.S. 15, 45 (1885) ("[N]o legislation can be supposed more . . . necessary in the founding of a free, self-governing commonwealth . . . than that which seeks to establish it on the basis of the idea of the family, as consisting in and springing from the union for life of one man and one woman in the holy estate of matrimony; the sure foundation of all that is stable and noble in our civilization; the best guaranty of that reverent morality which is the source of all beneficent progress in social and political movement."); Maynard v. Hill, 125 U.S. 190, 205 (1888) ("Marriage, as creating the most important relation in life, as having more to do with the morals and civilization of a people than any other institution, has always been subject to the control of the legislature"); Skinner v. Oklahoma, 316 U.S. 535, 541 (1942) ("Marriage and procreation are fundamental to the very existence and survival of the race"); Griswold v. Connecticut, 381 U.S. 479, 486 (1965) ("Marriage is a coming together for better or for worse, hopefully enduring, and intimate to the degree of being sacred. It is an association that promotes a way of life, not causes; a harmony in living, not political faiths; a bilateral loyalty, not commercial or social projects. Yet it is an association for as noble a purpose as any involved in our prior decisions").

8. *See, e.g.*, Kenneth L. Karst, *The Freedom of Intimate Association*, 89 Yale L.J. 624 (1980); William N. Eskridge, Jr., *A History of Same-Sex Marriage*, 79 Va. L. Rev. 1419, 1421, 1447–1454, 1484 (1993); William M. Hohengarten, Note, *Same-Sex Marriage and the Right of Privacy*, 103 Yale L.J. 1495, 1496, 1523–1530 (1994); Craig W. Christensen, *Legal Ordering of Family Values: The Case of Gay and Lesbian Families*, 18 Cardozo L. Rev. 1299 (1997); Ariela R. Dubler, *Wifely Behavior: A Legal History of Acting Married*, 100 Colum. L. Rev. 957 (2000); William N. Eskridge, Jr., *Equality Practice: Liberal Reflections on the Jurisprudence of Civil Unions*, 64 Alb. L. Rev. 853 (2001).

9. *See generally* American Law Institute, *Principles of the Law of Family Dissolution: Analysis and Recommendations: Tentative Draft No. 4*, ch. 6 (April 10, 2000).

10. § 6.01(1).

11. § 6.03(1)–(5).

12. § 6.05.

13. § 6.06(1).

14. An Act Relating to Civil Unions, ARCU, § 1(1), 2000 Vt. Adv. Legis. Serv. at 68; see generally Vt. Stat. Ann. tit. 15, § 1201, 1204. *See generally Recent Legislation—Domestic Relations—Same-Sex Couples—Vermont Creates System of Civil Unions*, 114 Harv. L. Rev. 1421 (2001).

15. Vt. Stat. Ann. tit. 15, § 1204(a).

16. 114 Harv. L. Rev. at 1422 n.22, citing 2000 Vt. Adv. Legis. Serv. at 70–71, codified at Vt. Stat. Ann. tit. 15, § 1204(e).

17. *Id.*, citing 2000 Vt. Adv. Legis. Serv. at 70, codified at Vt. Stat. Ann. tit. 15, § 1204(c).

18. Law Commission of Canada, *Recognizing and Supporting Close Personal Relationships Between Adults*, (May 2000) http://www.lcc.gc.ca/en/forum/cpra (searched Jan. 15, 2001).

19. *Id.* at 3.

20. *Id.* at 38, citing B. Cossman & B. Ryder, Gay, Lesbian, and Unmarried Heterosexual Couples and the Family Law Act: Accommodating a Diversity of Family Forms 3, 5 (Toronto: Ontario Law Reform Commission, 1993).

21. Baker v. State, 744 A.2d 864 (Vt. 1999).

22. William N. Eskridge, Jr., *Comparative Law and the Same-Sex Marriage Debate: A Step-by-Step Approach Toward State Recognition*, 31 McGeorge L. Rev. 641 (2000); *see also* Eskridge, *Equality Practice, supra* note 8, at 854.

23. Irizarry v. Bd. of Educ., 251 F.3d 604, 608 (7th Cir. 2001), citing David Popenoe, Disturbing the Nest: Family Change and Decline in Modern Societies 173–174 (1988).

24. William J. Goode, World Changes in Divorce Patterns 318, 335–336 (1993).

25. Cere, *supra* note 2, at 30.

26. *Id.* at 31.

27. Linda J. Waite & Maggie Gallagher, The Case for Marriage: Why Married People Are Happier, Healthier, and Better Off Financially (2000). *See also* David Popenoe, Life Without Father: Compelling New Evidence That Fatherhood and Marriage Are Indispensable for the Good of Children and Society (1996); George W. Dent, Jr., *The Defense of Traditional Marriage*, 15 J. L. & Pol. 581 (1999); *Izararry*, 251 F.3d at 608.

28. Kenneth L. Karst, *The Freedom of Intimate Association*, 89 Yale L.J. 624, 629 (1980).

29. *Id.* at 637. "The freedom to choose our intimates and to govern our day-to-day relationships with them . . . is the foundation for the one responsibility among all others that most clearly defines our humanity." *Id.* at 692.

30. *Id.* at 682. "All the values of intimate association are potentially involved in homosexual relationships; all have been impaired, in various ways, by government restrictions." *Id.*

31. *See generally* Milton C. Regan, Jr., Family Law and the Pursuit of Intimacy 119–122, 185 (1993).

32. Brause v. Bureau of Vital Statistics, No. 3AN-95-6562 CI., 1998 WL 88743 (Alaska Super Ct., Feb. 27, 1998) (Memorandum and Order).

33. *Id.*

34. Roberts v. United States Jaycees, 468 U.S. 609, 617–618 (1984) (a voluntary business club is not protected intimate association); *see further* Board of Dirs. of Rotary Int'l v. Rotary Club, 481 U.S. 537, 545 (1987) (declining to hold that the relationships protected are limited to the family, but rejecting the claim that a service club is protected).

35. 468 U.S. at 620. Family relationships are identified by the Court as the paradigmatic example of protected intimate associations. *Id.*

36. *See, e.g.*, Planned Parenthood v. Casey, 505 U.S. 833, 851 (1992) ("At the heart of liberty is the right to define one's own concept of existence, of meaning, of

the universe, and of the mystery of human life"). *See also* Shahar v. Bowers, 70 F.3d 1218 (11th Cir. 1995).

37. Karst, 89 Yale L.J. at 692.

38. FW/PBS, Inc., v. City of Dallas, 493 U.S. 215, 237 (emphasis added).

39. *See* FW/PBS, Inc. v. City of Dallas, 493 U.S. 215, 237 (1990) (rejecting the claim that a law regulating motels offering rooms for less than ten-hour use interferes with protected intimate associations); City of Dallas v. Stangler, 490 U.S. 19, 24–25 (1989) (rejecting the claim that an ordinance regulating dance halls interferes with a protected right of intimate association); New York State Club Ass'n v. City of New York, 487 U.S. 1, 12 (private clubs do not involve intimate associations); Bd. of Dirs. of Rotary Int'l. v. Rotary, 481 U.S. 537, 545 (1987) (a civic service and social organization is not protected intimate association); Bowers v. Hardwick, 478 U.S. 186, 191 (1986) (homosexual conduct is not protected intimate association); Roberts v. U.S. Jaycees, 468 U.S. 609, 617 (1984) (a business club does not involve protected intimate associations). *See further* Rowland v. Mad River Local School District, 471 U.S. 1062 (1985) (denying certiorari in the case of a school-teacher fired for homosexuality); Boy Scouts of America v. Dale, 530 U.S. 640 (2000) (BSA may exclude gays as scoutmasters).

40. 478 U.S. at 189 (emphasis added).

41. Shahar v. Bowers, 70 F.3d 1218 (11th Cir. 1995); Shahar v. Bowers, 114 F.3d 1099 (11th Cir. 1997).

42. 114 F.3d at 1115.

43. Nancy J. Knauer, *Domestic Partnership and Same-Sex Relationships: A Marketplace Innovation and a Less Than Perfect Institutional Choice*, 7 Temp. Pol. & Civ. Rts. L. Rev. 337, 338 n. 4 (1998).

44. Brave New Family: G.K. Chesterton on Men and Women, Children, Sex, Divorce, Marriage and the Family 15 (Alvaro DiSilva ed. 1990).

# Response

# *Terms of Endearment*
## William N. Eskridge, Jr.

Professor Lynn Wardle is the leading academic opponent of state recognition for same-sex marriage. His essay in this volume is an important critique of state recognition for same-sex unions or domestic partnerships. There are a number of problems with his argument.

1. *The key arguments for same-sex unions are based on the equality principle, not a prepolitical right of intimate association.* Contrary to Wardle's apparent assumption, the starting point for legal arguments for same-sex unions is not some prepolitical irrevocable right to intimate association. Rather, the starting point is the equality principle: the state cannot arbitrarily discriminate in the apportionment of rights and duties in the polity. When the rights and duties are important (like the hundreds associated with marriage) or the discriminating criterion is a suspicious one like sex or race, courts will require a compelling reason for excluding some citizens. To use Wardle's examples, the state can exclude pedophile or polygamous relationships from recognized unions because there is good evidence that such relationships are harmful to minors and women, respectively. Contrary to Wardle, however, the state cannot constitutionally punish cigarette smokers by refusing to recognize their marriages.[1] Although such an exclusion might discourage people from activity that harms their health, the state cannot use civil marriage as an incentive or additional punishment without stronger justification.[2]

Wardle's "right of intimate association," therefore, is not a stand-alone reason for state recognition of same-sex marriages or unions. The argument, properly framed, starts with equality and invokes intimate association as a reason for heightened equal protection scrutiny. Thus the state is not obliged to provide civil recognition for anyone's "marriages," but once the state decides to recognize some marriages civilly, it cannot discriminate without a very good reason. Although the state has long excluded same-sex couples from civil marriage—just as it long excluded different-race couples—the state is having difficulty justifying that exclusion now that same-sex couples are demanding equal treatment.

2. *The state policies underlying relationship recognition apply to same-sex couples.* Wardle opposes same-sex marriage on essentially sectarian grounds: the religious natural law theory he subscribes to requires procreative possibility as a requirement for marriage. Because states recognize marriage without regard to procreative possibility and indeed protect the right of married couples to avoid or even abort procreation, no state in this country follows this particular natural-law value as the policy basis for marriage. The feature of marriage that triggers state recognition and protection is the unitive (commitment) and not the procreative feature of marriage. The state believes that mutual commitment is good because it makes the spouses happier and more secure, renders the spouses more socially productive and less likely to drain community resources, and provides a good environment in which to raise children (including adopted children and those borne of surrogacy and artificial insemination).[3]

Lesbian and gay couples are as capable as straight couples of enjoying the same kind of happiness and security and of raising children, and for that reason it makes sense for the state to extend to them the same kind of legal protections and recognitions. What is the evidence for this proposition? The best evidence is this: Get to know those of your lesbian and gay coworkers and relatives who have formed committed unions; in my view, you will find them to be just as capable of supporting one another, contributing to the community, and raising children as straight couples. If you want more systematic evidence, it is available from the social science studies of lesbian and gay households.[4] There is no solid scientific evidence to the contrary.[5]

3. *Opposition to same-sex marriage has weakened marriage by driving states to create new institutions.* Although it is inspired by either sectarian natural law (Wardle) or antigay prejudice or stereotyping (others), opposition to same-sex marriage has been successful in this country. But the success of opponents has actually weakened marriage. Consider three scenarios. (1) The state opens marriage to same-sex couples. More couples would marry than before, and there is no reason to believe that the divorce rate would go up.[6] (2) The state bows to traditionalist opposition and, instead, creates a new institution for same-sex couples. This scenario would attract some but not many people away from marriage, mainly gay or bisexual people who strongly desire a committed relationship. (3) The state creates new institutions open to different as well as same-sex couples. This scenario poses a significant threat to marriage, because many straight as well as bisexual or gay people will choose it—and its diluted reinforcement of the couples'

mutual commitments—over marriage. This scenario has already played out in the Netherlands, France, Hawaii, Vermont, and many municipalities.

By opposing state recognition of same-sex marriages, traditionalists like Wardle have contributed to a quickening reconfiguration of Western family law that offers an expanding menu of state recognition for different-sex as well as same-sex relationships.[7] The larger the menu, the more choices couples have, short of marriage. This undermines marriage and its ideal of state reinforcement of the spouses' commitment to one another and to their family. Note the irony. Wardle, the most articulate and sincere defender of marriage, is also an agent of its decline.

## NOTES

1. See Lynn D. Wardle, "Marriage, Relationships, Same-Sex Unions, and the Right of Intimate Association," p. 190 n. 39 (suggesting that "chemical dependency in tobacco" is similar to "homosexuality" and thus can be similarly stigmatized or penalized by the state).

2. *Turner v. Safley*, 482 U.S. 78 (1987) (the state cannot deprive convicted murderers and other criminals the right to civil marriage without a neutral justification).

3. On the state policies underlying civil marriage recognition, see David Chambers, "What If? The Legal Consequences of Marriage and the Legal Needs of Lesbian and Gay Male Couples," 95 *Mich. L. Rev.* 447 (1996).

4. See Lawrence Kurdek, "Relationship Outcomes and Their Predictors: Longitudinal Evidence from Heterosexual Married, Gay Cohabiting, and Lesbian Cohabiting Couples," 60 *J. Marr. & Fam.* 553 (1998), as well as the source cited in note 5 below.

5. See generally Carlos A. Ball & Janice Farrell Pea, "Warring with Wardle: Social Science, Morality, and Gay and Lesbian Parents," 1998 *U. Ill. L. Rev.* 253 (reviewing the literature and responding to Lynn D. Wardle, "The Potential Impact of Homosexual Parenting on Children," 1997 *U. Ill. L. Rev.* 833).

6. Cf. Darren Spedale, *Nordic Bliss: The Danish Experience with "Gay Marriage"* (1999 draft) (during the first decade after Denmark recognized same-sex partnerships, their divorce rate was much lower than that of different-sex married Danes, whose divorce rate also fell during that period).

7. See William N. Eskridge, Jr., *Equality Practice: Civil Unions and the Future of Gay Rights* ch. 3 (2002).

# Part III

## U.S. Constitutional Law Issues Concerning Same-Sex Marriage or Domestic Partnership

# Chapter 7

Essay One

# *Discrimination Against Gays Is Sex Discrimination*

## **Andrew Koppelman**

All laws that discriminate on the basis of sexual orientation thereby discriminate on the basis of sex and thus are subject to heightened scrutiny under the Equal Protection Clause of the Fourteenth Amendment. Since these laws are not substantially related to any important state interest, they are unconstitutional.

Owing to limitations of space in this volume, I cannot develop here the claim made in the second sentence of the preceding paragraph. That would require surveying the major claims made on behalf of discrimination against gays and showing that each is inadequate.[1] Here I will merely develop the claim made in the first sentence of the preceding paragraph and thereby show that such laws are presumptively unconstitutional.

My basic argument can be stated in two syllogisms.

## FIRST SYLLOGISM

1. Laws that make people's legal rights depend on their sex are sex-based classifications.

2. Laws that discriminate against gay people are laws that make people's legal rights depend on their sex.

*Illustrations:* If Lucy may marry Fred, but Ricky may not marry Fred, then (assuming that Fred would be a desirable spouse for either) Ricky is suffering legal disadvantage because of his sex. If a business fires Ricky, or if the state prosecutes him, because of his sexual activities with Fred, while these actions would not be taken against Lucy if she did exactly the same things with Fred, then Ricky is suffering legal disadvantage because of his sex.

Therefore:

3. Laws that discriminate against gay people are sex-based classifications.

## SECOND SYLLOGISM

1. Sex-based classifications are subject to heightened scrutiny.
2. From the first syllogism, laws that discriminate against gay people are sex-based classifications.

Therefore:

3. Laws that discriminate against gay people are subject to heightened scrutiny.

The argument has been subject to numerous objections.[2] The most common of these is that there is no discrimination, because both sexes are treated alike. Both sexes, the argument goes, are treated alike by sanctions against homosexuality, because no one of either sex may engage in sexual conduct with another person of the same sex.[3] Ricky cannot marry Fred, it is true, but Lucy likewise cannot marry Ethel.

This response happens to be the same one that was made on behalf of the laws against interracial sex or marriage: both races are equally forbidden to engage in the prohibited sexual conduct, so there is no race discrimination.[4] That argument was rejected in *McLaughlin v. Florida*, in which the Supreme Court unanimously invalidated a criminal statute prohibiting an unmarried interracial couple from habitually living in and occupying the same room at night.[5] "It is readily apparent," the Court held, that the statute "treats the interracial couple made up of a white person and a Negro differently than it does any other couple."[6] Racial classifications, it concluded, can only be sustained by a compelling state interest. Since the state had failed to establish that the statute served "some overriding statutory purpose requiring the proscription of the specified conduct when engaged in by a white person and a Negro, but not otherwise,"[7] the statute necessarily fell as "an invidious discrimination forbidden by the Equal Protection Clause."[8]

*McLaughlin* stated the obvious. If prohibited conduct is defined by reference to the actor's own race or sex, the prohibition is not neutral with reference to that characteristic.[9] Indeed, in the states that specifically prohibit homosexual sex, the defendant's own sex would appear to be one of the essential elements of the crime that the prosecution must prove.[10]

Another response that has been made is that parallel discriminations, while impermissible in the race context, are just fine in the sex context. Thus David Orgon Coolidge has argued that sex-discrimination doctrine should apply only to "classifications that disadvantage individuals on the basis of preferring one sex over another."[11] But this does not explain the Court's hostility to, say, single-sex schools.[12] Could a state require all girls and women to attend one set of schools, and boys and men to attend another, and then defend the law by arguing that there is no sex discrimination because members of both sexes are equally required to attend same-sex public schools?

The fact of classification itself raises constitutional difficulties. The Court has held that "the party seeking to uphold a statute that classifies individuals on the basis of their gender must carry the burden of showing an 'exceedingly persuasive justification' for the classification."[13] "The burden of justification is demanding and it rests entirely on the State."[14]

Lynn Wardle points out that the Court has upheld sex-based classifications when they are based on "physiological" or "demonstrable" differences between men and women.[15] The laws upheld in these decisions, however, reflected accurate empirical rather than normative generalizations. More important, the generalizations they reflected were exceptionless. If it were otherwise—if a sex-based classification could be justified by what is usually the case, or what is true about most members of either sex—then the constitutional doctrine would be eviscerated, because even the most invidiously sexist laws have been justifiable in terms of some argument of this sort.

Thus, for example, in *Michael M. v. Superior Court*, the Court upheld a statutory rape law that punished the male, but not the female, participant in intercourse when the female was under eighteen and not the male's wife.[16] "Because virtually all of the significant harmful and inescapably identifiable consequences of teenage pregnancy fall on the young female," Justice William Rehnquist's plurality opinion explained, "a legislature acts well within its authority when it elects to punish only the participant who, by nature, suffers few of the consequences of his conduct."[17] Thus, Rehnquist claimed, the statute did not rest merely on "the baggage of sexual stereotypes."[18] Rehnquist nowhere suggests that such stereotyping is permissible; instead, he relies on the fact that "this Court has consistently upheld statutes where the gender classification is not invidious, but rather realistically reflects the fact that the sexes are not similarly situated in certain circumstances."[19]

Rehnquist's reasoning relies on the fact that no young males, not even a single one, can become pregnant. This is an exceptionless generalization about the sexes. It is a long leap from the holding of *Michael M.* to the conclusion that the state can impose sex-based classification on the basis of generalizations that are only statistically accurate, such as the generalizations that many heterosexual couples produce children and same-sex couples tend to be childless.[20] Such generalizations have been relied on by courts seeking justifications for denying gays the right to marry.[21] But such generalizations have also been relied on to justify all forms of sex discrimination.[22] It is now firmly established that generalizations of this sort, even if they are largely accurate, can never justify sex-based classifications. The Court has held that the justification for a sex-based classification "must not rely on overbroad generalizations about the different talents, capacities, or preferences of males and females."[23] "[G]eneralizations about 'the way women are,' estimates of what is appropriate for most women, no longer justify denying opportunity to women whose talent and capacity place them outside the average description."[24]

Some have objected that an interpretation of sex discrimination doctrine that applied heightened scrutiny to "mirror-image restrictions" would entail, absurdly, that single-sex toilets are unconstitutional.[25] The Court has (to my knowledge) only considered the issue of single-sex toilets once, and that indirectly, when in *United States v. Virginia* it declared that admitting women to a previously all-male residential college, as the Constitution required, "would undoubtedly require alterations necessary to afford members of each sex privacy from the other sex in living arrangements."[26] The Court thus assumed without explanation that these were innocuous, while holding that sex-based classifications were presumptively invalid as a general matter.[27]

Even if one accepted as an unshakable premise that single-sex toilets must be permissible, however, this hardly entails that such facilities do not classify on the basis of sex. The sign "MEN" on the door plainly indicates that only males may enter. Moreover, if it is insisted that mirror-image treatment keeps something from being a classification, then this insulates from scrutiny not only miscegenation prohibitions, but also the separate-race toilets that were one of the most insulting manifestations of segregation in the Jim Crow South.

A defense of single-sex toilets under heightened scrutiny would doubtless rely on the widespread desire for "privacy from the other sex in living arrangements." The basis for this desire is obscure, psychologically complex, and culturally contingent. (Sex-segregated toilets are not universal even in the United States.) Part of it is the felt need to preserve a sense of secrecy about the genitalia of the other sex, and women's fear of male violence also has something to do with it. Whatever the roots of this desire, single-sex toilets satisfy it at little tangible or intangible cost. The tangible burden of sex-segregated restrooms is fairly de minimis.[28] Intangible costs matter as well: single-race toilets were generally understood to connote that blacks were filthy, animal-like, and too polluted to be permitted to perform intimate functions in the same space as whites. Single-sex toilets, however, do not connote the inferiority of women.[29] All these considerations, taken together, should satisfy intermediate scrutiny.

No one who has raised this objection has explained just how the toilet exception to the sex-discrimination prohibition could be generalized to include antigay discrimination. Two possibilities present themselves.

One might read the exception to mean that the law should accommodate widespread, deeply felt anxieties about sexual boundaries. Sex-segregated toilets reflect these anxieties, and so does the prohibition of homosexual sex. But this principle proves far too much. All sex discrimination has sometimes reflected such anxieties. This exception would swallow the rule.

A second possibility is to say that the interest protected by sex-segregated toilets is freedom from the unwanted sexual gaze. That same interest is protected by some antigay rules, such as the exclusion of gays from the military, which shields soldiers from being seen naked by persons who might regard them as sexual objects. This argument, too, proves too much. It, like the other, has been used to justify all kinds of sex discrimination. It is impossible for any policy to shield persons from the sexual gaze, and it can be destructive to try. Humanity cannot neatly be divided into "homosexuals" and "heterosexuals." In situations in which women are unavailable for prolonged periods (such as the military in wartime), men sooner or later will start staring at each other in the shower. A policy that zealously strove to eradicate the sexual gaze would require an Orwellian regime of extraordinarily minute surveillance.[30] Acceptance of sex-segregated toilets hardly entails this.

The principal difference between the segregated-toilet exception to the prohibition of sex discrimination and any form of antigay discrimination is that the toilet exception does not impose any serious burden or insult on anyone. Discrimination against gays is always stigmatizing, and it usually involves serious tangible disadvantages as well, such as the military exclusion. If sex-segregated restrooms had such consequences, they, too, would be unconstitutional.

Some concede that discrimination against gays is formally a kind of sex discrimination, but argue that it is not the kind of discrimination that sex-discrimination law prohibits, because it has nothing to do with the subordination of women. This objection depends on a false legal premise. A party challenging a sex-based classification is not required to show anything about the relation between the statute and the subordination of women. The Supreme Court has never asked anyone who challenged a sex-based statute to make such a showing; given the difficulties of demonstrating such complex propositions of social causation, no plaintiff could possibly satisfy such a demand. A requirement of this sort would be tantamount to minimal scrutiny.

Those who make this objection note that *Loving v. Virginia*, the case that invalidated prohibitions on interracial marriage, noted a connection between the miscegenation prohibition and racism, declaring that the prohibition was "designed to maintain White Supremacy."[31] But *Loving* was preceded by, and relied on, *McLaughlin*. *McLaughlin*, not *Loving*, was the groundbreaking case that laid the equal application argument to rest, and *McLaughlin*, not *Loving*, is the crucial precedent on which the sex-discrimination argument relies.[32]

Still, there is a valid worry about the formal argument. Even if discrimination against gays is, as a formal matter, a kind of sex discrimination, is this argument merely a sort of clever lawyer's trick, or does protecting gays from discrimination really further the underlying purposes of sex-discrimination law? If the argument is a mere trick, then even if the rejection of the sex-discrimination argument would require the courts to carve out a new, ad hoc exception to the general rule against sex-based classifications, perhaps the exception should be made.

The answer depends on what one thinks sex-discrimination law is for. If the purpose of the law is to prevent the imposition of gender classifications on people's life choices,[33] then the argument is over; this is just what the formal argument shows that antigay discrimination does. If, however, one thinks that it exists in order to end the subordination of women, then one would have to demonstrate some link between antigay discrimination and the subordination of women.

Here, as in other areas of antidiscrimination law, the facial classification reveals something important about purpose. The link between heterosexism and sexism is common knowledge if anything is. Most Americans learn no later than high school that one of the nastier sanctions that one will suffer if one deviates from the behavior traditionally deemed appropriate to one's sex is the imputation of homosexuality. It is an obvious cultural fact that the stigmatization of homosexuality is closely linked to gays' supposed deviation from the roles traditionally deemed appropriate to persons of their sex. Moreover, both stigmas have gender-specific forms that imply that men ought to have power over women. Gay men are stigmatized as effeminate, which means insufficiently aggressive and dominant. Lesbians are stigmatized as too aggressive and dominant; they appear to be guilty of some kind of insubordination. The two stigmas, sex inappropriateness and homosexuality, are virtually interchangeable, and each is readily used as a metaphor for the other. The findings of scholarship reinforce what common sense already tells us. Numerous studies by social psychologists have found that support for traditional sex roles is strongly correlated with (and, in some studies, is the best single predictor of) disapproval of homosexuality. Historians chronicling the rise of the modern despised category of "the homosexual" have found similar connections with sexism.[34]

The connection is also a particularly malign one. The homosexuality stigma is part and parcel of some of sexism's worst manifestations. Christine Korsgaard observes that

whenever individuals deviate very far from gender norms, gender ideals become especially arbitrary and cruel. Human beings are fertile inventors of ways to hurt ourselves and each other, and gender ideals are one of our keenest instruments for the infliction of completely factitious pain. People are made to feel self-conscious, inadequate, or absolutely bad about having attributes that in themselves are innocuous or even admirable.[35]

If one were to search for illustrations of Korsgaard's concluding sentence, one could hardly find more telling examples than those involving the stigmatization of homosexuality. Men who are patient, aware of others' feelings, good with children, or appreciative of beauty or women who are active and competent, athletic, or good with tools are always in danger of being labeled "queer." The fear of this type of stigma plays a potent role in inducing members of both sexes to adhere to the roles traditionally assigned to their own sex—roles that are, of course, structured hierarchically.

A final worry about the sex-discrimination argument is that it marginalizes what is distinctive about the moral claims that gays are making. Jack Balkin writes that the sex-discrimination argument implies "that discrimination against homosexuals is merely a 'side effect' of discrimination against women, and therefore somehow less important."[36] John Gardner writes that "those committed to the moral wrongfulness of sexuality discrimination should not be at all happy to find this wrongfulness appended to the moral margins of somebody else's grievance, namely the grievance of those who are victims of sex discrimination."[37] William Eskridge writes that the sex-discrimination argument has "a transvestite quality," because "[i]t dresses a gay rights issue up in gender rights garb."[38]

All these concerns are valid. One can make the same point about the interracial couple that was prosecuted under the miscegenation laws: the racist system primarily harmed blacks, but the white husband's interests were hardly unimportant.

The problem here is the problem with any legal claim. Law always picks and chooses among facts in the world, deeming some relevant and ignoring others. It thus flattens the richness of human life. Law is not literature. When we evaluate a human life, we do not just ask whether the person followed the rules. Othello and Iago both killed their wives; the law would make no distinction between them, even though any reader of Shakespeare's play knows that the two men lived in different moral universes. Facts are messy; legal categories make them clean, usually by stripping off all the living flesh. We have already seen the danger that the causal claim behind the sex-discrimination argument will be taken to be stronger than it actually is. There is a similar danger, which should always be resisted, that stories deemed irrelevant for legal purposes will be deemed irrelevant simpliciter.

The sex-discrimination argument relies on settled law that was established for the benefit of women, not of gays. It can be relied on because it is settled, but it is settled only because it was devised without thinking about—to some extent, by deliberately ignoring—the claims of gays. Accepting and relying on the sex-discrimination argument thus means accepting and relying on a view of the world in which gays are at best marginal.

On the other hand, the marginalization of gays is precisely why the argument has the comparative advantages that it does. Each of the other principal arguments for gay equality, the privacy and suspect-classification arguments, depends on an extension of existing law to cover gays. The sex-discrimination argument does not depend on any extension of existing rules. On the contrary, it is its opponents who must ask for legal innovation by carving out an exception to a rule that is settled.

The argument's strengths are not accidental. The relation between the stigmatization of gender nonconformity and that of homosexuality is too close for the argument to be dismissed as a mere technical trick. But it does abstract from the particularity of gays' lives.

It also abstracts from the particularity of some conservatives' objections to homosexuality. The objection from the left that I have just considered, in its insistence on particularity, resembles the objection from the right that has been articulated by Lynn Wardle:

The heterosexual dimension of the relationship is at the very core of what makes marriage a unique union and is the reason why marriage is so valuable to individuals and to society. The concept of marriage is founded on the fact that the union of two persons of different genders creates a relationship of unique potential strength and inimitable potential value to society. The essence of marriage is the integration of a universe of gender differences (profound and subtle, biological and cultural, psychological and genetic) associated with sexual identity. . . . Legalizing same-sex marriage, on the other hand, would send a message that a woman is not absolutely necessary and equally indispensable to the socially valued institution of marriage, weakening rather than strengthening equality for the vast majority of women.[39]

Wardle's complaint is oddly similar to those of Balkin, Gardner, and Eskridge, all of whom are his political adversaries. He, too, complains that the sex-discrimination argument ignores social meanings that are salient in his culture. And the aspects of his culture to which the claims do not correspond should be acknowledged, even if they are legally irrelevant.

Conservative critics of the sex-discrimination argument have never addressed the evidence that heterosexism and sexism are culturally linked, just as they have never deigned to notice in print that gay people are the objects of insane hatred in the United States. It would be unfair to attribute sexism or hatred to these writers; the conservative Christianity that they all endorse condemns both the oppression of women and violence against gays. On the other hand, I do not suppose that they would attempt to deny that these vicious tendencies are at least reinforced by laws that discriminate against gays. There are men whose conceptions of heterosexual masculinity is very much bound up with rage toward women; the statistics on wife battering teach us that there are quite a few men of this sort. Violence against gays is a fact of life throughout the United States.[40]

The conservatives' argument must be that even if these unwelcome phenomena are made more likely by laws that discriminate against gays, and even if such laws get some of their support from people who have these immoral prejudices, these laws nonetheless reflect benign purposes. This defense of laws that reinforce invidious prejudices would resemble the doctrine of double effect in Catholic casuistry: it is morally permissible to bring about a bad result, such as someone's death, so long as that result is not what you intend either as end or as means, but is only an unwelcome side effect of your act. Even if one accepts this doctrine, however, the doctrine requires "that the good effect or aspect, which is intended, should be proportionate (say, saving someone's life), i.e. sufficiently good and important relative to the bad effect or aspect."[41] That is, the purpose being served by laws that discriminate against gays would have to be shown to be not merely rational, but so important that it justifies the reinforcement of sexism. Perhaps another way of saying this is that such laws would have to withstand heightened scrutiny. I do not think that they can survive such scrutiny, but that, as I have said, is an argument to be developed in a different place.

## NOTES

1. See Andrew Koppelman, The Gay Rights Question in Contemporary American Law, 72–93 (2002).

2. I cannot enumerate or respond to all of these objections here. See Andrew Koppelman, The Gay Rights Question in Contemporary American Law, 53–71; Andrew Koppelman, *Defending the Sex Discrimination Argument for Lesbian and Gay Rights: A Reply to Edward Stein*, 49 UCLA L. Rev. 519 (2001).

3. See Singer v. Hara, 52 P.2d 1187 (Wash. App. 1974); Smith v. Liberty Mut. Ins. Co., 395 F. Supp. 1098, 1099 n.2 (N.D. Ga. 1975), aff'd, 569 F.2d 325, 327 (5th Cir. 1978); DeSantis v. Pacific Tel. & Tel. Co., 608 F.2d 327, 331 (9th Cir. 1979); State v. Walsh, 713 S.W.2d 508, 510 (Mo. 1986); Phillips v. Wisconsin Personnel Comm'n, 482 N.W.2d 121, 127–28 (1992); Dean v. District of Columbia, 653 A.2d 307, 363 n.2 (D.C. 1995) (Steadman, J., concurring); Baker v. State, 744 A.2d 864, 880 n. 13 (Vt. 1999); X and Y v. UK, 5 E.H.R.R. 601 (1983); R. v. Ministry of Defence, ex parte Smith (1995), [1996] Q.B. 517; Smith v. Gardner Merchant, [1998] 3 All ER 852; Grant v. South-West Trains, E.C.J. Case C-249/96, ECR I-621, 1998 ECJ CELEX LEXIS 3673 (1998); see also Valdes v. Lumbermen's Mut. Cas. Co., 507 F. Supp. 10 (S.D. Fla. 1980) (discrimination against lesbians may constitute actionable "sex-plus" discrimination, but an employer can rebut the charge by showing that it discriminates equally against gay men).

4. See Pace v. Alabama, 106 U.S. (16 Otto) 583, 585 (1883).

5. 379 U.S. 184 (1964).

6. Id. at 188.

7. Id. at 192.

8. Id. at 192–93.

9. A complex, but fundamentally misconceived, objection to this claim has been raised by John Gardner. See John Gardner, *On the Ground of Her Sex(uality)*, 18 Oxford J. Leg. Stud. 167, 180 (1998). I describe and answer it in *The Miscegenation Analogy in Europe, or Lisa Grant meets Adolf Hitler*, in Legal Recognition of Same-Sex Partnerships: A Study of National, European, and International Law 623 (Robert Wintemute and Mads Andenaes, eds., 2001).

10. See Ark. Stat. Ann. § 5-14-122; Kan. Stat. Ann. § 21-3505; Mo. Ann. Stat. § 566.090.1(3); Mont. Code Ann. §§ 45-2-101(20), 45-5-505; Nev. Rev. Stat. Ann. § 201.190; 1989 Tenn. Acts ch. 591; Tex. Penal Code Ann. § 21.06. See also Schochet v. State, 580 A.2d 176, 184 (Md. 1990) (holding that facially gender-neutral sodomy statute does not apply to "consensual, noncommercial, heterosexual activity between adults in the privacy of the home" and expressly distinguishing cases involving homosexual activity); Post v. State, 715 P.2d 1105, 1109 (Okla. Crim. App. 1986) (invalidating facially gender-neutral sodomy statute in case of different-sex sodomy, but noting that "[W]e do not reach the question of homosexuality since the application of the statute to such conduct is not an issue in this case"). Cf. Jones v. Commonwealth, 80 Va. 538, 542 (1885): "To be a negro is not a crime; to marry a white woman is not a crime; but to be a negro, and being a negro, to marry a white woman is a felony; therefore, it is essential to the crime that the accused shall be a negro—unless he is a negro he is guilty of no offense." See generally Andrew Koppelman, Note, *The Miscegenation Analogy: Sodomy Law as Sex Discrimination*, 98 Yale L.J. 145, 149–51 (1988).

11. David Orgon Coolidge, *Same-Sex Marriage?* Baehr v. Miike *and the Meaning of Marriage*, 38 S. Tex. L. Rev. 1, 82 (1997).

12. See United States v. Virginia, 518 U.S. 515 (1996); Mississippi University for Women v. Hogan, 458 U.S. 718 (1982).

13. Mississippi University for Women v. Hogan, 458 U.S. 718, 724 (1982); see also United States v. Virginia, 518 U.S. 515, 531 (1996) (quoting same).

14. United States v. Virginia, 518 U.S. at 533.

15. Lynn Wardle, *A Critical Analysis of Constitutional Claims for Same-Sex Marriage*, 1996 B.Y.U. L. Rev. 1, 84, quoting Michael M. v. Superior Court, 450 U.S. 464, 481 (1981) (Stewart, J., concurring).

16. 450 U.S. 464 (1981).

17. Id. at 473.

18. Id. at 476, quoting Orr v. Orr, 440 U.S. 268, 283 (1979).

19. Id. at 469.

20. It is, I hope, unnecessary to dwell on the inappropriateness of relying on generalizations that are not even statistically accurate, such as the canard that gay people make worse parents than heterosexuals do. Lynn Wardle has offered the most sustained argument for that claim; see Lynn D. Wardle, *The Potential Impact of Homosexual Parenting on Children*, 1997 U. Ill. L. Rev. 601, but it has been systematically refuted in Carlos Ball & Janice Farrell Pea, *Warring with Wardle: Morality, Social Science, and Gay and Lesbian Parents*, 1998 U. Ill. L. Rev. 253, who show Wardle's work to be pervaded by sexist and heterosexist assumptions that lead him to systematically misinterpret the evidence on which he relies. It is most unfortunate that some courts have relied on Wardle's work to justify denying child custody to gay parents. See Judith Stacey & Timothy J. Biblarz, *(How) Does the Sexual Orientation of Parents Matter?*, 66 Am. Soc. Rev. 159, 161 (2001).

21. See, e.g., Singer v. Hara, 522 P.2d 1187, 1195 (Wash. Ct. App. 1974).

22. Thus Justice Joseph Bradley's notorious concurrence in Bradwell v. Illinois, 83 U.S. 130 (1873), defended the exclusion of women from the practice of law on the grounds that "[t]he natural and proper timidity and delicacy which belongs to the female sex evidently unfits it for many of the occupations of civil life," that "[t]he harmony, not to say identity, of interest and views which belong, or should belong,

to the family institution is repugnant to the idea of a woman adopting a distinct and independent career from that of her husband," and that "[i]t is true that many women are unmarried and not affected by any of the duties, complications, and incapacities arising out of the married state, but these are exceptions to the general rule." Id. at 141; see also id. at 141–42 ("the rules of civil society must be adapted to the general constitution of things, and cannot be based upon exceptional cases"). In recent Supreme Court opinions, Bradley's concurrence has repeatedly been cited as an instance of precisely the type of sexist stereotyping that the Fourteenth Amendment is now understood to prohibit. See Mississippi University for Women v. Hogan, 458 U.S. 718, 725 n.10 (1982); Dothard v. Rawlinson, 433 U.S. 321, 344 n.2 (1977) (Marshall, J., concurring in part and dissenting in part); Frontiero v. Richardson, 411 U.S. 677, 684–685 (1973) (plurality opinion).

23. United States v. Virginia, 518 U.S. at 533.

24. Id. at 550.

25. Craig M. Bradley, *The Right Not to Endorse Gay Rights: A Reply to Sunstein*, 70 Ind. L.J. 29, 30 n.9 (1994); Wardle, *A Critical Analysis*, at 85.

26. United States v. Virginia, 518 U.S. 515, 550 n.19 (1996). This requirement was agreed to by the parties, and so the issue of its constitutionality was not before the Court, but the Court's easy acceptance of it is nonetheless notable.

27. The Court did say that such classifications were permissible in three narrow circumstances:

Sex classifications may be used to compensate women "for particular economic disabilities [they have] suffered," to "promot[e] equal employment opportunity," to advance full development of the talent and capacities of our Nation's people.

Id. at 533, citations omitted. A footnote at the end of the quoted sentence made it clear that the last category was intended to allow evidence that single-sex schools may help to dissipate traditional gender classifications. It is not clear how single-sex toilets could fit into any of these categories, but they all seem to allow some accommodation of women's needs, which single-sex toilets arguably do. It is, however, hard to imagine how any burden on homosexual conduct could be shoehorned into any of these categories.

28. To the extent that this is not the case, so that, for instance, lines outside women's rest rooms are burdensomely longer than those outside men's rest rooms, then heightened scrutiny will and should be harder to satisfy.

29. See Richard A. Wasserstrom, *Racism, Sexism, and Preferential Treatment: An Approach to the Topics*, 24 UCLA L. Rev. 523, 592–594 (1977).

30. As, in fact, the military's policy has. See Janet E. Halley, Don't: A Reader's Guide to the Military's Anti-Gay Policy (1999); Andrew Koppelman, *Gaze in the Military: A Response to Professor Woodruff*, 64 UMKC L. Rev. 179 (1995).

31. 388 U.S. 1, 11 (1967).

32. Opponents of the sex-discrimination argument typically ignore *McLaughlin* and only talk about *Loving*. See, e.g., Wardle, *A Critical Analysis*, at 75–82; Baker v. State, 744 A.2d 864, 880 n.13 (Vt. 1999). I take the argument's power to be vindicated by the fact that those who seek to refute it find it necessary first to mischaracterize it.

33. See Mary Anne Case, *Unpacking Package Deals: Separate Spheres Are Not the Answer*, 75 Denver U.L. Rev. 1305 (1998).

34.  I have developed the claims made in this paragraph at much greater length in Andrew Koppelman, *Why Discrimination Against Lesbians and Gay Men Is Sex Discrimination*, 69 N.Y.U. L. Rᴇᴠ. 197 (1994).

35.  Christine M. Korsgaard, *A Note on the Value of Gender-Identification*, in Women, Culture, and Development: A Study of Human Capabilities 402–403 (Martha Nussbaum and Jonathan Glover eds. 1995).

36.  J.M. Balkin, *The Constitution of Status*, 106 Yale L.J. 2313, 2362 (1997).

37.  Gardner, *On the Ground of Her Sex(uality)*, at 183.

38.  William N. Eskridge, Jr., The Case for Same-Sex Marriage 172 (1996).

39.  Wardle, *A Critical Analysis*, at 39, 87.

40.  See Kendall Thomas, *Beyond the Privacy Principle*, 92 Colum. L. Rev. 1431, 1462–1470 (1992).

41.  John Finnis, *The Rights and Wrongs of Abortion*, in The Rights and Wrongs of Abortion 103 (Marshall Cohen et al. eds. 1974).

# Response

# *Reply to "Discrimination Against Gays Is Sex Discrimination"*

## Richard G. Wilkins

Andrew Koppelman (using slightly different rhetoric) asserts,[1] "If state law forbids Fred to marry Henry, aren't they denied equal protection when the law permits Tom and Jane to marry?"[2] As Judge Robert Bork has noted, "the argument is simplistic."[3]

The minor premises of Professor Koppelman's first and second syllogisms—that is, "[l]aws that discriminate against gay people are laws that make people's legal rights depend on their sex" and "[l]aws that discriminate against gay people are sex-based classifications"—conflate, confuse, and ignore the numerous distinctions between status and conduct.[4] This is a serious error. Courts do not equate sexual status with sexual conduct but, rather, distinguish between sex as an immutable biological reality (status) and sex as a personal idiosyncratic choice (conduct).[5] The difference between status and conduct cannot be dismissed. Professor Koppelman's refusal to recognize this vital distinction results not only in a complete misreading of established discrimination jurisprudence, but in the utter failure of his syllogisms to prove their conclusion: that courts should subject classifications based on sexual conduct to heightened scrutiny.

There is not—and never has been—heightened judicial scrutiny for sexual conduct. Professor Koppelman cites *McLaughlin v. Florida* as an example of the Supreme Court striking down a criminal statute that prohibited unmarried interracial couples from cohabiting.[6] *McLaughlin*, however, applied strict scrutiny because the prohibition turned upon an immutable biological trait—race. Racial status is not a choice, and, stating the obvious, race is a trait that never changes. Therefore, the court in *McLaughlin* applied strict scrutiny to racial status and invalidated the criminal statute.

The reasoning of *McLaughlin* is the same as that used in *Michael M. v.*

*Superior Court,*[7] where Professor Koppelman correctly states, "Rehnquist's reasoning relies on the fact that no young males, not even a single one, can become pregnant. This is an exceptionless generalization about the sexes."[8] Similarly, no white person has ever become black, and no black person has ever become white. Likewise, no two men (however sexually involved with each other) and no two women (whatever their sexual proclivities, and without some form of male involvement) have the potential to produce a child.[9] This is the very "exceptionless generalization" that supports society's unquestionably vital interest in preferring and protecting potentially procreative heterosexual marriage over homosexual relationships.

Indeed, courts and lawmakers have always recognized the difference between status and conduct. Surely Professor Koppelman would not argue that incest laws that prohibit siblings from marrying each other should be invalidated because of sexual discrimination. Yet under his argument, siblings would have the right to enter nuptial vows, sons would have the constitutional right to marry fathers,[10] mothers to marry sons or daughters, and groups of people to marry each other. There are also assertions in psychological and homosexual literature regarding (from the writers' viewpoint) the advantages of man/boy sexual relationships and the unmet desires of boys and men to have sex with each other.[11] Although Professor Koppelman would undoubtedly protest that the assertion is absurd, there are even those (including self-styled gay sex experts) who assert that sex with animals should no longer be considered taboo.[12] Should a man, therefore, be able to marry his dog? A young man a pederast? Professor Koppelman's argument would give positive answers to all of these questions. His argument, therefore, proves far too much. Sexual conduct, not status, is involved in all regulations of human sexuality, including marriage.[13]

Professor Koppelman also suggests that advocates of traditional marriage are merely "homophobic" and "sexist." But to dismiss evidence about the differences between homosexual and heterosexual behavior with such rhetoric displays an absolute lack of the rigorous analysis that must accompany sound legal argument. Sound social science evidence shows that homosexual parenting results in different outcomes for children,[14] and homosexual conduct exposes adults to serious and unique risks.[15] This evidence is too demanding to be dismissed with mere verbal swipes at sexism. Contrary to claims made by advocates of same-sex marriage, the homosexual lifestyle is a far cry from the lifestyle of the vast majority of married heterosexual couples.[16]

Finally, the assertion that there is no compelling state interest validating traditional marriage is clearly erroneous and terribly shortsighted.[17] There is no interest of greater importance to the nation than the maintenance of healthy families. As set out in my opening essay and reiterated by Judge Bork, "[T]raditional marriage and family have been the foundations of every healthy society known in recorded history."[18] Precedent, experience, and plain common sense show that it is in society's best interest to preserve the traditional institution of marriage, on which the very future of human society depends. Professor Koppelman to the contrary, the perpetuation of the state unquestionably qualifies as a "compelling state interest."

## NOTES

1. Andrew Koppelman, *Discrimination Against Gays Is Sex Discrimination*. To be absolutely fair, Professor Koppelman states his argument in somewhat different terms: "If Lucy may marry Fred, but Ricky may not marry Fred, then (assuming that Fred would be a desirable spouse for either) Ricky is suffering legal disadvantage because of his sex."

2. Robert H. Bork, *Stop Courts from Imposing Gay Marriage*, Wall St. J., Aug. 7, 2001, at A14.

3. *Id.*

4. Koppelman, *supra* note 1 at 709–210.

5. *Michael M. v. Superior Court*, 450 U.S. 464 (1981)

6. *McLaughlin v. Florida*, 379 U.S. 184 (1964).

7. *Michael M. v. Superior Court*, 450 U.S. 464 (1981).

8. Andrew Koppleman, *Discrimination Against Gays Is Sex Discrimination*, 8.

9. I.e., through artificial insemination or in vitro fertilization. A man is involved at some point in both of these medical procedures.

10. Claims by sons of a right to marry their fathers cannot be dismissed out of hand, if one is to take the writings of professed gay sex experts seriously. *See, e.g.*, Charles Silverstein & Felice Picano, The New Joy of Gay Sex at 48–49 (1st Harper Perennial ed. 1993) (discussing "the importance of the erotic attachment of gay sons to their fathers"). If the "erotic attachment of gay sons to their fathers" is indeed "important," courts and states that recognize gay marriage should brace themselves for the claims of sons and fathers who decide to demand social recognition of this "important relationship."

11. If claims for same-sex marriage between adults are accepted now, it will only be a short time before similar claims by pederasts of a "right" to marry a young boy gain acceptance. Indeed, homosexual psychological literature already touts the purported benefits of "intergenerational sexual intimacy." *See, e.g.*, Edward Brongersma, *Boy-Lovers and Their Influence on Boys: Distorted Research and Anecdotal Observations*, 20 Journal of Homosexuality (1990), at 145, 160:

Rossman (1976) gives several examples of social workers achieving miracles with apparently incorrigible young delinquents—not by preaching to them but by sleeping with them. Affection demonstrated by sexual arousal upon contact with the boy's body, by obvious pleasure taken in giving pleasure to the boy, did far more good than years in reformatories. [Referring to P. Rossman, *Sexual Experience Between Men and Boys* (New York: Association Press, 1976).]

Amsterdam juvenile judge Cnoop Koopmans openly advocated this form of social therapy in a public speech (1982). I personally know of cases brought before this man. In one, a boy who had been arrested several times for shoplifting, who had been a terror at home and a failure in school, suddenly turned over a new leaf, gave up crime, started getting good marks at school and became a national champion in his favorite sport. All of this occurred after a boy-lover had been asked officially to take care of him.

*Also see, e.g.*, Charles Silverstein & Felice Picano, The New Joy of Gay Sex 192 (1st Harper Perennial ed. 1993) ("There are some teenagers who prefer sex with adults. They do so for a number of reasons. Instead of bumbling around with friends their own age, they want a man who is sexually experienced and will patiently teach them").

12. *See, e.g.*, Silverstein & Picano at 171 ("Moralists condemn sex with animals as disgusting, immoral, and generally horrible. . . . We disagree with the moralists. . . . Like other inexperienced city dwellers, we may not so readily fathom the mechanics of cow-, sheep- or horse- ——ing, but see no reason to condemn it out of hand. We hope it doesn't become the *only* sexual contact in a man's life"). Modern "moralists," moreover, no longer universally condemn bestiality. *See, e.g.*, Peter Singer, "Heavy Petting," http://www.nerve.com/Opinions/Singer/heavyPetting.

13. Koppelman suggests that homosexuality is akin to race because it is immutable. Andrew Koppelman, *Discrimination Against Gays Is Sex Discrimination*, 4–5. There is, however, a wealth of evidence refuting the claim that homosexuality is immutable. *See, e.g.*, I. Bieber, Homosexuality: A Psychoanalytic Study 319 (Basic Books 1962); J. Clippinger, *Homosexuality Can Be Cured*, 21 Corrective and Social Psychiatry and Journal of Behavior Technology Methods and Therapy 22 (1987); A. Ellis, *The Effectiveness of Psychotherapy with Individuals Who Have Severe Homosexual Problems*, 20 Journal of Consulting Psychology 194 (1956); R. Fine, Male and Female Homosexuality: Psychological Approaches 85–86 (Hemisphere Publishing, Louis Piamaut ed. 1987); H. Kaye et al., *Homosexuality in Women*, 17 Archives of General Psychiatry 634 (1967); H. MacIntosh, *Attitudes and Experiences of Psychoanalysts*, 42 Journal of the American Psychoanalytic Association 1183 (1994); J. Nicolosi, *Beliefs and Practices of Therapists Who Practice Sexual Reorientation Psychotherapy*, 86 Psychological Reports 689–702 (2000); J. Satinover, Homosexuality and the Politics of Truth (Baker 1996); C. Tripp & L. Hatterer, *Can Homosexuals Change with Psychotherapy?* 1 Sexual Behavior 42–49 (1971).

14. While it has long been claimed that there are "no differences" in behavioral outcomes for children raised by homosexual (as compared to heterosexual) parents, a recent reanalysis of prior studies challenges this conclusion. Two researchers sympathetic to the cause of homosexual households have now concluded that the "[e]vidence . . . does not support the 'no differences' claim." Judith Stacy & Timothy J. Biblarz, *(How) Does the Sexual Orientation of Parents Matter?*, 66 American Sociological Review 159, 176 (April 2001). These researchers conclude that "[c]hildren with lesbigay parents appear less traditionally gender-typed and more likely to be open to homoerotic relationships. In addition, evidence suggests that parental gender and sexual identities interact to create distinctive family processes whose consequences for children have yet to be studied." *Id.* This research supports the argument, set out in my original essay, that the social costs of same-sex marriage are presently unknown, but are likely to be substantial. Society, therefore, should be exceptionally careful before dramatically restructuring the very foundation of society itself: marriage and the family.

15. Homosexual sex involves risky behavior. Anal intercourse is especially conducive to HIV infection. Warren Winklestein, Jr., et al., *Sexual Practices and Risk of Infection by the Human Immunodeficiency Virus*, Journal of the American Medical Association 321, 325 (Jan. 16, 1987); Mads Melbye & Robert J. Biggar, *Interactions Between Persons at Risk for AIDS and the General Population in Denmark*, 135

American Journal of Epidemiology, 601 (Mar. 15, 1992). Anal sex increases the exposure to human feces and correspondingly a large number of related diseases. Lawrence Corey & King K. Holmes, *Sexual Transmission of Hepatitis A in Homosexual Men*, 302 New England Journal of Medicine 425–438 (Feb. 21, 1980); Janet R. Daling et al., *Sexual Practices, Sexually Transmitted Diseases, and the Incidence of Anal Cancer*, 317 New England Journal of Medicine 973–977 (Oct. 15, 1987); Thomas C. Quinn et al., *The Polymicrobial Origin of Intestinal Infections in Homosexual Men*, 309 New England Journal of Medicine 576–582 (Sept. 8, 1983). "Gay bowel" syndrome is another problem associated with homosexual behavior. Glen E. Hastings & Richard Weber, *Letter to the Editor*, 49 American Family Physician 581 (Feb. 15, 1994).

Homosexual conduct also has consequences for mental health. There is a well-documented correlation between homosexuality and suicide and mental illness. *See, e.g.*, Theo B.M. Sandfort et al., *Same-Sex Sexual Behavior and Psychiatric Disorders: Findings from the Netherlands Mental Health Survey and Incidence Study*, 58 Archives of General Psychiatry 85 (Jan. 2001) ("The findings support the assumption that people with same-sex behavior are at greater risk for psychiatric disorders"); Richard Herrell et al., *Sexual Orientation and Suicidality*, 56 Archives of General Psychiatry 867 (Oct. 1999) ("Same-gender sexual orientation is significantly associated with each of the suicidality measures" and "is unlikely to be due solely to substance abuse or other psychiatric co-morbidity"); David M. Fergusson et al., *Is Sexual Orientation Related to Mental Health Problems and Suicidality in Young People?,"* 56 Archives of General Psychiatry 876 (Oct. 1999) ("Findings support recent evidence suggesting that gay, lesbian, and bisexual young people are at increased risk of mental health problems, with these associations being particularly evident for measures of suicidal behavior and multiple disorder"). While some may argue that these findings are "caused by societal oppression" (J. Michael Bailey, *Homosexuality and Mental Illness*, 56 Archives of General Psychiatry 883, 884 (Oct. 1999), this is not the only possible explanation. The survey of findings from the Netherlands Mental Health Survey and Incidence Study found a significantly greater risk for psychiatric disorders among homosexuals, even though "the Dutch social climate toward homosexuality has long been and remains considerably more tolerant" than most of the world. Theo B.M. Sandfort et al., above, at 89. Other possible explanations include hypotheses that "homosexuality represents a deviation from normal development and is associated with other such deviations that may lead to mental illness," and that "increased psychopathology among homosexual people is a consequence of lifestyle differences associated with sexual orientation." J. Michael Bailey, above, at 884.

16. As one homosexual advocate recently stated, "Our culture is, at its heart and soul, a sexual one: it is what we do in bed that connects us. The rest is gravy." Garth Kirby, *The Future Is Ours to Take*, Capital Xtra! Information, Aug. 1998 (last revised 27 Aug. 98) (visited Oct. 16, 2001), http://www.capitalxtra.aa.psiweb.com/queer capital/cx/CX60/MIXED/cx_MM60_queering.html. The level of promiscuity among the gay population is also very different from that in mainstream society. The Kinsey Institute published a study showing that 28 percent of male homosexuals have had sexual encounters with 1,000 or more partners, with over half having more than 500 different sexual partners in a lifetime. Joseph Nicolosi, Reparative Therapy of Male Homosexuality 124 (Jason Aronson 1991).

17. Andrew Koppelman, *Discrimination Against Gays Is Sex Discrimination*, 1.

Koppelman claims that since same-sex-marriage prohibitions "are not substantially related to any important state interest, they are unconstitutional."

18. Robert H. Bork, *Stop the Courts from Imposing Gay Marriage*, Wall St. J., Aug. 7, 2001, at A14.

Essay Two

# The Constitutionality of Legal Preferences for Heterosexual Marriage

## Richard G. Wilkins

Throughout the ages, marriage between man and woman has been essential to individual development, social progress, and communal prosperity.[1] Because of the important roles it has played in the evolution of modern society, marriage has become a "highly preferred" legal relationship.[2] Marriage's unique status is reflected in the numerous statutory and other legal preferences that have been created for the marital relationship, ranging from special tax and employment benefits to laws dealing with property ownership and intestacy.[3]

Today, however, the "highly preferred" status of marriage is under attack on several fronts. In the face of mounting divorce and abuse rates and the increasingly large number of children born out of wedlock,[4] some question whether marriage has any continuing social value.[5] Others (often building upon the increasingly low esteem in which modern marriage is held) question why the historic legal preferences conferred on husbands and wives should not be conferred upon alternative partnership arrangements, such as two men and two women, who wish to enjoy the benefits of a "marital" relationship. These advocates, in fact, often assert that federal and state constitutions mandate the conferral of marital benefits on such partnerships.

This essay answers the following question: Must the various legal preferences conferred on traditional marriage be extended to alternative partnership arrangements? The answer is no. The legal lines that have been drawn to protect and encourage the marital union of a man and a woman are principled and essential to furthering society's compelling procreative interest. Indeed, once outside the union of a man and a woman, there is no principled constitutional basis for distinguishing between (or among) any form of consensual sexual behavior. Recognition of a constitutional right to same-sex marriage, therefore, would open the door to legally mandated conferral of all legislative preferences now reserved for marriage upon any form of consensual sexual coupling, no matter how idiosyncratic. Society should not encourage (nor perhaps could it endure) such an outcome.

## CONSTITUTIONAL FRAMEWORK

Before analyzing the most common constitutional claims made by proponents of same-sex marriage, I would like to address one oft-made but inapt assertion. Television and radio talk shows, along with newspaper opinion columns, are often filled with variants of the submission that laws preferring heterosexual marriage "impose the morals of some upon all, and the law has no business answering moral questions."[6] This unfocused claim ignores the reality that any and all legal schemes enforce some moral code. Must we enjoin all provisions of state and federal criminal codes that reinforce the moral and religious precept that "[t]hou shalt not steal"?[7] Of course not. As Justice Byron White wisely noted in disposing of the argument that sodomy laws reflect an unconstitutional moral judgment, "[T]he law . . . is constantly based on notions of morality, and if all laws representing essentially moral choices are to be invalidated . . . , the courts will be very busy indeed."[8]

Once beyond the alleged impropriety of legislative actions reflecting a moral judgment, advocates for the judicial recognition of alternative marital partnerships generally focus upon two constitutional provisions: the Due Process and Equal Protection Clauses of the Fourteenth Amendment to the U.S. Constitution.[9] Under both clauses, the constitutional analysis of legislative action is quite similar. If legislative line drawing intrudes upon a "fundamental right" or "suspect classification," the challenged regulation will be subjected to close judicial scrutiny. By contrast, if a "fundamental right" or "suspect classification" is not involved, the legislative judgment (in the vast majority of cases) will be sustained.

The ongoing debate whether legislative and other legal preferences for heterosexual marriage pass constitutional muster has already consumed thousands of pages in the law reviews.[10] Somewhat surprisingly, however, virtually all of the literature concludes—on the basis of some variant of the due process or equal protection analyses explored in the proceeding paragraph[11]—that current statutory or legal preferences for heterosexual marriage are either irrational or subject to purportedly fatal strict scrutiny.[12]

With due respect, and knowing that my opinion is in the decided academic minority, I submit that this consensus is seriously flawed. Laws preferring heterosexual marriage are not subject to strict scrutiny. This is because statutory and other legal preferences for heterosexual marriage do not intrude upon any established constitutional right subject to rigorous judicial oversight and, in any event, further the most imperative of all governmental interests: "the very existence and survival of the race."[13] Current widespread statutory and legal preferences for heterosexual marriage, therefore, are plainly constitutional.

## PREFERENCES FOR HETEROSEXUAL MARRIAGE DO NOT TRIGGER STRICT SCRUTINY

Far from suggesting that statutory preferences for heterosexual marriage should be subjected to strict scrutiny, a straightforward reading of the opinions of the U.S. Supreme Court establishes that rational-basis review is the relevant judicial benchmark. Legislative preferences for heterosexual marriage do not intrude upon any fundamental right or impermissibly harm any suspect class. Accordingly, statutory and other legal preferences for heterosexual marriage need only be reasonably related to a rational objective, a hurdle that is readily cleared.

Any claim that preferences for heterosexual marriage intrude upon a "fundamental right" necessarily rest upon some variation of an assertion made by a plurality of the Supreme Court in *Planned Parenthood of Southeastern Pennsylvania v. Casey*.[14] In the course of reaffirming the abortion right first announced in *Roe v. Wade*, Justices Sandra Day O'Connor, Anthony Kennedy, and David Souter wrote that "[a]t the heart of liberty is the right to define one's own concept of existence, of meaning, of the universe, and of the mystery of human life."[15] Advocates of same-sex marriage essentially submit that this broadly phrased notion of liberty guarantees them the right to demand that the label "marriage"—as well as all of the statutory and legal preferences that follow that label—be attached to their own idiosyncratically defined sexual couplings. But while such arguments might get an A for rhetoric, they flunk the demands of established constitutional law.

Not every personal preference connected with "one's own concept of existence," "meaning," and "mystery" can (or ought to) be recognized as a "fundamental right." State policy makers, for example, can require policemen to adhere to dress and grooming standards, no matter how mysterious and meaningful a ponytail or beard might be to a particular law enforcement officer.[16] Were it otherwise, our Constitution would cease to be the written document construed by Chief Justice John Marshall in *Marbury v. Madison*[17] and would become, instead, a vessel into which a bare majority of the Supreme Court could pour their personal predilections at will. The Supreme Court has never adopted such a freewheeling notion of review under the Due Process Clause.

Accordingly, and far from protecting all notions of liberty that may be central to an individual's definition of "existence" and the "mystery of life," the Due Process Clause protects only "those fundamental rights and liberties which are, objectively, 'deeply rooted in this Nation's history and tradition' "[18] and " 'implicit in the concept of ordered liberty,' such that 'neither liberty nor justice would exist if they were sacrificed.' "[19] Moreover, the Court has required a " 'careful description' of the asserted fundamental liberty interest."[20] In short, even deeply held contemporary notions of "existence," "meaning," and "mystery"[21] do not provide the judicial map for substantive due process excursions. Rather, "[o]ur Nation's history, legal traditions, and practices provide the crucial 'guideposts for responsible decision making.' "[22]

Nothing in our nation's history, legal traditions, or practices supports the notion that "marriage" has been or should be expanded beyond the notion of a consensual coupling of a man and a woman.[23] To the contrary, in the course of adjudicating marital rights or opining on the marital relationship, the Supreme Court has consistently linked its opinions to the traditional family structure of a man, a woman, and their children by emphasizing the marital functions of conception,[24] procreation,[25] child rearing and education,[26] and traditional family relationships in general.[27]

This analysis forecloses, I believe, any serious assertion that statutory preferences for heterosexual marriage unconstitutionally impinge upon a fundamental right under the Due Process Clause of the U.S. Constitution. Other scholars have persuasively shown that the same conclusion is warranted for the assertion that such preferences unconstitutionally target a "suspect class" under the Equal Protection Clause.[28] Legal preferences for heterosexual marriage, therefore, are *not* subject to strict (and generally fatal) judicial scrutiny.

## ESTABLISHED MARITAL PREFERENCES FURTHER COMPELLING SOCIAL INTERESTS

Even if my foregoing analysis is flawed, traditional heterosexual marriage readily survives intrusive judicial review. Marriage between a man and a woman provides the very foundation of society. The Supreme Court has had frequent opportunities to expound upon the fundamental importance of marriage to society.[29] More than a century ago, the U.S. Supreme Court called marriage "the most important relation in life . . . having more to do with the morals and civilization of a people than any other institution."[30] More recently, the Court described marriage as an "association that promotes a way of life, not causes; a harmony in living, not political faiths; a bilateral loyalty, not commercial or social projects."[31] But, however ornate the rhetoric, the Supreme Court's discussions of marriage emphasize again and again a surpassingly important reality that (quite curiously) is often overlooked in the modern debates surrounding same-sex marriage: the unquestionable biological and historical relationship between marriage, procreation, and child rearing.

As the Supreme Court noted in *Skinner v. Oklahoma*, "Marriage and procreation are fundamental to the very existence and survival of the race."[32]

The Court reemphasized this connection between marriage, procreation, and child-rearing in *Zablocki v. Redhail*.[33] There the Court placed the "decision to marry" on "the same level of importance as decisions relating to procreation, childbirth, child-rearing, and family relationships" precisely because "[if the] right to procreate means anything at all, it must imply some right to enter" the marital relationship.[34] The very conception of marriage, in sum, is indissolubly linked to the societal imperatives of procreation and child rearing.

As a result, organized society has a substantial interest in drawing legal lines that responsibly channel and encourage procreation. This theme has dominated Supreme Court decisions from the beginning. All the family cases, from the earliest to the latest, recite that individuals have a unique interest in marriage because of its close connection to procreation and child rearing.[35] Judicial recognition of this individual right to marriage and procreation, however, necessarily demands recognition of a correlative social interest held by the state: a substantial—indeed surpassing—interest in channeling and promoting responsible procreative behavior. Only individuals marry and procreate, but society has a profound interest in the conduct and outcome of these individual behaviors because these activities are fundamental to society's "very existence and survival."[36]

These interests continue to survive despite modern claimants for alternative marital unions who seek to sever sexuality completely from any relationship to procreation and child rearing. Such a severance of sexuality from reproduction has significant legal, sociological, moral, and philosophical consequences that have been discussed by, among others, Professors Robert George and Gerard Bradley[37] and Hadley Arkes.[38] According to these scholars, heterosexual relationships (and, in particular, marital relationships) differ significantly from other possible sexual acts. Sexual relations between a man and a woman bound in marriage are described as an "intrinsic (or . . . 'basic') human good."[39] This is due, in large part, to the fact that a heterosexual marital relationship has the biological potential for reproduction. Indeed, stripped of this reproductive potential, sexual relationships become nothing more than physically (and emotionally) agreeable genital stimulation.

One need not dispute that mutually agreeable genital stimulation can have emotional, mental, and physical overtones. Such stimulation may be the result of—or perhaps result in—intense attachments to a sexual partner. Nevertheless, absent any relation to procreation, the sexual act is reduced to a purely sensory experience (whether the sensation is physical, mental, or emotional).[40]

At this point, homosexual activists might argue that if marital law exists to further society's procreative imperative, why should legal protection be extended to infertile (whether by choice or otherwise) heterosexual unions? The argument, however, is wide of the mark. Traditional marriage, unlike any other sexual relationship, furthers society's profound interest in the only sexual relationship that has the biological potential for reproduction: union between a man and a woman.

Procreation requires a coupling between the two sexes. Sexual relations between a man and a woman, therefore, even if they are infertile, fundamentally differ from homosexual couplings. Homosexual couplings do not have the biological potential for reproduction: children are possible only by means of legal intervention (e.g., adoption) or medical technology (e.g., artificial insemination). Accordingly, and by their very nature, sexual relationships between a man and a woman (even if they are infertile) differ in kind from couplings between individuals of the same sex: heterosexual couplings in general have the biological potential for reproduction; homosexual couplings always do not. This potential procreative power is the basis for society's compelling interest in preferring potentially procreative relationships over relationships founded primarily upon mutually agreeable genital stimulation.[41]

The institution of marriage furthers not mere sensory experience, but society's "very . . . survival."[42] The law, moreover, has never been ignorant of the vital distinction between purely sensory experience and procreation. Constitutional law, for its part, must take cognizance of this biologically obvious distinction. Constitutional decision making, above all other forms of judicial decision making, must be grounded in both principle and reason.[43] When it comes to the constitutional definition of marriage, the undeniable and well-grounded principle that has guided mankind for generations (including state legislatures and the Supreme Court since this country's founding) is straightforward: there is a fundamental difference between procreative sexuality and nonprocreative sexuality.

Reproduction is the only human act for which the two genders undisputably require each other. A woman can do everything in her life without a man except reproduce. Vice versa for a man. Thus the sexuality that unites a man and a woman is unique in kind. This uniqueness, in fact, is the very basis of the religious, historical, and metaphysical notion that "marriage" indeed joins two fleshes in one.[44]

Furthermore, should constitutional law abandon the principle that reproductive sex has a unique role, we will be left with no basis upon which to draw principled constitutional distinctions between sexual relations that are harmful to individuals and/or society and relations that are beneficial. In fact, the same arguments that would seemingly require constitutional protection for same-sex marriage would also require constitutional protection for any consensual sexual practice or form of marriage. After all, once the principled line of procreation is abandoned, we are left with nothing more than sex as a purely sensory experience. The purely sensory experience cherished by any given sexual partnership will be no more or less precious than the purely sensory experience valued by another sexual partnership, no matter how socially repugnant. Should courts depart from the established heterosexual definition of marriage, there will be little (if any) principled ground upon which to deny marital status to any and all consensual sexual groupings.[45] Bigamy, group marriage, and—yes—even consensual incestuous coupling could all (and probably would all) accurately lay claim to the same legal entitlements.

Advocates of same-sex marriage may nonetheless argue that denying same-sex couples the opportunity to marry is really just sex discrimination.[46] This assertion conflates (and/or confuses) the concepts of "sex" (a biological status) and "sexual conduct" (the way one uses the genitalia provided by a person's biological status). The law has indeed provided substantial protection against unthinking or stereotypical classifications based on sex.[47] But these decisions simply reflect the biological reality that (except for rather rare genetic anomalies such as hermaphroditism)[48] the human race is composed of women and men who, for the most part, are similarly situated and who, therefore, may not be treated differentially. Thus the rules for buying beer must be the same for women as they are for men,[49] and a military school may not admit men but not women without a compelling justification.[50]

These decisions, however, do not protect, nor have they ever protected, sexual conduct. Rather, the well-established and well-defined line of sex-discrimination cases protects women and men from unthinking or unfounded classifications based upon the biological status of being a woman or a man. Any assertion that classifications based on sexual conduct are "sex based" ignores the vital distinction between status (i.e., femaleness or maleness) and conduct (i.e., heterosexuality, homosexuality, bisexuality, incest, or bestiality).[51]

Proponents of same-sex marriage may nevertheless argue that they should be allowed to marry because a constitutional "zone of privacy" mandates that they be allowed to marry. This "zone of privacy," according to Justice William O. Douglas, is a concept even "older than the Bill of Rights."[52] But while it is true that a zone of privacy prevents society from policing certain bedroom behavior, the privacy argument, applied to same-sex marriage, proves too much. Privacy rights prevent governmental interference with relationships that are indeed private. Therefore, to the extent that homosexual relationships are private, they may properly be shielded (at least to some extent)[53] by the "zone of privacy" from government intrusion. But to transform a privacy shield into a policy sword turns the concept of "privacy" on its head: the assertion becomes, not that homosexual conduct is private, but that it must be publicly acknowledged, condoned, recognized, and normalized.

Same-sex advocates also assert that homosexual behavior harms no one, so the government has no interest in denying same-sex marriage. Nobody will be worse tomorrow, the argument goes, because their homosexual neighbors are married today. While this submission may have some appeal, it is shortsighted. No one knows what impact same-sex marriage will have on society. Moreover, it certainly has not been shown that society will be improved by same-sex marriage. For centuries, societies have been built upon the foundation of traditional families.[54] As the family is weakened, so is society.[55] For instance, in the 1970s one could argue that the loosening of divorce laws would inflict relatively minor pain on society. But thirty years later, the evidence tells a compelling story of the increased injury society endures every time the divorce rate rises and the traditional family is weakened.[56]

Making divorce easier to obtain seemed progressive in the 1970s, but thirty years later, when divorce has become a national norm and most households consist of unmarried individuals with no children, we begin to grasp that the divorce revolution has imposed high social costs indeed.[57] It may, in fact, be impossible to show, now, that same-sex marriage will cause immediate harm to society or to individuals in society, but it is undeniable that same-sex marriage is not based on procreation and a commitment to new life and future generations. The assertion that any sexual relationship (no matter how idiosyncratic and no matter how far removed from the continuation of life) has the same benefit as traditional marriage is simply unproved. Same-sex marriage, moreover, may well have severe long-term social consequences that cannot be predicted or foreseen at this time. One thing, however, does seem clear: as society becomes increasingly focused on individual and immediate transitory desires, rather than on the perpetuation of life and a commitment to the future, the consequences of same-sex marriage may be severe indeed.

The judicial system should not be tempted to stray from the course marked by history and tradition, a course that is soundly built on society's interest in procreation. As Justice White astutely noted in rejecting the asserted constitutional right to consensual sodomy, "[I]t would be difficult, except by fiat, to limit the claimed right to homosexual conduct while leaving exposed to prosecution adultery, incest, and other sexual crimes. . . . We are unwilling to start down that road."[58] American courts, both at the state and federal levels, should be similarly unwilling to begin the task of judicially defining which sexual partnerships—among all the possibilities ranging beyond that of a man and a woman—must be legitimated with the long-honored title of "marriage."

## CONCLUSION

Because legislative preferences for heterosexual marriage do not infringe upon fundamental rights or target a suspect class, such preferences need only reasonably further a rational objective: a legal test that virtually answers itself. Society has an undeniable interest in preferring heterosexual marriage over alternative sexual relationships. Heterosexual marriage, unlike same-sex partnerships, has the biological potential for procreation. There is no gainsaying the importance of this societal interest. As the Supreme Court has recognized, procreation involves the "very existence and survival" of mankind.[59] Laws protecting and preferring heterosexual marriage are a principled and necessary means of furthering this most imperative of all governmental objectives.

## NOTES

I would like to express my thanks to R. Chad Hales and Adam Becker for their able assistance in preparing this essay.

1. *See, e.g.*, Brigitte Berger, *The Social Roots of Prosperity and Liberty*, 35 SOCIETY 44 (Mar.–Apr. 1998) (available on WestLaw at 1998 WL 11168752).

2. Lynn D. Wardle, *A Critical Analysis of Constitutional Claims for Same-Sex Marriage*, 1996 B.Y.U. L. REV. 1, 29.

3. *See* Akiko Kawamura, *The Constitution and Family Values*, 1 J.L. & FAM. STUD. 89, 94 (1999):

Justice O'Connor, writing for the majority [in *Turner v. Safley*], articulated the reasons why marriage is "especially important to constitutional conceptions of liberty and citizenship" [citation omitted]. First, marriage is a precondition for government benefits like social security. Second, marital status guarantees certain property rights under intestate succession laws. Third, in some states, marriage is a precondition for the legitimacy of children. Lastly, marriage is an expression of commitment that carries "spiritual significance" because it is often "an exercise of religious faith as well as an expression of personal dedication."

(quoting *Turner v. Safley*, 107 S.Ct. 2254 [1987]); *see also* Todd Foreman, *Nondiscrimination Ordinance 101, San Francisco's Nondiscrimination in City Contracts and Benefits Ordinance: A New Approach to Winning Domestic Partnership Benefits*, 2 U. PA. J. LAB. & EMPLOYMENT L. 319, n.3 (1999) ("The many benefits of marriage include immigration rights, property rights, tax benefits, and employment benefits such as 'partner insurance coverage, pension survivorship plans, and sick and bereavement leave.' ") (quoting Philip S. Horne, *Challenging Public- and Private-Sector Benefit Schemes Which Discriminate Against Unmarried Opposite-Sex and Same-Sex Partners*, 4 LAW & SEXUALITY 35, 48 [1994] [citation omitted]).

4. *See, e.g.*, Maria Sophia Aguirre, *Family, Economics, and the Information Society—How Are They Affecting Each Other?*, available at http://www.world congress.org/gen99_mspeakers/ gen99_aguirre.htm (last visited Feb. 28, 2000) ("For instance, one out of every three children born in the United States and over half of all children in Scandinavia are born out of wedlock").

5. Some of the fiercest criticism regarding the continuing social utility of marriage comes from gay rights activists who seek to "deconstruct" the very concept of marriage. *See, e.g.*, Wardle, *supra* note 2, at 3 n.2 (noting that both supporters and opponents of same-sex marriage agree "that it could dramatically alter the core social institutions of marriage and the family, as well as gender relations, sexual practices, and general social stability") (citing authority). Other more subtle, but perhaps more damaging, devaluation of marriage comes from modern academicians who consis-

tently cast marriage in a negative light. For example, a recent survey of twenty college textbooks discussing marriage found that "current textbooks convey a determinedly pessimistic view of marriage," repeatedly suggesting "that marriage is more a problem than a solution." Norval D. Glenn, *Closed Hearts, Closed Minds: The Textbook Story of Marriage*, 35 SOCIETY 69 (Mar.–Apr. 1998) (available on WestLaw at 1998 WL 11168753).

6. For example, consider this excerpt published by a local Utah newspaper in its "Opinion" section:

> Equal rights for gay people. There is not a single, truly non-secular reason for denying same-sex couples the right to marry, to adopt children or to be foster parents, that can withstand any real objective scrutiny. It is simply a majority using the government to impose their unverifiable, religious beliefs on the many reasonable and responsible people with different religious beliefs and practices regarding God's plan for us all. This denial is therefore an establishment of religion specifically prohibited by the U.S. Constitution, and an immoral infringement on the fundamental and equal rights of gay people. Stuart McDonald, Salt Lake City.

Daily Herald, Feb. 11, 2000, at A6.

7. *Exodus* 20:15 (King James).

8. Bowers v. Hardwick, 478 U.S. 186, 196 (1986).

9. The Fourteenth Amendment provides in relevant part: "No State shall make or enforce any law which shall . . . deprive any person of life, liberty, or property, without due process of law." U.S. CONST. amend. XIV. The key word in this passage is "liberty," which has long been settled to be a substantive word—one conferring independent constitutional rights not otherwise expressly provided for in the text of the Constitution or its amendments. *See* Planned Parenthood of Southeastern Pennsylvania v. Casey, 505 U.S. 833, 846 (1992).

This essay does not address claims based upon state constitutional law. Because the federal courts generally have been unreceptive to the submission that the U.S. Constitution provides special protection for homosexual conduct (*see, e.g.*, Bowers v. Hardwick, 478 U.S. 186 (1986)), litigants of late have rested same-sex-marriage claims on state constitutional provisions, where success has been more forthcoming. *See, e.g.*, Baker v. Vermont, 744 A.2d 864 (Vt. 1999) (same-sex couples are entitled to receive the same marital benefits as heterosexual couples); Brause v. Bureau of Vital Statistics, No. 3AN-95-6562 CI, 1998 WL 88743 (Alaska Super. Ct. Feb. 27, 1998) (holding that one has a fundamental right to choose a life partner and that current marriage statutes constituted sex-based discrimination subjecting them to strict scrutiny); Baehr v. Lewin, 852 P.2d 44 (Haw. 1993) (Hawaii's marriage statute discriminated on the basis of sex and was therefore subject to strict scrutiny); Baehr v. Miike, CIV. No. 91-1394, 1996 WL 694235 (Haw. Cir. Ct. Dec. 3, 1996) (concluding after remand of Baehr v. Lewin that Hawaii's marriage statute was unconstitutional). *But see* ALASKA CONST. art. I, § 25 ("To be valid or recognized in this state, a marriage may exist only between one man and one woman") (enacted in response to *Brause*); HAW. CONST. art. I, § 23 ("The legislature shall have the power to reserve marriage to opposite-sex couples") (enacted in response to Baehr v. Lewin and Baehr v. Miike). Alaska's article 1, § 25 was upheld in Bess v. Ulmer, 95 P.2d 979, 988 (Alaska 1999). The issue in Baehr v. Lewin was ultimately rendered moot by the Hawaiian state legislature. Baehr v. Miike, 994 P.2d 566 (1999). While state courts may prove more receptive to same-sex-marriage claims than the federal judiciary, an analysis of the possible claims arising out of fifty state constitutions is well beyond the purview of a 5,000-word essay. Moreover, the federal due process and equal protection analysis set out here is generally applicable to the outcome of legal arguments based upon analogous state constitutional provisions.

10. *See, e.g.*, Wardle, *supra* note 2, at 18–20 (noting the extent of the literature on the subject).

11. Professor Wardle specifically examines due process claims based upon the "right to marry," the "constitutional zone of privacy," and the "right of intimate association" and equal protection claims that flow from analogies to racial and gender-based discrimination. *Id.* at 26–95.

12. *See, e.g., id.* at 26, 62 (surveying the literature).

13. Skinner v. Oklahoma, 316 U.S. 535, 541 (1942).

14. 505 U.S. 833, 851 (1992) (plurality opinion of O'Connor, Kennedy, and Souter, JJ.).

15. *Id.*

16. Kelly v. Johnson, 425 U.S. 238 (1976).

17. 5 U.S. (1 Cranch) 137 (1803).

18. Washington v. Glucksberg, 521 U.S. at 720–721 (quoting Moore v. City of East Cleveland, Ohio, 431 U.S., at 494, 503 (1977)). *Accord* Hawkins v. Freeman, 195 F.3d 732, 739 (4th Cir. 1999):

> The first step in [substantive due process analysis] is to determine whether the claimed violation involves one of those fundamental rights and liberties which are, objectively, deeply rooted in this Nation's history and tradition, and implicit in the concept of ordered liberty, such that neither liberty nor justice would exist if they were sacrificed. The next step depends for its nature upon the result of the first. If the asserted interest has been determined to be "fundamental," it is entitled in the second step to the protection of strict scrutiny judicial review of the challenged legislation. If the interest is determined not to be "fundamental," it is entitled only to the protection of rational-basis judicial review. [internal quotes and citations omitted]

19. 521 U.S. at 720–21 (quoting Palko v. Connecticut, 302 U.S. 319, 325 (1937)).

20. *Id.* (citing Reno v. Flores, 507 U.S. 292, 302 (1993); Collins v. City of Harker Heights, Texas, 503 U.S. 115, 125 (1992); Cruzan v. Director, Missouri Department of Health, 497 U.S. 261, 277–278 (1990)).

21. 505 U.S. at 851 (plurality opinion).

22. *Glucksberg*, 521 U.S. at 721 (quoting *Collins*, 503 U.S. at 125). Michael H. v. Gerald D., 491 U.S. 110 (1989), is a powerful example of the limits of "responsible decision making." There the Court addressed the constitutionality of a century-old California statute granting a nearly irrefutable presumption that a child born to a married woman was the child of the woman's husband. *See* CAL. EVID. CODE ANN. § 621(a) (West 1989). The plaintiff established a 98 percent probability of paternity. Nevertheless, the lower courts, consistent with California law, refused to allow the plaintiff to establish a relationship with the child. In affirming, the Supreme Court denied the plaintiff's substantive due process argument because, when analyzed in accordance with history and tradition, the values protected by the California law—namely, the sanctity of the marriage relationship—outweighed any individual rights the biological father might have had in a child conceived out of wedlock. 491 U.S.

at 126–130. Emphasizing the power of the legislature to govern and protect the marital union, the Court stated: "Where . . . the child is born into an extant marital family, the natural father's unique opportunity conflicts with the similarly unique opportunity of the husband of the marriage; and it is not unconstitutional for the State to give categorical preference to the latter." *Id.* at 129.

23. Professor Eskridge has suggested that while same-sex marriage has not been recognized in the West, it has been practiced and accepted in other cultures and countries throughout the world. *See* William N. Eskridge Jr., *A History of Same-Sex Marriage*, 79 VA. L. REV. 1419, 1511 (1993). In his article, however, Professor Eskridge carelessly assumes that a state-sanctioned "same-sex union" and "same-sex marriage" are the same thing. A state-sanctioned union and marriage are not the same, and recent research supports the proposition that nations and cultures of the world recognize that marriage is between a man and woman. *See* Peter Lubin & Dwight Duncan, *Follow the Footnote or the Advocate as Historian of Same-Sex Marriage*, 47 CATH. U.L. REV. 1271, 1325 (1998).

24. *See* Griswold v. Connecticut, 381 U.S. 479, 496 (1965) (calling the "traditional relation of the family" a "relation as old and as fundamental as our entire civilization").

25. *See* Skinner v. Oklahoma, 316 U.S. 535, 541 (1942) ("Marriage and procreation are fundamental to the very existence and survival of the race"); *see also* Planned Parenthood of Southeastern Pennsylvania v. Casey, 505 U.S. 833, 851 (1992) ("Our law affords constitutional protection to personal decisions relating to marriage, procreation").

26. *See* Pierce v. Society of Sisters, 268 U.S. 510 (1925).

27. *See* Prince v. Massachusetts, 321 U.S. 158, 165 (1944); Cutshall v. Sundquist, 193 F.3d 466 (6th Cir. 1999) (stating that activities implicit in the concept of ordered liberty were "matters relating to marriage, procreation, contraception, family relationships, and child rearing and education") (quoting Paul v. Davis, 424 U.S. 693, 701 (1976)).

28. In general, a "suspect class" is characterized by an immutable trait (such as race) that subjects the class to unique social disadvantages. While some state courts have recently applied this analysis to same-sex marriage (Tanner v. Oregon Health Sciences University, 971 P.2d 435 (Or. App. 1998); Baker v. Vermont, 744 A.2d 864 (Vt. 1998)), any claim that homosexuality is "immutable" or that "gayness" (in today's social milieu) imposes unique social disadvantages is unpersuasive. As Professor Lynn Wardle correctly states, while race—the classic suspect class—"is *passive*, homosexual behavior is active. Race is undeniably an immutable, *biologically determined* condition, which homosexual behavior has *not* been shown to be. Intuitively, there is a distinction between immutable racial classifications, which are logically irrelevant to legitimate policies, and personal sexual behavior choices, which are of substantial social concern, especially regarding marriage." Wardle, *supra* note 2, at 82 (emphasis added). *See also id.* at 75. *See also* Joseph Nicolosi, A. Dean Byrd, & Richard W. Potts, *Retrospective Self-Reports of Changes in Homosexual Orientation: A Consumer Survey of Conversion Therapy Clients*, 86 PSYCHOLOGICAL REPORTS 1071, 1083 (June 2000) (study concludes that "20% to 30% of the participants [in voluntary conversion therapy] said they shifted from a homosexual orientation to an exclusively or almost exclusively heterosexual orientation") (belying any assertion that homosexual orientation is "immutable").

29. *See* Griswold v. Connecticut, 381 U.S. 479, 486–499 (1965) (Goldberg, J., concurring); Reynolds v. United States, 98 U.S. 145, 164–65 (1878); *see also* Lynn D. Wardle, Loving v. Virginia *and the Constitutional Right to Marry, 1790–1990*, 41 How. L.J. 289, 301 (1998) (noting that *Griswold* "underscored that marriage is linked with, and the basis for, the traditional family and child-rearing").

30. Maynard v. Hill, 8 S.Ct. 723, 726 (1888).

31. *Griswold*, 381 U.S. at 486.

32. 316 U.S. 535, 541 (1942).

33. 434 U.S. 374 (1978).

34. *Id.* at 386.

35. *See supra* notes 30–34.

36. Skinner v. Oklahoma, 316 U.S. 535, 541 (1942).

37. Robert P. George & Gerard V. Bradley, *Marriage and the Liberal Imagination*, 84 Geo. L.J. 301, 302 (1995).

38. Hadley Arkes, *Questions of Principle, Not Predictions: A Reply to Macedo*, 84 Geo. L.J. 321 (1995).

39. George & Bradley, *supra* note 37, at 301–302.

40. Professors George and Bradley argue that the notion of sex as pure sensory experience compromises the important values of personal dignity and integrity:

[M]arriage provides a noninstrumental reason for spouses, whether or not they are capable of conceiving children in their acts of genital union, to perform [sexual] acts. In choosing to perform nonmarital orgasmic acts, including sodomitical acts—irrespective of whether the persons performing such acts are of the same or opposite sexes (and even if those persons are validly married to each other)—persons necessarily treat their bodies and those of their sexual partners (if any) as means or instruments in ways that damage their personal (and interpersonal) integrity; thus, regard for the basic human good of integrity provides a conclusive moral reason not to engage in sodomitical and other nonmarital sex acts.

*Id.*

41. *See supra* note 23 on Professor Eskridge argues that, while same-sex marriage is not sanctioned in the West, it has been recognized and accepted in other non-Western cultures and countries. However, careful review of Eskridge's work reveals that other cultures have *tolerated* same-sex unions, but never *sanctioned* same-sex marriage. *See* Peter Lubin & Dwight Duncan, *Follow the Footnote or the Advocate as Historian of Same-Sex Marriage*, 47 Cath. U.L. Rev. 1271, 1325 (1998).

42. Skinner v. Oklahoma, 316 U.S. 535, 541 (1942).

43. *See supra* notes 30–34 and accompanying text; *see also* Learned Hand, The Bill of Rights 70 (1958) ("For myself it would be most irksome to be ruled by a bevy of Platonic Guardians, even if I knew how to choose them, which I assuredly do not").

44. Robert P. George, *Public Reason and Political Conflict: Abortion and Homosexuality*, 106 Yale L.J. 2475, 2497 (1997):

Professor Bradley and I defend an alternative conception of marriage—one which we believe to be reflected in traditional American and British marriage law, especially in the law governing consummation of marriage. We argue that marriage is a one-flesh (i.e., *bodily*, as well as emotional, dispositional, and spiritual) union of a male and a female spouse consummated and actualized by sexual acts that are reproductive in type. Such acts consummate and, we maintain, actualize the intrinsic good of marriage whether or not reproduction is desired by the spouses in any particular marital act, or is even possible for them in a particular act or at all. [emphasis added]

45. Professors George and Bradley cogently ask how society can, in principle, reject the claim of the pederast once it accepts the marital claim of the homosexual couple. *See* George & Bradley, *supra* note 37, at 311.

46. *See* Andrew Koppleman, *Discrimination Against Gays Is Sex Discrimination*, infra at 209.

47. United States v. Virginia, 518 U.S. 515 (1996).

48. Hermaphroditism is a rare condition among humans, with few recorded incidences. WORLD BOOK ENCYCLOPEDIA, *Hermaphrodite* 211 (2001); MOSBY'S MEDICAL, NURSING, AND ALLIED HEALTH DICTIONARY 732 (Kenneth N. Anderson ed., 4th ed., Mosby 1994).

49. Craig v. Boren, 429 U.S. 190 (1976).

50. United States v. Virginia, 518 U.S. 515 (1996).

51. See *supra* note 28 on claims that "gayness" is an immutable, nonchosen behavior.

52. 381 U.S. 479, 486 (1965).

53. Bowers v. Hardwick, 478 U.S. 186, 196 (1986).

54. *See* Peter Lubin & Dwight Duncan, *Follow the Footnote*, 47 CATH. U.L. REV. at 1325 (1998).

55. *See* Brigette Berger, *The Social Roots of Prosperity and Liberty*, 35 SOCIETY 44 (Mar.–Apr. 1998) (available on WestLaw at 1998 WL 11168752).

56. JUDITH S. WALLERSTEIN, JULIA M. LEWIS, & SANDRA BLAKESLEE, THE UNEXPECTED LEGACY OF DIVORCE 294–316 (1st ed., Hyperion 2000) (asserting, among other things, that modern easy access to divorce "has increased the suffering of children." *Id.* at 294).

57. *Id.* As Dr. Wallerstein explains, during the past thirty years,

we've created a new kind of society never before seen in human culture. Silently and unconsciously, we have created a culture of divorce. It's hard to grasp what it means when we say that first marriages stand a 45 percent chance of breaking up and that second marriages have a 60 percent chance of ending in divorce. What are the consequences for all of us when 25 percent of people today between the ages of eighteen and forty-four have parents who divorced? What does it mean to a society when people wonder aloud if the family is about to disappear? What can we do when we learn that married couples with children represent a mere 26 percent of households in the 1990s and that the most common living arrangement nowadays is a household of unmarried people with no children? These numbers are terrifying. But like all massive social change, what's happening is affecting us in ways that we have yet to understand.

*Id.* at 295–296.

58. Bowers v. Hardwick, 478 U.S. 186, 196 (1986).

59. Skinner v. Oklahoma, 316 U.S. 535, 541 (1942). *See also* Zablocki v. Redhail, 434 U.S. 374, 383, 386 (1978) (recognizing that the "right to marry is of fundamental importance" because "[i]f the right to procreate means anything at all, it must imply some right to enter the only relationship in which [the State] allows sexual relations legally to take place").

Response

# Reply to "The Constitutionality of Legal Preferences for Heterosexual Marriage"

## Andrew Koppelman

Richard Wilkins thinks that the state has a compelling interest in denying gay people the right to marry because heterosexual relationships are often good. The "because" in the previous sentence is a mysterious thing. Even if it is true that many or most heterosexual marriages are good and have many social benefits, this entails nothing about how the law ought to deal with other relationships.

The indisputable datum on which he relies is the divorce rate, which is higher than it was for most of American history. Perhaps it is too high, although Wilkins offers no convincing evidence for that proposition.[1] But what does that have to do with same-sex marriage?

His causal claims appear to be these. Legal recognition of same-sex marriage would damage some entity or institution called "the family," and this damage would then result in more divorces. What "the family" is, what its characteristics are, and how the damage would occur are not explained. "The family" is evidently not identical with any particular family, and it is not clear what this term refers to.[2] Perhaps he means the set of institutions that "responsibly channel and encourage reproduction." It is good for children to grow up in stable, loving households, but we are not told what this indicates about relationships between gay people, many of whom have stable loving households of their own and are raising children very competently. How can recognition of same-sex marriages possibly affect the rate of heterosexual divorces? We are not given a clue.

Gay people appear to be in some way associated in Wilkins's mind with social trends that he dislikes, and that justifies legal treatment that disadvantages them. This is the kind of thinking that produced the Salem witch trials. Salem in 1692, historians Paul Boyer and Stephen Nissenbaum have argued, was in the throes of social and economic upheaval as an older agrarian order was being replaced by a new commercial one. Those who were accused of witchcraft were, for the most part, much more involved in the commercial activities of the nearby port than their accusers were. Unable to understand the forces that were transforming their world, the Salem villagers "lashed out with accusations not only against those who seemed in one way or another to represent the new order, but also against those who reminded them how far they, themselves, had already been seduced from their traditional moorings."[3] They hanged nineteen people and had more than 100 other suspects in jail when the trials ended. It did no good. The commercial and secular world continued its inexorable advance. Magical thinking is a poor basis for public policy. Wilkins likes to talk about morality, but his eagerness to scapegoat innocent people for social problems that they have nothing to do with has moral implications of its own.

Wilkins competently attacks the very weakest arguments for same-sex marriage. The substantive due process argument for gay equality is indeed rife with difficulties, though it has many prominent defenders.[4] More impressive is the argument that gay people are an oppressed minority, like blacks, who warrant special judicial protection. Wilkins mentions and rejects this argument so summarily that a response would have to begin by fully stating the argument, and this is not the place for that.[5]

His main essay never takes up the constitutional argument I do endorse, that discrimination against gay people is a form of sex discrimination. His response to me completely mischaracterizes that argument. He attributes to me claims that I do not make and do not believe and then proceeds to attack those claims. When I write that Ricky, denied the right to marry Fred, "is suffering legal disadvantage because of his sex," I do not mean that Ricky is suffering legal disadvantage because of his homosexual activity. I mean that he is suffering legal disadvantage because he is a man. He would not be denied the right to marry Fred if he were a woman. A woman could marry Fred even if they did not plan to engage in sexual activity, and Ricky may not marry Fred even if they do not plan to engage in sexual activity. My argument has attracted many criticisms since I first made it in 1988, but this is the first time that anyone has managed to misunderstand it so thoroughly. Wilkins offers no criticisms of the arguments that I actually make.

## NOTES

1. A divorce rate of zero would certainly be too low, since there are some terrible marriages that are best ended quickly. The question of when divorces are or are not appropriate is one not easily answered from the armchair, and I would hesitate to substitute my judgment for those of the persons immediately concerned. Nor is it sufficient to rely, as Wilkins does, on the alarming claims of Judith Wallerstein, who has extensively studied a small sample (with no control group) of divorced families

who were preselected because they had already been experiencing emotional problems when they were referred to her clinic. See Andrew Cherlin, *Generation Ex-*, NATION, Dec. 11, 2000. James Q. Wilson, who shares many of Wilkins's substantive views, notes that Wallerstein's study "is not so much a work of social science as a collection of biographies linked with therapeutic suggestions." James Q. Wilson, *Marriage Matters*, NATIONAL REVIEW, Oct. 9, 2000, at 49.

2. At a few points Wilkins tries to bolster his argument with that developed by Robert P. George and Gerard V. Bradley, which treats marriage as an ineffable metaphysical essence, but their defense of the heterosexuality requirement has nothing to do with consequences and so fits uncomfortably with that of Wilkins. For a critique of George and Bradley, *see* ANDREW KOPPELMAN, THE GAY RIGHTS QUESTION IN CONTEMPORARY AMERICAN LAW 79–93 (2002).

3. PAUL BOYER & STEPHEN NISSENBAUM, SALEM POSSESSED: THE SOCIAL ORIGINS OF WITCHCRAFT 212 (1974).

4. See KOPPELMAN, THE GAY RIGHTS QUESTION, *supra* note 2, at 35–52.

5. The argument that Wilkins is rejecting here is a good deal more complex and nuanced than he represents it to be, and no reader should imagine that he has adequately summarized it. See Watkins v. United States Army, 847 F.2d 1329 (9th Cir. 1988); Carol Steiker, Note, *The Constitutional Status of Sexual Orientation: Homosexuality as a Suspect Classification*, 98 HARV. L. REV. 1285 (1985); KOPPELMAN, THE GAY RIGHTS QUESTION, *supra* note 2, at 6–34.

# Chapter 8

## Essay One

# Civil Marriage and the First Amendment

## David B. Cruz

Across the nation a battle rages for control of one of U.S. society's most potent symbols, marriage—what it means, who has the right to use it, and for what purposes. Proponents of same-sex marriage or "marriage expansionists," for ease of exposition, have been arguing since at least the 1970s that the U.S. Constitution bars government from restricting marriage to mixed-sex couples.[1] Marriage expansionists' most common constitutional arguments for abolition of the mixed-sex requirement for civil marriage rely on fundamental-rights doctrine and the guarantee of equal protection of the laws. The mixed-sex requirement imposes upon many lesbigay couples an absolute barrier to the fundamental right to marry and cannot be justified under the heightened scrutiny mandated by the Due Process[2] and Equal Protection Clauses.[3] It also defines access to the institution of civil marriage by sex and/or sexual orientation, and this classification cannot withstand the ensuing heightened scrutiny under the Equal Protection Clause.

Despite the force of these arguments, in recent years both the federal government and some thirty states have amended their marriage laws or otherwise adopted measures designed to fortify the limitation of civil marriage to mixed-sex couples.[4] Yet the discourse on same-sex marriage and the national understanding of the issues in this area have been deficient without sustained attention to a core component of the value of civil marriage: its expressive potential. When many, although far from all, of the rights, obligations, and privileges of marriage may be enjoyed by unmarried couples, with whatever expense and forethought, the choice to marry civilly arguably takes on even greater symbolic meaning than it has in the past.[5] This expressive character of marriage lies behind much of the ostensibly secular opposition to extending civil marriage to same-sex couples, and understanding that civil marriage is a unique expressive resource opens the possibility of a First Amendment challenge to the mixed-sex requirement.

Civil marriage is nearly always an act and expression of commitment. Marital commitment is expressed not simply by ceremonies, rings, and gifts. It is also expressed by the act of undertaking and continuing to live under the responsibilities of civil marriage and by letting it be known that one is living as a part of a civil marriage. A proposition of (civil) marriage is an invitation to a partner to join a publicly valued institution, not simply to maintain a relationship in the realm of the private. One's statements of marital commitment gain additional credibility from the civil status.

Some of the literature on same-sex marriage notes marriage's importance to lesbigay self-conceptions, but marriage is obviously very important to many heterosexually identified individuals' personal identities. I do not wish to overstate this claim, given the high incidence of nonmarital births and child rearing, but at least normatively, marriage is held out to the heterosexually identified as an appropriately important aspect of their adult identity. In some instances, "in our culture, by just being married, a woman gains an identity, an acceptability, a legitimacy that you often don't get as a single woman."[6] While gender may make marriage especially salient for many women's identities, spousal identity is also important to men. As a general matter, a person "comes to define herself through a history of relationships and affiliations."[7]

It is not simply the interpersonal relationship between two people in love that may form part of their identities; the formal legal status of being civilly married may do so as well. Civil marriage carries with it numerous legal rights or privileges, reliance on which may form the backdrop of a couple's ongoing relationship and process of mutual self-constitution. In this respect, the relationship between two people who are married at law does differ from the relationship between people only married before their god, with the two relationships supporting different expectations that in turn can influence one's "sense of self" differently. As Judge Richard Posner has recognized, marrying civilly is one way in which couples might "signal[ ] the extent of their commitment."[8]

With marriage, and in particular civil marriage with its common state-sanctioned monopoly on lawful intercourse, one also communicates to the world (however accurately or not) that one's sex life is simply one facet of one's life, incorporated into a presumptively balanced whole. Indeed, one of the cultural consequences of civil marriage is the submergence of sexuality into (inter)personality: Couples believed to be civilly married thus enjoy the privilege of respectful privacy, whereby their sexuality is far from the most salient feature of their relationship but instead merely one component of an integrated life. In contrast, same-sex couples, precluded by the mixed-sex requirement from using civil marriage to express the integrity of their sexuality, are subjected to the "sex-as-lifestyle" presumption powerfully critiqued by Marc Fajer.[9] This differential treatment emphasizes the value of civil marriage's ability to allow one to contextualize sexuality, affording those who have access to it greater ability to control their messages about their intimate relationships.

Hence civil marriage, and not just private marriage ceremonies or religious marriage, should be understood as expressive. Access to the status relationship that is civil marriage provides couples with an important and unique resource with which they can, if they choose, express themselves and constitute their identities. Denials of access to civil marriage thus implicate the First Amendment's guarantees of freedom of expression. This perspective on the debate over civil marriage and its mixed-sex requirement provides important insight into the unconstitutionality of denying same-sex couples access to civil marriage.

The kinds of public expression enabled by civil marriage are high-value speech constitutionally protected by the First Amendment. Constitutional law expert Laurence Tribe "has accurately commented that the values of privacy are matched by equally important 'outward-looking aspects of self'; 'freedom to have impact on others—to make the "statement" implicit in a public identity—is central to any adequate conception of the self.' "[10] This is eminently true of the noble public expression of commitment and identity that marrying is for most people. Access to the expressive resource of civil marriage should accordingly receive strong constitutional protection.

Not only is civil marriage a uniquely powerful expressive resource, but the purposes of the mixed-sex requirement are also expressive. Specifically, concern with what the institution of civil marriage—as distinguished from individual civil marriages—might express or be capable of expressing underwrites the mixed-sex requirement throughout the United States. Although there may be other purposes that the mixed-sex requirement partially serves, however well or poorly, consideration of the mixed-sex requirement in its contemporary legal and social context reveals that government is indeed restricting access to the unique expressive resource of civil marriage in significant part on an expressive basis.

In various debates, marriage conventionalists have recurred to a riot of reasons alleged to support the mixed-sex requirement. While some conventionalist arguments invoke public welfare purposes[11] or the supposed immorality of sexual activity between people of the same sex, many of the arguments are expressive or symbolic in nature: the argument that marriage simply "means" a man and a woman, so that allowing same-sex couples to marry civilly would change the "meaning" of marriage; nebulous arguments that insist that the mixed-sex requirement is necessary to preserve the "specialness" of marriage;[12] claims that the mixed-sex requirement is needed to ward off threats to the "institution" of marriage; and the insistence that the mixed-sex requirement not be abolished lest government give a "stamp of approval" to "homosexuality." These contentions primarily reflect a view of civil marriage as an important symbolic institution, one whose expressive meaning should not, in these advocates' views, be changed.

Perhaps the most dramatic evidence that the mixed-sex requirement for civil marriage relates to expression comes from Vermont. In the waning days of the twentieth century, the Supreme Court of Vermont unanimously held in *Baker v. State* that the state's limitation of civil marriage to mixed-sex couples violated that state's constitution.[13] (The Common Benefits Clause of the Vermont Constitution provides, in pertinent part, "[t]hat government is, or ought to be, instituted for the common benefit, protection, and security of the people, nation, or community, and not for the particular emolument or advantage of any single [person], family, or set of [persons], who are a part only of that community.")[14] The court's opinion directed the state to enact legislation granting same-sex couples access to all the benefits and obligations that Vermont confers upon mixed-sex couples who marry. In response, the Vermont legislature passed and the governor signed legislation creating "civil unions." Vermont's "Act Relating to Civil Unions" specifies that "[p]arties to a civil union shall have *all* the same benefits, protections and responsibilities under law . . . as are granted to spouses in a marriage."[15] Thus, to the extent that the incidents of civil marriage are subject to control by one state, Vermont has adopted a separate legal status of "domestic partnership" that is virtually identical to marriage except in name, as even opponents of civil union in Vermont have recognized. "Mere" symbolic or expressive difference between mixed-sex civil marriage and same-sex civil unions thus has to a degree become reality in the United States.

The coexistence of such a domestic partnership regime with civil marriage from which it differs solely in name shows that the same-sex-marriage debates are about symbolic expression. The most plausible defense of such "separate-but-equal" regimes would seem to be one relying on the importance of naming, of keeping the meaning or symbolism of "marriage" as it is and distinct from institutions embracing same-sex couples, and of the connection between the symbolic meaning of "marriage" and personal identity, rather than any public welfare justification. These are clearly governmental purposes intimately related to expression.

Certainly in Vermont there should be no doubt that the dual regime of civil marriage for mixed-sex couples and civil unions for same-sex couples must be justified, if at all, by an expressive purpose or purposes. But a similar purpose should be understood to undergird (albeit not necessarily exclusively) the mixed-sex requirements in the other forty-nine states and the federal government. Given the ubiquity of compulsory heterosexuality,[16] one should be deeply skeptical that the people of the state of Vermont are psychologically constituted differently from the other people of the nation. In addition, Vermont pressed the same sorts of justifications in the *Baker* litigation that marriage conventionalists have been urging generally.[17] This highlights that both public welfare justifications and symbolic justifications undergird the mixed-sex requirement, so that even in states that offer same-sex couples no domestic partnership benefits whatsoever (let alone the valuable "civil-union" status offered in Vermont), the mixed-sex requirement should be understood to rest at least in significant part upon similar expressive grounds. Accordingly, the mixed-sex requirement for civil marriage must survive stringent constitutional analysis to be adjudged consistent with the First Amendment.

Even if the purpose of the mixed-sex requirement for civil marriage were deemed unrelated to expression, the fact that the mixed-sex requirement regulates access to a unique expressive resource and thus has an effect on expression that varies with respect to the expression's content should suffice to trigger some heightened judicial scrutiny, even if not the most strict. Given the substantial over- and underbreadth of the various public welfare purposes offered for the mixed-sex requirement, that heightened scrutiny suffices to show that the mixed-sex requirement violates the First Amendment.

The question remains, precisely how should First Amendment principles constraining regulation of civil marriage be treated by courts? No ready-made doctrine is available to handle the First Amendment questions that the mixed-sex requirement raises.[18] Nonetheless, relevant principles can be extracted from existing First Amendment doctrine and theory and combined to fashion constitutional doctrine adequate for analyzing the constitutionality of the mixed-sex requirement for civil marriage.

Some might think that civil marriage should be analyzed as itself a form of governmental "speech." That is, the institution of civil marriage might be examined as a way in which governments symbolically express a message of approbation—and thus legitimacy—of certain valued activities and relationships. Yet civil marriage is a means by which people—individual couples—variously express themselves and constitute their identities, not just a mode of government speech. Because individual civil marriages are themselves expressive resources, analyzing civil marriage as merely or primarily state speech would overlook something vitally important to individuals' lives and to society. Private parties—not government agents (employees or deputized recipients of government funds)—are speaking through civil marriage.[19]

Civil marriage should thus be analyzed as a unique expressive resource. It is important under the First Amendment that such resources be maintained in a nondiscriminatory fashion: "An important material dimension of public discourse is that there be a wide circulation of 'similar social stimuli.' This circulation creates a public communicative sphere by making common experiences available to those who would otherwise remain unconnected strangers."[20] In particular, civil marriage should be made available on a viewpoint-neutral basis, and content-based regulations of the expressive resource of civil marriage should be tolerated only insofar as they are justified by a nonexpressive compelling governmental interest and afford adequate alternative expressive resources.[21]

One of the most basic neutrality commands of the First Amendment is that of viewpoint neutrality. "If there is a bedrock principle underlying the First Amendment, it is that the Government may not prohibit the expression of an idea simply because society finds the idea itself offensive or disagreeable."[22] The disfavoring of viewpoint-discriminatory regulations may be due to concerns about government interference with either the "expressive marketplace" or equal freedom of expression and "the symbolic (as much as any other) endorsement by the authority of one side of the controversy."[23] Accordingly, the viewpoint-neutrality imperative should apply to governmental regulation of marriage, a uniquely powerful expressive resource that is of paramount importance in contemporary U.S. culture and politics.

Furthermore, even viewpoint-neutral regulations that are content based are constitutionally suspect under the First Amendment.[24] As the Supreme Court announced in *Police Department v. Mosley*, "[A]bove all else, the First Amendment means that government has no power to restrict expression because of its message, its ideas, its subject matter, or its content."[25] Because ruling majorities can easily impede equality of communicative opportunity and distort public discourse by amplifying speech favored by the majority, and because these skewing effects are potentially magnified where a unique expressive resource is at issue, content-based regulations of unique expressive resources should trigger closer First Amendment scrutiny. Hence if the mixed-sex requirement is found to be content based, it should be subjected to heightened purpose and means scrutiny.

Moreover, an expressive governmental purpose cannot count as "compelling" for purposes of overriding First Amendment constraints on regulation of a unique expressive resource such as civil marriage. To allow governmental symbolism or other expression to count as compelling would grant a majority the power to abridge unpopular speech based on its own desire to express something different, a move that would greatly undermine the purposes of the First Amendment.

Because the mixed-sex requirement for civil marriage rests at least in significant part upon a purpose related to the suppression of expression, it must survive heightened scrutiny under the First Amendment doctrine I have proposed for such unique expressive resources. The mixed-sex requirement, however, fails this analysis because it lacks the neutrality required by the Constitution. Gay or lesbian couples simply may not use civil marriage to express their belief that same-sex couples can love each other, that committed same-sex relationships are valuable to society, and that gay and lesbian people can form families deserving of respect and support. The mixed-sex requirement reflects viewpoint discrimination because in practice it makes civil marriage available to some people to make statements about love and commitment—those who marry heterosexually—thus not excluding these entire subject matters but privileging certain speakers who correspond strongly with a certain viewpoint on love and commitment due to a virtually definitional connection between sexes and sexual orientations.[26]

The discrimination embodied in the mixed-sex requirement for civil marriage has the effect of skewing public debate about lesbigay people and our rights. It distorts public discourse about the capacity of lesbigay people for fidelity and commitment by providing the heterosexually identified with a uniquely powerful tool for expressing to the world their interpersonal bonds while denying that tool to lesbigay persons.

The fact that majorities might defend the discriminatory mixed-sex requirement for access to the expressive resource of civil marriage as an attempt to protect the current meaning of marriage cannot save the requirement from invalidation under the First Amendment, for it is unconstitutional for government to limit symbolic expression in that fashion. The "meaning of marriage" is an important public or common symbolic resource: As a unique expressive resource, civil marriage functions as a sign or symbol, a way by which people can convey to each other and to the world their commitment and identity as a couple; preserving the symbol's current meaning cannot justify denying it to same-sex couples either by offering no legal status comparable to civil marriage or by fencing such relationships into a separate legal status such as domestic partnership.

The inconsistency of the mixed-sex requirement's attempt to preserve the symbolic meaning of the institution of civil marriage with constitutional principles of free expression may be illuminated by the U.S. Supreme Court's "flag-burning" decisions, *Texas v. Johnson* and *United States v. Eichman*.[27] These cases reject the proposition that government may seek to preserve the current meaning of a symbol by precluding its use by persons who may take a different view of its meaning and wish to use it to convey a message different from the majority's.

*Johnson* and *Eichman* presented challenges to state and federal laws prohibiting certain actions with respect to the U.S. flag such as "desecrating" or "physically defil[ing]" it, which the state and federal prosecutors argued were justified as efforts to protect the flag's symbolic meaning. In *Johnson*, the state of Texas argued "that it has an interest in preserving the flag as a symbol of nationhood and national unity, a symbol with a determinate range of meanings."[28] In *Eichman*, the United States argued that it had "an interest in 'protect[ing] the physical integrity of the flag under all circumstances' in order to safeguard the flag's identity ' "as the unique and unalloyed symbol of the Nation." ' "[29]

The Supreme Court accepted that government may have a legitimate interest in the meaning of at least some symbols, yet held that these anti-flag-burning laws violated constitutional guarantees of free expression, not simply because the government was interested in protecting the dominant meanings of the U.S. flag, but because of the way the laws had gone about serving that symbolic interest: by restricting contradictory expression with that symbol. The problem was that the laws at issue precluded others from using the flag as a symbolic resource to express dissenting views. As the Court observed in *Johnson*, "[W]e never before have held that the Government may ensure that a symbol be used to express only one view of that symbol or its referents."[30] In both cases, the Court held that the First Amendment barred government from doing so.

Similarly, free-expression principles should invalidate the mixed-sex requirement for civil marriage that denies that expressive or symbolic resource to same-sex couples. Even if admitting same-sex couples to the institution of civil marriage modulates the messages that marrying might convey, that is the consequence of our expansive commitment to expressive freedom. It is not constitutional for government to reserve civil marriage for mixed-sex couples to try to keep the term "marriage," the symbol that "marriage" is, or the social notion of "marriage" from coming to be understood as in principle embracing same-sex couples. Many same-sex couples do consider themselves already married, although not yet legitimately so in the eyes of the law. That some political majority takes a contrary position does not authorize it to enshrine in law a requirement that denies the expressive resource of civil marriage to those with whom it differs. If the mixed-sex requirement is not adjudged outright unconstitutional as a viewpoint-discriminatory condition on access to the expressive resource of civil marriage, at the least it is content based and so must survive strict scrutiny, and it must do so on the basis of some purpose other than preserving the current symbolic meaning of marriage.[31]

The stock "definitional" argument, variants of which are espoused by a current generation of natural-law scholars, holds that the mixed-sex requirement does not discriminate or deny any rights to anyone because marriage simply *means* one man and one woman. Yet this claim is patently unresponsive to the challenge that constitutional principles render such a legal definition of marriage impermissible. Indeed, it is circular, effectively saying that the reason government may adopt a definition of marriage excluding same-sex couples is that the definition of marriage excludes same-sex couples.

Beyond the circular definitional argument, marriage conventionalists also commonly advance a slew of public welfare arguments in support of the mixed-sex requirement: protecting the public fisc, procreation, child rearing, and so forth. These aims, however, do not satisfy heightened scrutiny and thus also do not justify denying the expressive resource of civil marriage to same-sex couples.

For example, despite Jean Bethke Elshtain's dogmatic contention that "marriage . . . is and always has been about the possibility of generativity,"[32] in-house procreation—procreation requiring only genetic material contributed by the two spouses—should not be considered a viable defense of the mixed-sex marriage requirement. A man and a woman need not have children to continue to be civilly married, need not intend to have children, and need not even be capable of having children. The procreation rationale fits the mixed-sex requirement like a square peg fits a round hole. Some marriage conventionalists attempt to defend this grossly poor fit between the mixed-sex requirement and procreation on the grounds that no same-sex couple can procreate in-house and that it would be intrusive to ask the questions of mixed-sex couples that would be necessary to limit civil marriage solely to those who will procreate in-house. That rationale, however, does not survive heightened scrutiny, for it would indefensibly privilege modest intrusions on heterosexual privacy over the major First Amendment infringement represented by the mixed-sex requirement's denial of the expressive resource of civil marriage to same-sex couples.

To the extent that society properly cares about future generations, the pressing issue is child rearing, not child production, but such concerns cannot justify the mixed-sex requirement. Claims about a supposed adverse impact on the development of children have been rejected by, for example, the trial court in the Hawaii litigation, based on the social science literature.[33] Speculative in its predictions of harm, the objection that same-sex couples do not provide role models of each sex to children should be understood as maintaining that they cannot constitute role models of each sex, for same-sex couples frequently do socialize with members of the other sex. There is, however, no convincing evidence that a child raised by gay or lesbian parents cannot look to others for gender role models in any psychologically necessary sense.[34] Thus this argument too fails heightened scrutiny.

As to the objection (made, for example, by Vermont in the *Baker* litigation) that there would be an adverse impact on recognition of a state's marriages were it to eliminate the same-sex requirement, I have seen no plausible argument that a state's authorizing same-sex marriages would lead other states to disregard the first state's mixed-sex marriages. The prospect that the extrastate effects of a same-sex marriage might be limited does not make sense as a reason not to recognize such marriages within the state.

An additional common defense of the mixed-sex requirement adverts to morality, claiming that a majority's view that same-sex conduct or relationships are immoral justifies the restriction of civil marriage to mixed-sex couples. Marriage conventionalists in the legal academy have pressed morality arguments in defense of the mixed-sex requirement, and morality arguments are a staple in marriage conventionalist writings in newspapers throughout the country.

Such morality arguments do not provide a sufficiently compelling basis for overriding lesbigay people's First Amendment right to share access to the expressive resource of civil marriage. First, morality arguments often are themselves expressive justifications for laws. Thus Justice Lewis Powell maintained that "[t]he State, representing the collective expression of moral aspirations, has an undeniable interest in ensuring that its rules of domestic relations reflect the widely held values of its people."[35] As expressive interests, morality arguments cannot provide a compelling governmental interest of the kind (i.e., nonexpressive) needed to trump what would otherwise be a First Amendment violation.

Second, and more fundamentally, claims that homosexuality or same-sex sexual conduct are immoral cannot plausibly be justified in secular terms by any interests subject to empirical disproof. Arguments resting on the supposed immorality of lesbigay relationships or sexual acts thus rest on "bare" assertions of morality, which should be understood not to provide an "important," "substantial," or "compelling" reason to override First Amendment rights.[36] Admittedly, the Court has previously rejected claimed constitutional rights on the basis of bare assertions of morality. In *Bowers v. Hardwick*, the Court rejected a due process challenge to Georgia's law criminalizing oral and anal sex on the basis of "the presumed belief of a majority of the electorate in Georgia that homosexual sodomy is immoral and unacceptable."[37] However, as Justice Antonin Scalia later observed, *Bowers* did not hold "that those [morality] concerns were particularly 'important' or 'substantial,' or amounted to anything more than a rational basis for regulation."[38]

The purpose that the mixed-sex requirement best serves is preserving the current symbolic meaning of civil marriage by denying this expressive resource to same-sex couples. If such efforts are not justified as an end in themselves (which the flag-burning cases would then invalidate), their object might be the protection of heterosexually identified persons from the unsettling effects of sharing the institution of civil marriage with same-sex couples. Or it might be the desire to keep marriage from being questioned in a time when many old values are under reexamination and free-floating anxieties fill the national psyche like smog in Los Angeles. But even these instrumental attempts by government to insulate the meaning of this important symbol from contestation should be regarded as impermissible under the First Amendment.

Denying the expressive resource of civil marriage to same-sex couples due to the potentially discomfiting effect on some heterosexually identified persons is antithetical to basic First Amendment principles. In particular, a strong current of First Amendment jurisprudence identifies the "heckler's veto"—whereby government limits expression out of concern with how it will be received—as inconsistent with our national commitment to robust discourse even at significant cost to peace of mind.[39] Protection of minority expression is a fundamental object of the First Amendment as it is understood today. Psychic upset is the unavoidable—and perhaps in many circumstances desirable—consequence of our constitutional protection of free expression. In trying to protect how some heterosexually identified persons think and feel by denying the expressive resource of civil marriage to same-sex couples, government again runs afoul of a type of neutrality norm embodied in the First Amendment: "Where the designed benefit of a content-based speech restriction is to shield the sensibilities of listeners, the general rule is that the right of expression prevails."[40] That general rule should govern here.

In addition, marriage conventionalists occasionally argue that same-sex couples should continue to be forbidden to marry civilly in order to keep marriage "unquestioned." Regardless of the fact that it may well be too late for that, in light of the current incidence of unmarried cohabitation and of unmarried women becoming pregnant, as well as the striking national debate about same-sex marriage, the aim is nonetheless profoundly antidemocratic and at odds with basic First Amendment principles. If marriage really is the foundation for society and a crucial training ground for new citizens, then along with the importance of the institution to society comes a greater importance in allowing questioning of that institution. Moreover, with only narrow and rare exceptions, the First Amendment should be interpreted to prohibit government from passing laws with the aim of fostering ignorance, even as a means to some generally permissible goal.

Assuming that the preceding arguments are correct, marriage practices in America will have to change. It is unconstitutional for the vast majority of states and the federal government to provide people in committed mixed-sex relationships with the expressive resource of civil marriage while denying it to committed same-sex couples.[41] It is even unconstitutional for California, Hawaii, and Vermont to provide heterosexually identified couples with the option of civil marriage while relegating lesbigay couples to the distinctly less legally or symbolically powerful domestic partnerships,[42] reciprocal-beneficiary arrangements,[43] or civil unions[44] offered, respectively, by these states. None of these marriage substitutes is an adequate alternative to the uniquely powerful expressive resource that civil marriage is. It may well be that the Vermont Supreme Court could also ultimately conclude that the expressive capacity of civil marriage is one of the "benefits" that the Vermont Constitution requires be provided equally.[45] Neither of these conclusions, however, would necessarily mean that same-sex couples must be allowed to marry civilly.

Vermont, for example, may choose whether to abolish the mixed-sex requirement (and thus to extend civil marriage to same-sex couples), or instead to abolish civil marriage itself.[46] Either course should comport with Vermont's Common Benefits Clause, for if civil marriage were abolished, its expressive capacity would not be available to anyone, and thus there would be no question of whether it was being improperly reserved to "a part only" of the populace. Similarly, both extension of civil marriage and its abolition would be consistent with the First Amendment, for neither would regulate a unique expressive resource on any ground related to the content (let alone the viewpoint) of expression; rather, the resource would simply no longer exist were civil marriage abolished. Recall in this regard that the U.S. Supreme Court has never intimated that government is constitutionally mandated to establish and to maintain civil marriage.

What seems clear, however, is that giving up civil marriage would deprive the heterosexually identified of the expressive resource that civil marriage is. It would cost single-earner married couples the "marriage bonus" in their federal income tax. It would leave them to worry about inheritances, hospital visitation and medical decision making, no longer being able to hold property by the entirety, loss of the testimonial privilege, and a host of other fairly "concrete" benefits. It might say to them that they are no longer the "special favorite of the laws."[47] I cannot know, but it is at least plausible that enough marriage conventionalists would, if faced with this choice, prefer to "suffer" the symbolic association with lesbigay people rather than give up all of that. At least they would still retain a bundle of privileges and valuable obligations, even if these were now shared with slightly more people.

## NOTES

This essay is based on a longer article, *"Just Don't Call It Marriage": The First Amendment and Marriage as an Expressive Resource*, 74 SO. CAL. L. REV. 925 (May 2001). I am grateful to my research assistant Mike Bermudéz and my spouse Steve Greene for their assistance in producing this essay from that article.

1. Baker v. Nelson, 191 N.W.2d 185 (Minn. 1971), *appeal dismissed*, 409 U.S. 810 (1972).

2. U.S. CONST. amend. XIV, § 1 ("No State shall . . . deprive any person of life, liberty, or property, without due process of law").

3. U.S. CONST. amend. XIV, § 1 ("No State shall . . . deny to any person within its jurisdiction the equal protection of the laws").

4. *See* A Historic Victory: Civil Unions for Same-Sex Couples 7, at http://www.lambdalegal.org/sections/library/marriage/whatsnext.pdf (last modified July 6, 2000) (enumerating states with "mini-DOMAs" as of June 20, 2000).

5. Kenneth L. Karst, *The Freedom of Intimate Association*, 89 YALE L.J. 624, 636 (1980) ("Indeed, as the legal consequences of a couple's living together come to approximate those of marriage, and as divorce becomes more readily available, marriage itself takes on a special significance for its expressive content as a statement that the couple wish to identify with each other").

6. Jeanne M. Eck, *The Shun Factor*, Wash. Post, Oct. 21, 1997, at D5 (focusing on the power culture in Washington, D.C.).

7. MORRIS B. KAPLAN, SEXUAL JUSTICE: DEMOCRATIC CITIZENSHIP AND THE POLITICS OF DESIRE 222–23 (1997) (characterizing Justice Harry Blackmun's view of the individual as reflected in his dissent in Bowers v. Hardwick, 478 U.S. 186 (1986)).

8. RICHARD A. POSNER, SEX AND REASON 312 (1992).

9. Marc A. Fajer, *Can Two Real Men Eat Quiche Together? Storytelling, Gender-*

*Role Stereotypes, and Legal Protection for Lesbians and Gay Men*, 46 U. MIAMI L.
REV. 511, 513–514, 537–570 (1992).

10. Karst, *supra* note 5, at 670 n.209 (quoting LAURENCE H. TRIBE, AMERICAN
CONSTITUTIONAL LAW 887–888 (1978)).

11. I take the phrase "public welfare purposes" from Peter M. Cicchino, *Reason
and the Rule of Law: Should Bare Assertions of "Public Morality" Qualify as Legitimate
Government Interests for the Purposes of Equal Protection Review?*, 87 GEO. L.J. 139
(1998). " 'Bare public morality' arguments defend a law by asserting a legitimate
government interest in prohibiting or encouraging certain human behavior without
any empirical connection to goods other than the alleged good of eliminating or
increasing, as the case may be, the behavior at issue. 'Public welfare' arguments, in
contrast, defend a law by asserting that the law avoids harms or realizes goods other
than the good of eliminating or increasing the behavior or characteristic that defines
the classification the law creates—for example, health, safety, or economic prosperity." *Id.* at 140–41.

12. Thus, for example, marriage conventionalists object to allowing same-sex couples to marry because currently married couples "have the right to know that . . .
[marriage] is something special . . . that has true meaning." Jon R. Perry, Editorial,
*Specious Allegations*, SALT LAKE TRIB., Oct. 22, 1999, at A14.

13. 744 A.2d 864 (Vt. 1999). The decision is dated December 20.

14. VT. CONST., ch. I, art. 7.

15. An Act Relating to Civil Unions, No. 91 § 3 (codified at VT. STAT. ANN. tit.
15, § 1204(a) (Supp. 2000)) (emphasis added).

16. *See generally* Adrienne Rich, *Compulsory Heterosexuality and Lesbian Existence*,
5 SIGNS 631 (1980).

17. State of Vermont's Motion to Dismiss, Baker v. State, 744 A.2d 864 (Vt.
1999) (No. S1009–97Cnc), http://www.vtfreetomarry.org/vtmotiontodismiss.
html.

18. Richard F. Duncan suggests that I say that government has "somehow created
some kind of public forum for private expression." Duncan, *Reflections on the Emperor's Clothes*. As I explain at great length in my article, with which he is presumably
familiar since he quotes a passage from its final page, neither public forum doctrine
nor any of the extant constitutional doctrines are well suited to addressing the expressive resource that civil marriage is. *See* Cruz, *supra* unnumbered note, at 971–
987.

19. Thus Duncan's reliance on Rust v. Sullivan, 500 U.S. 173 (1991), to make
precisely this government speech argument, *see* Duncan, *Reflections on the Emperor's
Clothes*, is misplaced, as I explain in detail in Cruz, *supra* unnumbered note, at 985–
986.

20. Robert Post, *Recuperating First Amendment Doctrine*, 47 STAN. L. REV.
1249, 1276 (1995) (citation omitted).

21. Because of considerations of length, I do not here address the adequate-
alternatives element of this test. The interested reader may consult Cruz, *"Just Don't
Call It Marriage," supra* unnumbered note.

22. Texas v. Johnson, 491 U.S. 397, 414 (1989). *See also, e.g.*, Perry Educ. Ass'n
v. Perry Local Educators' Ass'n, 460 U.S. 37, 62 (1983) (Brennan, J., dissenting)
("Viewpoint discrimination is censorship in its purest form and government regula-

tion that discriminates among viewpoints threatens the continued vitality of 'free speech.' ").

23. Wojciech Sadurski, *Does the Subject Matter? Viewpoint Neutrality and Freedom of Speech*, 15 CARDOZO ARTS & ENT. L.J. 315, 324 (1997). Sadurski concludes that "[g]overnmental partisanship is . . . the main First Amendment sin targeted by the principle of viewpoint neutrality." *Id.* at 331.

24. "Content-based restrictions also have been held to raise Fourteenth Amendment equal protection concerns because, in the course of regulating speech, such restrictions differentiate between types of speech." Burson v. Freeman, 504 U.S. 191, 197 n.3 (1992) (citing Police Dep't v. Mosley, 408 U.S. 92 (1972)).

25. 408 U.S. 92, 95 (1972).

26. U.S. society defines sexual orientations in terms of the sex(es) to which a person is attracted. The overwhelming majority of same-sex couples who would wish to make a long-term marital commitment to each other would include two lesbian, gay, or bisexual persons.

27. Texas v. Johnson, 491 U.S. 397 (1989), and United States v. Eichman, 496 U.S. 310 (1990).

28. 491 U.S. at 413.

29. 496 U.S. at 315.

30. 491 U.S. at 417.

31. I note that Justice Anthony Kennedy believes it improper to uphold most content-based laws simply because they may survive strict scrutiny. In his view, with certain narrow, categorical exceptions, content-based laws automatically violate the First Amendment. However, strict scrutiny may sometimes be useful to identify whether a particular law is in fact content based. Burson v. Freeman, 504 U.S. 191, 212 (1992) (Kennedy, J., concurring in the judgment) ("The [compelling-interest] test may have a legitimate role, however, in sorting out what is and what is not a content-based restriction"). *See also* Eugene Volokh, *Freedom of Speech, Shielding Children, and Transcending Balancing*, 1997 SUP. CT. REV. 141, 147 n.20.

32. Jean Bethke Elshtain, *Against Gay Marriage*, COMMONWEAL, Oct. 22, 1991, reprinted in SAME-SEX MARRIAGE: PRO AND CON 57, 59 (Andrew Sullivan ed. 1997).

33. *See* Baehr v. Miike, No. 91-1394, 1996 WL 694235 (Haw. Cir. Ct. Dec. 3, 1996).

34. *See* Judith Stacey & Timothy J. Biblarz, *(How) Does the Sexual Orientation of Parents Matter?*, 66 AMERICAN SOCIOLOGICAL REVIEW 159 (2001).

35. Zablocki v. Redhail, 434 U.S. 374, 399 (1978) (Powell, J., concurring) (emphases added).

36. *See* Cicchino, *supra* noted 11, at 143 (actually arguing that such "bare" assertions of morality are not even a rational basis for legislation, let alone compelling).

37. 478 U.S. 186, 196 (1986) (concluding that "majority sentiments about the morality of homosexuality" are "[ ]adequate" in due process suit).

38. Barnes v. Glen Theatre, Inc., 501 U.S. 560, 580 (1991) (Scalia, J., concurring in the judgment). *See, e.g., Bowers*, 478 U.S. at 196.

39. *See generally* Paul Siegel, *Second Hand Prejudice, Racial Analogies, and Shared Showers: Why "Don't Ask, Don't Tell" Won't Sell*, 9 NOTRE DAME J.L. ETHICS & PUB. POL'Y 185, 190–93 (1995).

40. United States v. Playboy Entm't Group, 529 U.S. 803, 813 (2000). *But see*

Post, *supra* note 20, at 1266 ("Although this focus on 'listeners' reaction' could be a powerful and far-reaching principle, it is not at all clear what it means").

41. Richard Duncan dubs me a "partial expansionist" based upon what he asserts is "his [i.e., Cruz's] definition of civil marriage," arguing that certain marriages are "discriminated against under Cruz's proposal" and accusing me of not being "open to permitting consenting adults to enter into incestuous 'marriages.' " Duncan, *Reflections on the Emperor's Clothes*, this volume. Yet the present essay and the article on which it is based merely address one legal restriction on civil marriage, the mixed-sex requirement, and present a detailed analysis why that restriction rests on an expressive basis (*see* Cruz, *supra* unnumbered note, at 945–964); I advance no definition or "model of civil marriage" (Duncan, *supra*) whatsoever. Any unconstitutionality of other restrictions, such as the dyad limitation or consanguinity limitations, would result from those restrictions' inconsistency (if any) with the First Amendment, not from the abolition of the mixed-sex requirement advocated herein. As a modestly careful reading of the article from which this essay is drawn shows, I am quite willing to live with whatever may be the consequences of my First Amendment theory and arguments, and thus insinuations of inconsistency are wholly unjustified. *See* Cruz, *supra*, at 1004–1005 & nn.409–411 (discussing polygamy and incest, citing same scholar cited by Duncan, *supra*, at note 8, and noting possible "self-serving selectivity in [some marriage conventionalists'] insistence on principle"), 1024–1025 (discussing a possible even more thoroughgoing commitment to neutrality as applied to the expressive resource of civil marriage).

42. *See* CAL. FAM. CODE §§ 297, 299.5–6 (West Supp. 2001); CAL. HEALTH & SAFETY CODE § 1261 (West 2000).

43. *See* HAW. REV. STAT. ANN. §§ 572C-1 to 572C-7 (Michie 1999).

44. *See* VT. STAT. ANN. tit. 15, §§ 1201–1207 (Supp. 2000).

45. Because the Vermont Supreme Court has already given same-sex couples so much and would face even greater political uproar were it to adopt the arguments of this article to require same-sex marriages, I believe that, at this time, litigation to test my arguments judicially would be premature. Nonetheless, I believe that it is vitally important for the arguments to enter the public dialogue on marriage in the twenty-first-century United States, and I believe that Richard Duncan is mistaken in characterizing my arguments as "dead on arrival in the real world of constitutional jurisprudence," Richard F. Duncan, *Reflections on the Emperor's Clothes: A Response to Professor Cruz's Theory on Marriage and the First Amendment*, this volume. I know that he is mistaken when he arrogantly insists that I "know[]" my theory has no "chance of winning." Indeed, my article and its marital-expression argument have been cited by the plaintiffs in marriage litigation under the Massachusetts state constitution, in the appeal of which I was asked to co-author an amicus brief expounding the argument. See *Brief of Amicus Curiae Professors of Expression and Constitutional Law* et al. in Support of Appellants' Brief in Goodridge et al. v. Department of Public Health et al., no. SJC–08860 (Mass. Sup. Judicial Ct. Nov. 8, 2002). (Duncan also falsely attributes to me an "acknowledg[ment]" that current doctrine "do[es] not support [my] analysis," *id.* at note 2. What I acknowledge is that "[i]t may well be that the country's current constitutional doctrines *and legal institutional cultures* will render *acceptance* of this analysis *difficult* for courts, legislatures, and legal scholars." Cruz, *supra* unnumbered note, at 1125.) (emphasis added)

46. Abolishing civil marriage would not abolish marriage tout court, but rather would simply "disestablish" it, eliminating governmental preferences for that social relationship form.

47. The Civil Rights Cases, 109 U.S. 3, 25 (1883).

Response

# Reflections on the Emperor's Clothes: A Response to Professor David B. Cruz's Theory on Marriage and the First Amendment

## Richard F. Duncan

Professor David Cruz has done splendid work in his contribution to this book on "Civil Marriage and the First Amendment" and, at much greater length, in his *Southern California Law Review* article on the same subject.[1] However, notwithstanding my admiration for his talent and work ethic, my analysis of his thesis about "civil marriage as a unique expressive resource" leads me to conclude that "the emperor has no clothes."

Just as a great deal of hard work and effort can be expended on fruitless arguments about the unconstitutionality of the income tax and the unconstitutional establishment of the religion of secular humanism in the public schools, Professor Cruz has likewise devoted himself to an argument that is dead on arrival in the real world of constitutional jurisprudence. To his credit, Cruz acknowledges that his argument, which concludes that the marriage laws of all fifty states are invalid under the Free Speech Clause of the U.S. Constitution, is not ready for a prime-time airing in actual litigation.[2] This is very good judgment on his part, because he knows that he has no more chance of winning on his theory than the tax protestors and anti-secular-humanists have of prevailing on theirs. However, my task here is to briefly respond to his theory, and I will do so by explaining exactly why Cruz's thesis is a nonstarter.

Cruz takes the position that the government's recognition and support for civil marriage have somehow created some kind of public forum for private expression (what he calls "a unique expressive resource") and that by denying same-sex couples access to civil marriage the government engages in unconstitutional viewpoint suppression of speech. Thus he argues that the marriage laws of all fifty states are invalid under the First Amendment unless they are amended to eliminate viewpoint discrimination by allowing same-sex couples equal access to civil marriage.

It is certainly black-letter First Amendment law that the government may not "discriminate against speech on the basis of viewpoint" by excluding persons with unpopular perspectives from government buildings and facilities that have been opened to the public for expressive meetings and discussions.[3] Thus the Supreme Court recently held that a public school violated the Free Speech Clause when it excluded a Christian youth group from an after-school forum open to other youth groups solely because of the religious viewpoint of the Christian group's expressive activities.[4]

However, it is equally clear that the government is free to adopt any viewpoint it wishes when it goes about its own activities and communicates its own position on governmental programs, subsidies, and policies. As the author of a leading casebook on the First Amendment has put it, "[T]he government itself can say pretty much whatever it wants . . . , even if this favors one viewpoint over another."[5] Thus, as the Supreme Court made clear in *Rust v. Sullivan*, government may act to recognize, subsidize, or otherwise encourage "certain activities it believes to be in the public interest" without providing similar preferences to other activities that take a different approach to the issue.[6] In so doing, the government does not engage in impermissible viewpoint discrimination; rather, it properly expresses its own view that certain activities are preferable to others.[7]

State laws defining marriage as a state-licensed relationship between one man and one woman do not create any kind of public forum for the expression of private speech. Rather, marriage laws constitute government speech and communicate the government's views about the meaning and importance of the institution of marriage. Thus the government has the power to express its view of what marriage is and to act on that view by defining and regulating civil marriage accordingly.

But suppose that I am wrong and Professor Cruz is right about the expressive character of marriage laws. In other words, let us assume for the moment that marriage laws are not government speech, but rather create some kind of public forum for private expression. Under this assumption, free speech doctrine would require civil marriage to be open to all viewpoints concerning marriage. Now, even Professor Cruz's proposal to expand marriage to include same-sex couples is too narrow to cure the unconstitutional viewpoint discrimination. There are more than two viewpoints about what civil marriage is. There is the traditional one-husband-and-one-wife viewpoint. There is the "expansionist" viewpoint advanced by Professor Cruz that takes civil marriage as it exists and merely expands it to cover two persons of the same gender. But Cruz is only a partial expansionist, and his definition of civil marriage also excludes certain "marriages" on the basis of viewpoint. For example, the plural- or group-"marriage" viewpoint is excluded under Cruz's proposal. Nor does his proposal allow consenting adults to enter into incestuous "marriages" and thereby to participate in the unique expressive resources of civil marriage. Thus, under Cruz's proposed First Amendment rule, even the "expansionist" model of civil marriage is unconstitutional because it discriminates on the basis of viewpoint against plural marriages, incestuous marriages, and perhaps even other nonmainstream "marital" relationships. If we take Professor Cruz's free-speech arguments seriously, viewpoint neutrality would require civil marriage to be expanded to include "marriages" composed of any number of persons and characterized by any kind of relationship. In conclusion, Professor Cruz's theory about marriage and the First Amendment is implausible and self-defeating. If he wishes to constitutionalize a right to same-sex marriage, he will need to search someplace other than the Free Speech Clause.

## NOTES

1. *See* David B. Cruz, "*Just Don't Call It Marriage*": *The First Amendment and Marriage as an Expressive Resource*, 74 So. Cal. L. Rev. 925 (2001).

2. In his contribution to this book, Professor Cruz acknowledges that "at this time, litigation to test my arguments judicially would be premature." [at 259, n. 45]. *See also* Cruz, *supra* note 1, at 1025 (acknowledging that "the country's current constitutional doctrines" do not support his analysis).

3. *Good News Club v. Milford Central School*, 121 S. Ct. 2093, 2100 (2001).

4. *Id.* at 2102.

5. Eugene Volokh, *The First Amendment: Problems, Cases, and Policy Arguments* 435 (2001).

6. 500 U.S. 173, 193 (1991).

7. *Id.*

Essay Two

# Hardwick's *Landmark Status,* Romer's *Narrowness, and the Preservation of Marriage*

## Richard F. Duncan

One of my favorite stories for children is the one about the little Dutch boy from the city of Haarlem who, on his way home from visiting a friend, noticed water trickling through a small hole in the dike. The young boy realized that unless he acted immediately, the small hole would grow and the sea would burst through the dike and flood the city. As most of you know, the Dutch boy acted heroically and placed his finger in the hole to stop the leak and give others time to repair the dike.[1]

This story always reminds me of one of the great justices ever to serve on the Supreme Court of the United States, Byron White, and of his landmark opinion in *Bowers v. Hardwick.*[2] In *Hardwick,* Justice White placed his finger in the hole in the dike and may well have saved the institution of marriage from a radical transformation imposed not by the people, and not by the Constitution, but by a body of unelected lawyers exercising "raw judicial power."[3] At the very least, White's *Hardwick* opinion bought time for the people to learn of the threat to marriage brewing in the courts and to shore up the legal defenses protecting this most basic building block of human civilization.

Many law professors abhor *Hardwick*—Professor William Eskridge calls it "the most uniformly criticized Supreme Court decision in [his] lifetime"[4]—and feel contempt and enmity for the justice who authored the majority opinion.[5] But I am here to praise *Hardwick,* not to bury it. *Hardwick*'s critics are wrong. I believe that it reached the right result for the right reasons. I do not believe that it should be overruled. I believe that it is unlikely that the Court will overrule it. Even if *Hardwick* is overruled, I believe the opinion will likely be a narrow one that will not threaten laws defining marriage as a relationship between one man and one woman.

## THE EMINENT RESPECTABILITY OF *HARDWICK*

In order to understand the eminent respectability and rightness of Justice White's opinion in *Hardwick*, one needs to take a step back and think about the idea of substantive due process. The Constitution does not contain any language protecting any kind of sexual conduct. In *Hardwick*, the plaintiff was seeking to have the Court declare that the right to engage in homosexual conduct was a fundamental right given a heightened degree of substantive protection by the Due Process Clause of the Fourteenth Amendment. The concept of substantive due process is a constitutional oxymoron,[6] one that, as Robert Bork has eloquently urged, always carries with it the risk of judicial tyranny:

Since the clause was designed only to require fair procedures in implementing laws, there is no original understanding that gives it any substantive content. Thus, a judge who insists upon giving the due process clause such content must make it up. That is why substantive due process, wherever it appears, is never more than a pretense that the judge's views are in the Constitution.[7]

To other legal scholars, judicial rule is a good thing—so long, of course, as the justices share the political and moral beliefs of the law professor class. Michael McConnell refers to this view of the Constitution as the "moral philosophic" approach and points out that this view of constitutional law is the one that gave us *Roe v. Wade* and the judge-made liberty of abortion.[8] Although this position is widely held among legal scholars, perhaps it is Ronald Dworkin who has best articulated the duty of judges to rule and the rest of us to follow under what he calls "the moral reading" of the Constitution.[9] Dworkin says that under this approach to constitutional law

it falls to judges to declare . . . what the basic liberties really are. But that means that judges must answer intractable, controversial, and profound questions of political morality that philosophers, statesmen, and citizens have debated for many centuries, with no prospect of agreement. It means that the rest of us must accept the deliverances of a majority of the justices, whose insight into these great issues is not spectacularly special.[10]

Dworkin's understanding of the relationship between the Court and citizens under the "moral" constitution is frighteningly similar to the O'Connor-Kennedy-Souter plurality opinion in *Planned Parenthood of Southeastern Pennsylvania v. Casey*, in which the troika proclaimed that the abortion debate was over because the Court had spoken.[11] Specifically, the *Casey* triumvirate declared that when the Court decides cases involving intensely divisive controversies, as it did in *Roe*, "the Court's interpretation of the Constitution calls the contending sides of a national controversy to end their national division by accepting a common mandate rooted in the Constitution."[12] In other words, the abortion debate is over. If you believe that abortion is wrong, don't have one. Otherwise, shut up and obey. Thus spake Zarathustra.[13]

Justice White's undeservedly much-maligned opinion in *Hardwick* demonstrates his sensitivity to the danger of judicial tyranny inherent in the "moral philosophic" approach to the Constitution. "The Court is most vulnerable and comes nearest to illegitimacy," he said, "when it deals with judge-made constitutional law having little or no cognizable roots in the language or design of the Constitution."[14] Thus, in order to establish some reasonable limits on the Court's role in constitutional lawmaking[15] and to reassure both "itself and the public that announcing rights not readily identifiable in the Constitution's text involves much more than the imposition of the Justices' own choice of values"[16] on a self-governing people, the Court has developed a sensible test based on history and tradition to identify those truly fundamental liberties that qualify for strict scrutiny under substantive due process analysis. As such, only liberties that are deeply rooted in an established consensus of the community are highly protected substantively under the Due Process Clause.[17]

Justice White applied this test in *Hardwick* and concluded that it is obvious that the right to engage in homosexual conduct is not one of our historically respected fundamental liberties.[18] If the historical pedigree of homosexual sodomy is the appropriate test, surely *Hardwick* is an easy case, and Justice White's matter-of-fact opinion for the majority is perfectly appropriate.

One line of attack on the *Hardwick* opinion is to suggest that it neglected to follow earlier cases, such as *Roe*, that recognized a fundamental right of privacy under the Due Process Clause. This was one of Justice Harry Blackmun's complaints in his dissenting opinion in *Hardwick*.[19] This criticism of *Hardwick* is unpersuasive. Even if the decision in *Roe* is correct because there is a historical consensus supporting a fundamental right for women to make choices about pregnancy and childbirth, that is a completely different question from the one before the Court in *Hardwick*.[20] Abortion and homosexuality are very different kinds of behavior with distinct historical records. If the historical respectability of homosexual conduct is the appropriate test, Justice White's opinion in *Hardwick* is clearly correct. Indeed, Justice Blackmun's dissenting opinion, far from demonstrating that the majority's historical analysis was erroneous, bitterly denounced the longstanding consensus of the community with respect to homosexuality: "I cannot agree that either the length of time a majority has held its convictions or the passions with which it defends them can withdraw legislation from this Court's scrutiny."[21]

In effect, Blackmun has confessed judgment against his own position. The historical tradition he denounces does not withdraw sodomy laws from the

Court's scrutiny; rather, it decisively resolves the Court's threshold test for fundamental rights by clearly demonstrating that homosexual conduct has been disfavored in American history and tradition and thus that the right to engage in such conduct is not a fundamental liberty under the Due Process Clause.

Another line of attack on the reasoning in *Hardwick* amounts to an intellectual version of the shell game, because it seems designed to subvert the Court's historical approach to substantive due process while appearing to apply it. This argument takes the position that "[t]he Court's error in *Hardwick* was that it used the wrong level of generality to conceptualize the plaintiff's claim of liberty and to test its pedigree."[22] According to Laurence Tribe, for example, "in asking whether an alleged right forms part of a traditional liberty, it is crucial to define the liberty at a high enough level of generality to permit unconventional variants to claim protection along with mainstream versions of protected conduct."[23] Under this approach, *Hardwick*'s historical analysis should not have focused on the particular conduct engaged in by Hardwick—homosexual sodomy—but rather on "whether private, consensual, adult sexual acts partake of traditionally revered liberties of intimate association and individual autonomy."[24] I call this approach a shell game because the entire purpose of the exercise is to disregard relevant historical facts in order to reach results favored by legal theorists. Tribe would recognize Hardwick's behavior as within a "traditionally revered" category even though he admits that "the history of homosexuality has been largely a history of opprobrium."[25] This is an intellectual sleight of hand worthy of the most streetwise practitioner of the shell game.

I suggest that even if the Court had adopted Tribe's higher level of generality when framing the question in *Hardwick*, an honest historical inquiry would have produced the same result. What is the honest answer to the question whether our society has "traditionally revered" a broad-based liberty of consenting adults to engage in a multitude of sexual acts to include not only marital intimacy but also, as in *Hardwick*, mutual fellatio between two men consummating a one-night stand? Clearly, the only truthful and accurate answer to this question is that our society has not "traditionally revered" a liberty broad enough to include Hardwick's "unconventional" sexual practices. Whether the historical inquiry focuses on homosexual sodomy in particular or on the breadth of Tribe's more general formulation, the answer should be the same—unless someone slips the pea out from under the shell.

## THE TRIUMPH OF *HARDWICK* AND THE END OF THE *ROE* ERA

Thus the debate over *Hardwick* revolves around two issues. First, should the Court look to history and tradition or to its own understanding of political morality when deciding which unenumerated liberties are fundamental rights entitled to heightened protection under substantive due process? Second, if history is the proper approach, should the Court frame the historical inquiry with specificity or at a high level of generality to include unconventional variants of the asserted liberty?

The Supreme Court recently answered both of these questions conclusively in *Washington v. Glucksberg*,[26] a significant decision that vindicated Justice White's understanding of substantive due process and, as Michael McConnell suggests, quietly "marked the end of an era characterized by cases, like *Roe*, in which the Justices took upon themselves the right to decide contentious issues of moral and social policy, independent of text, history, or democratic judgment."[27]

In *Glucksberg*, the plaintiffs waged a substantive due process attack on state laws prohibiting assisted suicide. Specifically, the question before the Court was whether the liberty "specially protected by the Due Process Clause includes a right to commit suicide which itself includes a right to assistance in doing so."[28] The judgment in *Glucksberg* was unanimous in rejecting the asserted right to commit suicide, and most significantly for purposes of substantive due process doctrine, Justice William Rehnquist's majority opinion commanded "a solid five votes" in support of a methodological test based upon an objective and precise analysis of "historical fact rather than on normative judgment."[29]

Specifically, although the *Glucksberg* majority recognized that the Due Process Clause does provide "heightened protection against government interference with certain fundamental rights and liberty interests,"[30] the opinion made clear that the Court has always been very reluctant to "break new ground" in the field of substantive due process because this risks substituting the "policy preferences of the Members of [the] Court" for those of a free and self-governing people.[31] This understanding of the proper role of the judiciary in a democratic society echoes the wisdom of Justice White's views as expressed in *Hardwick*.[32]

The doctrine of *Glucksberg* also vindicates Justice White's substantive due process methodology. The Court held that "[o]ur established method of substantive-due-process analysis" requires the party challenging state action to meet a two-part test as a "threshold requirement" before being entitled to heightened protection.[33] First, the claimant must establish that his claim implicates a fundamental right that is "objectively, 'deeply rooted in this Nation's history and tradition.' "[34] Second, the relevant historical inquiry must be based upon "a 'careful description' of the asserted fundamental liberty interest."[35] The Court's objective historical methodology is designed "to rein in the subjective elements that are necessarily present in due process judicial review."[36] As Professor McConnell has observed: "This means that the 'liberty interest' must be described with specificity. Airy generalities like 'the right to be left alone,' or to make choices 'central to personal dignity and autonomy,' which mean almost anything or almost nothing, are too imprecise to support legal analysis."[37] Although the Court did not specifically base its holding on *Hardwick*, perhaps reflecting its desire to focus on the issue of assisted suicide far from the noise and heat of the homosexuality front of the culture wars, *Glucksberg* represents a total victory for Justice White's substantive due process methodology over that of Justice Blackmun and Professors Tribe and Dworkin.

Of course, it is possible that, over time, an old tradition might fade and a new one develop. Although the Court did not expressly say so in *Glucksberg*, "the opinion implied that even a traditional norm could come to violate substantive due process if it is subsequently abandoned or rejected by a new stable consensus."[38] However, until a new national consensus develops and withstands the test of time, the *Glucksberg* methodology counsels the Court to defer to the give-and-take of the democratic process and to the judgment of Congress and state legislatures.[39]

Under the methodology of *Glucksberg*, the essential holding of *Hardwick*—that there is no fundamental right to engage in consensual acts of homosexual sodomy—seems unassailable. The most that can be said in support of the asserted claim is that our society's historical rejection of homosexual conduct is currently in flux. There is certainly increasing social tolerance for private homosexual behavior, but that inchoate attitude has not yet hardened into a stable national consensus, and *Glucksberg* suggests that the Court should remain on the sidelines and accept "the possibility of a multiplicity of approaches, and of regional variation in light of differences in social and moral perceptions."[40]

But suppose that I am wrong and the Court decides that the judgment in *Hardwick* must be reversed because a new consensus has developed in support of a fundamental right of sexual privacy for consenting adults. Does this mean that same-sex couples also have a fundamental right to state recognition of homosexual "marriage"? This is an easy question, and the answer is no.

Under *Glucksberg*, persons challenging the dual-gender requirement for marriage will be required to establish that an objective historical inquiry based upon a "careful description" of the asserted liberty interest supports their claim. In other words, they will be required to establish that our society has rejected its traditional concept of marriage as a relationship between one man and one woman and has formed a new national consensus in support of the equal validity of homosexual marriage.

This is an impossible task. Indeed, the mere possibility that an activist judiciary in a state such as Hawaii might open a window for some homosexual marriages to occur has stimulated a national dialogue about the modern meaning of marriage. This national conversation has resulted in a reaffirmation by acclamation of the traditional concept of marriage as a unique two-person "community defined by sexual complementarity."[41] In

1996, the U.S. Congress passed and President Clinton signed the Defense of Marriage Act (DOMA), a law that recognizes and clearly represents a bipartisan national consensus that understands marriage as a union of one man and one woman.[42] Under DOMA, it is clear beyond doubt that for purposes of national law and policy marriage "means only a legal union between one man and one woman as husband and wife."[43] Moreover, approximately thirty states have passed similar laws affirming and defending the traditional meaning of marriage.[44] Although some states and municipalities provide some recognition for same-sex "civil unions" or "domestic partnerships," no state recognizes homosexual relationships as marriages.

Quite simply, there is no chance that homosexual marriage could be declared a fundamental right under the substantive due process methodology established in *Glucksberg*. Thus laws defining marriage as a dual-gender relationship will be evaluated and upheld under a deferential rational-basis test. Justice White's approach to substantive due process has weathered the storms coming from the law reviews, and for this our polity owes Justice White a great debt of gratitude.

## *ROMER,* RATIONALITY, AND "ANIMUS"

Some proponents of same-sex marriage cite *Romer v. Evans*[45] and argue that the law's refusal to recognize homosexual marriage cannot withstand rationality review because that refusal is based simply upon "animus" directed at homosexuals and thus serves no legitimate state interest.[46] This argument is implausible, because it is based upon a fundamental misunderstanding of both the reasoning of *Romer* and the eminent reasonableness of the international consensus on the meaning of marriage.

In *Romer*, the Supreme Court invalidated an amendment to the state constitution of Colorado—popularly known as "Amendment 2"—under the Equal Protection Clause of the Fourteenth Amendment of the U.S. Constitution. If Amendment 2 had been allowed to go into effect, it would have provided:

No Protected Status Based on Homosexual, Lesbian or Bisexual Orientation. Neither the State of Colorado, through any of its branches or departments, nor any of its agencies, political subdivisions, municipalities or school districts, shall enact, adopt or enforce any statute, regulation, ordinance or policy whereby homosexual, lesbian or bisexual orientation, conduct, practices or relationships shall constitute or otherwise be the basis of or entitle any person or class of persons to have or claim any minority status, quota preferences, protected status or claim of discrimination. This Section of the Constitution shall be in all respects self-executing.[47]

The Court's decision in *Romer* was a very narrow one. *Romer* did not hold that homosexuals are a suspect or quasi-suspect class entitled to heightened

protection under the Equal Protection Clause. It did not overrule or undermine either the judgment or the reasoning of *Hardwick*. It did not hold
that the law may not reflect a moral preference for one kind of personal
relationship over other kinds of personal relationships.

The constitutional flaw in Colorado's Amendment 2 was its extreme overbreadth, not the identity of the group it adversely affected. The majority in
*Romer* applied the lowest standard of review—the rational-basis test—and
found that no legitimate purpose reasonably fit the infinitely broad sweep
of the disability imposed by the amendment.[48] It was the "sheer breadth"
of Amendment 2, not any presumed animus against homosexuals, that resulted in the law's facial invalidation.[49] The case would have been decided
in exactly the same way if Amendment 2 had affected smokers, insurance
salesmen, or any other targeted group instead of homosexuals.

Colorado's Amendment 2 prohibited all attempts by all levels of government to protect homosexuals against any kind of discrimination. The extreme breadth of this provision made it possible to imagine instances in
which it would bar policies designed to protect homosexuals from harms
that all would acknowledge to be wrongful.[50] For example, at oral argument
Justice Kennedy described Amendment 2 as creating a classification
"adopted to fence out . . . [a] class *for all purposes*." He then remarked,
"I've never seen a statute like that."[51] Various justices expressed concern
that under the amendment homosexuals would be helpless to protect themselves against exclusion from public libraries, police protection, and even
lifesaving treatment at public hospitals.[52] Justice Kennedy's majority opinion
in *Romer* concluded that the "unprecedented" flaw of Amendment 2 was
that it identified persons by "a single trait"—any trait—and then "denie[d]
them protection across the board."[53] The amendment imposed "a broad
and undifferentiated disability on a single named group" by denying "specific protection" against "exclusion from an almost limitless number of
transactions and endeavors that constitute ordinary civic life in a free society."[54]

The Court in *Romer* did not presume that Amendment 2 was tainted by
an impermissible disapproval of homosexual conduct. Rather, the Court applied a conventional rational-basis test, found that no legitimate purpose
reasonably fit the infinitely broad sweep of the amendment's coverage, and
only then concluded that this extreme overbreadth "seems inexplicable by
anything but animus toward the class it affects."[55] Thus *Romer* is not a case
in which the Court inferred an invidious intent based upon the identity of
the group disadvantaged. Rather, the Court drew an inference of animus
from the unlimited breadth of the disability created by Amendment 2 and
from the fact that no legitimate state interest was reasonably related to the
infinitely broad sweep of the law's coverage.

If *Romer* governs the constitutionality of laws defining marriage as a relationship between one man and one woman, these laws certainly will be

upheld because they are sufficiently narrow and focused to enable the Court to ascertain their eminent reasonableness. As the Court explicitly said in *Romer*, such laws will be "sustained" so long as they are "narrow enough in scope and grounded in a sufficient factual context for us to ascertain some relation between the classification and the purpose it serve[s]."[56]

Traditional marriage laws are completely unlike Colorado's Amendment 2. Marriage laws do not target a class of persons and deny that class the opportunity to protect itself politically against a limitless number of discriminatory harms and exclusions. These laws define and regulate the institution of marriage, but they do not forbid any individual or group from seeking the law's protection against any kind of public or private discrimination.

As William Eskridge has observed, it is true that marriage is a preferred relationship, and many "ongoing rights and privileges" are associated with marriage.[57] Marriage laws, however, do not prohibit those ineligible to marry from seeking to amend tax, immigration, welfare, and other laws privileging marriage in order to acquire these benefits. For that matter, homosexual couples and others ineligible to marry are not forbidden from using the political process to change marriage laws.[58] Everyone remains free to use the democratic process to right any perceived wrong or to acquire any desirable benefit.

Thus, under *Romer*, conventional marriage laws are sufficiently narrow to enable a court to apply the traditional rational-basis test.[59] Under this test, social legislation is presumptively valid, and the states are allowed "wide latitude" to create classifications designed to carry out ordinary legislative purposes.[60] As the Court clearly stated in *Federal Communications Commission v. Beach Communications, Inc.*, "[I]n areas of social and economic policy, a statutory classification that neither proceeds along suspect lines nor infringes fundamental constitutional rights must be upheld against equal protection challenge if there is any reasonably conceivable state of facts that could provide a rational basis for the classification."[61] The Equal Protection Clause "is not a license for courts to judge the wisdom, fairness, or logic of legislative choices."[62] Although a detailed analysis of the rationality of the international consensus on the meaning of marriage is beyond the scope of this essay, it is obvious that conventional marriage laws reasonably advance many legitimate governmental interests.[63] Those who seek to use *Romer* to overturn conventional marriage laws are tilting at windmills.

## CONCLUSION

Justice White's landmark opinion in *Hardwick* has survived both the test of time and the many slings and arrows of outraged scholarship launched at it by law professors who believe that the Constitution should be interpreted as codifying the political morality of the *Kama Sutra*. The eminent respectability and rightness of Justice White's methodology and reasoning in *Hard-*

*wick* were completely vindicated in *Glucksberg*, the Supreme Court's latest—and one of its most significant—decisions on the meaning of fundamental rights protected by substantive due process.

In *Glucksberg*, the Supreme Court reaffirmed an objective historical methodology, based upon a careful and precise description of the asserted liberty interest, for determining whether a substantive due process claim implicates a fundamental right entitled to heightened protection. Under this approach, the essential holding of *Hardwick*—that there is no fundamental right to engage in acts of homosexual sodomy—seems unassailable. Moreover, there is no possibility that homosexual marriage could qualify as a fundamental right under this test.

Nor does the Court's opinion in *Romer* advance the cause of those who seek to employ the Constitution to invalidate the law's traditional definition of marriage as an inherently heterosexual union. The constitutional flaw of the law struck down in *Romer* was its extreme overbreadth, not the identity of the group it adversely affected. The Court did not hold or even suggest that all laws that make distinctions on the basis of sexual orientation are tainted by irrational animus. The *Romer* majority applied the lowest standard of review—the rational basis test—and found that no legitimate purpose reasonably fit the infinitely broad sweep of the disability imposed by Colorado's Amendment 2.

If *Romer* governs the constitutionality of laws defining marriage as a relationship between one man and one woman, these laws certainly will be upheld. Traditional marriage laws serve many legitimate interests, any one of which by itself is sufficient to support these laws under *Romer* and the rational-basis test. Our society's understanding of the essential nature of marriage is deeply rooted not only in history, but also in the common sense and experience of the community. Thankfully, marriage as we have always understood it has nothing to fear from the Court's decision in *Romer*.

## NOTES

This essay is a revised version of my article "They Call Me 'Eight Eyes' ": Hardwick's *Respectability*, Romer's *Narrowness, and Same-Sex Marriage*, 32 Creighton L. Rev. 241 (1998).

1. Mary Mapes Dodge, Hans Brinker; or, The Silver Skates 129–33 (1946).

2. 478 U.S. 186 (1986).

3. *Doe v. Bolton*, 410 U.S. 179, 222 (1973) (White, J. dissenting). Justice White's powerful dissent in *Doe* also served as his dissent to the majority opinion in *Doe*'s companion case, *Roe v. Wade*, 410 U.S. 113 (1973), in which the Court created a new constitutional right to abortion. Justice White referred to *Roe* as imposing a judicially created "barrier to state efforts to protect human life" and as creating a corresponding right for pregnant women and their doctors "to exterminate" human life. *Bolton*, 410 U.S. at 222 (White, J., dissenting).

4. William N. Eskridge, Jr., *Democracy, Kulturkampf, and the Apartheid of the Closet*, 50 Vand. L. Rev. 419, 426 (1997).

5. *See* Charles Fried, *A Tribute to Justice Byron R. White*, 107 Harv. L. Rev. 20 (1993).

6. *See* Michael W. McConnell, *The Right to Die and the Jurisprudence of Tradition*, 1997 Utah L. Rev. 665, 667.

7. Robert H. Bork, The Tempting of America: The Political Seduction of the Law 43 (1990).

8. 410 U.S. 113 (1973). *See* McConnell, *supra* note 6, at 668.

9. *See* Ronald Dworkin, Freedom's Law: The Moral Reading of the American Constitution (1996).

10. Ronald Dworkin, *Unenumerated Rights: Whether and How Roe Should Be Overruled*, in G. Stone et al., The Bill of Rights in the Modern State 381, 383 (1992). *See* McConnell, *supra* note 6, at 668.

11. 505 U.S. 833 (1992).

12. *Id.* at 867.

13. *See* Friedrich Nietzsche, *Thus Spake Zarathustra* (Manuel Komroff ed., Thomas Common trans., Tudor Publishing Co. 1933).

14. *Hardwick*, 478 U.S. at 194.

15. *See id.* at 190.

16. *Id.* at 191.

17. *Id.* at 191–192.

18. *Id.* at 192–196.

19. *See id.* at 204–205 (Blackmun, J., dissenting)

20. I do not concede that Justice Blackmun's account in *Roe* of the history of abortion was accurate or even fair. For an excellent critique of the Court's historical analysis in *Roe*, see Dennis J. Horan, Clark D. Forsythe, & Edward R. Grant, *Two Ships Passing in the Night: An Interpretavist Review of the White-Stevens Colloquy* on Roe v. Wade, 6 St. Louis U. Pub. L. Rev. 229, 272–310 (1987).

21. *Hardwick*, 478 U.S. at 210 (Blackmun, J., dissenting).

22. Laurence H. Tribe, American Constitutional Law 1427 (2d ed. 1988).

23. *Id.* at 1428.

24. *Id.*

25. *Id.* at 1427.

26. 521 U.S. 702 (1997).

27. McConnell, *supra* note 6, at 708.

28. *Glucksberg*, 521 U.S. at 723.

29. *See* McConnell, *supra* note 6, at 672–673.

30. *Glucksberg*, 521 U.S. at 720.

31. *Id.*

32. *See* text accompanying notes 14–17 *supra*.

33. *Glucksberg*, 521 U.S. at 720, 722.

34. *Id.* at 720–21.

35. *Id.* at 721.

36. *Id.* at 722.

37. McConnell, *supra* note 6, at 671.

38. *Id.*

39. *See id.* at 682–691.

40. *Id.* at 687.

41. *See* David Orgon Coolidge, *Same-Sex Marriage?* Baehr v. Miike *and the Meaning of Marriage*, 38 S. Tex. L. Rev. 1, 29 (1997).

42. Defense of Marriage Act, Pub. L. No. 104–199, 110 Stat. 2419 (1996) (codified at 1 U.S.C. § 7 and 28 U.S.C. § 1738C). The act passed by a vote of 342–67 in the House of Representatives and 85–14 in the Senate. *See* Coolidge, *supra* note 41, at 4 n.8.

43. 1 U.S.C. § 7 (2000).

44. For a list of these states, *see* David Orgon Coolidge, *Playing the* Loving *Card: Same-Sex Marriage and the Politics of Analogy*, 12 B.Y.U. J. Pub. L. 201, 228 (1998).

45. 517 U.S. 620 (1996).

46. *See* Richard F. Duncan, *The Narrow and Shallow Bite of* Romer *and the Eminent Rationality of Dual-Gender Marriage: A (Partial) Response to Professor Koppelman*, 6 Wm. & Mary Bill of Rts. J. 147, 156 (1997).

47. *Romer*, 517 U.S. at 624.

48. *Id.* at 631–635.

49. *Id.* at 632.

50. *See* Duncan, *supra* note 46, at 149.

51. *See id.* at 150.

52. *See id.*

53. *Romer*, 517 U.S. at 633.

54. *Id.* at 631–632.

55. *Id.* at 632.

56. *Id.* at 632–633.

57. William N. Eskridge, Jr., The Case for Same-Sex Marriage 67 (1996).

58. Homosexuals are not the only class excluded by the conventional definition of marriage. Children below a certain age may not marry, and, even in the case of consenting adults, plural "marriages" and incestuous "marriages" are not allowed. Eskridge, *supra* note 57, at 144. Moreover, many committed and loving relationships that lack a sexual-romantic character—such as friendships, family relationships, and religious fellowships—are also denied many benefits and privileges granted under law to marriage relationships. *See* David L. Chambers, *What If? The Legal Consequences of Marriage and the Legal Needs of Lesbian and Gay Male Couples*, 95 Mich. L. Rev. 447, 489–490 (1996).

59. *See Romer*, 517 U.S. at 631–633.

60. *City of Cleburne v. Cleburne Living Ctr., Inc.*, 473 U.S. 432, 440 (1985). Under this test, "the Equal Protection Clause requires only a rational means to serve a legitimate end." *Id.* at 442.

61. 508 U.S. 307, 313(1993).

62. *Id.*

63. For my analysis of the eminent rationality of traditional marriage laws, *see* Duncan, *supra* note 46, at 156–165.

Response

# Social and Judicial "Just So" Stories
## David B. Cruz

Richard Duncan's essay opens with his fondness for stories—appropriately enough, for his contribution is rife with just-so stories purporting to describe and justify the jurisprudential and sociolegal status quo with respect to civil marriage. While *Bowers v. Hardwick* calls the story of the little Dutch boy to Professor Duncan's mind, his essay makes me think of Chicken Little, with its suggestion that *Bowers* "may well have saved the institution of marriage"—"this most basic building block of human civilization"—"from a radical transformation" as a result of "the threat . . . brewing in the courts," echoing that famous fowl's warning that "the sky is falling!" Indeed, nowhere does Duncan even identify the nature of the supposed impending threat to civil marriage, treating it as self-evident. Besides that omission, many other aspects of Duncan's essay cry out for response.

In Duncan's view, Justice Byron White's *Bowers* opinion staved off an exercise of "raw judicial power" by activist liberal judges, yet "raw judicial power" is exactly what White wielded there. Michael Hardwick's federal lawsuit brought a facial challenge to Georgia's criminal law against anal and oral sex, yet White on his own initiative transformed the claim into one that the law violated "the fundamental rights of homosexuals."[1] That obsessive focus on Hardwick's status was wholly improper in a nation of laws, not men or women, a nation governed by a Constitution that protects the rights of citizens and persons, not of "homosexuals" and "heterosexuals."

For that reason, among many others, the tremendously widespread scholarly criticism of *Bowers* is, pace Duncan, entirely justified. Consider, for example, the essay's claim that *Bowers*'s narrow "history and traditions" approach to rights protected under the Constitution's Due Process Clauses was proper. Duncan notes but misapprehends the objection that *Bowers* was and remains inconsistent with *Roe v. Wade*.[2] He is correct that it is logically possible for history to support an abortion right but not a right to engage in consensual oral or anal sex. The inconsistency argument, however, is that *Roe* precisely did not make *Bowers*'s narrow test of past practices the measure of liberty protected under the Due Process Clauses of the Constitution. White's interpretive approach—that of his dissent in *Roe* (against the views of seven members of the Court)—would conclude that one's freedom to choose abortion is not constitutionally protected. At the time of *Bowers*, however, the right of abortion choice was treated by the Court as a fundamental constitutional right. The Court's use of the narrow historical methodology in *Bowers* thus was inconsistent with its (non)use in other cases. Therefore, the "history and traditions" approach should not have been treated as mandatory or necessary for a fundamental right to exist, as Justices Sandra Day O'Connor and Anthony Kennedy (as well as many others) recognized in *Michael H. v. Gerald D*.[3] For reasons such as this, *Bowers* represents an "aberrant" decision.[4]

Nor has the inconsistency been eliminated or important interpretive questions "conclusively" resolved by the Court's decision in *Washington v. Glucksberg*, notwithstanding the repetition of Professor Michael McConnell's laughable characterization of William Rehnquist's slimmest-of-majorities *Glucksberg* opinion as "command[ing] 'a solid five votes.' " Rarely does such a bare majority settle contentious fundamental constitutional questions, as Duncan's slings and arrows at *Roe* and *Planned Parenthood v. Casey* ironically or at least unself-consciously demonstrate. (Indeed, *Casey*'s reaffirmation of *Roe* similarly commanded a "solid five votes" and not just the three upon which Duncan focuses.)

McConnell's jubilant view,[5] echoed by Duncan, holds that the Court's opinion in *Glucksberg* constitutes "a decisive shift in constitutional doctrine regarding unenumerated rights."[6] The question is, how can this be, if in fact the right to choose an abortion recognized by *Roe* "remains," as McConnell concedes, "secure"?[7] Rather than offer any explanation for how the Court might legitimately repudiate *Roe*'s reasoning and adhere to its basic result (thus "limit[ing] *Casey* to its facts"), McConnell simply speculates that the Justices might feel that they were burned by "the Court's sweeping decision" in *Roe*.[8] Yet this atheoretical, picking-and-choosing approach to constitutional rights seems dangerously close to an "excercis[e of] judgment and discretion of a sort that is properly reserved to legislatures," to use McConnell's condemnatory description of the *Lochner* Court's jurisprudence (McConnell's characterizations presume industrial freedom of Krabst due process),[9] and not an adequate basis for answering the question whether the judiciary should recognize same-sex couples' claims of a constitutional right to marry.

In denying such a right, Duncan purports to apply *Glucksberg* to formulate a narrow specification of the claimed right, yet this approach dramatically ignores the Supreme Court's lesson in *Loving v. Virginia*,[10] which invalidated the laws against interracial marriage of Virginia (and fifteen other states) on independent equal protection and substantive due process grounds. Were *Glucksberg*'s methodology applied to *Loving*, one might have to characterize the liberty at issue as the right of two people of different races to marry (much as Duncan wants to describe the claimed right at issue today as that of two people of the same sex to marry). But if one accepted that characterization, one would see that this was not a historically protected liberty in 1967, and so Richard and Mildred Loving would not have had their claim accepted by the Court. If instead it is not appropriate to take enduring characteristics of persons into account in the framing of fundamental rights, as *Loving* and common sense suggest, then, absent a functional justification for the mixed-sex requirement (of which there is no persuasive one available), the sexes of the parties to a civil marriage should not form part of the description of the right.[11]

Duncan rejects the argument that the mixed-sex requirement as enshrined in DOMA and state mini-DOMAs, for example, reflects antilesbigay animus and thus is unconstitutional under *Romer v. Evans*: 116 Sct 1620 (1996), an argument ably pressed by other scholars.[12] I would note, however, that Duncan ambiguously says that *Romer* announced that "such laws" would be sustained under rational-basis review, apparently meaning "laws defining marriage as a relationship between one man and one woman." Yet what *Romer* said is that laws implicating no fundamental rights and no suspect or quasi-suspect classifications are subject to rational-basis end-means review.[13] The fact that in *Romer* the Supreme Court was able to invalidate Amendment 2 using (as Duncan reports) only "the lowest standard of review—the rational-basis test" meant that it did not have to—and it did not—decide whether strict scrutiny should apply to governmental discrimination on the basis of sexual orientation. It should, as many scholars and jurists have persuasively explained.[14] Even apart from that, the mixed-sex requirement is a facial sex classification subject to very demanding if perhaps not strict scrutiny under the Court's classificationist approach to equal protection and *United States v. Virginia*.[15]

That Duncan does not address these issues may be attributable in part to the space considerations under which all of this volume's contributors labored. Nonetheless, the narrow arguments Duncan presents are a sideshow distracting us all from the serious questions implicated by the constitutional challenges to current marriage laws. Duncan erases most lesbigay persons as well as the great many heterosexually identified sympathizers who think same-sex couples should be allowed to marry civilly when he invokes "[o]ur society's understanding of the essential nature of marriage," "the common sense and experience of the community," and "marriage as we have always understood it" as reasons to exclude same-sex couples from the important public institution of civil marriage. But readers should not be surprised by this, for such expulsion of lesbigay persons from full membership in the social and political community is precisely what the secular opposition to dropping the mixed-sex requirement is about.

## NOTES

The title of this response is inspired by Jeanne L. Schroeder, *Just So Stories: Posnerian Methodology*, 22 CARDOZO L. REV. 351 (2001), and Pamela S. Karlan, *Richard Posner's Just-So Stories: The Phallacies of Sex and Reason*, 1 VA. J. SOC. POL'Y & L. 229 (1993).

1. Bowers v. Hardwick, 478 U.S. 186, 189 (1986).

2. 410 U.S. 113 (1973).

3. 491 U.S. 110, 132 (1989) (O'Connor, J., joined by Kennedy, J., concurring in part).

4. Compassion in Dying v. Washington, 79 F.3d 790, 813 n.65 (9th Cir. 1996) (en banc), *rev'd sub nom.* Washington v. Glucksberg, 117 S. Ct. 2258 (1997).

5. *See* Michael W. McConnell, *The Right to Die and the Jurisprudence of Tradition*, 1997 UTAH L. REV. 665, 702 (opining that the likelihood of the great influence of the *Glucksberg* methodology "is cause for celebration").

6. *Id.* at 708.

7. *Id.* at 666.

8. *Id.* at 700, 701.

9. *See id.* at 696 n.142.

10. 388 U.S. 1 (1967).

11. Because two people need not procreate, intend to procreate, or even be capable of procreating in order to marry civilly, procreation simply cannot form a functional justification for the mixed-sex requirement that might justify building the parties' sexes into the definition of the right.

12. The interested reader may consult, for example, Samuel A. Marcosson, *Romer and the Limits of Legitimacy: Stripping Opponents of Gay and Lesbian Rights of Their "First Line of Defense" in the Same-Sex Marriage Fight*, 24 J. CONTEMP. L. 217 (1998).

13. 116 S. Ct. at 1627.

14. *See, e.g.*, sources cited in Walter J. Walsh, *The Fearful Symmetry of Gay Rights, Religious Freedom, and Racial Equality*, 40 HOW. L.J. 513, 526 n.52 (1997); Watkins v. United States Army, 875 F.2d 699, 711–728 (9th Cir. 1989) (Norris, J., concurring in the judgment).

15. 518 U.S. 515 (1996). *See, e.g.*, Andrew Koppelman, *Why Discrimination Against Lesbians and Gay Men Is Sex Discrimination*, 69 N.Y.U. L. REV. 197 (1994).

# Part IV

## Issues of State Constitutional Law and International Law Concerning Marriage and Same-Sex Unions

# Chapter 9

Essay One

# Vermont Civil Unions:
# A Success Story

## Greg Johnson

> I have an opinion about the gay marriage issue—boy, I could get myself
> into trouble here. . . . I think that you're playing with something that is
> a tradition and an institution to a certain majority of people. Why go
> there? Create a new language, create a new tradition. . . . Instead of fit-
> ting into something that's not ours, we have to build our own culture.
>
> k.d. lang[1]

The lesbian and gay civil rights movement entered a new era on July 1,
2000. On that day Vermont's civil unions law took effect. At a time when
setbacks seemed to outweigh positive developments in the struggle for same-
sex marriage, Vermont managed to buck the trend, and in a big way. In the
late 1990s many states passed so-called defense-of-marriage laws, and in
1998 voters in Hawaii and Alaska resoundingly overturned pro-marriage
judicial decisions. But at the dawn of the new millennium, the Vermont
legislature passed a law that is truly unprecedented, at least in this country:
the civil unions law that grants same-sex couples "all the same benefits,
protections and responsibilities under law . . . as are granted to spouses in a
marriage."[2]

This achievement has led to howls of protest from religious leaders, politicians, and conservatives who favor "traditional" marriage. That was expected, but the lesbian and gay community has also criticized the civil unions
law. Noted gay author Andrew Sullivan unleashed a broadside against civil
unions in a cover story in the *New Republic*. Sullivan calls the civil unions
law "an act of pure stigmatization." He compares the civil-unions law to
the miscegenation laws in the Old South: "Like the miscegenation laws,
civil union essentially creates a two-tiered system, with one marriage model

clearly superior to the other."[3] Evan Wolfson, the former head of the Marriage Project at Lambda Legal Defense and Education Fund, echoes this theme. He has said, in reference to civil unions, "We've gone down the path of two lines at the clerk's office, or two drinking fountains before. We've done separate and equal; it was a mistake and should not be repeated."[4] Professor Mark Strasser has suggested that the civil unions law may be unconstitutional because "civil unions are less likely than marriages to be recognized in other jurisdictions." Strasser also thinks that Vermont's attempt at marital equality is stigmatizing: "Even if one sets aside the fact that same-sex civil union partners will not receive the benefits that they might have received had they been married, the stigmatization that occurs by setting up a separate civil union system for same-sex couples alone suffices to establish that the separate system does not pass constitutional muster."[5]

Taken together, these are some weighty charges. In this essay, I will defend civil unions against them. I do not see the civil unions law as an act of "pure stigmatization." The law is admittedly a political compromise, but that does not necessarily mean that it is homophobic. Although it is often profitable to second-guess a legislature's motives, all the evidence suggests that the civil unions law was passed by a legislature with the best of intentions. In creating a parallel system, the Vermont legislature was not trying to stigmatize gays and lesbians; rather, it was making a heroic and historic attempt to recognize the reality and worth of lesbian and gay families. I could not support the civil unions law if I did not think that it offered at the least the chance or opportunity for marriage equality. I have fought for same-sex marriage for years. I was cocounsel on *Brause v. State*, Alaska's same-sex-marriage case. I moved to Vermont from Alaska in July 1997, by pure coincidence a mere week before *Baker* was filed. As a professor at Vermont Law School, I have lectured and spoken publicly in favor of same-sex marriage. I also testified in favor of same-sex marriage before the Vermont House Judiciary Committee when it was fashioning a response to the *Baker* mandate. At the time, I was dubious that anything other than marriage could satisfy *Baker*. But the Vermont legislature opened my eyes to new possibilities. I have come to believe that civil unions are equal to marriage in law and in status. I will use my essay here to try to prove that.

I will also suggest that civil unions can become another symbol of power and pride for the lesbian/gay community, like the pink triangle and the rainbow flag. In a sense, civil unions are the best of both worlds. Couples in a civil union have the same rights and responsibilities as couples in a marriage, yet at the same time the lesbian and gay community can retain and nurture a little of what is uniquely its own with the new institution. Some might argue that only marriage is worth fighting for, since the term *marriage* carries with it so much status and tradition, but I see the newness of civil unions as one of their strengths. Why borrow every term and tradition from heterosexual culture? Why not create a new language of marriage?

## CIVIL UNIONS SHOULD BE RECOGNIZED FOR MARITAL BENEFITS IN OTHER STATES

The civil unions law was passed in response to the Vermont Supreme Court's mandate in *Baker v. State*. In *Baker*, the court held that denying same-sex couples the benefits and protections of the marriage laws violated the Common Benefits Clause of the Vermont Constitution.[6] The court told the legislature that it could either amend the marriage laws to include same-sex couples or "establish an alternative legal status to marriage for same-sex couples."[7] The legislature chose the latter route. After much rancor and outcry, it passed the civil-unions law as a legal alternative to marriage for same-sex couples.

The best argument for recognizing civil unions in other jurisdictions begins with the plain language of the statute. It is worth repeating that the civil unions law entitles same-sex couples to "all the same benefits, protections and responsibilities" offered to spouses in a marriage.[8] All the same. How could the legislature's intent be any clearer? It did not say "most" or "many"; it said "all." "All" means "every,"[9] so under any fair reading of the plain text this must mean that the legislature intended to offer same-sex couples whatever benefits, protections, and responsibilities it offers to couples married in Vermont. Vermont cannot control what the federal government or other states do, but to the extent that other states care to honor the intent of the Vermont legislature in passing the civil-unions law, it is unmistakable that the legislature intended to treat opposite-sex couples and same-sex couples exactly the same.

The analogy to marriage by no means ends with the rights and responsibilities offered to couples in a civil union. The registration process is the same for civil unions and marriage. Both same-sex couples and opposite-sex couples begin the process by applying for a license from the town clerk.[10] Couples then have sixty days to solemnize a marriage or certify a civil union by a justice of the peace, a member of the clergy, or a judge.[11] Upon filing with the town clerk, marriage licenses and civil-union licenses are both converted into "certificates."[12]

Equality between marriage and civil union continues throughout the course of the respective relationships. The law mandates that parties to a civil union are to be included in "any definition or uses of the terms 'spouse,' 'family,' 'immediate family,' 'dependent,' 'next of kin,' and other terms that denote the spousal relationship, as those terms are used throughout the law."[13] The parties are "responsible for the support of one another to the same degree and in the same manner as prescribed under law for married persons."[14] If a civil union should dissolve, the family court has jurisdiction, and the same law governing the dissolution of a marriage applies, "including annulment, separation and divorce, child custody and support, and property division and maintenance[.]"[15]

The legislature withheld no marital benefit and spared no marital responsibility with the civil unions law. But the civil unions law does more than just track the marriage code. It also recognizes lesbian and gay couples as families entitled to the same rights and respect as heterosexual couples. Here are two of the legislative findings in the act:

(7) The state has a strong interest in promoting stable and lasting families, including families based upon a same-sex couple.
(9) . . . Despite longstanding social and economic discrimination, many gay and lesbian Vermonters have formed lasting, committed, caring and faithful relationships with persons of their same sex. These couples live together, participate in their communities together, and some raise children and care for family members together, just as do couples who are married under Vermont law.[16]

Does that sound demeaning or stigmatizing? Hardly. I would call it inclusive and welcoming.

These findings, the scope of the benefits and protections offered, and the lengthy legislative record make clear that the legislature, in responding to *Baker*, was well intentioned and sensitive to the needs and dignities of same-sex couples. The evidence suggests that the legislature was trying to do as much as or more than the bare constitutional minimum required by *Baker*. The legislature did not challenge or test the court by doing nothing or too little; rather, in fashioning a parallel marital system for same-sex couples, it did the best it possibly could, given the political reality. When one appreciates the tremendous opposition to the bill and the backlash that followed, it is not too strong to call the work of the Vermont legislature heroic.

If Vermont treats couples in a civil union the same as couples in a marriage, why shouldn't other states? Professor Strasser and others have persuasively argued that same-sex marriages, if they ever come to be, should be recognized in other states and by the federal government.[17] But so far scholars have yet to explain adequately why this same reasoning, which is based on full faith and credit, the right to travel, comity, and other theories, should not also apply to Vermont civil unions. This is understandable. Since the institution is so new, it takes time to think about it.

Strasser, for one, rests his argument that civil unions would not be recognized outside of Vermont largely on the unsupported assertion that "[c]ivil union partners would presumably be treated like domestic partners[.]"[18] I contest this premise. Civil unions are not at all like domestic partnerships. "Domestic partnership" is a generic term used to describe the benefit programs offered to same- and opposite-sex couples by a growing number of municipalities, states, and private employers. Some programs are better than others, but no domestic partnership program grants all the benefits and protections of marriage. No domestic partnership program requires registration at the town clerk's office and the blessing of the state, as with marriage and civil unions. No domestic partnership program allows for intestate succession. No domestic partnership program bestows the testimonial privilege. No domestic partnership program allows partners to adopt. No domestic partnership program allows couples to own property as tenants by the entirety, a right reserved for couples in a marriage or civil union. Importantly, no domestic partnership program imposes obligations on dissolution like those imposed by marriage and civil union. Civil union is meant to be a legal equivalent to marriage; that is decidedly not the intent behind any of the proliferating domestic partnership plans across the country.

Once one appreciates the many ways in which a civil union really is like a marriage,[19] then it might not be quite so hard to come up with arguments for interstate recognition of civil unions. Litigants can rely on the plain language of the law to argue for interstate recognition. For example, let us say that a Vermont couple joins in civil union and then moves to some other state. Let us also say that, tragically, one of them dies on the operating table. Can the surviving spouse sue the doctor for wrongful death? The answer should be yes. Most states allow a wrongful death claim to be brought by, among others, a decedent's surviving spouse. The civil unions law says that parties to a civil union are to be included in the definition of "spouse" wherever that word might appear in the law. The civil unions law also states explicitly that parties to a civil union may bring "causes of action related to or dependent upon spousal status, including an action for wrongful death, emotional distress, [and] loss of consortium[.]"[20] Clearly the surviving spouse of a Vermont marriage would be able to sue for wrongful death in some other state. By the same reasoning, the surviving spouse in a Vermont civil union should also be able to sue.

A major hurdle to recognizing both same-sex marriages and civil unions in other jurisdictions will be the "strong-public-policy" exception to the rule of universal marital recognition.[21] This will be especially true in states that have so-called Defense-of-Marriage acts (DOMAs). In those states, parties will have to mount a constitutional challenge to the DOMA before their same-sex marriage or civil union will be recognized. In those states that do not have a DOMA, the argument for recognition of civil unions will be much easier. The plain language of the civil-unions law gives courts in those states more than enough interpretative wiggle room to rule in favor of same-sex couples. Litigants can also use in their favor arguments made against recognizing civil unions in DOMA states. In 2000 the attorney general of Illinois (which is a DOMA state) issued an opinion in which he concluded that "the State of Illinois is not required to recognize same-sex civil unions entered into under the laws of Vermont." Attorney General James Ryan reached this conclusion based on his presumption that civil unions were essentially same-sex marriages and therefore not to be recognized under the Illinois DOMA:

> The Vermont Legislature . . . opted to provide marital benefits to same-sex partners through a system of civil unions rather than by permitting same-sex marriages. The difference between a civil union in Vermont and a same-sex marriage, however, is merely a matter of nomenclature. Pursuant to the Vermont civil union legislation, parties to a same-sex civil union are entitled to all benefits, protections and responsibilities under Vermont law as are spouses in a marriage. Moreover, Vermont same-sex couples must meet all of the formalities of marriage. Same-sex couples must obtain a civil union license, the civil union must be certified and the certificate of civil union must be registered in the same way as a marriage license. It is my opinion, therefore, that Vermont same-sex civil unions are equivalent to same-sex marriages, for purposes of Illinois law. Consequently, under both State and Federal law, same-sex civil unions entered into pursuant to Vermont law are not recognized under Illinois law.[22]

In a non-DOMA state, a court could use this exact same analysis but reach an opposite result in the final sentence, namely, that civil unions are so much like marriages that they should be recognized for marital benefits and responsibilities. Obviously a court disinclined to rule in favor of same-sex couples will not have to, given the strong-public-policy exception to the recognition rule. But outside of that exception, the jurisprudence would seem to favor recognizing civil unions to the same extent that Vermont marriages are recognized.

## CIVIL UNIONS ARE NOT STIGMATIZING

I think that it is inaccurate and unfair to compare the civil unions law to the Jim Crow laws struck down in *Brown v. Board of Education* and its progeny. Jim Crow laws established segregated facilities that infringed on the rights of African Americans gained through the Civil War amendments. Conversely, the civil-unions law is expansive legislation, extending a host of rights to lesbian and gay couples that they never had before. Jim Crow laws were passed with malice by racist legislatures hell-bent on subjugating African Americans. The civil unions law was passed by a legislature earnestly trying to do the right thing. Jim Crow laws pandered to the masses and to the white establishment—they were meant to be stigmatizing. The civil-unions law represents a courageous attempt by a legislature to vote its conscience in the face of fierce protest and outrage. Some legislators lost their seats because of their vote in favor of civil unions. I doubt that that was ever true for anyone who voted in favor of Jim Crow laws. This is not to say that one might still not chafe at the thought of a separate institution. My point is that before scholars apply the equal protection precedent from *Brown* and its progeny to the civil-unions law, they would do well to appreciate the difference between the civil unions law and the laws struck down in those cases.[23]

There is more than just the legislative record to suggest that civil unions might not be stigmatizing in the way segregated facilities in the South were. We can also look to the response of the many couples who have joined in civil union. In just one year since the law took effect, Vermont town clerks issued 2,479 civil-union certificates. Couples came from forty-six states to obtain their civil union. The only four states not yet represented are Mississippi, Montana, North Dakota, and Wyoming. Couples also came from Canada, England, Venezuela, Mexico, the Philippines, Australia, the Netherlands, Germany, India, and Guatemala.[24] I do not think that many of these couples consider their civil union to be stigmatizing. To the contrary, an emerging theme among couples who have joined in civil unions is how they have been surprised by the intensity of their reaction to the event. Keith Ribnick, a member of the Vermont Freedom to Marry Task Force, captured what I would call the prevailing attitude of those who have joined in civil union. He called his civil union with his partner of sixteen years, David Van Duyn, a "powerful moment." "We thought we loved each other as much as we possibly could, even before we'd ever heard of civil unions or the Baker case. . . . But when you go into a ceremony and hear a justice (of the peace) say, 'By the power vested in me,' it truly was the most joyous experience I'd ever had[.]"[25] Stan Baker, the man who agreed to be the named plaintiff in Vermont's same-sex-marriage case, eventually joined in civil union with his partner, Peter Harrigan. He has called his civil union "spiritual," "meaningful," and "powerful." He said that their families "understood the legal connection. They got it right away."[26]

What does this say about the new institution of civil unions? I would never deny the possibility of a "false consciousness" about all this, but I honestly do not think that the couples who fought for marriage but accepted civil unions have been deceived or have compromised too much. To me, the outpouring of support for civil unions suggests that many in the lesbian and gay community, even those who are fighting for marriage, would agree with Professor William Eskridge that, at least for now, "Vermont got it right[.]"[27]

## THE SPECIAL "QUEER QUALITY" OF CIVIL UNIONS

The civil unions law "does not 'bestow the status of marriage' on same-sex couples,"[28] but the reverse is also true: The law does not bestow the status of civil unions on opposite-sex couples. This is what I mean by the "queer quality" of civil unions. Since civil unions are open only to same-sex couples, the lesbian and gay community has a chance to "own" them, to turn them into a viable and vibrant institution, to be proud of them.

I do not doubt that most of those who have joined in civil union would prefer to have married. At the same time, it is important to recognize that some couples might prefer civil unions to marriage. Carey Goldberg, who has covered the civil unions story for the *New York Times*, interviewed several couples who said that "though they wanted the rights and responsibilities of marriage, they liked the fact that the Vermont bill did not use the word, because it left them with the image that they were creating a different kind of partnership, more egalitarian and perhaps more successful."[29] One woman who had been married to a man and "vowed never to marry again" said, "I see marriage as very patriarchal and very much about property and ownership . . . but I see civil union as a completely level playing field; Theresa and I are equal partners and we are willingly doing this as equals."[30] Paula Ettelbrick, who famously criticized the movement for same-sex marriage in her 1989 article "Since When Is Marriage a Path to Liberation?,"[31] said, "I will admit to being very awed by the developments in Vermont, and just personally, it has made me rethink the opportunity it might provide for me and for my children."[32]

The civil-unions law thus resurrects a debate and tension evident in the lesbian and gay community since Stonewall. Is the goal of the legal and political struggle for equal rights to be exactly like the straight community, to blend in and eventually disappear, or is it to achieve equality while at the same time celebrating identity? Put another way, if in the future all forms of discrimination against lesbians and gays were eradicated, would the idea of a "lesbian and gay community" become irrelevant?

Some think so. Take, for example, Neil Tennant, a member of the pop band Pet Shop Boys:

Because some people have sex with people of the same sex, an entire culture has been created, broadly speaking, out of oppression. Which in a rational world would not be an issue. . . . The idea of "gay"—it's a big subject. To me, it's like a '70's response to political repression; as political equality is achieved, the idea of "gay" should evaporate. I am always very suspicious of gay communities or communities based on people's ethnic origins or what have you. . . . I think we should be one community.[33]

To the contrary, I am just as suspicious of "one community." I subscribe to the "cornucopia" vision of America rather than the "melting pot." America's strength is its diversity. In its struggle for equality, one would hope that the lesbian and gay community is not totally subsumed into straight culture. The lesbian and gay community may have grown out of oppression and discrimination, but over time I think that the community has grown to like what it has created, and most would be sorry to see it go. Most lesbians and gays are proud of their community; we might be shy to admit it, but we like being different.

Professor David Chambers addresses the "sameness/difference" debate in his thoughtful introduction to the issue of the *Vermont Law Review* devoted to *Baker* and civil unions. Chambers discounts the suggestion that the legislature and Governor Howard Dean felt that same-sex unions and opposite-sex couples were truly identical but merely bowed to political reality in selecting civil unions over same-sex marriage. He believes that Governor Dean and many legislators "really do think that gay relationships are different from theirs and, though worthy, not quite equal." But Chambers does not attribute the choice of a term other than marriage "solely to the discomfort of liberal heterosexual legislators."

They were not the only ones who accepted relegating gay people to a "different but equal" institution. Liberal homosexual Vermonters in large numbers, including me, comfortably accepted the relegation. Of course, we would have preferred "marriage," but when it became clear that we weren't going to get it, only a few of us experienced "civil union" as an affront. Many of us, as pragmatists, were delighted to take what we could get for now, especially from a legislature that had demonstrated such good will. Nonetheless, I believe that some part of our comfort with "civil union" has a deeper explanation. It is that just as heterosexuals see themselves as different from us, we too see ourselves as different from them. Even the most self-assured among us grew up feeling different in some essential way from our parents and from most of our peers. . . . The irony in the end is that our comfort provided comfort to the liberal legislators of Vermont when they named our marriages something else.[34]

Professor Michael Mello has also noted this irony, but with some sharper words. He had this to say when the Vermont Freedom to Marry Task Force said that it could support the civil-unions bill:

I see a downside in the gay community's supporting any legislation short of marriage, because it provided legislators, Governor Dean, and perhaps even a supreme court justice or two political cover in compromising for domestic partnerships: These folks could point proudly to the second-class citizenship conferred by domestic partnerships, and say, "see, even the gay leadership thinks domestic partnership is enough." With gay support behind a domestic partnership statute, the supreme court would have a tougher time voiding that statute in favor of requiring same-sex marriage.[35]

Was it a mistake to support civil unions? I do not think so, since it gave same-sex couples rights they badly needed. But on top of that, what is wrong with being different? The presumptions behind Mello's position may be that no lesbian or gay couple could possibly want something other than what heterosexual couples have, and that marriage is the pinnacle, the summit, the only form of state recognition worth pursuing—the key to equality and happiness. I would hope that the struggle for same-sex marriage is about more than imitation and emulation. Civil unions give the lesbian and gay community a chance to be different, a chance to celebrate its identity.

The courts will decide legal questions such as whether civil unions are portable to other states, but it is up to the lesbian and gay community to decide on a political and cultural response. Perhaps the community can use the new name and the new institution of civil unions to rekindle some of that healthy rebellion that characterized and motivated some of the pioneers of the same-sex-marriage movement. The first same-sex-marriage case was brought by Jack Baker and Michael McConnell in 1970, shortly after Stonewall. Baker said that they hoped to "cause a cultural revolution!"[36] Much has changed since 1970 (except the name Baker), and today the same-sex-marriage movement is seen by most as "mainstreaming." But the community still has time to consider whether all this effort is about nothing more than being "just like them." Maybe with civil unions the community can cause a bit of a cultural revolution. *Vive la différence.*

## NOTES

1. Michele Kort, *k.d., a Woman in Love*, Advocate, June 20, 2000, at 51, 59.

2. An Act Relating to Civil Unions, Vt. Stat Ann. tit. 15 § 1204(a) (Supp. 2000).

3. Andrew Sullivan, *State of the Union*, New Republic, May 8, 2000, at 18, 20.

4. Evan Wolfson, *Interview: Why the Boy Scouts Case Went Down*, Gay and Lesbian Review Worldwide, Jan.–Feb. 2001, at 17.

5. Mark Strasser, *Mission Impossible: On Baker, Equal Benefits, and the Imposition of Stigma*, 9 William and Mary Bill of Rights J. 1, 2–3 (2000).

6. *Baker v. State*, 744 A.2d 864, 867 (Vt. 1999).

7. *Id.* at 886.

8. Vt. Stat. Ann. tit. 15 § 1204(a).

9. Webster's 7th New Collegiate Dictionary 23 (1970).

10. *Compare* Vt. Stat. Ann. tit. 18 § 5131(a) *with* Vt. Stat. Ann. tit. 18 § 5160(a).

11. *Compare* Vt. Stat. Ann. tit. 18 § 5131(b) *with* Vt. Stat. Ann. tit. 18 § 5160(b).

12. *Compare* Vt. Stat. Ann. tit. 18 § 5131(b) *with* Vt. Stat. Ann. tit. 18 § 5160(b).

13. Vt. Stat. Ann. tit. 15 § 1204(b).

14. *Id.* at § 1204(c).

15. *Id.* at § 1204(d).

16. An Act Relating to Civil Unions, 2000 Vt. Acts & Resolves 91 § 1(7) and (9) (legislative findings).

17. *See, e.g.*, Mark Strasser, The Challenge of Same-Sex Marriage (1999).

18. Strasser, *Mission Impossible*, *supra* note 5, at 2.

19. To cite but one interesting example, couples in a civil union in Vermont are allowed to file their state income-tax return "in the same manner as married couples[.]" Vermont Department of Banking, Insurance, Securities, & Health Care Administration, in collaboration with the Vermont Department of Taxes, *Information for Civil Union Partners in Vermont* (January 2001). Since Vermont "piggybacks" its state income tax on a filer's federal tax (24 percent of the federal tax), couples in a civil union wishing to file jointly must first fill out a "shadow" federal 1040 form "using federal rules as they apply to married couples." *Id.* An income-tax specialist for the Department of Taxation has said, "The income tax of parties to a civil union in Vermont is as if the federal law recognized civil union as marriage." Joanne Pencak,

*Businesses Must Respond to Civil Union Act by Extending Coverage of Employee Benefits*, Valley Business Journal, Oct. 2000, at 31. This means that in Vermont some lesbian and gay couples in a civil union will receive a tax break with the end of the so-called marriage penalty.

20. Vt. Stat. Ann. tit. 15 § 1204(e)(2).

21. *See* Restatement (Second) of Conflicts of Laws § 283(2) (1971) ("A marriage which satisfies the requirements of the state where the marriage was contracted will everywhere be recognized as valid unless it violates the strong public policy of another state").

22. Ill. Ag Op. 2000 WL 33152171 at *4.

23. Professor William Eskridge has also concluded that the civil-unions law is not comparable to the Jim Crow laws:

I am a classical liberal and a gay person who supports legal recognition of same-sex marriages. My last book criticized the twentieth century legal regime that created an "apartheid of the closet" for lesbian, bisexual, gay, and transgendered people. Yet I do not think the civil unions law is apartheid. . . . Nor do I believe the analogy to Plessy holds up: formally, the law is neither separate nor equal; functionally, the law ameliorates, rather than ratifies, a sexuality caste system. The racial apartheid adopted by southern state legislatures and upheld in Plessy were very different from the new institution suggested by Baker and adopted by the Vermont legislature.

William N. Eskridge, Jr., *Equality Practice: Liberal Reflections on the Jurisprudence of Civil Unions*, 64 Albany L. Rev. 853, 863 (2001).

24. Vermont Civil Union Review Commission, Report of December 31, 2000, available at www.leg.state.vt.us/baker/cureport.htm.

25. David Mace, *On First Anniversary, Ripples Said to Be Wide*, Rutland Herald, July 1, 2001.

26. Ross Sneyd, *A Year After Baker*, Rutland Herald, Dec. 18, 2000.

27. Eskridge, *supra* note 23, at 878.

28. An Act Relating to Civil Unions, 2000 Vt. Acts & Resolves 91 § 1(10) (legislative findings).

29. Carey Goldberg, *Gay Couples Are Welcoming Vermont Measure on Civil Union*, N.Y. Times, Mar. 18, 2000, at A1.

30. *Id.*

31. Paula L. Ettelbrick, *Since When Is Marriage a Path to Liberation?*, Out/Look National Gay and Lesbian Quarterly, issue 6, at 8 (Fall 1989), *reprinted in* Lesbians, Gay Men, and the Law 401 (William B. Rubenstein ed. 1993).

32. Goldberg, *supra* note 29, at A1.

33. Interview, *West End Boys*, Advocate, July 17, 2001, at 47–48.

34. David L. Chambers, *The Baker Case, Civil Unions, and the Recognition of Our Common Humanity: An Introduction and a Speculation*, 25 Vermont L. Rev. 5, 12–13 (2000).

35. Michael Mello, *For Today I'm Gay: The Unfinished Battle for Same-Sex Marriage in Vermont*, 25 Vermont L. Rev. 149, at n.450 (2000).

36. Kay Tobin & Randy Wicker, The Gay Crusaders 144 (1972).

Response

# Are Civil Unions Mandated by Constitutional Law? A Response to Greg Johnson

## William C. Duncan

In his essay, Professor Johnson makes a forthright defense of the status of "civil unions" in Vermont against the claim that allowing same-sex couples to contract civil unions but not marry creates a "separate-but-equal" status that is fundamentally unjust. I believe that Professor Johnson is right to suggest that the Vermont legislature did not enact the civil-unions law with the intent to stigmatize same-sex couples. I also agree (although I understand that our interpretation of this fact will lead to different conclusions) that the different nature of same-sex and opposite-sex relationships justifies differential treatment of the two by the law. Indeed, this difference seems to be essential to a rebuttal of the claim that constitutional guarantees of equality require the redefinition of marriage to include same-sex couples. What Professor Johnson does not spend much time on, the constitutional justification for civil unions, seems to me to be of great importance and would lead to a different conclusion than he reaches on the question of whether other states should recognize civil unions.

Professor Johnson is correct in noting that civil unions have great symbolic significance (in addition to the practical significance for Vermont residents). This explains the popularity of civil unions among nonresidents of Vermont who may or may not receive recognition of the status in their home states. The question is whether this symbolic gesture is constitutionally required. Defenders of civil unions conveniently ignore that question by pointing out that the Vermont legislature created civil unions, and it is clearly within its power to do so. The reality, though, is that the legislature would not have done so at this time without a very strong motivation given that a majority of Vermonters opposed the enactment of the civil-union law. Something beyond legislative goodwill was at work, and that something was the Vermont Supreme Court's decision in *Baker v. Vermont*.[1] That decision included an order from the court to the legislature to redefine marriage to include same-sex couples or "establish an alternative legal status to marriage for same-sex couples."[2] More ominously, the court announced that it would retain jurisdiction over the case until the legislature acted to ensure that the legislature did the job right. If it did not, the court would consider holding the marriage law unconstitutional and thus mandating same-sex marriage itself.[3] The legislative approach to civil unions should be understood in this context of duress.

Thus it can be said that the Vermont Supreme Court never actually ruled on the constitutionality of the marriage law—the very subject at issue in the case. Instead, it made the nebulous pronouncement that there is no difference between same- and opposite-sex couples and that the benefits available to one should be available to the other. I have already critiqued the court's purported constitutional justification for this decision, but it is important to revisit some of the questions this kind of decision raises.

Inherently, the decision has a form of constitutional reasoning but lacks any substance. This is true because the court lacked any authority to make its decision. The responsibility to decide what relationships ought to have state sanction is not a judicial one. The judiciary was being asked in *Baker* to settle the question of whether the definition of marriage reflected in the law of Vermont was constitutional. Implicitly, the court made this decision—it ruled that it was (by not striking down the law). Then, in a stunning move, the court ignored its authority and made the kind of decision associated with legislative power: it put forward a compromise—the legislature could create a new kind of status for same-sex couples. No one would deny that the legislature could, at any point, have advanced the idea of civil unions, but it did not. The court did that for it and threatened another result if it did not. It was as if a legislator had threatened that if he did not get his way on a particular bill, he would enact even more stringent legislation. Of course, no legislator could do that, but the court managed, through a remarkable sleight of hand, to do just that. How the court would have justified reversing its holding that the marriage law was constitutional as anything other than a raw legislative power play would have been interesting, but the legislature blinked, so we may never know.

The fact that the Vermont legislature's enactment of civil unions was forced by a court decision that flagrantly violated the principle of separation of powers and clearly exceeded the court's constitutional authority calls into question any argument that other states have a legal obligation to recognize Vermont civil unions. To argue otherwise would be to allow a rogue court to redefine marriage not only for one state, but potentially for the rest of the country. In addition, if the Vermont legislature is constitutionally justified in differentiating between same-sex couples and married couples, presumably other state legislatures (such as the vast majority of states that have

enacted statutes prohibiting the recognition of out-of-state same-sex marriages) can do the same without offending their state constitutions. In conclusion, while the Vermont compromise has important lessons to teach
about the constitutional relationship between marriage and same-sex relationships, it can only be understood in the context of the Vermont Supreme
Court decision that forced it to be made.

## NOTES

1. 744 A.2d 864 (Vt. 1999).
2. *Id*. at 886.
3. *Id*. at 887.

Essay Two

# Imposing the Same-Sex-Marriage Template on State Constitutional Law: The Implications for Marriage, Constitutional Theory, and Democracy

## William C. Duncan

One helpful result of the same-sex-marriage debate in the United States is the renewal of interest in state constitutional law, because the law of marriage is an issue where states have near-exclusive power. This is appropriate because state governments are closer to the people who are most intimately affected by matters that touch on the intersection of the family and the law. State legislatures, in particular, are likely to be best equipped to respond to the varying contexts that exist in the diverse states. This is not to say that the story of the same-sex-marriage debate in the United States is a story about differing legislative responses to claims for same-sex marriage. It is not. In fact, the story is much more complex. It raises questions of governmental authority, constitutional rights, and the meaning of marriage. This essay will briefly discuss the history of state constitutional jurisprudence in the same-sex-marriage context and describe how advocates of redefining marriage to include same-sex couples and the judges who have accepted their theories have advanced a novel and, finally, unjust theory of state constitutional law.

## STATE CONSTITUTIONAL CLAIMS FOR SAME-SEX MARRIAGE

The attractiveness of state courts to proponents of same-sex marriage is not surprising. State legislatures generally have opposed the legalization of same-sex marriages. "To date, 35 states have enacted legislation clarifying that same-sex 'marriages' contracted in other jurisdictions will not be recognized in those states."[1] Additionally, there has been a movement in the last few decades to secure a wider range of individual rights by recourse to novel interpretations of state constitutions. This movement, spurred on by the encouragement of Justice William J. Brennan, Jr., and the example of Oregon Supreme Court Justice Hans Linde, has made some state courts an increasingly attractive forum for activists who believe that they are unlikely to get a sympathetic hearing from the federal courts.[2] The experience of activist supporters of same-sex marriage has indicated the wisdom of avoiding federal courts while pursuing their claims in the state courts. In the one instance where the issue has been addressed by a federal court, the claim for same-sex marriage was rejected out of hand.[3] Proponents have gotten much further in state courts.

## Same-Sex Marriage in State Courts

In 1993, the Hawaii Supreme Court held that under the Hawaii Constitution the state's marriage law "discriminated on the basis of sex" under the state's Equal Rights Amendment, because the sex of the parties entering into marriage was taken into account and was therefore subject to strict scrutiny, requiring the state to provide a compelling state interest in order to justify the law.[4] Applying this standard, a Hawaii trial court found the law unconstitutional in 1996.[5] In 1997 meanwhile, the legislature passed, and in 1998 the citizens of Hawaii approved, an amendment to the state constitution protecting their power to restrict marriage to the union of a man and a woman.

In early 1998, while the appeal of the 1996 Hawaii decision was pending before the Hawaii Supreme Court, a trial judge in Alaska held that the Alaska Constitution created a fundamental right to "choose a life partner."[6] The court identified the source of this right as the state constitution's privacy provision. The court then announced that there would be a trial to determine whether the state had a compelling interest that would justify the marriage law's violation of the right to privacy. In response, as in Hawaii, the Alaska legislature approved, and the people of the state ratified, a state constitutional amendment defining marriage as the union of a man and a woman.

Shortly after the Hawaii legislature voted to put the marriage amendment on the general election ballot, groups seeking to redefine marriage filed a similar lawsuit in Vermont. After the trial court dismissed the lawsuit, the plaintiffs appealed to the Vermont Supreme Court. On December 20, 1999, the court decided that the Vermont Constitution's Common Benefits Clause required the state to offer all the benefits of marriage to same-sex couples, even though the actual status of marriage could still be reserved for opposite-sex couples.[7] The court did not, as the plaintiffs urged, strike down the marriage law, but instead effectively ordered the Vermont legislature to provide a way for same-sex couples, to enjoy the benefits of marriage. In response, the legislature created a new status, "civil unions" for same-sex couples, allowing them to register and gain all of the benefits of marriage. Now a lawsuit is pending in the Massachusetts supreme judicial court in which seven same-sex couples are appealing a lower court rejection of their challenge to the state marriage law under various provisions of the state constitution's Declaration of Rights in order to get a decision that these provisions require that marriage licenses be issued to same-sex couples.

### The Template Imposed by Same-Sex-Marriage Advocates

Why the major difference between state and federal court outcomes? There are a number of possible reasons for this. Proponents claim that it is because state constitutions provide more protection of individual rights than the federal constitution. Skeptics point to judicial activism, arguing that sympathy toward same-sex marriage and related legal concepts is much more pronounced in the judiciary and the legal profession than in other parts of the population and that the lack of conservative precedent in some state courts guarantees that activists will have more success there.[8] There is some truth in both accounts. State constitutions are different and may provide more protections than the U.S. Constitution does. On the other hand, there are good reasons to be skeptical about the new rights found in state constitutions by judges who are clearly more sympathetic to the claims made by same-sex-marriage proponents than in other states with similar constitutional provisions.

What is at work here is the acceptance by state courts of a specific view of state constitutional law advanced by those who would redefine marriage to include same-sex couples. This view serves as a template for evaluating constitutional claims made by activists.

## ANOTHER VIEW OF STATE CONSTITUTIONALISM

The problem with the template that advocates of redefining marriage are trying to impose on state constitutional law is the distorting effect it has on marriage and state constitutions.

### The Redefinition of Marriage

In their attempt to advance a particular view of equality, proponents of same-sex marriage see the state as the most fundamental unit of society, which can and should reshape the rights of citizens and civil society in a way that overturns laws that perpetuate domination by one group over others. The decisions noted earlier have run roughshod over traditional understandings of marriage that rely on an understanding of marriage as more than a mere contract, an understanding that is characterized by certain essential elements: (1) the requirement of a man and a woman, (2) perma-

nence, (3) mutual faithfulness between spouses, and (4) openness to the
potential for the creation of new life. Instead, all of the decisions in favor
of same-sex marriage have included one or more of the following assumptions about marriage:

1. Marriage has nothing to do with sexual difference. This idea is implicit in the
   Hawaii decision since the very reference to sex in the marriage statute is held
   unconstitutional. The Alaska decision reconfigures the right to marry as "the fundamental right to choose one's life partner."[9] The Vermont court held that same-
   sex couples were "no differently situated" with respect to the goals advanced by
   marriage laws than opposite-sex couples.[10]
2. Marriage is a wholly malleable social institution that is created by the state solely
   to achieve certain goals. The Hawaii Supreme Court baldly stated that the state
   is the "exclusive progenitor of the marriage relationship."[11] The Vermont court
   described marriage as part of "the family of State-sanctioned human relations."[12]
3. Marriage is a policy device to promote stable relationships. In the *Baker* decision,
   the majority opinion said: "The state's interest in extending official recognition
   . . . to the professed commitment of two individuals to a lasting relationship of
   mutual affection is predicated on the belief that legal support of a couple's commitment provides stability for the individuals, their family, and the broader community."[13] As noted earlier, the Alaska decision effectively redefines marriage as
   a "life partnership."
4. Marriage is a policy device to protect children, and same-sex couples are as capable
   of protecting children as opposite-sex couples. In addition to arguing that marriage is meant to promote stability in relationships, the Vermont court also argued
   that the state recognizes marriage in order to "promote the security" of children
   raised by couples.[14] It further argued that same-sex couples are no different from
   married couples in this regard. This claim was also important to the outcome of
   the Hawaii trial court decision.[15]
5. Marriage, or at least the benefits thereof, is something to be equally distributed
   by the state as a matter of basic fairness. The *Brause* decision holds that the very
   choice of a partner is the crucial right "whether the decision results in a traditional
   choice or a nontraditional choice. . . . The same constitution protects both."[16]
   The Vermont court says: "The extension of the Common Benefits Clause to
   acknowledge plaintiffs as Vermonters who seek nothing more, nor less, than legal
   protection and security for their avowed commitment to an intimate and lasting
   human relationship is simply, when all is said and done, a recognition of our
   common humanity."[17]

These assumptions reflect a dramatic redefinition of marriage, which has
traditionally been based on very different understandings. These include an
understanding that marriage is intrinsically a relationship between a man
and a woman and that it is unique as such, because the relationship between
a man and a woman is qualitatively different than the relationship between
two men or two women.

Another reality shortchanged by the same-sex-marriage template is that marriage preexisted the state and is recognized (not created) by the state because of its intrinsic value. This is not a theological point. Whether one understands that marriage preexisted state recognition as a matter of religious belief or whether one believes that marriage has developed from the machinations of a "selfish gene," one thing is clear—marriage did not come into being by statute (some state marriage statutes do not even define marriage). It is not, therefore, wholly malleable. It has internal limits and characteristics that the state ignores at the risk of damaging the nature of marriage itself.

Marriage law has also recognized the reality that only the sexual relationship of a man and a woman can result in the conception of a child. This creates a state interest in the marital relationship that just does not exist in other relationships. Of course, some will argue that children are born to parents in same-sex relationships, and therefore the same interest is at work, but there is an inherent difference between a relationship in which, by definition, children can enter only through the exercise of the will and the use of reproductive technology and relationships in which (barring unrelated disability) children are a natural product of the union even when the parents do not intend their relationship to result in the begetting of a child. This difference is that the latter relationship creates a vulnerability for women (because they may become pregnant) and children (who need stability in their parents' relationship) that does not exist in the former relationships where all procreation must be planned.[18]

Finally, marriage has always been understood to require a man and a woman because the unique contributions of men and women to child rearing cannot be duplicated by any other contexts in which child rearing takes place. Even some who believe that same-sex couples are as good as or better than married couples at raising children admit that there is a significant difference between children raised by same-sex couples and those raised by opposite-sex married couples.[19]

## The Distortion of Constitutional Law

The next problem with the view of state constitutions that sees in them only a way of creating ever-expanding benefits is the distorting effect this has on the substantive meaning of state constitutions. Constitutional provisions have been reconfigured to justify results that the language and meaning of the provisions cannot reasonably support. One manifestation of this is the fact that different state courts have used substantially similar provisions to achieve completely opposite results. For instance, Judge Peter Michalksi in Alaska based his decision on that state's privacy provision (article I, section 22). In Hawaii, that state's privacy provision (article I, section 6) was expressly rejected as the source of a right to same-sex marriage. Similarly, in

Hawaii, the supreme court ruled that the marriage statute was an unconstitutional sex-based classification, relying on its Equal Rights Amendment (article I, section 5), but in Washington State, which has a similar amendment (article 31, section 1), the sex-discrimination claim was explicitly rejected in an early same-sex marriage case.[20]

The holding of an Alaska trial court judge that the Alaska Constitution's privacy protection included a fundamental right to "choose one's life partner" is a prime example of this distortion of constitutional meaning.[21] The concept of privacy is stretched beyond reason when it is held to mean that the state must privilege private choices about private behavior. The precedents the court relied on in its decision both involved private behavior that was prohibited (either criminally or by school rules) and no claim that state benefits should be extended based on the behavior.[22] The marriage law of Alaska did not prohibit same-sex relationships; it merely defined marriage. In its decision, the court changed the substantive meaning of the constitutional right of privacy from a right to be left alone to a right to not be left alone if one wanted state recognition.

Another example is the Hawaii court's interpretation of the equal protection provision that yielded the improbable conclusion that marriage is sex discrimination. Case law based on federal and state constitutions has long recognized that statutes that disadvantage one sex over the other constitute sex-based classifications that are subject to heightened scrutiny. The Hawaii decision took a different approach, arguing that any distinction that even touches upon sex is inherently subject to heightened scrutiny whether it treats men and women exactly the same, as marriage laws do, or whether it disadvantages one sex. This approach ignores the salient reality noted by Justice Ruth Bader Ginsburg that "a community made up exclusively of one [sex] is different from a community composed of both."[23] It turns the concept of equality on its head by treating the sexes as fungible and perpetuating a truly unequal approach where one sex is permanently excluded from some marriages. Marriage law has always been a source of true equality because it inherently requires a partner of each sex, thus putting the opposite-sex partners on a footing of absolute equality since the marriage could not exist without both of them.

One of the most confusing aspects of the equal protection discussions in these decisions is trying to nail down the actual class that the court alleges is being discriminated against. Since both men and women are in both the class that is presumably being discriminated against and in the class that is being privileged at the expense of the other, it hardly makes sense to allege that sex discrimination is at work since both sexes are treated exactly the same. Nor does the attempt to identify the affected class as "couples of the same sex" avoid this problem since the problem remains that one sex is not privileged over the other by the law. Some would argue that the affected class could be identified by "sexual orientation," but this ignores the fact that the marriage statutes say nothing about the "orientation" of the parties involved in the marriage.

Similarly, provisions such as those in the Vermont (chapter I, article 7) and Massachusetts (part I, articles 6 and 7) Constitutions that are meant to proscribe governmental favoritism cannot plausibly support the redefinition of marriage. The Vermont clause relied on by the court for its decision states: "That government is, or ought to be, instituted for the common benefit, protection, and security of the people, nation, or community, and not for the particular emolument or advantage of any single man, family, or set of men, who are part only of that community."[24] This provision is clearly aimed at preventing government favoritism such as hereditary titles. It vests rights in the community rather than in individuals and directs that state actions must not benefit individuals at the expense of the general community. In fact, past Vermont Supreme Court decisions had never construed this clause as having any implications for marriage before the *Baker* decision.

It should also be noted that in each of these cases, the constitutions relied on by activist courts to yield the holding that marriage laws are unconstitutional were all believed to be consistent with constitutional law before the challenges were brought. In contrast to questions about slavery and race relations that plagued the U.S. Constitution and state constitutions from their very inauguration, the idea that state constitutions could be construed to overturn marriage laws recognizing marriage as the union of a man and a woman are entirely novel. Surely, decades of totally uncritical acceptance of the consistency of marriage and other constitutional guarantees can be taken at least as evidence that the constitutional provisions at issue were not meant to have the effect given them by these decisions.

Finally, if we take state constitutional law seriously, why would we limit our inquiry to what rights and benefits a constitution may provide to individuals? If state constitutions can provide greater protection to women or criminal defendants, they can surely provide a higher level of protection to marriage as it has been traditionally understood. In fact, it can be argued that the Massachusetts Constitution does just that by withholding jurisdiction over the definition of marriage from state courts.[25] A very plausible understanding of constitutional equality assumes that individuals, social institutions, and government all exist in their own right and all ought to be treated fairly by the law, and that the mere presence of difference is not a sign of oppressive social relations the law must transform.[26]

The real problem is that advocates of the redefinition of marriage want a constitution that can't say "no." Whether it is Hawaii's equal protection clause, Alaska's privacy provision, or Vermont's (or Massachusetts's) Common Benefits Clause, to advocates of judicial redefinition of marriage, they all provide the same outcome—a right to marriage licenses or marital benefits for same-sex couples. This is a result of the template they would impose on the state constitutions: a paradigm in which the sole purpose of the constitution is to secure the greatest possible recognition of individual autonomy and the most radically egalitarian outcome possible. Their view of state constitutions is strictly utilitarian. To them, state constitutions are helpful to the degree to which they can be construed to give out benefits and dispense new statuses. On the other hand, aspects of state constitutions that are not susceptible to these claims are discounted or ignored. In fact, when the people of Hawaii and Alaska amended their state constitutions (as some Vermont legislators proposed doing) to prevent a judicial redefinition of marriage, some commentators who favored the expansive view of state constitutional law that provided for a finding of a right to same-sex marriage attacked these amendments as violating federal constitutional provisions.[27] The attraction of federalism began to fade when state constitutional law cut the other way.

## The Threat to Constitutional Democracy

Potentially the greatest problem with the template being imposed on state constitutions in the matter of same-sex marriage is the fact that it fundamentally misinterprets the very nature of the state constitutions and thus threatens democracy. As Professor Donald Lutz has noted, "A constitution provides a definition for a way of life. . . . Reading properly and carefully, one can glean from a constitution the balance of political forces, a structure for preserving or enhancing that balance, a statement of the way people should treat each other, and the values that form the basis for the people's working relationship, as well as the serious, remaining problems in the political order."[28] As opposed to a tool for the extraction of novel political and social rights, "constitutions should be taken seriously as architectonic plans," as Professor Lutz counsels.[29] State constitutions are not mere lists of benefits available to citizens, but are primarily principles for limiting the power of government to affect its citizens in the enjoyment of rights not provided by the government but recognized in the constitutions as inalienable. Thus the template advanced in the same-sex-marriage cases strikes at the very nature of constitutional law and theory. Specifically, the same-sex-marriage template threatens the structural and procedural provisions of state constitutions. By going to the state courts to get constitutional interpretations that benefit a radically egalitarian agenda, the proponents of this view threaten crucial constitutional concepts such as separation of powers and accountability to the people.

The same-sex-marriage template offends the constitutional principle of separation of powers that in many state constitutional provisions is more explicitly stated than in the federal constitution.[30] It requires that courts rather than the legislature make important policy decisions regarding the family, although the legislature is the branch of government constitutionally empowered to make such policy. It also ignores the reality that state legislators are also responsible to advance and protect the principles of the constitutions. Pursuant to that authority, the vast majority of states have enacted legislation specifying that marriage is the union of a man and a woman and/or providing that same-sex marriages from one state will not be recognized in their state. In the case of Vermont, the judicial usurpation of the legislative prerogative was particularly egregious because the supreme court effectively ordered the legislature to enact a system that gave marital benefits to same-sex couples. In Hawaii and Alaska, though, the same usurpation was at work as the crucial question of the definition of marriage was removed from the people's representatives. What is at work here is an "amendment by interpretation" of the state constitutions of Vermont, Hawaii and Alaska.

State constitutions, maybe more than the federal constitution, derive their authority directly from the people of those states. This is particularly obvious in a state like Massachusetts where the constitution (which predates the U.S. Constitution) comes out of a long tradition of compacts and covenants between those who will be governed by them.[31] The attempt to take the definition of marriage out of the normal legislative process and have it reinterpreted by the courts defeats the fundamental constitutional purpose of creating a government accountable to the governed.[32] It then leaves citizens no recourse but to amend their constitution, as was done after these principles were violated by courts in Alaska and Hawaii. The strongly held opinions of the people of the states should not be ignored in the name of discovering novel political rights. Ironically, this is the counsel of the very constitutions relied on to ignore the will of citizens. For instance, the Common Benefits Clause relied on by the Vermont Supreme Court in the *Baker* decision includes these words: "that the community hath an indubitable, unalienable and indefeasible right, to reform or alter government, in such manner as shall be, by that community, judged most conducive to the public weal." The Massachusetts Constitution specifies in a similar clause that the people "alone" have the right to alter government.[33]

Activist supporters of redefining marriage have ignored this principle. They have attempted to get court decisions made by judges whose accountability to the people is attenuated and whose decrees are difficult or impossible to reverse. Advocates of redefining marriage have shown something akin to "democratophobia." When a proposed constitutional amendment was put forward in Alaska, activists, including the plaintiffs in the *Brause* case, sued in an attempt to prevent the amendment from being voted on. In California, a similar ballot initiative was subject to litigation by the Lambda Legal Defense and Education Fund, trying to modify its ballot description to take the position that the proposition was "discriminatory." The certification by the attorney general of a proposed amendment to define marriage in Massachusetts has been vigorously opposed (with two lengthy letters to and two meetings with the attorney general's office) by the Gay and Lesbian Advocates and Defenders (GLAD), the group advocating the overturning of the state's marriage law. GLAD's argument has been that the proponents of the amendment should not even be allowed to collect signatures that would eventually result in its placement on the ballot because GLAD does not believe that the secular justifications of the amendment put forward by its proponents are valid and, therefore, it must be assumed that the amendment unconstitutionally constitutes mere religious dogma since some religious groups' beliefs about marriage coincide with the definition of marriage in the proposed amendment. Certainly, great harm is done to our system of government when the most important questions of public life are removed from the authors of the very constitutions being relied upon to subvert the public will.

## CONCLUSION

There is much to discuss and debate about state constitutions and their relation to same-sex "marriage," but if we are to be true to the principles of state constitutionalism, we must respect these constitutions—their limitations, their meaning, and the structure and process they provide. Fundamentally, this means that we must work out deep policy disagreements about marriage and the family in a way that respects the reality that these involve differences of viewpoint, not attempts at victimization, and allow the people from whom the authority of the constitutions derives to have their say on these weighty issues. We should have "an abiding faith in the wisdom of all the people."[34] The autonomy approach turns the issue into a stark contrast between the "rights" of same-sex couples and the "bigotry" of opponents of same-sex marriage. This is not good for marriage, it is not good for federalism, and it is not good for state constitutions.

## NOTES

1. Marriage Law Project, *State Information, available at* http://marriage law.cua.edu/State_in.htm (updated June 19, 2001).

2. *See* William J. Brennan, Jr., *State Constitutions and the Protection of Individual Rights,* 90 HARV. L. REV. 489 (1977); William C. Duncan & David Orgon Coolidge, *Marriage and Democracy in Oregon: The Meaning and Implications of* Tanner v. Oregon Health Sciences University, 36 WILLAMETTE L. REV. 503 (2000).

3. *Adams v. Howerton,* 486 F.Supp. 1119 (C.D. cal. 1980), affd 673 F.2d 1036 (9th Cir. 1982), *cert. denied,* 458 U.S. 1111.

4. *Baehr v. Lewin,* 852 P.2d 44 (Haw. 1993).

5. *Baehr v. Miike,* 1996 WL 694235, 1996 Civ. No. 91-1394 (Haw. Cir. Ct. 1996).

6. *Brause v. Bureau of Vital Statistics,* 1998 WL 88743 (Alaska Super. 1998).

7. *Baker v. Vermont,* 744 A.2d 864 (Vt. 1999).

8. *See* William C. Duncan, *"A Lawyer Class": Views on Marriage and "Sexual Orientation" in the Legal Profession* 15 B.Y.U. J. PUB. L. 137 (2001).

9. *Brause v. Bureau of Vital Statistics*, 1998 WL 88743, *5 (Alaska Super. 1998).

10. *Baker v. Vermont*, 744 A.2d 864, 884 (Vt. 1999).

11. *Baehr v. Lewin*, 852 P.2d 44 (Haw. 1993).

12. *Baker v. Vermont*, 744 A.2d 864, 889 (Vt. 1999).

13. *Id.*

14. *Id.* at 884.

15. *Baehr v. Miike*, 1996 WL 694235, 1996 Civ. No. 91-1394 (Haw. Cir. Ct. 1996).

16. *Brause v. Bureau of Vital Statistics*, 1998 WL 88743, *6 (Alaska Super. 1998).

17. *Baker v. Vermont*, 744 A.2d 864, 889 (Vt. 1999).

18. This insight comes from Professor Teresa Stanton Collett at the South Texas College of Law.

19. Judith Stacey & Timothy J. Biblarz, *(How) Does the Sexual Orientation of Parents Matter?*, 66 AM. SOC. REV. 159 (Apr. 1, 2001).

20. *Singer v. Hara*, 522 P.2d 1187, 1189 (Wash. App. 1974), *review denied*, 84 Wash. 2d 1008 (1974).

21. *Brause v. Bureau of Vital Statistics*, 1998 WL 88743 (Alaska Super. Ct. 1998).

22. *Breese v. Smith*, 501 P.2d 159 (Alaska 1972) (school hair-length requirement); *Ravin v. State*, 537 P.2d 494 (Alaska 1975) (possession of marijuana in home).

23. *United States v. Virginia*, 518 U.S. 515, 518 (1996) (quoting *Ballard v. United States*, 329 U.S. 187, 193 (1946)).

24. The Massachusetts provisions are very similar, but are even more clearly related to issues of favoritism.

25. The argument relies on a provision in the Massachusetts Constitution that states: "All causes of marriage, divorce, and alimony, and all appeals from the judges of probate shall be heard and determined by the Governor and Council, until the Legislature shall, by law, make other provision." MASS. CONST. pt. 2, ch. 3, art. 5. The argument is that since the legislature has not provided the courts jurisdiction over the definition of marriage, the current challenge to Massachusetts's marriage law, *Goodridge v. Dept. of Public Health*, Docket 2001–1647A (Suffolk Cty. Ct. 2002.), should be dismissed.

26. William C. Duncan & David Orgon Coolidge, *Marriage and Democracy in Oregon: The Meaning and Implications of* Tanner v. Oregon Health Sciences University, 36 WILLAMETTE L. REV. 503 (2000).

27. ALASKA CONST. art. I, sec. 25; HAW. CONST. art. I, sec. 23. For arguments against these and similar proposed amendments, *see* Gil Kujovich, *In Opposition to Amending the Vermont Constitution*, 25 VT. L. REV. 278 (2000); Mark Strasser, *From Colorado to Alaska by Way of Cincinnati: On* Romer, Equality Foundation, *and the Constitutionality of Referenda*, 36 HOUSTON L. REV. 1193 (1999); Mark Strasser, *Statutory Construction, Equal Protection, and the Amendment Process: On* Romer, Hunter, *and Efforts to Tame* Baehr, 45 BUFFALO L. REV. 739 (1997).

28. DONALD S. LUTZ, THE ORIGINS OF AMERICAN CONSTITUTIONALISM 3 (1988).

29. *Id.*

30. MASS. CONST. pt. 1, art. 30 ("In the government of this commonwealth, the legislative department shall never exercise the executive and judicial powers, or either of them, the executive shall never exercise the legislative and judicial powers, or either of them, the judicial shall never exercise the legislative and executive powers, or either

of them, to the end it may be a government of laws and not of men"); VERMONT CONST. ch. II, sec. 5 ("The Legislative, Executive and Judiciary departments, shall be separate and distinct, so that neither exercise the powers properly belonging to the others").

31. *See generally* DONALD S. LUTZ, THE ORIGINS OF AMERICAN CONSTITU-TIONALISM 23–34 (1988); MASS. CONST. Preamble ("The body politic is formed by a voluntary association of individuals: it is a social compact, by which the whole people covenants with each citizen, and each citizen with the whole people, that all shall be governed by certain laws for the common good").

32. *See* MASS. CONST. pt. 1, art. 5 ("All powers residing originally in the people, and being derived from them, the several magistrates and officers of government, vested with authority, whether legislative, executive, or judicial, are their substitutes and agents, and are at all times accountable to them"); MASS. CONST. pt. 1, art. 10 ("[T]he people of this commonwealth are not controllable by any other laws than those to which their constitutional *representative* body have given their consent") (emphasis added); ALASKA CONST. art. I, sec. 2 ("All political power is inherent in the people. All government originates with the people, is founded upon their will only, and is instituted solely for the good of the people as a whole"); HAWAII CONST. art. I, sec. 1 ("All political power of this State is inherent in the people and the responsibility for the exercise thereof rests with the people. All government is founded on this authority").

33. MASS. CONST. pt. 1, art. 7.

34. J. Reuben Clark, Jr., *Address*, 26 ABA JOURNAL 901 (Dec. 1940).

# Response

# *Reply to William C. Duncan*
## **Greg Johnson**

I agree with William Duncan that states have "near-exclusive power" over marriage law. That is what makes the federal Defense of Marriage Act so unprecedented and so suspect. The use of state constitutions in the struggle for same-sex marriage is appropriate because states create family law, and because state constitutions best reflect the values of a state. This is the promise and strength of our federal system. Justice Hans Linde is rightly credited with being an early champion of state constitutional law, but in Vermont another influential jurist was Judge Frank G. Mahady. In his 1988 essay *Toward a Theory of State Constitutional Jurisprudence: A Judge's Thoughts*, Judge Mahady recognized that "[i]n our heterogeneous national society, the ethical, sociological, and economic concerns of the citizens vary greatly from state to state."[1] For this reason, he felt that the "soul of one state" should not be treated as interchangeable with that of another.[2] Judge Mahady said that the "development of state constitutional jurisprudence requires creative thought with attention to the unique character of each state."[3] In particular, Judge Mahady encouraged Vermont courts to abandon the federal "three-tiered" equal protection analysis in favor of an independent Common Benefits Clause jurisprudence befitting the clause's unique history and purpose. This is precisely what the Vermont Supreme Court did in *Baker*. As the court noted in an earlier opinion, the Vermont Constitution "predates the federal counterpart, and it extends back to Vermont's days as an independent republic."[4] It is altogether fitting that the state constitution have its own jurisprudence.

While same-sex couples have scored a string of favorable decisions under state constitutions since the mid-1990s, the "same-sex-marriage story" is not a story about judicial activism. Courts in Hawaii, Alaska, and Vermont did nothing more than examine the constitutionality of statutes, something courts have been doing since *Marbury v. Madison*, so that should not be news. These courts, though, were fairly timid when it came to announcing a remedy. In fact, no court has ever ordered a legislature to do anything on same-sex marriage. In Hawaii and Alaska, the legislatures preempted the judicial process by authorizing referenda to amend their state constitutions before any mandate issued from the courts. The Vermont Supreme Court in *Baker* boldly proclaimed "our common humanity" but then deferred to the legislature to fix the constitutional infirmity. Although some may rightly rankle at putting fundamental rights up to a vote, that is how the same-sex-marriage issue has played out. Victories in court are not enough. Favorable court decisions may have jump-started the discussion, but the people, through their elected representatives, have had the final say.

The *Baker* decision is a model of judicial restraint, not judicial activism. The court, after noting the outcomes in Hawaii and Alaska, acknowledged that "judicial authority is not ultimate authority."[5] By bringing the legislature into the process, the court acted not so much as the dictator of a result but as it did as a catalyst for change. In her dissent, Justice Denise Johnson criticized the court for declaring a right without providing a remedy and for throwing the plaintiffs into "an uncertain fate in the political cauldron."[6] While that cauldron proved fiery indeed, we know now that the result was a positive one. Rather than creating a combative atmosphere between the two branches, the court's collaborative approach empowered the legislature to fashion its own just and constitutional remedy.

Make no mistake, the civil unions law was the product of legislative free will. The legislature passed the civil unions law because it wanted to, not because it had to. A legislature with a different disposition could have started the process to amend the constitution, just as in Hawaii and Alaska, but that did not happen. The legislature could also have called the court's bluff and done nothing. More than a few legislators argued for this approach then and continue to argue for it now. Finally, the legislature could have tested the court's mettle by passing a law akin to Hawaii's Reciprocal Beneficiaries Act, which gave same-sex couples substantive marital rights but held back on key components of marriage such as state certification.[7] But the legislature did not want to test the court; rather, it wanted to do as much as was politically possible. In a sense, the legislature "outenvisioned" the court by going well beyond the domestic partnership laws cited as examples in *Baker*. There is absolutely nothing in *Baker* that would have required the legislature to find, as it did, that "many gay and lesbian Vermonters have formed lasting, committed, caring and faithful relationships with persons of their same sex," and that these couples "live together, participate in their communities together, and some raise children and care for family members together, just as do couples who are married under

Vermont law."[8] The legislature said this and other uplifting things because it sought to make its own grand statement on lesbian/gay civil rights.

Opponents of civil unions have charged that the legislature and governor were not "listening" to Vermonters, but this charge is not borne out by the results of the November 2000 election. That election, which saw "the single highest voter turnout in Vermont history,"[9] can fairly be called a plebiscite on civil unions. Although some anti-civil unions candidates were elected, most of the legislators who voted in favor of civil unions and ran for ree-lection retained their seats. The statewide results are even more telling. Every statewide office, from lieutenant governor to secretary of state to state auditor, went to candidates who favored civil unions. Governor Dean, who signed the civil-unions bill into law one day after it was passed, received 52 percent of the vote in a three-way race. The Progressive candidate, Anthony Pollina, who spoke openly and ardently in favor of civil unions, received 10 percent. Republican Ruth Dwyer, who adamantly opposed civil unions, was only able to capture 38 percent of the vote, less than she had received in her previous run against Dean.[10] Vermonters have spoken, and in large part they have said "yes" to civil unions.

As the issue of same-sex marriage moves to other states, results will vary depending on the constitutional provisions involved and the political makeup of each state. In some states, progress will be slow, but in other states, those with a willing populace and a constitution as "inclusive" as Vermont's,[11] equality may come soon. Marriage law has never been static. It has changed throughout history to reflect changes in society. At one time, for example, it was universally true that women lost their legal identity when they married. Married women are now no longer thought of as the property of their husbands. Women fought for and obtained equal rights in marriage one state at a time, and through that struggle the definition of marriage changed, for the good. In the not-too-distant past, laws against interracial marriage were common. Despite "decades of totally uncritical acceptance" of these laws, everyone now knows that civil society was much better off when the definition of marriage was broadened to include interracial cou-ples. The same thing should happen with same-sex marriage and civil unions over time. The Vermont legislature was right. Gays and lesbians really do contribute to the community just like everyone else and they deserve the same rights.

## NOTES

1. 13 VT. L. REV. 145, 149 (1988).
2. *Id.*
3. *Id.* at 152.
4. State v. Badger, 450 A.2d 336, 347 (Vt. 1982).
5. Baker v. State, 744 A.2d 864, 888 (Vt. 1999).

6. *Id.* at 898 (Johnson, J., concurring and dissenting).

7. In 2001 the Vermont House of Representatives narrowly passed a bill which would repeal the civil unions law and replace it with an arrangement called "reciprocal partnerships." *See* H.502, 2001–2002 Leg. Sess. (Vt. 2001) available at http:// www.leg.state.vt.us/docs/2002/bills/house/h-502.htm. The bill was not considered by the Vermont Senate. *See* Alex Hanson, *Civil Unions Stay; Foes' Last Hurrah?*, Valley News, May 29, 2001 at A1 ("[S]tate Senate leaders and the governor have said they do not intend to take up the [reciprocal partnership] measure.").

8. 2000 Vt. Acts & Resolves 91 § (1).

9. David Ross and Heather Rider, *A Note from the Editors: A Vermont Law Review Milestone, a Landmark Case, and a Vermont Election*, 25 Vt. L. Rev. 1, 2 (2000).

10. *Id.*

11. *See Baker*, 744 A.2d at 875 ("The words of the Common Benefits Clause . . . do not, to be sure, set forth a fully-formed standard of analysis for determining the constitutionality of a given statute, but they do express broad principles which usefully inform that analysis. Chief among these is the principle of inclusion").

# Chapter 10

Essay One

# *Applying the Usual Marriage-Validation Rule to Marriages of Same-Sex Couples*

**Barbara J. Cox**

Simply by looking at my immediate family, the need for interstate recognition of marriage can readily be understood. Both my sisters and my parents live in Kentucky, but none was married there. My older sister married her husband in South Carolina while on vacation with his family. They had been dating for several years and decided suddenly to marry at the beach. None of us, including me, who had been researching interstate recognition of marriage for several years, even considered that their marriage might not be valid in Kentucky. My younger sister was married in Tennessee in 1981 after she and her husband realized, at the last minute, that they did not have enough days before their formal wedding in Lexington to obtain a Kentucky marriage license. Discovering that Tennessee had no waiting period, they drove all night to Tennessee with two friends, were married by a justice of the peace, and returned home in time to be "remarried" in the church before their family and friends. Again, no one wondered whether their marriage in Tennessee would be recognized in Kentucky. Finally, my parents were married in Evanston, Illinois, moved immediately to Milwaukee, Wisconsin, and then to Kentucky following my father's job transfer in 1961. It mattered little that they married in my mother's hometown, had their first marital domicile in another state, and moved nine years later to Kentucky. Their marital status remained constant throughout these changes in their domiciles.

None of this is remarkable because interwoven in our societal culture is an expectation that American citizens can move from state to state, and can easily travel through all fifty states without their marital status changing. (I originally used "our" when referring to "marital status" in the preceding sentence, but because I remain unable to marry my same-sex partner in any state, clearly this expectation does not include me and others in same-sex relationships that continue to be denied legal recognition across our country.) Those of you who have the freedom to marry have probably never considered whether your marriage would be permitted in your domicile or whether your marital status would survive a vacation or business trip or a change of domicile. But once same-sex couples win the freedom to marry, that is the question awaiting us. We will face the same question that interracial couples once faced, both in trying to find a state where they could marry and making decisions about whether they could move or even travel without their marriages being challenged. Interracial couples knew, however, that if they lived in a state where their marriage was valid and recognized, they could freely move to most other states without fear that their marital status would not travel with them. Only those who were prevented from marrying in their own domicile, married in another state to evade that law, and returned to their original domicile seeking recognition of their marital status encountered difficulties. Even then, many of these marriages were recognized, despite constitutional or statutory provisions declaring the marriage void and imposing criminal penalties for violating those provisions.[1]

Those of you who were underage and could not wait to marry until you reached the age of majority in your home state, or who wanted to remarry after divorce sooner than your domicile permitted, or who wanted to marry a first cousin, aunt, or uncle but were prevented from doing so in your home state, or who wanted to move from a state where your common-law marriage was permitted to a state where common-law marriages could not be created usually found that you could return to your domicile or move to another state without your marriage being declared invalid.[2] The majority of these marriages were recognized, despite statutes prohibiting them in the original domicile state.

They were upheld using the legal doctrines controlling these choice-of-law situations. Courts deciding whether to recognize a marriage entered into out-of-state begin with the general rule preferring validation of marriages, which exists with an "overwhelming tendency" in the United States. Under this rule, marriages will be found valid if there is any reasonable basis for doing so. There are such strong policy reasons behind this rule that it has become well entrenched in the substantive law of all the states. "The validation rule confirms the parties' expectations, it provides stability in an area where stability (because of children and property) is very important, and it avoids the potentially hideous problems that would arise if the legality of a marriage varied from state to state." The parties' expectations arise from the fact that the married couple needs to know "reliably and certainly, and at once, whether they are married or not." Additionally, the concern about uncertainty arises either because the couple is married in one state and not another or because the couple's marital status is ambiguous during the pursuit of litigation to determine it.[3]

In my nine years of researching whether the marriages of same-sex couples will be recognized by the different states, the question asked most often is why choice-of-law theories control this situation, rather than the Full Faith and Credit Clause of the U.S. Constitution.[4] This question continues to be asked because everyone understands that a couple's marital status should not vary from state to state. Many scholars believe that the Full Faith and Credit Clause should be used to resolve these questions; others are less convinced. Some think that the Clause requires every state to recognize marriages validly celebrated in other states; others do not.[5] People remain confused about the Clause's importance because courts addressing interstate recognition of marriage historically have not turned to the Constitution for an answer. Instead, courts have relied on choice-of-law theories to determine whether a marriage is valid either when the couple returns to their domicile from the state where their marriage was celebrated and seeks recognition of that marriage or moves from the state of domicile and celebration to another state.

Those courts following the Restatement of the Conflict of Laws refer to section 121, which states that "a marriage valid where celebrated is valid everywhere."[6] Although that section "indicates that the law of the domicile governs the domestic status of marriage, the differences between states' marriage laws would 'lead to great difficulty, if it were not for the fact that all Anglo-American states agree in creating the status of marriage (except in rare cases considered in sections 131 and 132) in every case where there is a contract of marriage valid in the state where the contract is made."[7] (Section 131 applies to remarriage after divorce, and section 132 applies to marriages void under domicile law.) "The courts are understandably reluctant 'to negate a relationship upon which so many personal and governmental considerations depend.' 'In fact, denying a normal incident of marriage to a validly married couple is a harsh measure that should be avoided unless enjoyment of that incident 'violently offends the moral sense of the community.' "[8]

Those who oppose marriages by same-sex couples argue that section 132 of the First Restatement permits courts to conclude that those marriages offend a state's moral sensibilities and refuse to recognize them. Section 132 states that polygamous, incestuous, interracial, and other marriages declared void by the parties' domicile can be held to be invalid, even if they were valid where celebrated.[9] But most courts have recognized these marriages.

The Restatement (Second) of Conflict of Laws was completed in 1971.[10] "When considering the validity of out-of-state marriages, the Second Restatement directs courts to consider the law of the state with the 'most significant relationship to the spouses and the marriage' and to the issue involved in the particular case."[11] What state has the "most significant relationship" is determined by consulting the factors in section 6: (*a*) the needs of the interstate and international systems; (*b*) the relevant policies of the forum; (*c*) the relevant policies of other interested states and the relative interests of those states in the determination of the particular issue; (*d*) the protection of the parties' justified expectations; (*e*) the basic policies underlying the particular field of law; (*f*) certainty, predictability, and uniformity of result; and (*g*) ease in the determination and application of the law to be applied.[12] "Having determined which state has this 'most significant relationship,' the court should, using section 283(2), then consider the marriage to be valid if it was valid where celebrated 'unless it violates the strong public policy' of the state with the most significant relationship to the marriage."[13] According to Professor Willis Reese, reporter of the Second Restatement, "the primary values involved are protection of the parties' expectations in intending to enter into a valid marriage and recognition of the general policy favoring validation of marriages."[14] "The Second Restatement, although clearly tending toward validation as a general rule, . . . would defer to the domiciliary state, as the state with the most significant relationship to the couple, to consider whether a given marriage violates its public policy."[15] "Again, this analysis potentially leaves the court significant discretion to determine whether such a strong public policy exists and, if so, what that policy is."[16]

The other major choice-of-law theories also instruct the courts to consider public policy in deciding whether to recognize an out-of-state marriage by that state's or another state's domiciliaries. "Governmental interest analysis, developed by [Professor] Brainerd Currie in the 1950's and 1960's, refers courts to policy considerations,"[17] as does Professor Robert Leflar's theory of "choice-influencing considerations."[18]

Although these theories permit courts to consider public policy when deciding whether to recognize a marriage, a recent move away from using public policy has occurred. Section 210 of the Uniform Marriage and Divorce Act is a model marriage validation provision stating that "[a]ll marriages contracted . . . outside this state, that were valid at the time of the contract or subsequently validated by the laws of the place in which they were contracted or by the domicile of the parties, are valid in this state."[19] Numerous states have statutes that essentially incorporate this language.[20]

The comments to the Uniform Marriage and Divorce Act indicate that section 210 was intended to validate marriages, even if the parties would not have been allowed to marry in their domicile. The section also states that section 210 "expressly fails to incorporate the 'strong public policy' exception of the Restatement [Second] and hence may change the law in some jurisdictions. *This section will preclude invalidation of many marriages which would have been invalidated in the past.*"[21]

Thus in states that have adopted section 210, the policy declared by those statutes—validation if the marriage was valid where celebrated—should prevent those courts from refusing to recognize the marriages of same-sex couples.

Additionally, "[u]ntil the recent wave of legislation attempting to prevent recognition of marriages by same-sex couples, . . . the modern trend has been away from" adopting marriage evasion statutes in general.[22] The Uniform Marriage Evasion Act was withdrawn as being inconsistent with the validation principle contained in the Uniform Marriage and Divorce Act.[23] Only four states adopted it during its short existence,[24] although several other states also have evasion statutes.[25] The current viability of the public policy exception remains in question today.[26]

As part of a national project organized by the Lambda Legal Defense and Education Fund, one of the nation's premier civil rights organizations for the lesbian, gay, bisexual, and transgendered communities, I reviewed and edited materials provided by more than seventy law professors, attorneys, and law students who had done in-depth research on how courts have interpreted these choice-of-law theories in out-of-state marriage-recognition cases in all fifty states. The conclusion I reached after completing that research is that "courts do not use a public policy exception to refuse to validate an out-of-state marriage even when the domicile has an explicit statutory prohibition against the marriage in question."[27] "Instead, courts repeatedly indicate that they have the discretion to use such a public policy exception but then validate the out-of-state marriage following the general rule in favor of recognition. Although a few states use the exception consistently, virtually all the rest recognize the existence of such an exception but rarely use it."[28]

The policies favoring validation of marriage "have led most courts to recognize the out-of-state marriages of opposite-sex couples even when they traveled to another state to marry, because their domiciliary state prevented them from doing so, and then returned to their domicile and requested recognition of their marriage."[29] "Basically, the law of the place of celebration will apply unless the marriage violates an important public policy of the domicile, in which case the domicile's law will apply and the marriage will be invalid."[30] "While this public policy exception has been used to refuse recognition of an out-of-state marriage by a state's domiciliary,[31] courts have not consistently done so even though the domiciliary state had an explicit statutory prohibition against that type of marriage."[32] "In numerous and repeated cases, courts have recognized out-of-state marriages even when the marriage violated the domicile's restrictions on underage marriages, on incestuous marriages (such as first cousin or uncle/niece marriage), on adultery or when divorced persons could remarry, and even on polygamous marriages for some limited purposes."[33] "The vast majority of cases recognize the out-of-state marriages, whether entered into by residents of the domicile who validly married under that state's laws and then moved to another state which prohibited their marriages, or entered into by residents who were prevented by their domicile's law from marrying but who married in another state where their marriage was legal and then sought recognition within their original domicile."[34] Only in states with antimiscegenation statutes can one find "consistent and repeated use of public policy exceptions to refuse to recognize otherwise valid out-of-state marriages, and even then only when the couple had not been validly married in its own domicile."[35] But other courts did validate these out-of-state, miscegenous marriages, in cases such as *Pearson v. Pearson* (1875) (recognizing an interracial marriage validly entered into in Utah despite a California law nullifying them); *Medway v. Needham* (1819) (recognizing an interracial marriage validly entered into in Rhode Island despite a Massachusetts law prohibiting them); and *Miller v. Lucks* (1948) (recognizing an interracial marriage validly contracted in Illinois for inheritance purposes despite a Mississippi state constitutional provision refusing recognition).[36]

At least fourteen states and the District of Columbia do not currently prohibit same-sex marriages by statute or have not excepted marriages by same-sex couples from the state's general validation statutes.[37] In those states, courts should recognize the marriages of same-sex couples based on the general rule of validation and established precedent recognizing the marriages of opposite-sex couples from other states. Additionally, the Vermont civil-union legislation indicates that "parties to a civil union shall have all the same benefits, protections and responsibilities under law, whether they derive from statute, administrative or court rule, policy, common law or any other source of civil law, as are granted to spouses in a marriage."[38] If civil unions do have all the same benefits and protections as marriages, then same-sex couples who travel to Vermont and enter into these unions should also be able to obtain recognition in their own domiciles, as should Vermont couples when they leave the state to move or travel across the country.[39]

If civil unions are the "equivalent statutory alternative" that the Vermont Supreme Court required the Vermont legislature to develop if it chose not to permit same-sex couples to marry,[40] then these civil unions should be recognized to the same extent that a marriage in Vermont would be recognized by other states. This is particularly true of those civil unions entered into by Vermont citizens. "Unlike questions that arise when an out-of-state couple travels to another state to obtain the marital status prohibited in the couple's home state, little question about the interstate recognition of marriage usually occurs when a couple enters into a valid marriage under the law of its own domicile. . . . From a public policy standpoint, while a court may refuse to recognize the out-of-state marriage or civil union entered into by its own domiciliaries attempting to evade restrictions on those marriages within their own domicile, it has little reason to refuse recognition of the marriage or civil union of another state's domiciliaries. . . . Usually courts recognize the out-of-state marriage in this context under principles of comity that are based on deference and respect for another state's authority to determine the status of its own residents."[41]

But "if we expected courts to hesitate before recognizing same-sex couples' marriages, we must now expect greater hesitancy when they are asked to recognize out-of-state civil unions—a status previously unknown in the law. Judges may decide that Vermont's statutorily-created status of 'civil union' does not extend beyond the state's border, unlike the clearly portable status of 'marriage.' This unknown portability of civil unions puts these same-sex couples at great risk: they no longer know whether the law considers them to be single or 'married' and whether their status in countless contexts, such as property ownership, intestacy, and responsibility for their partner's debts, changes after they leave Vermont."[42] Since both state and private institutions recognize marriages created in one state in other states, since civil unions were statutorily created to be equivalent to marriages, and since both are intended to change each person's legal status from single to coupled, then no principled basis exists for recognizing the Vermont marriage of an opposite-sex couple and not recognizing the Vermont civil union of a same-sex couple.

As domestic partnership statutes begin to provide state rights such as the right to sue for wrongful death or negligent infliction of emotional distress and the right to make health care decisions for an incapacitated partner, as is true in California since January 2002 when AB25 became effective, the need for these rights to be recognized by other states will become obvious. A couple who relies on the existence of these rights will also expect them to survive a trip across the state's border.

We must also consider whether the recent spate of antimarriage statutes aimed only at marriages and perhaps civil unions and domestic partnerships of same-sex couples will negate the overwhelming weight of precedent recognizing out-of-state marriages by opposite-sex couples even though these couples were also statutorily prohibited from entering into their marriages within their own domicile. When I wrote on this question in 1993, only Louisiana, Texas, Utah, and Virginia explicitly prohibited marriage between same-sex couples.[43] As of November 2002, thirty-six states had statutes that purport to prohibit marriages by same-sex couples or indicate that they will not recognize the out-of-state marriages of these couples.[44]

For example, in March 2000, California changed more than 120 years of settled law when its voters approved Proposition 22 amending Family Code section 308. Previously, its courts had repeatedly expressed the unquestioned public policy of California of respecting any validly contracted marriage, even though the out-of-state marriage was statutorily prohibited within the state.[45] California courts validated the following marriages: *Tatum v. Tatum* (1957) (common-law marriage); *Barrons v. United States* (1951) (proxy marriage); *In re Dalip Sing Bir's Estate* (1948) (polygamous marriage); *Colbert v. Colbert* (1946) (common-law marriage); *McDonald v.*

*McDonald* (1936) (remarriage after divorce); and *Pearson v. Pearson* (1875) (interracial marriage).[46] Family Code section 308 states: "A marriage contracted outside this state that would be valid by the laws of the jurisdiction in which the marriage was contracted is valid in this state."[47]

But Proposition 22 changed that settled law for the marriages of same-sex couples alone. It added section 308.5, which states: "Only marriage between a man and a woman is valid or recognized in California."[48] In a state where common-law, proxy, polygamous, and miscegenous marriages have been recognized despite statutes prohibiting each, only marriages by same-sex couples have been excluded from the broad validation policy that applies to all other marriages.

At least 35 other states have adopted statutes indicating that marriages by same-sex couples are not permitted in those states.[49] Many are similar to earlier statutes routinely ignored by courts in order to ensure that marriages by opposite-sex couples who were also statutorily refused permission to marry in their home states were validated. What is different about the others is that they purport to impose a "blanket rule of nonrecognition, under which states would 'ignore marriage licenses granted to same-sex couples in other states.' "[50] For example, the Minnesota statute states: "A marriage entered into by persons of the same sex, either under common law or statute, that is recognized by another state or foreign jurisdiction is void in this state and contractual rights granted by virtue of the marriage or its termination are unenforceable in this state."[51] The Florida statute indicates: "Marriages between persons of the same sex which are treated as marriages in any jurisdiction, are not recognized for any purpose in this state."[52] Georgia's statute is perhaps the most extreme:

No marriage between persons of the same sex shall be recognized as entitled to the benefits of marriage. . . . Any contractual rights granted by virtue of such [a marriage] license shall be unenforceable in the courts of this state and the courts of this state shall have no jurisdiction whatsoever under any circumstances to grant divorce or separate maintenance . . . or otherwise to consider or rule on any of the parties' respective rights arising as a result of or in connection with such marriage.[53]

Even when one reviews the cases involving interracial marriages, where courts frequently condemned those marriages with the same vehemence as some who oppose marriages by same-sex couples,[54] one cannot find such a blanket rule of nonrecognition. I imagine that opponents of same-sex marriage will gain little comfort from needing to use this universally condemned precedent to support an argument that same-sex couples can also be refused recognition of our marriages because we are not being treated any worse than interracial couples were in the South. But even those cases did not employ a blanket rule of nonrecognition. To argue that marriages by same-sex couples, even those lawfully celebrated in their own domicile, should receive worse legal treatment than interracial marriages did in Southern states at the height of the backlash against the civil rights struggle by African Americans proves that animus against these couples, like animus against interracial couples, underlies these statutes. In 1967, the U.S. Supreme Court in *Loving v. Virginia* finally acknowledged the racism and white supremacy underlying the antimiscegenation statutes and declared them unconstitutional.[55] Like those statutes before them, the statutes prohibiting same-sex marriage and exempting marriages by same-sex couples from the general rule of validation should also be declared unconstitutional.

In *Loving*, the Court struck down the anti-miscegenation statutes on equal protection and due process grounds, finding that these laws were based solely on racial distinctions.[56] Even using the less rigorous test declared in *Romer v. Evans*,[57] it is clear that laws singling out marriages by same-sex couples for worse treatment than any other marriage ever prohibited or denied recognition in the United States are based on animus against these couples.

While finding that Colorado's Amendment 2 imposed special disabilities on gay men and lesbians alone, the *Romer* Court held that "[h]omosexuals, by operation of state decree, are put in a solitary class with respect to transactions and relations in both the private and governmental spheres."[58] The Court continued: "Homosexuals are forbidden the safeguards that others enjoy or may seek without constraint. . . . These are protections taken for granted by most people . . . ; these are protections against exclusion from an almost limitless number of transactions and endeavors that constitute ordinary civic life in a free society."[59]

Only same-sex couples are excluded from the "almost limitless" benefits, protections, and responsibilities that come with marriage.[60] "Just like Amendment 2, many of these new [antirecognition] statutes impose a special disability on marriages by same-sex couples. . . . Only opposite-sex couples are permitted to marry under many of these new statutes, although that prohibition had, in many of these states, never been statutorily declared before. While it is true that most states prohibited other marriages, such as those by under-age persons, those between persons within certain degrees of consanguinity, and those by persons with more than one spouse, none of those defects exists for most same-sex couples. Most same-sex couples are disabled from marriage simply because both persons are of the same sex. Additionally, many of the new statutes refuse recognition of marriages by same-sex couples when entered into out-of-state, even though the general rule, whether stated by marriage validation statute or case law, has been to recognize out-of-state marriages if they were valid where celebrated, even when they violated the state's domestic marriage statutes."[61] "[W]hen combined with the previous non-prohibition of marriages by same-sex couples, the speed in passing anti-recognition statutes immediately once it became possible for those marriages to exist, and the case law in most states recognizing marriages that would be invalid if entered into in-state as long as they were valid where celebrated, it becomes clear that these statutes likely have the same constitutional defect as Colorado's Amendment 2, due to their focus on one group, and one group alone."[62]

As the Minnesota, Florida, and Georgia statutes cited earlier make clear, these statutes not only declare that marriages by same-sex couples are void in the state in question, "but they also state that any contractual rights granted by virtue of the marriage license are unenforceable within the state. Although some states do refuse to recognize out-of-state marriages that would violate their domestic marriage laws, my research has not found a single other statute that imposes a disability with such a broad sweep. In fact, even marriages that were prohibited by state statutes as incestuous, adulterous, interracial or polygamous have not generated such hostility."[63]

For example, in *Ethridge v. Shaddock*, the Arkansas court upheld an out-of-state marriage that violated the Arkansas statute prohibiting marriages by first cousins. Finding that such marriages do not create 'much social alarm,' it recognized the marriage since it was valid in the state in which it was celebrated. In *In re Estate of Lenherr*, the Court determined that violation of Pennsylvania's paramour statute which prohibited marriage of adulterous partners during the lifetime of the former spouse did not prevent recognition of the marriage for the limited purpose of receiving certain estate tax benefits. The strong public policy in favor of recognizing out-of-state marriages combined with the fact that denial of the tax exemption would not deter adulterous conduct or spare the aggrieved former spouse led the court to conclude that the marriage was valid for estate tax purposes. In *Miller v. Lucks*, the Court recognized an interracial couple's marriage for purposes of intestate succession, despite the presence of a provision in the Mississippi Constitution prohibiting interracial marriage, because the Court determined that the prohibition was intended to prevent interracial cohabitation in the state, not to void the marriage for all purposes. In *In re Dalip Singh Bir's Estate*, the Court determined that public policy would not be negatively affected by dividing property between two wives involved in a polygamous marriage validly entered into in India, although it would have been negatively affected had cohabitation in the state [of California] occurred. As these cases show, refusing to recognize marriages by same-sex couples for any reason, even the marriage's termination, goes beyond any refusal found in statutory or case law. The only conceivable reason for this difference in treatment is animus against marriages by same-sex couples which, under *Romer*, may be unconstitutional because it is directed against one group alone.[64]

The *Romer* Court applied a traditional equal protection analysis to Amendment 2. The Court, finding that the law "neither burdens a fundamental right nor targets a suspect class,"[65] stated that "[Amendment 2's] sheer breadth is so discontinuous with the reasons offered for it that the amendment seems inexplicable by anything but animus toward the class that it affects; it lacks a rational relationship to legitimate state interests."[66] Just as the *Romer* Court recognized the constitutional violation underlying

Amendment 2 from the breadth of the disability imposed by it, so too it may be possible to establish antigay animus by the breadth of the disability imposed by the antimarriage statutes recently passed. As noted earlier, many of these statutes refuse recognition of a marriage by a same-sex couple for any reason. Since some incestuous, adulterous, interracial, and polygamous marriages have been recognized generally or at least for receiving particular incidents of marriage, even though cohabitation within the state might have been rejected, there are no analogies in marriage law for the breadth of the disability imposed against marriages by same-sex couples. Withholding recognition of marriages of same-sex couples for any purpose speaks of the strong antigay animus behind these statutes.

Additionally, the statutes do not impose these disabilities only upon their own residents who, by marrying outside the state, seek to evade their domicile's domestic marriage statutes. These statutes are across-the-board prohibitions against recognition of the marriages of any same-sex couple for any purpose. . . . Their marriages, according to these statutes, will be given no effect, even though virtually any other marriage entered into outside the state by non-residents would be recognized by those states. The list of disabilities imposed is endless and is imposed only against same-sex couples.

. . .

By comparing their previous statutory and case law [in states with antirecognition statutes] to the changes now imposed against same-sex couples and their marriages alone, one can establish that anti-gay animus must be behind these statutory amendments. Anti-gay animus has no rational relationship to a legitimate state interest. The Supreme Court rejected animus as a constitutionally valid basis for Amendment 2 and may well reject it as a constitutionally valid basis for these new anti-same-sex marriage statutes.[67]

Just as my sisters and parents needed to have their marriages, entered into in a different state than their domicile, recognized by other states, so too will my partner and I. Once same-sex couples receive the freedom to marry, my partner and I will exercise that freedom and become legally married. When we travel across the country, visiting members of our immediate family who live in Minnesota and Georgia, will our marital status travel with us, or will it be lost? Only when our marriage is recognized in all fifty states and around the world will we have the same rights that the opposite-sex couples in my immediate family currently enjoy.

## NOTES

1. *See* Andrew Koppelman, *Same-Sex Marriage and Public Policy: The Miscegenation Precedents,* 16 Quinnipiac L. Rev. 105 (1996).
2. *See* Barbara J. Cox, *Same-Sex Marriage and the Public Policy Exception in*

*Choice of Law: Does It Really Exist?*, 16 Quinnipiac L. Rev. 61 (1996) [hereinafter Cox, *Public Policy Exception*], and cases cited therein.

3. *See* Barbara J. Cox, *Same-Sex Marriage and Choice of Law: If We Marry in Hawaii, Are We Still Married When We Return Home?*, 1994 Wis. L. Rev. 1033, 1064–1065 [hereinafter Cox, *If We Marry*] (citing William M. Richman et al., Understanding Conflict of Laws § 116 (2d ed. 1993), and Robert A. Leflar et al., American Conflicts Law § 220 (4th ed. 1986)).

4. U.S. Const. art. IV § 1.

5. Dean Patrick Borchers believes the Full Faith and Credit Clause should not control this question; others who do are cited in Cox, *If We Marry, supra* note 3, at 1041 n.23.

6. Restatement of the Conflict of Laws §121 (1934) [hereinafter First Restatement].

7. *See* Cox, *If We Marry, supra* note 3, at 1085 (citing First Restatement §121 cmt. d.).

8. *Id.* at 1085 (citing J. Philip Johnson, Note, *The Validity of a Marriage Under the Conflict of Laws*, 38 N.D. L. Rev. 442, 456 (1962), and Charles W. Taintor II, *Marriage in the Conflict of Laws*, 9 Vand. L. Rev. 607, 615 (1956)).

9. First Restatement § 132.

10. Restatement (Second) of Conflict of Laws (1971) [hereinafter Second Restatement].

11. Cox, *If We Marry, supra* note 3, at 1095 (citing Second Restatement § 283(1)).

12. *Id.*

13. *Id.* (citing Second Restatement § 283 (2)).

14. *Id.* (citing Willis Reese, *Marriage in American Conflict of Laws*, 26 Int'l & Comp. L.Q. 952, 967 (1977)).

15. *Id.*

16. *Id.* at 1095–1096.

17. Cox, *Public Policy Exception, supra* note 2, at 65 (citing Brainerd Currie, Selected Essays on the Conflict of Laws 187 (1963)).

18. *Id.* (citing Robert A. Leflar, *Choice-Influencing Considerations in Conflicts of Law*, 41 N.Y.U. L. Rev. 26, 282 (1996)).

19. Unif. Marriage and Divorce Act § 210, 9A U.L.A. 176 (1987).

20. Cox, *If We Marry, supra* note 3, at 1066–1068.

21. *Id.* at 1068 (citing Unif. Marriage and Divorce Act § 210) (emphasis added).

22. Cox, *Public Policy Exception, supra* note 2, at 94.

23. *Id.* (citing Uniform Marriage and Divorce Act § 210, 91 U.L.A. cmt. at 176–177 (1987)).

24. Cox, *If We Marry, supra* note 3, at 1074.

25. *Id.* at 1078 n.262.

26. Barbara J. Cox, *But Why Not Marriage: An Essay on Vermont's Civil Unions Law, Same-Sex Marriage, and Separate But (Un)Equal*, 25 Vt. L. Rev. 113, 139 (2000) [hereinafter referred to as Cox, *But Why Not Marriage*], citing Larry Kramer, *Same-Sex Marriage, Conflict of Law, and the Unconstitutional Public Policy Exception*, 106 Yale L.J. 1965 (1997).

27. Cox, *Public Policy Exception, supra* note 2, at 66.

28. *Id.* at 66–67.

29. Cox, *But Why Not Marriage*, *supra* note 26, at 138.

30. Mark Strasser, *Legally Wed: Same-Sex Marriage and the Constitution* 108 (1997).

31. *See* cases cited in Cox, *But Why Not Marriage*, *supra* note 26, at 138 n.117.

32. *Id.* at 138–139; *see also* Cox, *Public Policy Exception*, *supra* note 2, at 67–102; and Cox, *If We Marry*, *supra* note 3, at 1069–1083.

33. Cox, *But Why Not Marriage*, *supra* note 26, at 139.

34. *Id.* at 139 n.118.

35. *Id.* at 139.

36. Pearson v. Pearson, 51 Cal. 120 (1875); Medway v. Needham, 16 Mass. 157 (1819); Miller v. Lucks, 36 So. 2d 140 (Miss. 1948).

37. *See* National Gay and Lesbian Task Force Specific Anti-Same Sex Marriage Laws in the U.S., at http://ngltf.org/downloads/marriagemap.pdf (visited Dec. 5, 2002).

38. Vt. Stat. Ann. tit. 15, § 1204(a) (Supp. 2000).

39. *See* Cox, *But Why Not Marriage*, *supra* note 26, at 137–144.

40. Baker v. State, 744 A.2d 864, 867 (Vt. 1999).

41. Cox, *But Why Not Marriage*, *supra* note 26, at 140–141.

42. *Id.* at 140.

43. Cox, *If We Marry*, *supra* note 3, at 1070.

44. *See* National Gay and Lesbian Task Force, *supra* note 37.

45. Cox, *Public Policy Exception*, *supra* note 2, at 76 n.85.

46. Tatum. v. Tatum, 241 F.2d 401 (9th Cir. 1957); Barrons v. United States, 191 F.2d 92 (9th Cir. 1951); *In re* Dalip Sing Bir's Estate, 188 P.2d 499 (Cal. Dist. Ct. App. 1948); Colbert v. Colbert, 169 P.2d 633 (Cal. 1946); McDonald v. McDonald, 58 P.2d 163 (Cal. 1936); Pearson, v. Pearson, 51 Cal. 120 (1875).

47. Cal. Fam. Code § 308 (Devins 2003).

48. Cal. Fam. Code § 308.5 (Devins 2003).

49. *See* note 37, *supra*.

50. *See* Koppelman, *supra* note 1, at 106.

51. Minn. Stat. § 517.03(a)(4) (2002).

52. Fla. Stat. Ann. § 741.212(1) (West 2002).

53. Ga. Code Ann. § 19-3-3.1(b) (West 2002).

54. *See* the courts' language cited in Koppelman, *supra* note 1, at 114 and n.34.

55. 388 U.S. 1, 11 (1967); *see also* cases cited in Koppelman, *supra* note 1, at 114 n.34.

56. 388 U.S. at 11.

57. 517 U.S. 620 (1996).

58. *Id.* at 627.

59. *Id.* at 631.

60. *See* Cox, *But Why Not Marriage*, *supra* note 26, at 113 n.3 (hundreds of state benefits provided by the civil-unions law) and at 145 (indicating that 1,049 federal laws consider marital status).

61. Cox, *Are Same-Sex Marriage Statutes the New Anti-Gay Initiatives?*, National Journal of Sexual Orientation Law, http://metalab.unc.edu/gaylaw/issue4/cox 3.html, at 4–5.

62. *Id.* at 5 n. 44.

63. *Id.* at 5.

64. *Id.* at 5–6 (citations omitted).
65. *See id.* at 6 n.60 questioning that conclusion.
66. *Id.* at 6.
67. *Id.* at 6–7, 9.

# Response

# *Reply to Professor Barbara J. Cox*
## **Patrick J. Borchers**

I find a fair amount with which to agree in Professor Cox's interesting contribution on interstate marriage recognition, though we eventually part company. Let me begin by pointing out two important areas of agreement.

First, Professor Cox and I agree that courts have traditionally evaluated the validity of marriages contracted in other states by employing choice-of-law doctrine and not by reference to the Full Faith and Credit Clause or any other constitutional provision. Essentially she demurs on the question of whether the Full Faith and Credit Clause could be drafted into the battle over whether to recognize same-sex marriages. As I have argued, however—and Professor Cox does not take direct issue with me on this point—recasting the Full Faith and Credit Clause as the source of a rule of automatic recognition of out-of-state marriages would be inconsistent with the accepted understanding of the clause.

Second, I agree with her that choice-of-law doctrine tilts heavily toward the recognition of marriages that are valid where contracted. There are many good reasons for this validation preference, most of which she notes. Consistent treatment of marriages from state to state also accords with our instincts. A marriage is unlike a driver's license in the sense that a move to a new state generally requires getting a new driver's license but not a new marriage. Indeed, I believe that those state courts that are free to apply common-law choice-of-law doctrine to the question of recognition of an out-of-state same-sex marriage will probably, at least in some cases, give some effect to such unions.

Our disagreement seems to be on the question of whether this will eventually translate into broad legal acceptance of same-sex marriages. The most obvious problem for the prorecognition position is the slew of state statutes that directly address the choice-of-law question regarding same-sex marriages. Indeed, as she notes in her principal contribution and I note in mine, many of these statutes are models of drafting clarity at least insofar as they prohibit state courts from giving any effect to out-of-state same-sex unions.

Given the existence of these statutes, unless they are unconstitutional (a point to which I return later), they must trump common-law choice-of-law doctrine. The Second Restatement of Conflicts, upon which Professor Cox relies in part, makes the obvious point that judicially created choice-of-law doctrine applies only where choice-of-law statutes do not, and legislatures have long enacted specialized choice-of-law statutes, such as borrowing statutes that adopt another state's shorter limitation period in some cases.[1] Thus, when Professor Cox poses the question of whether these statutes will "negate" prorecognition choice-of-law doctrine or suggests that courts might "ignore" these statutes, this seems to be essentially a call to civil disobedience by the judiciary. Professor Cox seems to suggest that something like this took place with regard to those awful statutes that once prohibited interracial marriages, but those statutes seem not to have so clearly addressed the interstate recognition problem, and courts that recognized interracial marriages correctly anticipated the Supreme Court's 1967 decision in *Loving v. Virginia* holding interracial marriage prohibitions unconstitutional.[2]

The *Loving* case takes us to the last major point that Professor Cox makes, which is to argue that the statutes prohibiting recognition of same-sex marriages are unconstitutional. She bases this argument not on the Full Faith and Credit Clause, but rather on equal protection principles. In particular, she relies on the Supreme Court's decision in *Romer v. Evans*,[3] which— applying a rationality test—struck down a Colorado voter-approved initiative purporting to forbid gays and lesbians from employing the political process to obtain any special status. If one takes a step back from Professor Cox's argument, it becomes clear that it is but a variation on the theme that limitation of the marriage relationship to opposite-sex couples violates equal protection. Surely it cannot be that equal protection principles allow a state to limit marriages to opposite-sex couples but forbid that same state from denying recognition to an out-of-state same-sex marriage. If her equal protection argument is correct, then the interstate recognition question disappears, because the uniform national rule would then be that same-sex marriages must be permitted.

Others in this book address this equal protection argument in more depth, and one cannot do it justice in the context of discussing the interstate recognition question. It seems extremely unlikely, however, that *Romer* will bear the weight Professor Cox places on it. The rationality test invoked by *Romer* is generally not a difficult one for a state to surmount, and the Court's concern in that case was much more with access to the political process and far removed from revision of the traditional understanding of the marital relationship. Moreover, *Romer* does not overrule the Court's earlier decision in *Bowers v. Hardwick* upholding Georgia's criminal sodomy statute.[4] If states retain the ability to criminalize same-sex sex, it is impossible to see how they can be under a constitutional compulsion to allow same-sex marriages. Same-sex marriage may eventually have its *Loving v. Virginia*, but not unless *Bowers* is overruled.

I agree with Professor Cox that, as a matter of common-law conflicts doctrine, courts have shown a preference for validating out-of-state marriages, even if those marriages would not be permitted under the forum state's statutes. Thus if the question of recognition of out-of-state same-sex marriages were left to courts applying the *lex loci celebrationis* rule, it seems likely that a good number of courts would recognize them even though their marriage laws did not allow such unions.

The rub is that a majority of states now have statutes expressly forbidding their courts from recognizing such unions even if they were valid where celebrated. To choose randomly, here is the relevant language from Delaware's statute: "A marriage obtained or recognized outside the State between persons prohibited by subsection (a) of this section [which specifically prohibits marriages 'between persons of the same gender'] shall not constitute a legal or valid marriage within the State."[5] Here is Alaska's: "A marriage entered into by persons of the same sex, either under common law or under statute, that is recognized by another state or foreign jurisdiction is void in this state."[6] Here is Oklahoma's: "A marriage between persons of the same gender performed in another state shall not be recognized as valid and binding in this state as of the date of the marriage."[7]

Courts must follow choice-of-law statutes.[8] The only conceivable reason that a court might not follow a choice-of-law statute is if the statute were unconstitutional, as in the case of a statute voiding interracial marriages. Professor Cox apparently agrees with me that the Full Faith and Credit Clause provides no ground for finding statutes like Delaware's, Alaska's or Oklahoma's unconstitutional. In her principal contribution, Professor Cox suggests that these statutes might be unconstitutional on an equal protection theory. As I have stated in my reply, however, this cannot be so unless and until *Bowers v. Hardwick* is overruled.[9]

Thus, even if one or more states eventually recognize same-sex marriages, the result will not be a tide of successful claims for recognition in other states. The question of acceptance of same-sex marriage will continue to be a state-by-state question and will depend upon the political processes of individual states for its resolution.

## NOTES

1. Restatement (Second) of Conflict of Laws § 6(1) (1971) (courts must follow statutory directives of their home state regarding choice of law unless the statute is

unconstitutional); *see, e.g.*, N.Y. CPLR 202 (applying shorter statutes of limitation of the place in which the cause of action "accrues" if the plaintiff is a nonresident).

2. 388 U.S. 1 (1967).
3. 517 U.S. 620 (1996).
4. 478 U.S. 186 (1986).
5. 13 Del. Code Ann. § 101.
6. Alaska Stat. § 25.05.013(a).
7. 43 Okla. Stat. Ann. § 3.1.
8. Restatement (Second) of Conflict of Laws § 6 (1971).
9. 478 U.S. 186 (1986).

## Essay Two

# Interstate Recognition of Nontraditional Marriages

## Patrick J. Borchers

Even the casual reader of the popular press knows that there is a fierce ongoing debate as to the appropriate boundaries of the marital relationship. Most of it has been fueled by the recent push in several states to garner recognition for same-sex marriages. The first major victory for proponents of same-sex marriage was the Hawaii Supreme Court's decision in *Baehr v. Lewin*.[1] A plurality of that court decided on state constitutional grounds that the state's marriage statute, which limited marriage to heterosexual unions, might be unconstitutional, but that decision was effectively reversed by an initiative amending the state constitution before any same-sex marriages were recognized.[2] A similar case in Vermont ultimately prompted the Vermont legislature to enact a statute creating same-sex civil unions with essentially all of the benefits of a marriage.[3]

As might be expected, this drive to recognize same-sex marriages has coalesced a passionate opposition. A majority of the states now have statutes that expressly limit marriages to heterosexual unions and enjoin their state courts from giving any effect to same-sex marriages in other states.[4] The federal government also stepped into the fray by enacting the Defense of Marriage Act (DOMA).[5] In its relevant portion, the act provides:

No State, territory, or possession of the United States, or Indian Tribe, shall be required to give effect to any public act, record, or judicial proceeding of any other State, territory, possession, or tribe respecting a relationship between persons of the same sex that is treated as a marriage under the laws of such other State, territory, possession, or tribe, or right or claim arising from such relationship.

As the text of DOMA makes clear, its principal goal is to free states from any obligation to give effect to same-sex marriages in other states. It thus reflected the widespread belief that if one state began to recognize same-sex marriages, every other state would then be required to give full effect to these same-sex unions. The source of this perceived obligation was usually identified[6] as the Constitution's Full Faith and Credit Clause, which provides:

Full Faith and Credit shall be given in each State to the public Acts, Records, and judicial Proceedings of every other State. And Congress may by General Laws prescribe the Manner in which such Acts, Records and Proceedings shall be proved, and the Effect thereof.[7]

The problems presented are neither new nor are they limited to same-sex marriages. States have always had substantial differences with regard to the boundaries of permissible marriages, notably including age and consanguinity standards. The interstate recognition question is thus no different than if a state decided to allow polygamous or sibling marriages. Of course, the moral and political discourse would change considerably, but that ought not obscure the essential point that the same-sex-marriage debate has merely given new life to an old question in the conflict of laws.

As we shall see, the conflict-of-laws problems have been resolved on the side of state autonomy. Courts are free, absent some contrary direction from their state legislature, to recognize or not recognize nontraditional marriages celebrated in other states.[8] DOMA, therefore, despite all of the furor over its enactment, is essentially a restatement of what the law would be without it. Thus the question of whether a state will recognize same-sex or other nontraditional unions from other states is ultimately up to the recognizing state.

## TANGLED STRANDS

Understanding the conflict-of-laws problems requires unwinding two strands of the discipline that have become tangled in the debate. One strand is choice-of-law doctrine. Choice-of-law issues arise when a court confronts a case with connections to more than one state. A New York court, for instance, must decide, in the case of a New Yorker who boarded a plane in New York and was killed in a crash landing in Massachusetts, whether to apply the New York or Massachusetts wrongful-death statute.[9]

Unsurprisingly, these questions come up with regard to marriage law. A New York court must decide whether to treat as married a couple who has lived together in New York for several decades.[10] They were married in Rhode Island, a state that allowed their marriage even though the wife was the husband's half niece. New York's marriage statute treats such unions as incestuous. The estate hangs in the balance because, if the couple is not married, the surviving "spouse" has no intestacy rights.

The other important strand of the conflict of laws is that of judgment recognition. A plaintiff in the courts of one state—usually denominated "F-1"—has recovered a judgment requiring the defendant to pay money or refrain from some action. The defendant or his assets, however, are in another state, and the plaintiff takes F-1's judgment to the courts of that other state—denominated "F-2"—and seeks the aid of F-2 in holding the defendant to his obligations under the judgment.[11] F-2 must decide whether to recognize F-1's judgment, and thus treat it as conclusive, or not, and thus force the plaintiff to relitigate the dispute.

## JUDGMENT RECOGNITION

Taking initially this latter strand of conflicts doctrine, judgment recognition, let us consider whether any aspect of it can be invoked to require courts in one state to recognize nontraditional marriages celebrated in another state. A good deal of law review commentary seems to argue in the affirmative,[12] but the arguments do not withstand close analysis. To begin with some basic propositions: The Full Faith and Credit Clause, and its implementing statute,[13] require litigated judgments of one state to be recognized in another state. This principle dates back to the founding of the Republic. In *Mills v. Duryee*, the U.S. Supreme Court rejected the common-law view that F-1's judgments had merely "evidentiary" effect, and settled upon what one might call a "mandatory" interpretation of the Full Faith and Credit Clause and the statute.[14] Under this mandatory interpretation, F-2 is required to treat F-1's judgments with the same respect that it would give its own judgments.

Because of the fixed and certain application of this principle, one commentator calls it the "Iron Law" of Full Faith and Credit.[15] Nonetheless, even this iron law has a few exceptions. Default judgments, that is, judgments taken without an appearance in the action by the defendant, remain open to attack on jurisdictional grounds in F-2.[16] A decree by F-1 purporting to convey title to land in the state in which F-2 sits apparently can be ignored by F-2.[17] The Supreme Court recently held that F-1's judgment could not force F-2 to take an "official act within the exclusive province of that other State or interfere[] with litigation [before F-2]."[18] But, as this same opinion also summarized, this iron law of full faith and credit for judgments is subject to only minor limitations and is not subject to a "roving 'public policy exception.'"[19] For our purposes, there are no limitations to the full-faith-and-credit principles regarding judgment recognition of direct relevance to the same-sex-marriage debate.

The question might then fairly be asked: Why doesn't the iron law require F-2 to treat a marriage celebrated in the state in which F-1 sits as if it were an F-2 marriage? The short answer is that marriages are not judgments, and therefore the iron law has nothing to say about the subject.

A good deal of the confusion about whether marriage licenses are "judgments" apparently stems from the full-faith-and-credit treatment of divorce decrees. A divorce decree rendered by F-1 is a judgment and must be recognized in F-2,[20] even if the divorce is granted on grounds not permitted by F-1's state law.[21] The proponents of interstate recognition of nontraditional marriages make the superficially appealing argument that a marriage license ought to get at least the same respect as a divorce decree.

While there is a certain surface symmetry to this position, it ignores the most crucial characteristics of a judgment. A divorce proceeding is a dispute or potential dispute. In order for a decree to be a judgment for full-faith-and-credit purposes, it must come before a tribunal that "has jurisdiction to act judicially," by which is meant "action taken in the name of the state by a duly authorized representative or representatives [usually a judge or judges] *in the adjudication of a controversy.*"[22] A divorce proceeding can and often does have this character. It can well be that one party wants a divorce, the other does not, and the court has to decide; even if both parties want a divorce, there can be significant factual disputes concerning serious wrongdoing—adultery, extreme cruelty, and the like—by one or both of the parties.

While a marriage can take place before a judicial officer, it need not, and it does not entail the resolution of a controversy in the legal sense. It is not as though one party wants to get married, the other does not, and they appear before a court for the purpose of obtaining a ruling on the question. Marriage quite obviously depends upon the mutual assent of the parties, and the state's involvement is limited to requiring the parties to attest to the limited prerequisites for entering into the relationship.[23]

Some prorecognition commentators, apparently realizing the difficulty with attempting to treat a marriage license as a judgment, have suggested that parties could simply follow the marriage ceremony with a trip to the courthouse to obtain a declaratory judgment affirming the validity of the marriage.[24] This suggestion, while clever, does nothing to bring the Full Faith and Credit Clause into play. First, there is a large practical problem, which is that declaratory-judgment statutes generally require the existence of an "actual controversy."[25] Without some opposing party to contest the validity of the marriage, it seems unlikely that courts would be willing to declare in the abstract the validity of the marriage. Second, even if some state courts were willing to make such abstract determinations, these decrees would lack the "in-controversy" aspect of a judgment necessary for such treatment for full-faith-and-credit purposes. Third, even if these problems could be overcome, the Supreme Court has held that even true judgments can bind only those who are parties to the action or in privity with them.[26] Indeed, to bind someone who had no opportunity to participate in the litigation is a violation of elementary due process principles.[27] Thus even a couple armed with a purported declaratory judgment from F-1 would find that document of no constitutional significance in their efforts to require F-2 to honor the marriage.[28] Ultimately, therefore, a marriage license simply is not a "judgment" for constitutional purposes, and the full-faith-and-credit principles regarding judgment recognition impose no obligation on states to recognize each other's marriages.

## CHOICE OF LAW

The question of F-2's treatment of a nontraditional marriage is therefore not a question of judgment recognition at all. Instead, it is a question that implicates our other strand of the discipline of the conflict of laws: choice-of-law doctrine. Choice-of-law doctrine regarding marriages is well developed. As far back as one cares to read reported decisions, couples have gotten married in one place, made their home in another, and managed to create close questions as to their marital status.

Although the so-called conflicts revolution has wrought enormous changes in some areas of choice-of-law doctrine, the principles surrounding recognition of marriages have remained fairly constant. As one surveys the literature, it becomes apparent that the general rule has long been that a marriage valid in the state in which it is celebrated is valid everywhere, subject to the limitation that states will not recognize marriages positively prohibited by their own laws or that offend their public policy. For example, Joseph Story's nineteenth-century treatise affirmed the place-of-celebration rule, but also noted exceptions, including "those respecting polygamy and incest; those positively prohibited by the public law of a country, from motives of policy."[29] Story also specifically described marriage as a relationship existing "between individuals of different sexes."[30] As we move forward to the 1930s, it becomes clear that the rule had changed little. The First Conflicts Restatement recognized the celebration rule but also recognized that the domicile of either party could refuse to recognize the marriage for certain reasons, including polygamy, incest of such a close degree as to be "contrary to the strong public policy of the domicile," and a statute voiding the marriage.[31] A leading treatise of that time also recognized various policy exceptions to the place-of-celebration rule.[32]

Pressing forward to more modern times, the Second Conflicts Restatement provides in its relevant portion that "[a] marriage which satisfies the requirements of the state where the marriage was contracted will everywhere be recognized as valid unless it violates the strong public policy of another state which had the most significant relationship to the spouses and the marriage at the time of the marriage."[33] Treatises of a more modern vintage also continue to endorse the place-of-celebration rule subject to essentially the same policy-based exceptions and the possibility of positive prohibitions on such marriages.[34]

Cases bear out these statements of the general rule. Marriages are usually validated if they conform to the celebration state's requirements.[35] On the other hand, courts have refused to recognize marriages that while valid in the celebration state were found to offend the recognizing state's strong notions of public policy.[36] Even in those cases in which courts have upheld marriages, their opinions have usually repeated in dictum the public policy limitation.[37]

The point here is that choice-of-law questions surrounding nontraditional marriages have been around for a long time and persist today. It is true, as has been noted by careful commentary, that courts usually uphold marriages that are valid under the celebration state's law.[38] But validation of such marriages is not an immutable rule. It depends, rather, upon the recognizing state's attitudes toward the marriage and whether that state has any positive prohibition on such marriages.

Indeed, many states now have statutes that clearly address the choice-of-law question and forbid recognition of same-sex marriages even if they are celebrated in a state that allows them. A 1998 survey found that twenty-six states had statutes that "include explicit language that foreign marriages between persons of the same sex will not be recognized."[39] The Pennsylvania statute is typical. It provides:

It is hereby declared to be the strong and longstanding public policy of this Commonwealth that marriage shall be between one man and one woman. A marriage between persons of the same sex which was entered into in another state or foreign jurisdiction, even if valid where entered into, shall be void in this Commonwealth.[40]

Thus it appears that a good many states will not recognize validly celebrated same-sex marriages either because they have a statute like Pennsylvania's or because their courts will invoke the common-law public policy exception to the place-of-celebration rule.[41] The only possible route, therefore, by which such states could be forced to recognize same-sex marriages is if there is some constitutional command to do so. As discussed in the previous section, the constitutional aspects of judgment-recognition law provide no mandate to recognizing states to validate out-of-state marriages. The only other possibility is that the constitutional aspects of choice-of-law doctrine would prohibit a state from enforcing a statute like Pennsylvania's or from applying the public policy exception to the place-of-celebration rule.

As it turns out, the constitutional aspects of choice of law provide no substantial support for the prorecognition arguments. The Supreme Court has held that the combined operation of the Due Process and Full Faith and Credit Clauses places some outer boundaries around state choice-of-law doctrine. However, the area within those boundaries is expansive and allows the states tremendous freedom to choose the applicable law. In its leading modern case, the Supreme Court in *Allstate Insurance Co. v. Hague* held that a state oversteps the constitutional boundaries only if it chooses the law of a state "which has no significant contact or aggregation of contacts, creating state interests, with the parties and the occurrence or transaction."[42] The application of this rule in *Allstate* was revealing, because the Supreme Court validated the Minnesota courts' application of Minnesota insurance-coverage law to a policy involving a Wisconsin decedent, a Wisconsin beneficiary, a Wisconsin vehicle, and a Wisconsin accident. The only real connection with Minnesota was that the decedent had been employed in Minnesota at the time of his death. In truth, the Minnesota Supreme Court's choice of Minnesota law appeared to be based on little more than its frank assertion that "[t]he Minnesota rule is better."[43]

Thus, once a state achieves even a slight connection with parties or the dispute, it is free to choose the applicable law in whole or in part based upon its policy judgments about the competing rules. Moreover, the Supreme Court has explicitly approved the application of traditional choice-of-law rules even in cases in which this minimal connection is not present. In *Sun Oil Co. v. Wortman*, the Supreme Court upheld the application of Kansas's statute of limitations to all aspects of a complicated case involving claims of underpayment for natural gas—even on claims arising from wells located outside of Kansas and not involving Kansas residents.[44] The reason the Supreme Court was willing to approve the application of the Kansas limitation rule was that application of the forum state's law in limitation matters was a choice-of-law rule well established at the time of the adoption of the Full Faith and Credit and Due Process Clauses.[45] As we have seen, the place-of-celebration rule and its accompanying limitations have a pedigree that extends well back in time, and thus application of traditional doctrine would be constitutional under *Wortman*.[46]

The net result is that the constitutional aspects of choice-of-law doctrine impose no relevant constraints on states. A state court called upon to pass judgment on the validity of a same-sex marriage would be free to apply its own law, which, in most cases, would result in nonrecognition of the marriage. A good deal of the commentary on the constitutionality of DOMA is thus beside the point because it proceeds from the assumption that states are under a constitutional duty to recognize each other's marriages.[47] The fact of the matter is that DOMA is essentially a restatement of existing law regarding recognition of out-of-state marriages. In the end, the Constitution simply cannot be invoked successfully to require states to honor out-of-state same-sex marriages. The question has been settled on the side of state autonomy with regard to marriage law and recognition.

Before concluding, a few words on Vermont's civil-union legislation. As noted earlier, Vermont's statute essentially creates a marital relationship available to same-sex couples, though it employs the term "civil union" in its place.[48] From the standpoint of choice-of-law analysis, it is hard to imagine any significant difference between marriages and civil unions. Both are voluntary relationships entered into without the resolution of any "actual controversy" and thus are not judgments. Whether any other state decides to recognize this relationship is that state's choice; the Constitution imposes no obligation. Seemingly Vermont recognizes as much because the civil union licenses that it issues state in capital letters: "in Vermont only."[49]

## CONCLUSION

Same-sex marriage, of course, is an emotional issue. Its emotional character, however, ought not cloud the legal issues. Marriage is a state-law matter. Its boundaries have always varied from state to state and thus reflect the varying policy choices of the states. The drive to allow same-sex marriage changes none of this, and efforts to invoke the Full Faith and Credit Clause or any other constitutional provision to create a de facto federal standard are simply unavailing. A marriage license is not a "judgment" for constitutional purposes and thus is not subject to the Full Faith and Credit Clause's mandate for unquestioning recognition as between states. Questions of marriage recognition as between states are in reality questions of choice-of-law doctrine. While choice-of-law doctrine has usually favored the recognition of marriages that are valid in the celebration state, this has never been an immutable rule and has long been subject to the public policy limitation and the possibility of positive law prohibitions in the recognizing state. More than half of the states now have statutes that positively prohibit recognition of same-sex marriages, and others may well apply the public policy limitation to the celebration rule. In the end, therefore, the appropriateness of allowing same-sex marriages will have to be decided state by state.

## NOTES

This essay draws upon Patrick J. Borchers, Baker v. General Motors: *Implications for Interjurisdictional Recognition of Non-Traditional Marriages*, 32 CREIGHTON L. REV. 147 (1998).

1. 852 P.2d 44 (Haw.), *reconsideration granted in part and mandate clarified*, 74 Haw. 645 (1993).

2. HAW. CONST. art I, § 23.

3. Baker v. State, 744 A.2d 864 (Vt. 1999); 15 Vt. Stat. Ann. § 1201.

4. David Orgon Coolidge & William C. Duncan, *Definition or Discrimination: State Marriage Recognition Statutes in the "Same-Sex Marriage" Debate*, 32 CREIGHTON L. REV. 3 (1998).

5. Pub. L. No. 104-199, 110 Stat. 2419 (1996). The important—for our purposes—portion of the act is codified at 28 U.S.C. § 1738C.

6. *See, e.g.*, Joan Biskupic, *Once Unthinkable, Now Under Debate: Same-Sex Marriage Issue to Take Center Stage in Senate*, Wash. Post, Sept. 3, 1996, at A1 (noting that some argue "that courts might deem same-sex marriages 'judgments,' forcing other states to accept them unless Congress intervened").

7. U.S. CONST. art. IV, § 1.

8. Throughout I will refer to courts as if we were speaking only of state courts. Even if, however, a case were to arise in federal court, the resolution would not change. In federal court cases based upon diversity of citizenship, *see* 28 U.S.C. § 1332, state law would control as to the marriage question. *See, e.g.,* Metropolitan Life Ins. Co. v. Chase, 294 F.2d 500 (3d Cir. 1961) (applying New Jersey state law to determine the question of marital status). To the extent that the term "marriage" is relevant for federal law purposes, another portion of DOMA, *see* 1 U.S.C. § 7, limits the federal definition of marriage to heterosexual unions.

9. *See* Kilberg v. Northeast Airlines, 172 N.E.2d 526 (N.Y. 1961).

10. *In re* May's Estate, 114 N.E.2d 4 (N.Y. 1953).

11. *See, e.g.,* Baker v. General Motors, 522 U.S. 222 (1998).

12. *See, e.g.,* Credence Fogo, *Cabining Freedom: A Comparative Study of Lesbian and Gay Rights in the United States and Canada,* 6 CARDOZO J. INT'L & COMP. L. 425 (1998); Mark Strasser, Baker *and Some Recipes for Disaster: On DOMA, Covenant Marriages, and Full Faith and Credit Jurisprudence,* 64 BROOKLYN L. REV. 307 (1998); Evan Wolfson & Michael F. Melcher, *Constitutional and Legal Defects in the "Defense of Marriage" Act,* 16 QUINNIPIAC L. REV. 221 (1996). There is a good deal of commentary, however, that rejects the assertion that the Full Faith and Credit Clause imposes any duty on states to recognize each other's marriages. *See, e.g.,* Linda Silberman, *Can the Island of Hawaii Bind the World? A Comment on Same-Sex Marriage and Federalism Values,* 16 QUINNIPIAC L. REV. 191 (1996); Thomas M. Keane, Note, *Aloha Marriage? Constitutional and Choice of Law Arguments for Recognition of Same-Sex Marriages,* 47 STAN. L. REV. 499, 508 (1995); Rebecca S. Paige, Comment, *Wagging the Dog—If Hawaii Accepts Same-Sex Marriage Will Other States Have To?: An Examination of the Choice of Laws and Escape Devices,* 47 AM. U.L. REV. 165 (1997).

13. 28 U.S.C. § 1738.

14. 11 U.S. (7 Cranch) 481 (1813).

15. William Reynolds, *The Iron Law of Full Faith and Credit,* 53 MD. L. REV. 412 (1994).

16. *See, e.g.,* Pennoyer v. Neff, 95 U.S. 714 (1877).

17. Fall v. Eastin, 215 U.S. 1 (1903).

18. *Baker,* 522 U.S. at 234.

19. *Id.* at 233.

20. Assuming that F-1 has jurisdiction, which is generally established by the domicile of either party. Restatement (Second) of Conflict of Laws § 71 (1971).

21. Williams v. North Carolina, 317 U.S. 287 (1942).

22. Restatement (Second) of Conflict of Laws § 92 & cmt. d (1971).

23. Proponents of interstate recognition for same-sex marriages point to some scattered lower court authority that mentions the Full Faith and Credit Clause in the context of deciding whether to give effect to a marriage from another state. Two commentators, *see* Beth A. Allen, *Same Sex Marriage: A Conflict-of-Laws Analysis for Oregon,* 32 WILLAMETTE L. REV. 619, 670 n.370 (1996), and Habib A. Bailan, Note, *'Til Death Do Us Part: Granting Full Faith and Credit to Marital Status,* 68 S. CAL. L. REV. 397, 403 (1995), for example, lean heavily on the New York state trial court decision of Ram v. Ramharack, 571 N.Y.S.2d 190 (Sup. Ct. 1991). That opinion, in the course of deciding to give effect to a common-law marriage that was apparently valid in Washington, D.C., mentioned the Full Faith and Credit Clause.

That case and others in the same vein are choice-of-law cases, not judgment-recognition cases. Indeed, in the case of a common-law marriage, it is impossible to see how an F-1 "decree" could possibly be treated as a "judgment." In any event, if the *Ram* court in that case meant to say that the Full Faith and Credit Clause imposes a rule of mandatory recognition on out-of-state marriages, it is against the great weight of authority. This point is treated extensively elsewhere. *See* Borchers, *supra* unnumbered note, at 165 n.121.

24. *See, e.g.,* Deborah M. Henson, *Will Same-Sex Marriages Be Recognized in Sister States: Full Faith and Credit and Due Process Limitations on States' Choice of Law Regarding the Incidents of Homosexual Marriage Following Hawaii's* Baehr v. Lewis, 32 U. LOUISVILLE J. FAM. L. 551, 584–587, 590 (1994); Jon-Peter Kelly, Note, *Act of Infidelity: Why the Defense of Marriage Act Is Unfaithful to the Constitution,* 7 CORNELL J.L. & PUB. POL'Y 203, 218 (1997).

25. *See, e.g.,* 28 U.S.C. § 2201(a).

26. *See, e.g.,* Martin v. Wilks, 490 U.S. 755, 759 (1989) ("the general rule [is] that a person cannot be deprived of his legal rights in a proceeding in which he is not a party").

27. *Id.* at 762 n.2.

28. This is not to say that F-1's courts could never enter a judgment regarding a couple's marital relationship that would have some effect in F-2. Suppose, for example, that a same-sex couple enters into civil union in Vermont and continues to live in Vermont. One of the couple is injured in an accident with a careless driver, and the uninjured partner then sues the careless driver for loss of consortium and obtains a money judgment in the Vermont courts. If the careless driver's assets are located in New York, ordinary principles of full faith and credit would require the New York courts to honor the Vermont judgment and not allow the careless driver to force relitigation in New York. DOMA arguably changes this result and allows the driver to force relitigation, although I have argued elsewhere that this is probably an unintended consequence of DOMA and would be an unfortunate result. *See* Borchers, *supra* unnumbered note, at 180–183. Note, however, that the decree binds only the careless driver. If the couple later decides to vacation in New York and there is another accident with another careless driver, the second careless driver cannot be bound by the earlier decree treating the couple as married. *See, e.g., Martin,* 490 U.S. at 759.

29. JOSEPH STORY, COMMENTARIES ON THE CONFLICT OF LAWS § 113 (7th ed. 1872).

30. *Id.* § 108.

31. Restatement (First) Conflict of Laws §§ 121, 132 (1934). The latter section also, unfortunately, contained a provision on recognition of interracial marriages. In Loving v. Virginia, 388 U.S. 1 (1967), the Supreme Court declared prohibitions on interracial marriages to be unconstitutional.

32. GEORGE W. STUMBERG, PRINCIPLES OF CONFLICT OF LAWS 255, 262 (1937).

33. Restatement (Second) of Conflict of Laws § 283(2) (1971).

34. EUGENE F. SCOLES, PETER HAY, PATRICK J. BORCHERS, & SYMEON C. SYMEONIDES, CONFLICT OF LAWS 548 (3d ed. 2000).

35. *See, e.g.,* Loughran v. Loughran, 292 U.S. 216 (1934) (prohibition on remarriage after divorce not given extraterritorial effect); *In re* May's Estate, 114

N.E.2d 4 (N.Y. 1953) (marriage between uncle and half niece recognized even though incestuous under forum's law).

36. *See, e.g.*, Metropolitan Life Ins. Co. v. Chase, 294 F.2d 500 (3d Cir. 1961) (common-law marriage not recognized because forum state did not allow for such marriages); Catalano v. Catalano, 170 A.2d 726 (Conn. 1961) (uncle-niece marriage held contrary to forum's public policy); Wilkins v. Zelichowski, 129 A.2d 459 (N.J. App. 1957) (marriage involving sixteen-year-old wife not recognized because to do so would offend forum's strong public policy).

37. *See, e.g.*, Leszinske v. Poole, 798 P.2d 1049, 1052, 1053 (N.M. 1990) (referring to an uncle-niece marriage celebrated under Costa Rican law: the challenge to its validity "raises a serious question," and although upholding the trial court's determination regarding custody, "[w]e need not decide whether New Mexico would recognize the marriage . . . in all circumstances and for all purposes").

38. Barbara J. Cox, *Same-Sex Marriage and the Public Policy Exception in Choice-of-Law: Does It Really Exist?*, 16 QUINNIPIAC L. REV. 61, 66 (1996). Professor Cox's research also shows that courts in some cases have managed to find ways around so-called marriage-evasion statutes and have upheld marriages that were inconsistent with forum law. *Id.* at 102. Many of the state statutes addressing recognition of same-sex marriages are, however, pellucidly clear that these states will not recognize such marriages. *See, e.g. infra*, text accompanying note 40. It thus seems unlikely that a court would refuse to apply such a statute unless it were persuaded that the statute is unconstitutional.

39. *See* Coolidge & Duncan, *supra* note 4, at 12.

40. 23 Pa. Consol. Stat. § 1704.

41. This is not to say that this will always be the result. Some courts, if not under a statutory obligation to do otherwise, may give same-sex marriages at least partial effect. *See* Borchers, *supra* unnumbered note, at 184–185.

42. 449 U.S. 302, 308 (1981) (plurality opinion).

43. Hague v. Allstate Ins. Co., 289 N.W.2d 43, 49 (Minn. 1979).

44. 486 U.S. 717 (1988).

45. *Id.* at 726.

46. *See Baker*, 522 U.S. at 233 ("A court may be guided by the forum State's 'public policy' in determining the *law* applicable to a controversy") (emphasis in original).

47. *See, e.g.*, Julie B. Johnson, Comment, *The Meaning of "General Laws": The Extent of Congress's Power Under the Full Faith and Credit Clause and the Constitutionality of the Defense of Marriage Act*, 145 U. PA. L. REV. 1611 (1997); Timothy Joseph Keeler, Note, *DOMA as a Defensible Exercise of Congressional Power Under the Full-Faith-and-Credit Clause*, 54 WASH. & LEE L. REV. 1635 (1997). The question of congressional power under the Full Faith and Credit Clause is of relevance only if DOMA is read to apply to litigated judgments in which a marriage is a necessary aspect of the judgment, such as a claim for loss of consortium. *See supra* note 28. It is not clear that DOMA will be so read, and even if it is read to cover judgments of this kind, it is probably constitutional because of the "effects" portion of the clause. This point is covered extensively in Borchers, *supra* unnumbered note, at 179–185, and is collateral to the larger and more straightforward question of a state's duty to recognize an out-of-state same-sex marriage.

48. 15 Vt. Stat. § 1201. Like marriage laws, the statute prohibits the entry into

a civil union if a party is already a party to another civil union or a marriage or if the parties have a close family relationship such as mother and daughter or brothers-in-law. 15 Vt. Stat. §§ 1202, 1203.

49. *State Not Ready for Gay Marriages: Omaha Women See an Answer; Initiative Backers See a Threat*, Omaha World-Herald, Sept. 17, 2000, at 1A.

Response

# Reply to Dean Patrick J. Borchers's Essay

## Barbara J. Cox

Half of Dean Borchers's essay discusses the Full Faith and Credit (FFC) Clause, whether it requires the interstate recognition of marriages by same-sex couples, and whether the Defense of Marriage Act (DOMA) impacts that question. I agree that the FFC Clause has had little importance in prior marriage-recognition jurisprudence. Whether it can and should play an expanded role in the future, I leave to other commentators who, armed with expertise I lack, have made such an argument.[1]

Dean Borchers states that "[c]ourts are free, absent some contrary direction from their state legislature, to recognize or not recognize nontraditional marriages celebrated in other states."[2] Despite being free to make this choice, most courts have recognized these marriages. The long-standing precedent in most states validates out-of-state marriages despite in-state prohibitions against them. Dean Borchers seems to imply that courts are free to ignore this precedent. I disagree. As he notes, "States have always had substantial differences with regard to the boundaries of permissible marriages, notably including age and consanguinity standards."[3] When addressing these differences, courts regularly recognize the nontraditional marriage valid in the state of celebration, regardless of whether it would have been permitted in the parties' domicile. This general rule has been followed with perhaps surprising consistency in most states even when dealing with controversial marriages such as those following divorce or underage, polygamous, incestuous, or interracial marriages. The general rule should also be followed when dealing with marriages by same-sex couples.

Even the most superficial review of family law history leads one to understand that the definition of marriage has changed greatly over the years. It was hugely controversial earlier in this century to divorce and then remarry. Many states imposed significant restrictions and time limits on re-marriage, if permission was granted at all. But couples defied these restrictions, married in other states that permitted remarriage after divorce, and returned home to find that their marriages were recognized. Even more controversial were marriages by interracial couples. The vehemence against these marriages found in state court opinions is shocking today. But many of these couples had their marriages recognized, at least for some purposes. Marriages by same-sex couples should not be treated differently than other controversial marriages. The usual standard recognized the marriage; the prior precedent underscored this standard in most states. The usual standard and the prior precedent must be followed.

I agree with Dean Borchers that it is not necessary to turn to the Full Faith and Credit Clause to find support for recognizing marriages of same-sex couples. One needs simply to read the prior precedent, as I have done for all fifty states, to know that courts have not given much credence to statutes preventing couples from marrying, even when they left their home state to evade those statutes. Many courts have simply ignored these statutes, confident that recognizing the marriage was the right choice, based on the general validation rule, based on the prior precedent in that state, and based on the policies underlying both: to protect valid marriages and avoid disputes about whether a couple is married.

Dean Borchers asserts that "the general rule has long been that a marriage valid in the state in which it is celebrated is valid everywhere, subject to the limitation that states will not recognize marriages positively prohibited by their own laws or that offend their public policy."[4] I question his claim that courts do not recognize marriages prohibited by their own laws. Without disproving that assertion here, my previous articles cite numerous cases where a marriage not permitted in the home state was recognized there.[5] Since courts recognized incestuous, underage, polygamous, and interracial marriages and remarriage after divorce despite statutes preventing them, then they must also recognize marriages by same-sex couples despite statutes preventing them.

Dean Borchers states that some courts have "refused to recognize marriages that while valid in the celebration state were found to offend the recognizing state's strong notions of public policy."[6] But most courts recognized these marriages, despite the public policy contained in statutes preventing them in the home state. Public policy did not stop previous courts. It should not stop them now.

Dean Borchers notes that "[e]ven in those cases in which courts have upheld marriages, their opinions have usually repeated in dictum the public policy limitation."[7] The limitation was repeated in dictum because it did not control these decisions. The courts did not use the public policy limitation to declare the marriage void; instead, they ignored the limitation and recognized the marriage even though it violated their own state statutes. Because they have done so consistently over time, it would be disingenuous now to upgrade public policy from its place as dictum in the prior precedent and use it to declare marriages by same-sex couples, valid where celebrated, to be invalid.

One can refuse to use the general rule, refuse to follow that precedent, and refuse to ignore the new anti-same-sex marriage statutes only if one can convince us that marriages by same-sex couples are more controversial than the other marriages recognized before them. But recognizing the relationships of same-sex couples continues to lessen in controversy. The Netherlands and Belgium permit marriage, numerous European nations provide registered partnerships, Vermont has civil unions, Hawaii has reciprocal beneficiaries, and California has domestic partnerships. Marriage by same-sex couples is just over the horizon in the United States. We should treat these marriages the same as other controversial marriages before them and recognize them if they were valid where they were celebrated.

I am delighted to agree with Dean Borchers's statement in his response to my essay that states free to apply common-law choice-of-law doctrine "will probably, at least in some cases, give some effect to such unions." Although I would exclude the limitations contained in his statement, I agree that recognition should be forthcoming in these states. In states with no statutes concerning marriages by same-sex couples, courts should follow the prior precedent in that state and, to the extent that out-of-state marriages by opposite-sex couples were recognized, they should also recognize the out-of-state marriages by same-sex couples.

Dean Borchers's reply, however, implies that all other states are free to refuse recognition of the marriages of same-sex couples validly celebrated in another state due to statutes passed by those states. Although he refers to them as "models of drafting clarity," many of these statutes say nothing about choice of law, and thus they can not trump the common-law precedent that controls this issue in these states. Many of these statutes simply provide the same limitations on same-sex couples marrying that other statutes did on underage, previously married, interracial, incestuous, and polygamous couples marrying. It would be inappropriate to give these new statutes more weight than state courts gave to earlier statutes restricting other types of marriages.

These statutes purporting to prevent recognition of the out-of-state marriages of same-sex couples are "models" of discrimination, masquerading as choice-of-law statutes. Many refuse recognition of the validly celebrated marriages of same-sex couples only, despite blanket validation of all other out-of-state marriages, even ones that violate other marriage statutes in that state. To single same-sex couples out for worse treatment than any other marriage is discriminatory. Other statutes prohibit any recognition of the relationship underlying the marriage for any purpose. But Dean Borchers in his principal contribution notes that the Supreme Court has essentially given blanket protection to judgments rendered in other states. Under that analysis, these statutes will not be permitted to trump the Full Faith and Credit Clause, which requires recognition of judgments, entered into in other states, based on the marriages or relationships of the couples in question. These statutes may try to impose such a limit on recognition, but they will be held to be too far-reaching if Dean Borchers's original discussion of the Full Faith and Credit Clause is accurate.

I agree with Dean Borchers that the interstate recognition question will disappear once the Supreme Court issues a *Loving*-type decision for same-sex couples. Until then, state courts should remain faithful to the precedent in their states recognizing marriages that were prohibited in that state but validly entered into in another state. They should also recognize the clear discriminatory effect of statutes purporting to create different choice-of-law rules for the marriages of same-sex couples alone.

Dean Borchers seems to misunderstand the equal protection argument made in my main essay. Contrary to his assertion, that argument did not address the overall issue of whether same-sex marriage must be permitted under the Constitution. Although I believe that to be true, my point was that it would violate the Equal Protection Clause for courts to recognize the out-of-state marriages of opposite-sex couples despite state statutes prohibiting them while refusing to recognize the out-of-state marriages of same-sex couples because of state statutes prohibiting them. Since courts have repeatedly established their willingness to ignore statutory prohibitions aimed at the marriages of opposite-sex couples, they are prevented by *Romer* from singling out the marriages of same-sex couples for different and much harsher treatment.

## NOTES

1. Three commentators whom Dean Borchers cites in his *Creighton Law Review* article are Evan Wolfson & Michael F. Melcher, *Constitutional and Legal Defects in the "Defense of Marriage" Act*, 16 Quinnipiac L. Rev. 221 (1996); Mark Strasser, *Loving the Romer out for Baehr: On Acts in Defense of Marriage and the Constitution*, 58 U. Pitt. L. Rev. 279 (1997); and Larry Kramer, *Same-Sex Marriage, Conflict of Laws, and the Unconstitutional Public Policy Exception*, 106 Yale L.J. 1965 (1997). *See also* Mark Strasser, *Baker and Some Recipes for Disaster: On DOMA, Covenant Marriages, and Full Faith and Credit Jurisprudence*, 64 Brooklyn L. Rev. 307 (1998), cited in Borchers's essay at n.13.

2. *See* Patrick Borchers, Interstates Recognition of Nontraditional Marriage, at 332 (citation omitted).

3. *Id.*

4. *Id.*

5. *See* Barbara J. Cox, *Same-Sex Marriage and Choice of Law: If We Marry in Hawaii, Are We Still Married When We Return Home?*, 1994 Wis. L. Rev. 1033;

and Barbara J. Cox, *Same-Sex Marriage and the Public Policy Exception in Choice-of-Law: Does It Really Exist?*, 16 Quinnipiac L. Rev. 61 (1996).

6. *See* Borchers, *supra* note 2, at 336.

7. *Id.*

# Chapter 11

Essay One

# The Inexorable Momentum Toward National and International Recognition of Same-Sex Relationships: An International, Comparative, Historical, and Cross-Cultural Perspective

**James D. Wilets**

This essay will discuss the growing recognition of same-sex relationships among the world's countries and will explore the interplay between cultural norms and national and international law as they pertain to same-sex relationships. In pursuit of this aim, this essay will (1) demonstrate that the recognition of same-sex relationships by a growing number of countries and/or sub-jurisdictions is not a new phenomenon, but rather has ample precedent cross-culturally and historically; (2) provide an overview of those jurisdictions that recognize the right of same-sex couples to marriage, partnership, and/or same-sex couple immigration; (3) demonstrate the very close relationship between contemporary recognition of same-sex relationships and recognition of gender equality in general; and (4) provide an analysis of the status of same-sex relationships under international law.

The bulk of this essay will be devoted to discussing the growing momentum toward national legal recognition of same-sex unions by the world's countries, since family law is primarily an issue of national law. This essay, however, will also discuss those increasing instances where international law has recognized that the principle of equal protection is not fully realized until it is applied to all aspects of an individual's existence, including family life.

This essay's central thesis is that the nondiscrimination principle found in international law and most national legal systems is increasingly leading to legal recognition of the basic human rights of same-sex couples to long-term intimate relationships. Indeed, those who criticize the growing trend toward recognition of same-sex relationships can only do so based upon at least one of two assumptions: (1) that gays and lesbians are not deserving of equal treatment and protection under the law or (2) that the denial of the right to marry is not an abridgment of equal treatment for individuals who are otherwise entitled to equal protection.

With respect to the first assumption, this essay will demonstrate that international law and the overwhelming majority of Western democracies have recognized, at least to some extent, the right of sexual minorities to equal protection. With regard to the second assumption, a growing number of jurisdictions are extending the right of nondiscrimination to the right of sexual minorities to enter into loving, long-term relationships with other adults. In Europe, the European Union and the Council of Europe have moved concretely in this direction, providing examples of the acceptance of this second assumption in international law as well.

## A CROSS-CULTURAL AND HISTORICAL PERSPECTIVE

This section of the essay will identify two principal phenomena: (1) the existence of same-gender sexual relationships in almost all cultures, cross-culturally and historically; and (2) the preponderance of societal recognition of these relationships in most societies cross-culturally and historically.

A brief cross-cultural and historical discussion of sexual minorities is useful in an analysis of the contemporary status of same-sex unions. Law is a culturally specific expression of the traditions and norms of a particular society. It is therefore difficult to engage in comparative legal analysis without exploring the differing cultural assumptions underlying each country's legal approach to a specific issue.

In order for same-sex relationships not to be dismissed as a response to a historically and geographically unique phenomenon, of little relevance to the rest of the world, it is important to recognize the substantial evidence that individuals with predominately homosexual, transgendered, or bisexual inclinations exist in every society, whether or not they are able to express these inclinations. To the extent that people perceive homosexuality, and sexual minorities in general, as strictly a product of a particular period in contemporary Western society, they are unlikely to accept that sexual minorities deserve legal protection on a national or international level. For example, Hawaii's traditional acceptance of same-sex unions played a role in the debate regarding same-sex marriage following the Hawaii Supreme Court decision in *Baehr v. Lewin*, which ruled that Hawaii's ban on same-sex marriages presumptively violated the state constitution's prohibition of sex discrimination.[1] Indeed, the Hawaii Constitution provides that lawmakers and courts give deference to traditional Hawaiian usages, customs, practices, and language.[2]

There is substantial evidence that same-sex relationships have existed and continue to exist in almost all, if not all, cultures.[3] Perhaps more relevant for the purposes of this anthology, however, it is important to recognize also that societal recognition of same-sex relationships has substantial precedent cross-culturally and historically. In 1951, in a seminal anthropological study, Yale professors Clellan S. Ford and Frank A. Beach found that "[i]n 49 (64 percent) of the 76 societies other than our own for which information is available, homosexual activities of one sort or another are considered normal and socially acceptable for certain members of the community."[4] Yale historian John Boswell provides extensive documentation that homosexual unions were present and even sanctioned in medieval Christian Europe until the twelfth century.[5] Yale professor William Eskridge has written of the existence of same-sex and/or transgenderal unions in nineteenth-century Nigerian society, pre-Columbian Native American societies, nineteenth-century Zuni society, ancient Egyptian, Greek, Roman, and Mesopotamian society, the Azande, Siwah, El Garah, Basotho, Venda, Meru, Phalaborwa, Nuer, Bantu, and Lovedu societies of Africa, and the Paleo-Siberian, Chinese, Vietnamese, Indian, Japanese, Burmese, Korean, and Nepalese societies of Asia and in what is now New Zealand and the Cook Islands.[6]

New York University sociology professor David Greenberg has documented the existence of societally sanctioned homosexual relationships in ancient Mesopotamian (e.g., Hittite, Assyrian, Babylonian), Chinese, Mayan, Incan, Aztec, Egyptian, Etruscan, Indian, Greek, and Roman cultures.[7] Frank and Beach, Greenberg, and other scholars have documented widespread recognition of same-sex relationships among Native American peoples in North, Central, and South America.[8]

Vivien Ng, professor of history and women's studies at the University of Oklahoma, notes that "male homosexuality has a long and documented history in China," as does societal recognition of these relationships. Ng cites from the third-century B.C. text *Chronicles of the Warring States* to describe one of the literary terms for homosexuality:

One of the expressions for male love, *longyang*, stems from the well-known homosexual relationship between Longyang Jun, a fourth-century B.C. minister, and the prince of Wei. From the *Chronicles*, too, we know about the affection between Duke Ling of Wei and his minister, Ni Xia. Once, when the two men were taking a stroll in an orchard, Ni picked a peach off one of the trees and took a bite off it. The fruit was so delicious that he offered the rest of it to the duke; a common euphemism for male homosexual love, *fen tao zhi ai* (literally, "the love of shared peach"), is derived from this account.[9]

Bret Hinsch documents lesbian "marriages" from the Qing dynasty:

After an exchange of ritual gifts, the foundation of the Chinese marriage ceremony, a feast attended by female companions served to witness the marriage. These married lesbian couples could even adopt female children, who in turn could inherit family property from the couple's parents.[10]

Greenberg notes that the broad and open acceptance of homosexuality in Western antiquity came to an end with the spread of ascetic philosophies such as the Judeo-Christian-Islamic faiths.[11] This would be especially true for Catholicism, which traditionally has prohibited all sex outside of procreation.

Nevertheless, as William Eskridge and other authors have amply demonstrated, past recognition of same-sex unions has generally (although clearly not always) occurred within relatively narrow gender constructs that mimicked the dominant-passive construct of "traditional" heterosexual relationships. Eskridge notes that "ancient cultures (Egypt, Mesopotamia, Greece and Rome), maintained strict patriarchal lines of authority over women yet also tolerated same-sex [male-male] homosexual union."[12] Those societies that recognized same-sex unions generally did so when gender roles were not threatened. Thus to the extent that societies are uncomfortable with homosexuality, it is usually because that activity is perceived as crossing gender rather than sexual boundaries. Eskridge notes that "[m]ore recent experience reveals a connection between intolerance of same-sex unions and suppression of women."[13] The Hawaii Supreme Court recognized this correlation when it applied strict scrutiny to the Hawaii marriage law prohibiting same-sex marriage in *Baehr v. Lewin*.[14] The majority held that Hawaii's marriage law constituted sex discrimination under the state Equal Rights Amendment because it prohibited women from doing something (marrying a woman) that men were entitled to do, and vice versa.[15] Thus how a society views gender roles often determines how it treats sexual minorities.[16] This correlation is one of the most distinctive patterns emerging from the contemporary comparative legal evidence. Romania was one of the last European countries to decriminalize homosexual relations. It also has a law that absolves all the individuals participating in a gang rape of a woman if one of the rapists later marries the victim.[17] Similarly, in the United States, the anti-sexual-minority rhetoric of the fundamentalist right is inextricably linked to the fundamentalists' view of the appropriate role for women. Randall Terry, cofounder of Operation Rescue, a conservative antichoice organization, has called for the death penalty for "practicing homosexuals." He has called homosexuals criminals and has said that they should be forced to wear a badge identifying their sexual orientation so that heterosexuals can avoid any physical contact with them.[18] An Ohio judge, citing "family values" (which are frequently used in U.S. political discourse to attack sexual minorities), sentenced a man convicted of domestic violence to marry the woman he physically abused.[19] The Southern Baptist Convention recently formalized the submissive role of women; it also is one of the most stridently antigay religious bodies in the United States. On January 29, 1993, Canada granted asylum to a Saudi feminist[20] who, more than coincidentally, comes from a country in which gays and lesbians may be legally sentenced to death simply for their orientation.[21]

## A COMPARATIVE PERSPECTIVE ON THE LEGAL RIGHT TO MARRIAGE, FAMILY, AND PARTNER BENEFITS UNDER NATIONAL LAWS

Legal recognition of same-sex relationships can be divided into three general categories: (1) jurisdictions that recognize same-sex unions as legally equal to heterosexual; and (2) jurisdictions that recognize certain limited benefits for same-sex relationships.

### Jurisdictions That Recognize Same-Sex Unions as Legally Equal to Heterosexual Marriages

In April 2001, the Netherlands became the first country to extend marriage to same-sex unions, recognizing no distinction between same-sex and different-sex marriages, even in name. At almost the same time, the state of Vermont statutorily established "civil unions" that fully extend the state law on marriage and divorce to same-sex unions, the only difference being the name applied to the unions.[22] In 2003, Belgium became the second country to extend marriage to same-sex couples.

Beginning in 1989, Denmark, Greenland, Finland, Iceland, Norway, and Sweden passed laws that provided for the application of existing marriage laws (and other related laws) to same-sex spouses on the same basis as these laws are applied to heterosexual couples, with several exceptions involving adoption and church involvement in the ceremony. Otherwise, these laws have the same legal consequences as entering into marriage, including the possibility of legally terminating the relationship.[23] Sweden has now removed those restrictions related to domestic adoption.

In its summary of the Norwegian partnership law, the Ministry of Children and Family Affairs noted:

The causes of homosexuality are still unclear, but there is good evidence that sexual orientation is established at a very early age. Homosexuality is an engrained [*sic*] and permanent part of the personality, and as inescapably a part of one's nature as heterosexuality. About 5 percent of the population is purely homosexual. Others have a tendency towards heterosexuality, in the same way that many who are mainly heterosexual have a tendency towards homosexuality. The predominant expert view is that apart from their sexual orientation homosexuals are as normal and as different individually as are heterosexuals.[24]

The ministry further added:

> A homosexual disposition is still, however, often the cause of great personal problems. Society's attitudes result in difficult lives and social isolation for many gays and lesbians. The possibility of public registration and statutory regulation, help to stabilize relationships between homosexuals and make their social lives easier, in addition to solving practical, legal and financial problems. . . . The relationships will also probably become more stable if they are met with the same expectations and attitudes as heterosexual relationships.[25]

In 1995, the Hungarian Constitutional Court granted relatively far-reaching recognition to same-sex unions when it obliged Parliament to extend material partnership rights to gays. Since then, gay couples have obtained all the privileges of a heterosexual partnership, such as those relating to taxation and inheritance.[26]

Canada is now on the brink of fully recognizing same-sex unions or marriage. On May 20, 1999, in the case of *M. v. H.*, Canada's Supreme Court declared, in an 8–1 vote, that for the purposes of family law, same-sex partners must be considered "spouses" with the meaning of section 29 of Canada's Family Law Act.[27] The court concluded that the limited definition of "spouse" in Canada's family law was an infringement of section 15(1) of the Canadian Charter of Rights "not demonstrably justified in a free and democratic society," and declared it of no force or effect.[28] Although the decision applied only in the context of spousal support in the care of common-law spouses, the reasoning of the Supreme Court has tremendous implications for future interpretations of the Canadian Charter of Rights. In 1999, Ontario amended its Human Rights Code to include "same-sex partnership status" as a separate protected ground in the act upon which to prevent discrimination.[29]

On July 22, 1997, the British Columbia legislature changed the definition of "spouse" in the Family Relations Act to include same-sex partners. The change in the law was met with approval by both the attorney general, Ujjal Dosanjh, and many Anglican bishops.[30] In October 1993, a Vancouver court ordered Canada's federal government to grant a gay couple the same family and bereavement benefits that heterosexual couples receive.[31]

In July, 2002, an Ontario Divisional Court unanimously held, in *Halpern v. Toronto* (City), 28 R.F.L. (5th) 41 (July 12, 2002), that the denial of a marriage license to same-sex couples violated the Canadian Charter of Rights. The Court gave the Canadian Parliament two years to change the law governing marriage or its decision would automatically nullify the offending law. Although the provincial government of Ontario declined to appeal the decision, the federal government has appealed the decision to the Canadian Supreme Court for clarification.

The same judgment was reached by the Quebec Superior Court in *Hen-*

*dricks c. Quebec* (Procureur General), 2002 WL 1608180 (Sept. 6, 2002). The court in that case unanimously found invalid all laws resulting in denial of same-sex marriage, but suspended the effective date of its judgment for a period of two years.

In 2000, the Canadian federal government passed Bill C-23, which extends many of the obligations and benefits of marriage to same-sex couples. British Columbia, Nova Scotia, Ontario and Quebec have similar legislation. Alberta, British Columbia, Ontario, Quebec, and Saskatchewan permit adoption by gay couples.[32]

### Jurisdictions That Recognize Certain Limited Benefits for Same-Sex Unions

Jurisdictions that legally recognize same-sex relationships on some level include numerous countries in Europe such as, among others, France, Belgium, Spain, Portugal, Germany, and the Czech Republic, not to mention the countries discussed earlier that have gone much further. More than 100 municipalities, counties, and states in the United States recognize same-sex partnerships, with varying degrees of benefits flowing from that recognition.[33] California recently passed domestic partner legislation for all same-sex couples in the state.

There are active movements in Brazil and other countries in Latin America, Africa, and Asia to create partnership registries or other partnership benefits. Only some of the more notable examples of this development are discussed here.

On November 15, 1999, France enacted the Civil Solidarity Pact (PACS), allowing unmarried heterosexual and homosexual couples to register their union "in order to organize their common life." The new law grants unmarried same-sex and heterosexual couples the rights to housing, social welfare, and payment of joint taxes and lighter inheritance taxes.[34] In August 2001, a new law came into force in Germany, granting same-sex couples "recognized life partnerships" and giving same-sex couples many of the rights and duties of traditional ones, including sharing a family name and legally sharing possessions and income.[35] In the Czech Republic, existing laws give surviving members of gay couples many of the rights of married survivors. For example, the surviving partner can inherit the deceased partner's property provided they have lived together for at least three years.[36] Similarly, in Belgium, the Flemish regional government has agreed to amend the tax requirements for registered same-sex partners of at least three years. Prior to the agreement, inheritance taxes were payable at a rate of 30 percent for nonrelated or unmarried couples. The corresponding rate of 10 percent applied for a surviving spouse. As of January 1998, a surviving registered partner had to pay any inheritance tax at the 10 percent rate of current "married couples."[37]

Despite the strong influence of the church, an increasing number of courts are handing down favorable decisions for gay partners in South America. In July 1997, an Argentinean court granted teacher Rafael Freda spousal rights for his partner. As a result of the decision, the government extended pension benefits to all lovers of deceased gays and lesbians. The Roman Catholic Church in Argentina reacted with anger. In a press release by the National Bishops Conference Family Secretary, the church said that gays are sick and abnormal.[38] In February 1998, a Brazilian High Court decision enabled a gay man to acquire half of his deceased partner's estate. The court stated that "[a] judge nowadays cannot deny that two people of the same sex can form family ties."[39] There is an ongoing battle for federal recognition of same-sex partnerships in the Brazilian Parliament.

Numerous countries recognize same-sex unions by granting the foreign partner of a citizen the right to immigrate. In addition to all of the countries that grant marriage or full partnership rights to same-sex partners, such as the Netherlands, Belgium, Sweden, Norway, Denmark, Finland, and Iceland, other countries grant the more limited right of immigration to same-sex partners. These countries include Australia, Belgium, Canada, Germany, Israel, New Zealand,[40] South Africa, and the United Kingdom.[41] In 1991, the Australian federal government introduced a new visa and permit category that allows common law and same-sex couples to achieve residency. Canada's Immigration and Refugee Protection Act (Bill C-31) provides the statutory basis for recognition of the right of same-sex partners to immigrate. In 2000, the Israeli Ministry of the Interior granted resident status to two same-sex partners of Israeli citizens. Israel recognized the status of *yedu'a ba-tzibur* (common-law spouse), and these couples obtained citizenship based on their "married" status.[42]

On December 2, 1999, the South African Constitutional Court decided that section 25(5) of the Aliens Control Act 96 of 1991 was unconstitutional. The court found that section 25(5) reinforced harmful stereotypes of gays and lesbians and related rights of equality and dignity to this case. The court further stated that it was an invasion of gays and lesbians' dignity to convey the message that gays and lesbians lack the inherent humanity to have their families' lives in such same-sex relationships respected or protected.[43] The court's decision now permits the immigration of same-sex partners.

## THE STATUS OF SAME-SEX RELATIONSHIPS UNDER INTERNATIONAL LAW

As noted earlier, family law is almost entirely an issue of national law. Nevertheless, international human rights law does set certain parameters that countries are bound to respect with respect to their own laws regarding marriage and the family. These parameters include the right of individuals to form a family[44] and nondiscrimination. In 1992, the United Nations Human Rights Committee, in *Toonen v. Australia*, ruled that Tasmania's sodomy law violated the right of sexual minorities to equal protection and privacy.[45] In March 2000, the European Parliament applied this principle of equal protection to family law and adopted a resolution urging the fifteen European Union nations to grant same-sex couples the same rights as heterosexual couples. The resolution, adopted 265–125, stated that the nations of the European Union should "guarantee one-parent families, unmarried couples and same-sex couples rights equal to those enjoyed by traditional couples and families, particularly as regards tax law, pecuniary rights and social rights."[46] In 1999, the European Court of Human Rights, with jurisdiction over almost every country in Europe, extended the principle of nondiscrimination to cover same-sex-couple rights in family law by ruling that the prohibition against discrimination contained in the European Convention on Human Rights and Fundamental Freedoms, when read together with the convention's respect for family life, required that a gay man be awarded custody over the objections of the child's mother.[47]

The process by which international human rights law recognizes certain rights as fundamental is a relatively slow dialectical process, as is appropriate for a legal system that seeks a consensus before determining whether certain rights are fundamental to all human beings. It is thus all the more surprising that the European human rights bodies have come as far as they have, given the wide "margin of appreciation" granted to the member countries' legal systems. These legal bodies have recognized the incoherence of recognizing the right of nondiscrimination without applying that fundamental right to one of the most basic rights of all: the right to form a family and to enter into a stable, loving relationship with another human being.

## CONCLUSION

As noted earlier, those opposing same-sex marriage can only do so based upon at least one of two assumptions: (1) that gays and lesbians are not deserving of equal treatment of the law or (2) that the denial of the right to marry is not an abridgment of that right. The sheer number of jurisdictions that have recognized the rights of sexual minorities to equal protection, including one of the principal United Nations adjudicative bodies, indicates that the first assumption has been firmly rejected as a principle of international law and of the legal systems of the great majority of industrialized democracies. As evidenced by the judicial opinions of numerous national courts and the judgment of the highest political body in the European Union, the principled application of the rules of nondiscrimination and equal protection require the application of this principle to those areas of law that are central to the inherent dignity of a person. The ability to love another human being is one of the greatest gifts God has given humankind, and the denial of that gift is a violation of a person's dignity and fundamental human rights that no principled legal system can let stand.

## NOTES

I would like to thank Bill Adams and Marilyn Cane for their insightful comments, and my legal spouse, Luis Font.

1. *Same Sex Unions Were Accepted in Hawai'i*, Honolulu Advertiser, June 13, 1993, at B3.

2. *See* Robert J. Morris, *Configuring the Bo(u)nds of Marriage After Bowers and Baehr: The Implications for Homogamy of Hawaiian Sovereignty and Culture* (1996) (draft manuscript on file with author). *See also* J. Van Dyke, M. Chung, & T. Kondo, *The Protection of Individual Rights Under Hawaii's Constitution*, 14 UNIV. HAW. L. REV. 311 (1992).

3. *See, e.g.*, David Gelman, *Born or Bred?*, NEWSWEEK, Feb. 24, 1992, at 46. *See also* FRANK & BEACH, PATTERNS OF SEXUAL BEHAVIOR 143 (1951).

4. FRANK & BEACH, at 130.

5. JOHN BOSWELL, SAME-SEX UNIONS IN PREMODERN EUROPE (1994); JOHN BOSWELL, CHRISTIANITY, SOCIAL TOLERANCE, AND HOMOSEXUALITY: GAY PEOPLE IN WESTERN EUROPE FROM THE BEGINNING OF THE CHRISTIAN ERA TO THE FOURTEENTH CENTURY (1980).

6. *See* William N. Eskridge, Jr., *The History of Same-Sex Marriage*, 79 VA. L. REV. 1419, 1437–1446, 1453–1469, 1510 (1993).

7. DAVID F. GREENBERG, THE CONSTRUCTION OF HOMOSEXUALITY 124–127, 127–135, 141–151, 152–171 (1988).

8. For North America, *see id.* at 41. For Central and South America, *See, e.g.*, FRANK & BEACH, *supra* note 3, at 131. *See also* GREENBERG, *supra* note 7, at 163–168.

9. Vivien W. Ng, *Homosexuality and the State in Late Imperial China*, in HIDDEN FROM HISTORY 77 (Martin Bauml Duberman et al. eds., 1989).

10. BRET HINSCH, PASSIONS OF THE CUT SLEEVE: THE MALE HOMOSEXUAL TRADITION IN CHINA 11–13 (1990), *cited in* Eskridge, *supra* note 6, at 1466, n.170.

11. GREENBERG, *supra* note 7, at 184.

12. *See* Eskridge, *supra* note 6, at 1510.

13. William N. Eskridge, Jr., *The History of Same-Sex Marriage*, 79 VA. L. REV. 1419, 1510 (1993).

14. *Baehr v. Lewin*, 852 P.2d 44 (Haw. 1993).

15. For a discussion of sexual-minority discrimination as gender discrimination, *see* Andrew Koppelman, *The Miscegenation Analogy: Sodomy Law as Sex Discrimination*, 98 YALE L.J. 145 (1988).

16. As used in this essay, the term "sexual minorities" includes all individuals who have traditionally been distinguished by societies because of their sexual orientation, inclination, behavior, or nonconformity with gender roles or identity.

17. *See* James D. Wilets, *Conceptualizing Private Violence Against Sexual Minorities as Gendered Violence: An International and Comparative Law Perspective*, 60 ALB. L. REV. 989, 1010.

18. *Go Home, Yankee, Gay Activists Yell*, Edmonton Journal, Apr. 23, 1995, at A4.

19. *See Ohio Judge Orders Abuser to Marry Woman He Punched*, Miami Herald, July 15, 1995, at 11A.

20. *See* Clyde H. Farnsworth, *Saudi Woman Who Fled Predicts Crackdown*, N.Y. Times, Feb. 7, 1993, at 19. *See also* Jennifer Bingham Hull, *Battered, Raped, and Veiled: The New Sanctuary Seekers*, L.A. Times, Nov. 20, 1994, at 26.

21. *See* Wilets, *supra* note 17, at 1010–1011.

22. *Baker v. State*, No. 98-032, 1999 Vt. Lexis 406, at 4.

23. *See, e.g.*, The Norwegian Act on Registered Partnerships for Homosexual Couples, Ministry of Children and Family Affairs (Aug. 1993).

24. *Id.* at 6.

25. *Id.* at 37.

26. Miklos Haraszti, *Gays and the Gay Rights Limbo*, BUDAPEST BUS. J., Aug. 6, 2001.

27. *M. v. H.*, [1999] 2 S.C.R. 3.

28. *Id.*

29. Canada Newswire, *Sexual Orientation Policy Released by Human Rights Commission*, Feb. 25, 2000.

30. Rex Wockner, *British Columbia Redefines "Spouse,"* INT'L NEWS 170 (July 30, 1997) http://qrd.org/qrd/www/world/wockner.html.

31. *See Canada Court Upholds Benefits for Gay Couples*, Reuters World Service, Oct. 1, 1993, *available in* LEXIS, World Library, Reuwld File.

32. *See* http://canadaonline.about.com/library/weekly/aa081002a.htm.

33. Editorial, *Have They Nothing Better to Do?* Wash. Post, Oct. 30, 2001, at A20 (113 state and local governments offer domestic partnerships).

34. *Bill Recognizing Unmarried Couples Becomes Law in France*, Agence France-Presse, Nov. 16, 1999.

35. *See Equality for Gays in Germany*, Chi. Sun-Times, Aug. 2, 2001, at 26.

36. *See* David Appell, *Gays Make Strides Toward Acceptance in the System*, Prague Post, June 30–July 6, 1993, at 4.

37. Alan Reekie, *Bill to Reduce Inheritance Tax for Registered Partners*, 51 EURO-LETTER (July 1997), http://www.qrd.org/qrd/www/orgs/ILGA/euroletter.html.

38. Rex Wockner, *Argentine Church Attacks Gay Teachers*, INT'L NEWS 169 (July 23, 1997), http://www.qrd.org/qrd/www/world/wockner.html.

39. *Gay Man Wins Property Rights Case in Brazilian High Court*, EMERGENCY RESPONSE NETWORK (ILGHRC, San Francisco, Cal.), Mar. 6, 1998.

40. Rex Wockner, *New Zealand OKs Gay Immigration*, Bay Area Rep., May 16, 1991.

41. As of October 2, 2000, the United Kingdom recognized the right of same-sex partners to immigrate as a result of the coming into effect of the Human Rights Act and a revamping of the Immigration Rules in general. See, e.g.,

42. Einat Fishbein, *Two Foreigners Recognized as Residents of Israel Based on Same-Sex Relationship*, Ha'aretz, Agudah News, Feb. 14, 2000 (translated by Lee I. Walzer).

43. *See National Coalition for Gay and Lesbian Equality and Others v. Minister of Home Affairs and Others*, Constitutional Court of South Africa, Front Page (Dec. 2, 1999). The court held that the subsection omits to give persons who are partners

in permanent same-sex life partnerships the benefits it extends to "spouses" under this section. http://www.law.wits.ac.za/archive.html.

44. *See* article 16 of the Universal Declaration of Human Rights, G.A. Res. 217 A(III), U.N. GAOR, 3rd Sess., U.N. Doc. A/810 (1948), and article 23 of the International Covenant on Civil and Political Right's G.Z. res. 2200 A (XXI), Dec. 16, 1966, 21 U.N. GAOR Supp. (No. 16) at 52, U.N. Doc. A/6316 (1996), 999 U.N.T.S. 171, *entered into force* Mar. 23, 1976.

45. *Nicholas Toonen v. Australia*, Case No. 488/1992, U.N. Hum. Rts. Comm., 15th Sess., U.N. Doc. CCPR/c/50/D/488/1992 (4 Apr. 1994).

46. *EU Parliament Urges Treating Gay Couples Same as Others*, Raleigh News & Observer (AP), Mar. 18, 2000. On February 11, 2003 the European Union Parliament voted to give same-sex partners the same residence rights in European Union countries enjoyed by those individuals in either their home or host countries. The term "spouse" with respect to residence rights was also broadened under EU law to include same-sex spouses.

47. *Salgueiro da Silva Mouta v. Portugal*, App. No. 33290/96, at http://www.echr.coe.int./Eng/Judgments.htm. See generally Bernard Oxman, & Laurence Helfer, *International Decisions*, 95 AM. J. INT'L L. 422 (2001).

Response

# *Reply to Professor James D. Wilets's Essay*

## **Robert John Araujo, S.J.**

Professor Wilets has written a passionate chapter in which he attempts to substantiate his claim about the recognition of same-sex marriages under international law. However enthusiastic he is, the justifications he employs fail to achieve his goal. As an initial matter, he confuses certain kinds of human relationships with marriage. Throughout his chapter, Professor Wilets offers no distinction between the meaning of "relationship" and the meaning of "marriage." This distinction is important, but it may be that to him all human relationships of two or more people might be akin to marriage. They are not.

The central thesis of his argument is founded on the principle of nondiscrimination. In several places, Professor Wilets employs the phrase "sexual minority" as a way of describing gay or lesbian people. Perhaps this is a method to reinforce his argument that prohibitions against certain conduct or activities based on this status of being a member of such a group or "minority" are suspect. However, for the sake of argument, if homosexuals are considered to be some sort of minority group, they are treated no differently from heterosexuals in the context of seeking the right to marry, as I have illustrated. There are at least two problems with this thesis as presented in his chapter. First of all, the chapter fails to acknowledge that many discriminations are lawful and serve important social functions that are protective of the human race and its individual members. Second, the arguments mustered to substantiate this thesis are based on two assumptions that are inapposite.

With regard to the first problem, his engaging chapter fails to acknowledge that not all discrimination is unlawful. Legal systems throughout the world do not brand as unlawful distinctions such as those based on certain age categorizations (e.g., the age at which one can vote, smoke, consume alcohol, marry, or drive a motor vehicle); physical characteristics (e.g., capabilities to perform certain functions essential to be a police officer, a soldier, or a firefighter); sex (e.g., bona fide qualifications that restrict applicants based on sex); and academic or professional qualifications (e.g., the ability to practice a profession or trade licensed by the state). With regard to long-standing legal practices that discriminate under matrimonial law, it has been and remains lawful to prohibit from marriage those who are under a certain age, those who are related in certain degrees of consanguinity, or those who are afflicted with certain physical ailments or diseases.

The second problem emerges from his two assumptions that he incorrectly attributes to any opponent of same-sex marriages that (1) "gays and lesbians are not deserving of equal treatment of the law" or (2) "the denial of the right to marry is not an abridgment of that right." As stated earlier, most people, including gays or lesbians, can find themselves being discriminated against on certain grounds that do not deny them equal treatment of the law. If his argument is that such a person is denied equal protection of the law simply because he or she is gay or lesbian, that would not seem to be the case. While neither may wish to do so, a gay man would be entitled to marry a woman and a lesbian would be entitled to marry a man. They would not be denied equal treatment of the law since they would be treated like anyone else regardless of the person's sexual orientation. There is no disparate treatment because neither the homosexual nor the heterosexual can marry a person of the same sex. Thus the gay or lesbian would be treated just like any heterosexual man or woman who might wish to marry a person of the same sex. Regardless of one's sexual orientation, the prohibition would be uniformly applied. The legal prohibition does not discriminate against the person who is homosexual or heterosexual. It treats each person the same. Therefore, Professor Wilets's suggested claim that gays and lesbians are denied equal treatment of the law dissolves. The same problem exists with the assumption that "the denial of the right to marry" is an abridgment of the right. Again, a gay man or lesbian is not denied the right to marry. Each is entitled to marry a person of the opposite sex just as anyone else who meets the criteria established by the state is so entitled. A heterosexual who wishes to marry a person of the same sex equally shares such abridgment.

In elaboration of his central thesis, Professor Wilets relies on a perspective that takes account of various "inclinations" in cultures throughout human history.[1] Human beings have, throughout their history, displayed a wide variety of biases that may be shared with some, but not all, members of the human race. However, a bias by itself cannot automatically be equated with a claim for protection under domestic or international law. For example, the inclinations of the Taliban, polygamists, or those who cohabit in sexual relationships and the expressions of such inclinations, no matter how deeply

held, are not automatically accorded the status of a right that must be protected under international law. The same limitation applies to the inclinations of persons who wish to be "married" to a person of the same sex.
Interestingly, Professor Wilets relies on John Boswell's assertions that "homosexual unions" were not only present but also sanctioned in medieval
Christian Europe until the twelfth century. However, his cited authority
conflicts with the long-standing tradition of the Christian Church that goes
back to the ancient texts of the Bible (see, e.g., Genesis 1:26–28 and 2:24;
Romans 1:24–27; 1 Corinthians 6:9; 1 Timothy 1:10) and to the canonical
tradition that extends back to St. Ignatius's writings to St. Polycarp in the
second century, which stated, "It is fitting that the groom and the bride
enter marriage with the advice of the bishop so that their marriage may be
according to God and not according to concupiscence."[2]

In the second part of his chapter, Professor Wilets furnishes a comparative
perspective of several national legal systems that presently extend particular
rights to members of same-sex relationships. Several points should be made
about these recognitions. First of all, they reflect the conclusions of positive
legal institutions—in some cases legislators, in others courts. However, Professor Wilets acknowledges that these institutions do not concur with one
another because they place the status of same-sex relationships into a minimum of three categories, which he identifies. In some instances, the positive
law appears to recognize same-sex unions as being equal to heterosexual
marriages "in all legal respects." I make this point in order to draw a distinction between a positive legal system that does not rely on the natural
law and one that does. A positive legal system that incorporates the natural
law would rely on human reason to ascertain first principles that are objective
and moral. If the positivist system were to rely on the use of reason to search
for objective first principles of the law that have a moral content, legislatures
and judges would be hard pressed to find a right to same-sex marriage. In
short, the application of the natural law would lead the lawmaker to conclude, through the application of reason, that the differences between the
male and female exist to further an objective reality, namely, procreation of
the species. Through the union of the complementary sexes, the species
continues; moreover, parents have a continuing obligation to nurture and
educate their children, who continue a part of the parents' natures after the
latter have died. None of this is possible in a homosexual union, be it male
or female. The second category, while applying some of the general law of
domestic relations to same-sex relationships, utilizes some restrictions. The
third and final category of municipal law identified by Professor Wilets accords "certain limited benefits for same-sex unions."

Several points need to be made regarding this component of his argument. First, the positive law of a domestic jurisdiction can state just about
anything that it wishes as long as the reviewing authority, usually judges,
concludes that the basic law of the state or applicable jurisdiction is not

violated. This is not to say that such positive law accords with the universal principles of human rights law. The laws of the United States, Nazi Germany, the Netherlands, apartheid South Africa, the People's Republic of China, the European Union, and virtually every other state or political entity past and present have contained principles that others have found to be inappropriate if not "unlawful." It may be the law in a particular jurisdiction, but it is not a right or principle that accords with the fundamental, universal understanding of the law that should apply to all peoples.

Second, Professor Wilets's analysis demonstrates the disagreement among those jurisdictions that have accorded some kind of legal recognition to homosexual relationships. The fact that he was required to develop a minimum of three categories of varying degrees of recognition makes one point very clearly: there is no universal recognition, even among those states that have accorded some privileges to homosexual unions, that these relationships are the same as the monogamous relationship of a man and woman who are united in their complementarity to found, nurture, and educate a family that results from their union with one another. No positive law can overcome this fundamental fact that is at the core of our human nature. The "right" to be accorded certain economic benefits granted to heterosexual couples may be granted by the lawmaker to the members of a homosexual relationship, but such "rights" cannot be given for the same reasons, that is, to found a family of the children of their union who shall in turn continue the human race into the next generation.

Last, in the third part, Professor Wilets makes the case for recognition of same-sex relationships under international law. As I have pointed out in my paired essay, Professor Wilets and others have already conceded that international law does not recognize same-sex marriages.[3]

In those cases where he has cited as authority decisions of the United Nations Human Rights Committee or the European Court of Human Rights, a critical reader must pay attention to what these bodies have said and what they have not. Perhaps this is evidence of the "relatively slow dialectical process" that he addresses. In the context of the Human Rights Committee or the European Court of Human Rights cases cited, the issues addressed custody of children or the criminalization of sodomy. None of these opinions recognized an international right to same-sex marriage.

In conclusion, there is no international birthright of any person to a same-sex marriage. The joining of the terms "same-sex" and "marriage" may not defy some people's inclinations, but they do defy international law. To assert otherwise is to advance an argument that is incoherent.

In his response to my "Marriage, Relationship, and International Law," Professor Wilets has once again provided readers with a robust attempt to support his position that international law recognizes same-sex marriages. As I have previously pointed out in my response to his essay, he and other advocates who hold his position have conceded that this is not the case.[4] In the final analysis, there is no inexorable momentum toward recognition of same-sex marriages. Rather, it is the relentless and rigid insistence of a small minority who yearn to have same-sex marriages recognized that is inexorable. Unlike Professor Wilets, who has raised issues not material to the general theme of this anthology, I shall address only the legal arguments he has presented in defense of his position and their soundness.

First, the international authorities cited in his response come from two sources: the United Nations Human Rights Committee, which is not a judicial body, and the European Human Rights Court. None of the proceedings from either body cited in his response has legitimated same-sex marriages. Rather, they have addressed other nonmatrimonial issues involving homosexual persons. These proceedings do not support, directly or indirectly, the claim that international law is on an inexorable or, for that matter, any other momentum toward recognition of same-sex marriage.

Second, he reiterates his previous thesis based on the theory of denial of equal treatment. I have already demonstrated in my response to his principal chapter why this argument fails. In recapping my argument, I demonstrated that homosexual persons are not denied equal protection of the law. To the contrary, they enjoy the same rights (the ability to marry a person of the opposite sex) and experience the same restrictions (the prohibition to marry a person of the same sex) as heterosexual persons. The allegation that homosexuals are denied equal treatment or protection under the law is imaginary.

Third, he criticizes what he identifies as my "breathtaking argument that 'prohibitions against same-sex marriages are exercises in the protection of international human rights.' " He further states that my view "is not only completely inconsistent with the underpinnings of human rights law as a check on abuses committed by 'sovereign' nations, it also runs counter to the decisions of the primary body charged with interpreting the ICCPR." What his vigorous avowal fails to acknowledge is that universal human rights principles cherish the ability of peoples to exercise legitimate self-determination.[5] Sadly, the Human Rights Committee of late has been enforcing an understanding of human rights that a variety of cultures and peoples from around the globe find not only not universal but also not right.[6] To argue that the Human Rights Committee, a political group with little if any accountability through democratic mechanisms, is an unimpeachable source of determining basic human rights duplicates the error.

In the final analysis, international law has not recognized, does not recognize, and cannot recognize a right to same-sex marriage. The claim that such a right exists is not inexorable but illusory.

## NOTES

1. *See* the first part of *The Inexorable Momentum Toward National and International Recognition of Same-Sex Relationships.*
2. *Ad Polycarpum,* ch. 5.

3. *See, e.g.*, nn. 12, 17, & 20 and their accompanying texts in my essay titled *Marriage, Relationship, and International Law*.

4. *See* nn. 12, 17, & 20 and accompanying texts in my principal essay.

5. *See, e.g.*, Charter of the United Nations, article 1.2. *See also* Robert John Araujo, *Sovereignty, Human Rights, and Self-Determination: The Meaning of International Law*, 24 FORDHAM INT'L L.J. 1477, 1492–1500 (2001).

6. By way of illustration, *see* Padraic P. Mcguinness, *Bending the Agenda of the UN's Democratic Deficit*, Sydney Morning Herald, Sept. 2, 2000.

Essay Two

# Marriage, Relationship, and International Law: The Incoherence of the Argument for Same-Sex Marriage

## Robert John Araujo, S.J.

The issue of sexual minorities' human rights is international in scope since individuals with gay, lesbian, bisexual, or transgender inclinations or identities appear to have been, and continue to be, present in every society. . . . In fact, it has been argued by some historians and legal commentators that much of the contemporary hostility towards sexual minorities is a direct result of Western colonialism, Judeo-Christian-Islamic homophobia, and communist doctrine, none of which is rooted in indigenous tradition.[1]

Marriage, in short, is the last legal bastion of compulsory heterosexuality. . . . It is the most blatant evidence that gay and lesbian citizens must sit in the back of the law bus, paying for a first-class ticket and receiving second-class service. . . . [A]ny serious agenda for homosexual rights must presumptively include marriage.[2]

During the past several years, there has been much celebration surrounding the fiftieth anniversary of the Universal Declaration of Human Rights (UDHR).[3] The UDHR was generated during a time in which many people of good will not only acknowledged the great sins committed by some against others in the name of racial, ethnic, and other "purities" but also decided to take steps within international law to ensure that the twentieth-century crimes against humanity would never be repeated. Johannes Morsink argues that the UDHR "was meant to be used as an educational text to tell people about all the inherent rights they already have."[4] As Professor Mary Ann Glendon has pointed out, the UDHR "is the single most important reference point for cross-cultural discussion of human freedom and dignity in the world today."[5] Yet it is apparent from the ensuing discussion over the years that there exists confusion about the nature of human rights under international law. While it would be fair to suggest that these rights involve the freedom and dignity of each person, it would also be vital to acknowledge that international human rights are subject to a hierarchical ordering and necessary limitation, as will be explained in greater detail later.[6]

It should come as no surprise that these principles of international human rights have been misconstrued in and misapplied to a fairly recent development. This development is the claim that same-sex relationships must be entitled to enjoy marital status and, further, that such a claim is recognized and protected under international law, which emerged from the traditions established by the UDHR. These claims for international protection are further justified by pointing to the changes in municipal law that recognize same-sex registered partnerships and civil unions.[7] While such relationships may be based on the love of two people who happen to be of the same-sex, there are many other types of love between and among humans that do not constitute the grounds for declaring such relationships to be marriage. Examples include the love between a parent and his or her children, the love between siblings, and the love between friends or distant relatives. The reader might imagine many kinds of love and many kinds of commitment leading to a variety of relationships. Some of these relationships are with people, some with animals, and some with inanimate objects. They may all be based on a person's love for the other, be the other a person, animal, or thing. But such kinds of love do not a marriage make. As the venerable *Oxford English Dictionary* states, the act of marrying is "to join for life as husband and wife." The claim that relationships between same-sex couples can be recognized as a marriage under international law is false. In order to substantiate this argument, an analysis of international law must now be undertaken.

## A PRIMER ON INTERNATIONAL HUMAN RIGHTS

The UDHR is not an international legal instrument per se, but it has supplied the essential components of the principal international human rights conventions, including the International Covenant on Economic, Social, and Cultural Rights of 1966 (ICESCR) and the International Covenant on Civil and Political Rights of 1966 (ICCPR). While the UDHR was not drafted to establish binding legal obligations, it is generally regarded as the principled source from which treaties having legal force would follow.[8]

Under these subsequent covenants, states have the primary duty of enforcing the international principles and legal norms designed to protect universally fundamental human dignities. This would obviously mean that constitutions or other basic laws would be the legal forum in which these dignities would be declared and protected by law. But states have often been the perpetrators responsible for violating these norms identifying and addressing human rights. An illustration of this last point would be the promulgation of the Nuremberg Laws by the Third Reich.

While the exercise of state sovereignty has led to the unwarranted and unjustifiable deprivation of human dignity to millions of innocent victims, it would be imprudent and erroneous to conclude that state sovereignty must be curtailed when it does not permit or outlaws same-sex marriages. Indeed, the prohibitions against same-sex marriages are exercises in the protection of international human rights recognized by the UDHR and protected under the two 1966 instruments. Furthermore, the movements both municipally and internationally to establish same-sex marriages are inconsistent with international law and its protection of basic or fundamental and universal human rights.[9] The undermining of the legal rights of communities who uphold the custom of marriage as a union between one man and one woman paves the way for the erosion of other basic human rights mentioned in the UDHR. This important point was recognized in *Rees v. United Kingdom*, where the European Court of Human Rights stated, "In the Court's opinion, the right to marry guaranteed by Article 12 [of the European Convention for the Protection of Human Rights and Fundamental Freedoms] refers to the traditional marriage between persons of the opposite biological sex. This appears also from the wording of the Article which makes it clear that Article 12 is mainly concerned to protect marriage as the basis of the family."[10]

The principal goal of this chapter is to examine the concept of marriage as it exists under international law. Included within this investigation are the related questions of whether international law recognizes same-sex unions/marriages or should recognize them. At this stage, it should be noted that advocates for the recognition of same-sex marriages have conceded that no such right exists under international law.[11] Nevertheless, their contentions will be examined in greater detail shortly. Essential to the scrutiny of this chapter is the need to ascertain whether same-sex unions/marriages are essential to the existing and developing human rights regime. This examination will lead to the ultimate conclusion that same-sex unions are not marriages under international law.

Even though exercises of sovereignty can be the source of violation of fundamental human rights (e.g., the racial-purity laws of Nazi Germany), they can also be equivalent to expressions of fundamental human rights.[12] In many instances, especially within democratic regimes, sovereignty and its exercise can be crucial to the protection of human rights because they can be an expression of how individuals and the communities that they form practice self-determination, which is constitutive of human rights. Nevertheless, there exist articulate opponents to this point of view. One of the better known, Professor William Eskridge of Yale Law School, has acknowledged the effectiveness of the judiciary and the academy in neutralizing or overriding the responsible exercise of popular sovereignty and the democratic process that are themselves indisputable objects of international human rights protection. As Professor Eskridge has stated, "For the judiciary, or the professorate, to tell traditionalist citizens that their time-tested family values count for nothing in the same-sex marriage debate is a time-tested path to political alienation or revolt."[13] While seemingly respectful of the rights of "traditionalist citizens" and their legal claims, he continues to assert that the "genius" of a particular state's movement toward recognizing same-sex marriages "is that the state insisted that traditional family values give way to the recognition of lesbian and gay rights, but lesbian and gay family values give way to accommodation of traditionalist anxieties *for the time being*."[14] In the same article, Professor Eskridge states that he is "a classical liberal and a gay person who supports legal recognition of same-sex marriages."[15] Of little comfort are his assertions to "traditionalist citizens" unless their concerns are only for the time being.

It should be noted that even under domestic law, advocates for same-sex marriage face difficulty in basing their claims on recognized legal principles. This reality may have led Professor Mary Becker to make a tenuous policy rather than a legal argument in defense of same-sex marriage.[16] The ends to which advocates of same-sex marriage would go are disturbing, unsettling, and menacing. For example, Sheila Rose Foster has stated, "I, along with others in same-sex monogamous life partnerships, would love to obtain the material benefits that accompany marriage—regardless of the means."[17] One means she appears to suggest is to make opposition to such "marriages" a form of discrimination that might then be made illegal—perhaps through hate-crime regulation or other means.[18] As she concludes, "As a first principle, achieving this dignity and respect means freedom, and protection from violence and discrimination just for being who we are. Until our victories [which remain ambiguous], as a movement, translate into these types of fundamental reforms, marriage will be a tokenistic privilege available only to the brave and the few."[19]

In the presentation of this chapter's thesis, the next part will examine the meaning of marriage under international law. The part after that will analyze same-sex relationships and conclude that they cannot be accorded the status of marriages under international law. Consequently, states have no obligation to consider same-sex marriages as a human right since the concept of the family (the "natural and fundamental group unit of society," as acknowledged by article 16.3 of the UDHR, article 23.1 of the ICCPR, and article 10.1 of the ICESCR) does not include a same-sex union.

## THE CONCEPT OF MARRIAGE IN INTERNATIONAL LAW

The quotation from the work of Professor William Eskridge that appears at the beginning of this chapter suggests an equality argument crucial to the legal claim for the recognition of same-sex marriages. However, a fundamental question must be raised as to whether this argument will pass the muster of international law. In order to address responsibly this issue, international law's understanding of marriage—that is, what it entails and what it does not—must be ascertained.

In discussing the applicability of the UDHR, same-sex-union advocate Vincent Samar notes that the rights to be protected are for "all people" regardless of who they are. He then states that these protections include, "*arguably*, sexual orientation."[20] By including the word "arguably," the author acknowledges that there is or may be some doubt surrounding the claim. He is joined by others who are sympathetic to the cause of same-sex marriage but must admit that it is not recognized under principles of public international law in spite of their fondest wishes. For example, Edward Sadtler must use qualifying language such as "International law *potentially* secures a right to same-sex marriage,"[21] or "same-sex marriage *may* develop as an international human right in the new millennium,"[22] or "the [ICCPR] does not explicitly recognize a right to same-sex marriage. In fact, no major human rights instrument explicitly addresses same-sex marriage, or even the rights of gays and lesbians generally."[23] While attempting to construct a theory that a reading of "sexual orientation," "sex," "or other status" would provide a foundation for arguing the case for international law's recognition of same-sex marriages, this author is forced to concede that "the argument is far from an unassailable principle of international law."[24] If it is not an "unassailable principle," it would be impossible to argue that it is a universal right protected by the UDHR or the ICCPR. Professor Wilets has argued that "[i]t is, unfortunately, highly unlikely that a court would interpret the criminalization of same-gender private sexual behavior, or other discrimination against sexual minorities, to be a violation of customary international human rights law. However, the eventual development of such a binding customary norm should not be ruled out."[25] He concedes that "international law has made almost no progress in following the example of those countries which have recognized some form of same-sex family rights, marriages or partnerships, although there are hopeful trends in this direction."[26] The Office of the United Nations High Commissioner for Human Rights and the Joint United Nations Programme on HIV/AIDS in their 1998 report "HIV/AIDS and Human Rights—International Guidelines" also admitted similar shortcomings when they stated, "Anti-discrimination and protective laws *should* be enacted to reduce human rights violations against men having sex with men. . . . These measures should include providing penalties for vilification of people who engage in same-sex relationships, giving legal recognition to same-sex marriages.[27] But relying on "rights" in international law does not mean that the UDHR and relevant international legal instruments, specifically the two 1966 covenants identified earlier, establish a right to have same-sex marriages recognized under the law of nations.

The UDHR establishes the foundation for two principal legal texts, the ICCPR and the ICESCR. All three texts address the subject of marriage and the family. In several important ways, these two subjects are inextricably linked. Upon completion of a careful analysis of the relevant texts of these three documents, it becomes unequivocal that a marriage is a union of one man and one woman for purposes that advance personal as well as public or state goals. The personal goals focus on the complementarity of the two sexes of male and female and their natural fulfillment in one another. This fulfillment does not occur when one person seeks satisfaction with either another person of the same sex or with a nonhuman sentient being. The public and social/state goals emerge from the personal and concern the need for the propagation of the human race from monogamous, lifelong commitments of a man and a woman. Elaboration of these two points—the unitive and the procreative—will follow.

The love between a man and a woman is fulfilled when they make a life commitment to each other. It is a love recognized and regulated by the state. Not only can the state preclude same-sex unions, it can and does preclude certain opposite-sex marriages because of specified impediments. These may include the degree of relation between the intended spouses (e.g., parents attempting to marry their children, or a brother attempting to marry a sister), age limitations, and medical reasons that concern the spread of communicable diseases that threaten personal and public health. The personal relationship of the man and the woman that is consummated in marriage leads to the establishing of a family that includes children who are the fruit of this complementary union that is vital to sustaining the human race. The husband and the wife become parents who have the principal responsibility of educating their children so that they, too, may become responsible members of society. The union of the man and the woman in matrimony evidences the complementary nature of their differences that attract one to the other. Neither a man nor a woman can naturally produce offspring by oneself—or, for that matter, with another member of the same sex or with an animal. It is through the complementary union of two members of the opposite biological sexes that a new generation of human beings comes into existence. This is the product of the natural relationship between the male and the female that naturally exists throughout all organic life. In essence, it is the nature of the complementarity of the two sexes that ensures the continuation of each organic species, including human beings. This is where the interests of society and the state intersect the interests of the man and the woman who are united in marriage. There is a further mutual interest to be considered in the debate on same-sex marriage in international law. As the husband and wife and the family they rear are protected by society and the state, so are the interests of society and the state protected by the husband, the wife, and the family they create from their complementary union.

The continuation of the human species is of vital concern to society and the state. Both need future generations to ensure that human civilization continues. Moreover, both the society and the state are assisted by the husband/father and wife/mother through the parental education of children. The society's and the state's respective responsibilities to educate children are built on the education given to children by their parents. The education of children by society or the state is not a substitute for the education provided by parents; rather, it is a correlative to the principal educational duty that belongs to parents and other members of families.

While human beings may love many things, including one another, these loving relationships are not the same as the loving relationship that is at the core of a marriage between a man and a woman. A person may love siblings, parents, other relatives, and friends. Such loving relationships are between members of the same sex and of the opposite sex as well. However, they are not constitutive of a marriage. Moreover, a person may love a thing—food, clothing, books, artwork, geological phenomena—or another living entity not a human, such as dogs, cats, whales, trees, and so on. But none of these loves for something else is marriage. Even if a person attempts to engage these things or living beings sexually, the procreation of the human species will not follow. That is no different than when one man engages another man sexually; moreover, the same is true when one woman engages another sexually. The result is the same: there may be a sense of pleasure and sexual gratification and intimate exchange evidencing affection for the other, but there is no possibility that such an encounter will produce another member of the human race. That is the principle of marriage shared by the personal and the social/state interests that have just been identified.

But what does international law have to say about the possibility of same-sex marriage? The answer follows.

## SAME SEX "MARRIAGES" ARE NOT RECOGNIZED OR PROTECTED UNDER INTERNATIONAL LAW

This part of the investigation must begin with the relevant provisions of the UDHR. Article 16.1 of the UDHR states, "Men and women of full age, without any limitation due to race, nationality or religion, have the right to marry and found a family. They are entitled to equal rights as to marriage, during marriage and at its dissolution." Article 16.3 addresses the issue of the family as introduced in article 16.1 and states that it "is the natural and fundamental group unit of society and is entitled to protection by society and the State." Professor Mary Ann Glendon has stated, "Article 16 . . . is a blend of old and new ideas with varying genealogies. It went far beyond most national legislation of the day with its affirmation of the principle of equal rights between the spouses both during marriage and at its dissolution. The idea that the family 'is entitled to protection by society and the state,' on the other hand, was familiar in many countries as legislative policy, had already appeared in several constitutions, and would shortly appear in many others."[28]

While article 16 on its face does not explicitly state that it is the union of a man and a woman that forms the marriage and founds a family, this is implied. Article 16 was drafted long before homosexual unions as marriages were discussed in the context of human rights law. The 1948 UDHR reflected the tradition of male-female marriages that can be traced back to ancient customs and norms such as those reflected in the Jewish natural law, the Noahide.[29] The Noahide is generally considered to include seven principles applicable to all people. The one pertinent here is this: Thou shall not engage in bestiality or incestuous, adulterous, or homosexual relations nor commit the act of rape. In addition, the in vitro procedures or surrogate parenthood that might allow a homosexual couple to "have" a child had not yet been discovered. Consequently, there could only be one way of founding a family under article 16, and that is through the union of a man and a woman who come together in marriage. Marriage may be considered many things, but for purposes of international law it is the complement of the personal and social/state purposes just identified in the previous section. The desire or attraction of two persons of the same sex (regardless of whether either or both are "transgendered") cannot fulfill the personal and social/state goals of marriage that have been previously identified and discussed.

Article 23.2 of the 1966 ICCPR makes this point by stating, "The right of men and women of marriageable age to marry and to found a family shall be recognized." The first subparagraph of this same article reiterates the protection to be accorded the family by stating, "The family is the natural and fundamental group unit of society and is entitled to protection by society and the State." Article 10.1 of the 1966 ICESCR reiterates these points in somewhat different language by stating in pertinent part, "The widest possible protection and assistance should be accorded to the family, which is the natural and fundamental group unit of society. . . . Marriage must be entered into with the free consent of the intending spouses."

Advocates of same-sex marriages might suggest that such a construction of these provisions is unlawful on two grounds. The first would be on the grounds of discrimination; the second would be based on their failure to provide or promote equal protection. But, as has been noted earlier, not all discrimination in the context of being prohibited from marriage is unlawful. Moreover, same-sex-union or marriage advocates have conceded that no international tribunal has "found that sexual orientation discrimination is a form of sex discrimination, let alone identified a right to same-sex marriage."[30] Lawful discrimination exists, as was pointed out in the previous section, on the basis of degree of relation, age considerations, and concerns about public and private health. Moreover, such discrimination does not violate any sense of equal protection under international law. An illustration of this last point is that article 4.2 of the ICCPR does not permit derogation of certain rights in times of public emergency involving the right to life (article 6); the right to be free from torture or cruel, inhuman, or degrading treatment or punishment (Article 7); the right not to be enslaved or subjected to certain kinds of servitude (articles 8.1 and 8.2); freedom from imprisonment for debt (article 11); freedom from prosecution under ex post facto laws (article 15); the right to be recognized as a person before the law (article 16); and the right to freedom of thought, conscience, and religion (article 18). Since religion fits into the category of nonderogable rights, it logically follows that forcing a religious community to accept same-sex marriages against its beliefs would constitute a violation of international human rights law. The imposition of same-sex marriages on religious communities would be a violation of the non-derogation clause of article 4.2 [article 18—religion]. However, it would appear permissible that other rights may be derogated under such circumstances as identified in article 4.1. Consequently, such a hierarchy of rights in the context of those that are derogable and those that are not would support the conclusion that there exists a lawful inequality among them.

Another important point made by advocates for the recognition of same-sex marriages under international law is that there can be no discrimination against people on the basis of "other status" as mentioned in article 2.1 and article 26 of the ICCPR and article 2 of the UDHR.[31] First of all, this phrase "other status" applies to individual persons, not to associations or groups of persons—such as same-sex couples. Consequently, while states may not discriminate against an individual solely on the basis that he or she is homosexual, there is no prohibition against the state prohibiting or regulating conduct or actions that emerge from this status. Therefore, the state may regulate homosexual conduct by prohibiting same-sex marriages.

Second, a proper construction must be given to this phrase "other status" that appears in the UDHR and the ICCPR. This phrase appears in the context of restraints upon states to preclude them from taking or making distinctions among individuals. Various qualities are then listed in each of the three cases. However, this does not mean that states are prohibited from making any distinction. If they were, they could not incarcerate people for committing crimes; they could not license individuals to drive cars, to be electricians, to perform brain surgery, or to practice law. Distinctions and discriminations are a part of life, and many are lawful. What is prohibited by the common language of the UDHR and the ICCPR is discrimination or distinction that is based on the person's race, color, sex (not sexual orientation, as some advocates for same-sex marriages argue), language, religion, political or other opinion, national or social origin, property, or birth. Otherwise, this would prohibit states from censuring individuals who engage in destructive, sometimes antisocial behavior. One illustration would be rapists who engage in violent and nonconsensual sex. Each of these lists of prohibitions from the two documents concludes with the phrase "or other status." However, as just mentioned, this cannot mean all possible other statuses because virtually any human characteristic, including those that can and must be regulated (being a rapist or being a homicidal maniac) would otherwise be protected by the UDHR and the ICCPR. To argue an expansive meaning of "other status," as advocates for same-sex marriage assert, would court aberration.

Consequently, this problematic phrase "other status" must be properly construed under accepted rubrics of legal construction or interpretation. One rubric that provides immense assistance is the canon of construction, *ejusdem generis*. The essence of this canon is that when a general word or phrase follows a list of specific persons or things, the general word or phrase will be interpreted to include only persons or things of the same type as those listed. The example used in *Black's Law Dictionary* (1999) to illustrate this canon is the phrase "horses, cattle, sheep, pigs, goats, or any other barnyard animal." The general language "or any other barnyard animal," despite its seeming breadth, would probably be held to include only four-legged, hoofed mammals (and thus would exclude chickens, geese, and ducks). This prudent rubric for legal interpretation would provide for restrictive rather than expansive definition of "other status." Otherwise, "other status" would include anything, including the worst antisocial behavior that would be criminal in any recognized legal system, municipal or international. For the phrase "or other status" to make sense, it must be read coherently with all the provisions, as well as their underlying intent and purposes, for the human rights regime to make sense and to be enforceable.

## CONCLUSION

Today the world of international human rights law is at a crossroads. On the one hand, there is the perspective that after so much struggle, all members of the human family—after generations of being oppressed by despots, oligarchs, and ruling classes—can now make their rightful claim to self-determination, the root of human rights. On the other hand, there are new oligarchs, new ruling elites who, under the guise of "human rights," are prepared to impose regimes that erode and neutralize the exercise of self-determination that says "no" to the movement to recognize same-sex marriage with the attending benefits traditionally given to opposite-sex marriages.[32]

The future of the human race is inextricably related to how individuals-in-community plan their future and the future of succeeding generations not yet born for the common good of the human race when they exercise their right of self-determination through democratic political institutions. For it is the common good of humanity, not the self-indulgent desires of isolated individuals, that will determine the successes of our race to sustain itself and develop in accord with our human nature. If we are to be satisfied that this current generation can determine for eternity how the rest of the race is to live and develop, why is it not just as true that a past or future generation can tell us with equal impunity that those of our time were wrong in the direction we took to plan for the future of the race?

It is the community of individuals fortified by the exercise of self-determination that guarantees that human rights—rights identified in and protected by the ICCPR and the ICESCR—flourish. They flourish because it is all members of the community who decide what the future should hold, not just some. It is these more traditional views that are at the heart of human rights and universally enforceable. While these traditional views seem to be secure for the time being, vigilance in the protection of universal human rights is essential, for, as this chapter should demonstrate, the advocates for same-sex marriages have been, are, and will likely continue to be busy.

Wise counsel might be derived from Alexander Pope, who once wrote:

> Vice is a monster of so frightful mien,
> As to be hated needs but to be seen;
> Yet seen too oft, familiar with her face,
> We first endure, then pity, then embrace.[33]

As the members of the Ramsey Colloquium noted in its 1994 commentary to Pope's verse:

To endure (tolerance), to pity (compassion), to embrace (affirmation): that is the sequence of change in attitude and judgment that has been advanced by the gay and lesbian movement with notable success. We expect that this success will encounter certain limits and that what is truly natural will reassert itself, but this may not happen before more damage is done to innumerable individuals and to our common life.[34]

Advocates of same-sex marriage first asked for tolerance of themselves as homosexuals who were entitled to privacy. When this privacy was recognized and protected, they sought the pity of legal institutions for being discriminated against when they entered the public sphere. When the discrimination was declared unlawful and they were favored with the compassion of the courts and legislatures, they demanded endorsement by legal recognition of their sexual practices as being the same as those of traditional, married couples consisting of one man and one woman. But this attempt at affirmation and legal acceptance to be the same as marriage is an absurdity, and the law of nations will have none of that—in the future or for the time being.

## NOTES

1. James D. Wilets, *International Human Rights Law and Sexual Orientation*, 18 HASTINGS INT'L & COMP. L. REV. 1, 4: 5 (1994) (citations omitted).

2. WILLIAM N. ESKRIDGE, THE CASE FOR SAME-SEX MARRIAGE, 65–66 (1996) (citations omitted).

3. *See, e.g.*, Symposium on the Future of International Human Rights, *The Mid-Life Crisis of the Universal Declaration of Human Rights*, 55 WASH. & LEE L. REV. 661 (1998).

4. *See* JOHANNES MORSINK, THE UNIVERSAL DECLARATION OF HUMAN RIGHTS: ORIGINS, DRAFTING, AND INTENT 325 (1999).

5. Mary Ann Glendon, *Knowing the Universal Declaration of Human Rights*, 73 NOTRE DAME L. REV. 1153 (1998).

6. *See, e.g.*, Oscar Schacter, *Human Dignity as a Normative Concept*, 77 AM. J. INT'L L. 848, 850 (1983); *see also* Michael Perry, THE IDEA OF HUMAN RIGHTS: FOUR INQUIRIES (1998).

7. *See* Wilets, *International Human Rights Law, supra* note 1, at 91–100. *See also* Edward H. Sadtler, *A Right to Same-Sex Marriage Under International Law: Can It Be Vindicated in the United States?* 40 VA. J. INT'L L. 405, 412–416 (1999).

8. Ian Brownlie, BASIC DOCUMENTS ON HUMAN RIGHTS 113 (3d ed. 1992); *see also* Ian Brownlie, PRINCIPLES OF PUBLIC INTERNATIONAL LAW 574–575 (5th ed. 1998).

9. *See* Theodor Meron, *On a Hierarchy of International Human Rights*, 80 AM. J. INT'L L. 1, 22 (1986), for an explanation of "basic" and "fundamental" human rights.

10. 9 Eur. H.R. Rep. 56, Par. 49 (1987).

11. *See, e.g.*, Wilets, *International Human Rights Law, supra* note 1, at 19, 91, 92, 93, 106; Sadtler, *A Right to Same-Sex Marriage Under International Law, supra* note 7, at 407–408, 418, 425.

12. *See, e.g.*, GA Res. 41/128 of 4 December 1986, Declaration on the Right to Development. *See also* Principle VIII of the Final Act of the Helsinki Conference.

13. William N. Eskridge, *Equality Practice: Liberal Reflections on the Jurisprudence of Civil Unions*, 64 ALB. L. REV. 853, 881 (2001).

14. *Id.* (emphasis added).

15. *Id.* at 863.

16. *See* Mary Becker, *Family Law in the Secular State and Restrictions on Same-Sex Marriage: Two Are Better than One*, 2001 U. ILL. L. REV. 1, 8 (2001).

17. Sheila Rose Foster, *The Symbolism of Rights and the Costs of Symbolism: Some Thoughts on the Campaign for Same-Sex Marriage*, 7 TEMP. POL. & CIV. RTS. L. REV. 319 (1998).

18. *Id.* at 326–327.

19. *Id.* at 327–328.

20. Vincent Samar, *Gay Rights as a Particular Instantiation of Human Rights*, 64 ALB. L. REV. 983, 993 (2001) (emphasis added).

21. *See, e.g.*, Sadtler, *A Right to Same-Sex Marriage Under International Law, supra* note 7, at 408 (emphasis added).

22. *Id.* at 408.

23. *Id.* at 418.

24. *Id.* at 425.

25. Wilets, *International Human Rights Law, supra* note 1, at 19.

26. *Id.* at 91.

27. HIV/AIDS and Human Rights—International Guidelines, HR/PUB/98/1, at 21 (emphasis added).

28. MARY ANN GLENDON, A WORLD MADE NEW: ELEANOR ROOSEVELT AND THE UNIVERSAL DECLARATION OF HUMAN RIGHTS 182 (2001).

29. For an instructive introduction to the Noahide, *see* David Novak, *Judaism and Natural Law*, 43 AM. J. JURIS. 117, 132–133 (1998).

30. Sadtler, *A Right to Same-Sex Marriage Under International Law, supra* note 7, at 429.

31. *See, e.g.*, Wilets, *International Human Rights Law, supra* note 1, at 50–52; and Sadtler, *A Right to Same-Sex Marriage Under International Law, supra* note 7, at 418, 427–428.

32. *See* Further Promotion and Encouragement of Human Rights and Fundamental Freedoms, Including the Question of the Programme and Methods of Work of the Commission, Replies Received from Governments, Commission on Human Rights, E/CN.4/1996/45/Add.1, Mar. 18, 1996, wherein Mexico reminded the membership of the United Nations that "any unilateral coercive measure is contrary to international law and in violation of the San Francisco [United Nations] Charter. Accordingly, the Government of Mexico . . . considers any such action reprehensible."

33. ALEXANDER POPE, AN ESSAY ON MAN IN FOUR EPISTLES: EPISTLE 2, V. (London: 1733–34).

34. *The Homosexual Movement, A Response by the Ramsey Colloquium*, FIRST THINGS, Mar. 1994, at 21.

# Response

# *Reply to Father Robert John Araujo's "Marriage, Relationship, and International Law: The Incoherence of the Argument for Same-Sex Marriage"*

## James D. Wilets

Father Araujo's essay fails to provide a coherent argument against same-sex marriage, except for those readers who are already imbued with a deep animus toward sexual minorities.[1] More problematically, his essay does little to address the concerns of the great majority of individuals in Western democracies who theoretically accept the right of sexual minorities to basic civil rights, but are reluctant to extend these rights to marriage. His argument relies on a dismissal of nonprocreative marriage that is likely to find little resonance among the great majority of the world's population that looks to marriage (or at least long-term relationships) as a central emotional and spiritual focus of their lives. Finally, his essay misstates the current status of international law on the subject and the role of human rights law in protecting the rights of the individual.

Father Araujo arrives at his conclusion that the legal argument for same-sex marriage is "incoherent" through reliance on two assumptions, both of which are at odds with an increasing body of national and international law. The first assumption is that gays and lesbians are not deserving of equal treatment of the law. The second assumption is that the denial of the right to marry is not an abridgment of the right to equal protection.

The U.S. Supreme Court in *Romer v. Evans* effectively addressed the first assumption when it ruled that simple animus against sexual minorities, unsubstantiated by empirical harm to society, does not constitute a legitimate state interest in discriminating against them.[2] The European Court of Human Rights went even further, ruling that the prohibition against discrimination contained in the European Convention on Human Rights and Fundamental Freedoms, when read together with the Convention's respect for family life, required that a gay man be awarded custody over the objections of the child's mother.[3] Father Araujo's position is quite clear that gay people, or at least their relationships, pose a real danger of "damage to innumerable individuals and to our common life."[4] The problem with this assumption is that it does nothing to address the concerns of many people who do not believe that gays and lesbians pose a danger to society, but who are still reluctant to go so far as to embrace state recognition of same-sex unions. In other words, Father Araujo's essay cannot explain or defend his second assumption: why a group that most people in the industrialized world, at least theoretically, believe is entitled to equal protection should be denied the right to the legal and financial benefits of state-recognized same-sex relationships.

With respect to this second assumption, Father Araujo argues that same-sex relationships are different from heterosexual relationships because of their nonprocreative nature. He compares adult same-sex relationships to relationships "with animals, and . . . with inanimate objects"[5] and with "the love between a parent and his or her children, the love between siblings, and the love between friends or distant relatives,"[6] and asks why same-sex relationships are more entitled to legal recognition than these other "nonprocreative" relationships. Putting aside the obvious point that nonprocreative heterosexual marriages are in fact legal, which alone renders a good portion of his essay moot, his analogies are too far removed from the reality of long-term adult intimate relationships to provide a coherent legal reason for not applying equal protection to these relationships. Even most people who are skeptical of the rights of sexual minorities can recognize the difference between a same-sex adult relationship and relationships with animals, siblings, and inanimate objects.

The author decries gay and lesbian individuals as "self-indulgent" individuals, presumably for insisting on the right to love another human being.[7] Yet this position that the claim for recognition of long-term adult relationships is "self-indulgent" is one that can only make sense in the context of conservative Catholic theology. Clearly the Catholic Church believes that its clergy is entitled to all other rights pertaining to the human race, but unlike most other religions, denies the basic right of loving another adult to its own hierarchy.

Professor Araujo attempts to defend his conclusion by resorting to an analysis of human rights that is completely outside any mainstream view of international human rights law. This analysis is also inaccurate on at least two counts.

First, he argues that international law provides "no prohibition against the state prohibiting or regulating conduct or actions that emerge from th[e] status [of sexual orientation]. Therefore, the state may regulate homosexual conduct by prohibiting same-sex marriages."[8] The author ignores the decisions by the United Nations International Human Rights Committee prohibiting criminalization of same-sex intimate relations under the equal protection clause of the International Covenant on Civil and Political Rights (ICCPR).[9] He has also ignored the numerous decisions by the European Court of Human Rights that have repeatedly struck down sodomy laws as a violation of human rights.[10]

Second, the author makes the breathtaking argument that "prohibitions against same-sex marriages are exercises in the protection of international human rights recognized by the UDHR and protected under [the ICCPR]." The author appears to be arguing that the human right being protected by banning same-sex marriage is that of "exercise . . . of sovereignty" and "self-determination."[11] The view of the author is not only completely inconsistent with the underpinnings of human rights law as a check on abuses committed by "sovereign" nations, it also runs counter to the decisions of the primary body charged with interpreting the ICCPR, the world's foremost human rights treaty. The author's view is also inconsistent with the decisions of the European Court of Human Rights and the European Parliament and the decisions of numerous national courts and legislatures.[12] Father Araujo thus seems to be suggesting that the actions of the European Parliament and the European Court of Human Rights recognizing same-sex relationships are violative of the sovereignty of European countries or Europe as a whole. Such an argument is nonsensical. It is also quite disingenuous, since it was the pope himself who attacked the sovereign, democratic decisions by the European Parliament and national parliaments regarding same-sex relationships, not gay groups, representing one of the rare times that the pontiff has attacked a political body directly.[13] It would appear presumptuous for a law professor to label the argument for legal recognition of same-sex relationships "an absurdity" when international and national courts and legislatures in Canada, the United States, Europe, and elsewhere have recognized those relationships. These sovereign and legal entities have recognized the logical and "coherent" connection between the equal rights of gay and lesbian citizens and their right to enjoy the birthright of all people: an intimate, long-term relationship with another human being.

The most effective response to Father Araujo's thesis that the argument for same-sex marriage is "incoherent" comes from his own response to my essay. Father Araujo bases his argument that gays and lesbians do not suffer from discrimination on the inapposite observation that

[w]hile neither may wish to do so, a gay man would be entitled to marry a woman and a lesbian would be entitled to marry a man. They would not be denied equal treatment of the law since they would be treated like anyone else regardless of the person's sexual orientation. . . . Thus the gay or lesbian would be treated just like any heterosexual man or woman who might wish to marry a person of the same sex. . . . The legal prohibition does not discriminate against the person who is homosexual or heterosexual. . . . Therefore, Professor Wilets's suggested claim that gays and lesbians are denied equal treatment of the law dissolves.[14]

If this is the basis for Father Araujo's argument that the equal protection argument for legal recognition of same-sex relationships "dissolves[,]" then it appears that the argument for same-sex marriage remains quite solid indeed.

Father Araujo then undercuts his equal protection argument by noting that there are many circumstances in which the law sanctions discrimination against differently situated individuals such as those based on age, physical characteristics, and so on. This obvious point is a basic assumption in equal protection analysis and simply points out its circularity: individuals have to be deemed similarly situated in order to receive equal protection under the law. The two assumptions contained in my chapter address this circularity by providing that the denial of the right to marriage is a violation of equal protection if one believes that gays and lesbians are fundamentally similarly situated to heterosexuals. Father Araujo has made it very clear in his chapter that he believes that gays and lesbians pose a danger to society and are thus certainly not similarly situated to other individuals. If one believes this, then it makes perfect sense to discriminate against gays and lesbians, including withholding the right to marry. His argument, however, provides no coherent anti-same-sex-marriage argument for those individuals who do not share his views. What makes his argument rather unique among anti-same-sex-marriage advocates, however, is his view of nonprocreative marriage itself as not a fundamental right. This view of marriage may be consistent with conservative Catholic theology, but it renders his argument all the more marginal in the debate over legal recognition of same-sex marriage.

In the context of international law, Father Araujo has argued that international law does not prohibit criminalizing homosexual "actions" (as opposed to status), and that international law does not prohibit discrimination against gays and lesbians. I have demonstrated earlier in this response that both assertions are simply inaccurate.

As for his response to the discussion of international and comparative law contained in my chapter, Father Araujo has been far too generous in his evaluation of what I have attempted to accomplish. I have never attempted to argue that international law currently recognizes gay marriage as a fundamental human right of universal application. My chapter's title and central thesis is simply that there is an inexorable momentum toward recognition of same-sex relationships in foreign and international law.

The European Court of Human Rights and the courts of South Africa, Canada, Vermont, Hawaii, and numerous European countries, among others, have applied equal protection principles to same-sex relationships in a variety of contexts. The European Parliament has also called upon the member nations of the European Union to extend many of the benefits of marriage to same-sex couples, and numerous European parliaments have done precisely that. It is quite a stretch for Father Araujo to label the reasoning of these esteemed legal bodies "incoherent" and to compare the legal legitimacy of the decisions of these esteemed courts and the positive law of the European Union to the Taliban and Nazi Germany. In fact, the momentum of national and international law toward recognition of same-sex marriage is not only a reality, it is firmly rooted in the logic and consistency of equal protection and the requisites for human dignity.

## NOTES

1. Robert Araujo, *Marriage, Relationship and International Law: The Incoherence of the Argument for Same-Sex Marriage, supra* at 367.

2. *See Romer v. Evans*, 517 U.S. 620, 116 S.Ct. 1620, 134 L.Ed. 2d 855 (1996).

3. *Salgueiro da Silva Mouta v. Portugal*, App. No. 33290/96, *available at* http://www.echr.coe.int./Eng/Judgments.htm. *See generally* Bernard Oxman and Laurence Helfer, International Decisions, 95 AM. J. INT'L L. 422 (2001).

4. *See* Araujo, *supra* note 1, at n. 34, citing FIRST THINGS, Mar. 1994, at 15–21.

5. *See* Araujo, *supra* note 1, at 2.

6. *Id.*

7. *See* Araujo, *supra* note 1, at 14.

8. *See* Araujo, *supra* note 1, at 12.

9. *See Nicholas Toonen v. Australia*, Case No. 488/1992, U.N. Hum. Rts. Comm., 15th Sess., U.N. Doc. CCPR/c/50/D/488/1992 (4 Apr. 1994).

10. *See, e.g., Modinos v. Cyprus*, 16 Eur. H.R. Rep. 485 (1993); *Norris v. Ireland*, 13 Eur. Ct. H.R. 186 (1991).

11. Araujo, *supra* note 1, at 4.

12. *See generally* Wilets, *The Inexorable Momentum Toward National and International Recognition of Same-Sex Relationships: An International, Comparative, Historical, and Cross-Cultural Perspective, supra*, at 349.

13. For example, on February 20, 1994, Pope John Paul II attacked the European Parliament for its earlier call for legal recognition of same-sex relationships. Alan Cowell, *Pope Deplores Gay Marriage*, N.Y. Times, Feb. 22, 1994, at A2. *See also Resolution Riles Pontiff*, ADVOCATE, Apr. 5, 1994, at 18.

14. Father Robert Araujo, *A Response to Professor Wilets's Essay*, at 2.

# Index of Cases

# Index

# About the Editors and Contributors

ROBERT JOHN ARAUJO, S.J., is Professor of Law at Gonzaga University in Spokane, Washington, where he teaches contracts, constitutional law, international law, and international organizations. Most of his publications explore the application of natural-law theory to public law issues. He is a legal advisor to the Holy See and regularly participates in meetings of the Sixth (Legal) Committee at the United Nations.

CARLOS A. BALL is Professor of Law at the University of Illinois. His book *The Morality of Gay Rights: An Exploration in Political Philosophy* was published in 2002. His articles have appeared in *Cornell Law Review, Georgetown Law Journal, Law and Social Inquiry, North Carolina Law Review,* and *UCLA Law Review,* among other journals.

PATRICK J. BORCHERS is Dean and Professor of Law at Creighton University. He is the coauthor of a leading U.S. treatise on the conflict of laws and the most widely adopted textbook on the same subject. His writings have appeared in *Texas Law Review, Wisconsin Law Journal, U.C. Davis Law Review, Creighton Law Review,* and many other law reviews.

TERESA STANTON COLLETT is a Professor of Law at South Texas College of Law in Houston, Texas, where she teaches professional responsibility, property, and constitutional law. She is a member of the American Law Institute and a widely published author on the topics of marriage, abortion, and professional responsibility.

DAVID ORGON COOLIDGE was Director of the Marriage Law Project at the Columbus School of Law, Catholic University of America, and also was affiliated with the Ethics and Public Policy Center in Washington, D.C., until his death in 2002, shortly before this manuscript was completed. He was coeditor and contributor to *Revitalizing the Institution of Marriage in the Twenty-First Century* (Praeger, 2001) and a contributor to Christopher Wolfe (ed.), *Homosexuality and American Public Life* (1999), and his law review articles on the leading same-sex cases in Hawaii, Alaska, Oregon, and Vermont and on "defense-of-marriage"-type state statutes were published in many journals. He was a graduate of the Georgetown Law School, Howard Divinity School, and Smith College.

BARBARA J. COX is a Professor of Law at California Western School of Law. A past chair of the Association of American Law Schools Section on Gay and Lesbian Issues, she has published extensively about sexual orientation and women's legal issues, including same-sex marriage issues.

DAVID B. CRUZ teaches constitutional law, federal courts, and law and identity at the University of Southern California Law School. A former federal appellate clerk and attorney in the Office of the Solicitor General of the United States, he has published numerous articles on sexual-orientation-related legal issues.

RICHARD F. DUNCAN is the Sherman S. Welpton, Jr., Professor of Law at the University of Nebraska College of Law. He is the author of numerous books and articles on religious liberty, same-sex marriage, and other constitutional issues.

WILLIAM C. DUNCAN is the former Acting Director of the Marriage Law Project at the Columbus School of Law, Catholic University of America. He is a graduate of the J. Reuben Clark Law School at BYU, and has published in legal journals and in other publications about same-sex marriage and domestic partnership and has testified before state legislative bodies concerning related issues.

WILLIAM N. ESKRIDGE, JR., is the John A. Garver Professor of Jurisprudence at Yale Law School. He has published extensively in the areas of constitutional law, legislation, and same-sex marriage. One of his recent publications is *Equality Practice: Civil Unions and the Future of Gay Rights* (2001).

MAGGIE GALLAGHER is a fellow at the Ethics and Public Policy Center, a nationally syndicated columnist, and one of the leading voices of the new marriage movement. She is the author (with Linda J. Waite) of *The Case for Marriage: Why Married People Are Happier, Healthier, and Better Off Financially* (2000) and *The Abolition of Marriage: How We Destroy Lasting Love* (1996). She was the principal drafter of *The Marriage Movement: A Statement of Principles* signed by more than 100 scholars and civic leaders from across the political spectrum (available at www.marriagemovement.org).

ROBERT P. GEORGE is McCormick Professor of Jurisprudence and Director of the James Madison Program in American Ideals and Institutions at Princeton University. He has served as a presidential appointee to the U.S. Commission on Civil Rights and a judicial fellow at the Supreme Court of the United States. He is the author of *In Defense of Natural Law* (2001).

GREG JOHNSON teaches dispute resolution, appellate advocacy, and sexual orientation and the law at Vermont Law School. He has written popular and scholarly articles on same-sex marriage and civil unions. He was co-counsel on *Brause v. Bureau of Vital Statistics*, Alaska's same-sex-marriage case. He is a graduate of Cornell University and Notre Dame Law School.

LYNNE MARIE KOHM is currently John Brown McCarty Professor of Family Law at Regent University School of Law and has published on family law, marriage, women's issues, marital oneness, reproductive issues, abortion, euthanasia, and children. She serves on the Virginia State Bar Family Law Section Board of Governors and was appointed to the Governor's Advisory Board on Child Abuse and Neglect for Virginia. She serves the Alliance Defense Fund and its National Litigation Academy on family law issues and has practiced law.

ANDREW KOPPELMAN is the George C. Dix Professor of Constitutional Law and an Associate Professor of Law and Political Science at Northwestern University. He has published extensively about equality and moral issues. His books include *The Gay Rights Question in Contemporary American Law* (2002) and *Antidiscrimination Law and Social Equality* (1996).

ARTHUR S. LEONARD, a professor at New York Law School, is a graduate of Cornell University and Harvard Law School. He produces the monthly newsletter *Lesbian/Gay Law Notes*, has written numerous articles and book chapters on gay law and AIDS law, and is a trustee of the Jewish Board of Family and Children's Services of New York.

STEPHEN MACEDO is Laurance S. Rockefeller Professor of Politics and the University Center for Human Values, and Director of the University Center for Human Values at Princeton University. He is the author of *Diversity and Distrust: Civic Education in a Multicultural Democracy* (2000); *Liberal Virtues: Citizenship, Virtue, and Community in Liberal Constitutionalism* (1990); and *The New Right v. the Constitution* (1987), as well as numerous scholarly articles and book chapters, and the editor of several volumes and several scholarly journals.

MARK STRASSER is the Trustees Professor of Law at Capital University Law School in Columbus, Ohio. He has written dozens of articles about issues in family law, constitutional law, and federalism. His two most recent books are *Legally Wed: Same-Sex Marriage and the Constitution* (1997) and *The Challenge of Same-Sex Marriage: Federalist Principles and Constitutional Protections* (1999). He is currently writing a book about civil unions, the marriagelike status for same-sex couples that was recently recognized in Vermont.

LYNN D. WARDLE is a Professor of Law at Brigham Young University's
J. Reuben Clark Law School. Most of his research and writing relates to
family law and biomedical ethics and law, including many articles and chapters about same-sex marriage and gay/lesbian adoptions. He is coauthor
(with Laurence C. Nolan) of *Fundamental Principles of Family Law* (2002),
and principal editor of a four-volume treatise, *Contemporary Family Law:
Principles, Policy, and Practices* (1988). He served as President of the International Society of Family Law (2000–2002).

JAMES D. WILETS is an Associate Professor of Law at Nova Southeastern
University and is Executive Director of the Inter-American Center for Human Rights. He has worked as an attorney for the International Human
Rights Law Group in Romania and as a representative of the National Democratic Institution in Liberia. He prepared, at the request of the United
Nations secretary-general, the first two drafts of a proposal for reforming
the human rights functions of the United Nations and assisted with drafting
a proposed basic law for a future Palestinian state. He writes extensively on
international and comparative law, with a particular focus on human rights.
His most recent article is titled "The Demise of the Nation-State: Towards
a New Theory of the State Under International Law," published in the
*Berkeley Journal of International Law.*

RICHARD G. WILKINS is a Professor of Law at the J. Reuben Clark Law
School and Managing Director of the World Family Policy Center at
Brigham Young University, Provo, Utah. He has written numerous articles
on constitutional issues and conducts an annual survey of Supreme Court
voting trends published by the *Hastings Constitutional Law Quarterly*. He
is a former assistant to the solicitor general, U.S. Department of Justice.

JOHN WITTE, JR., is the Jonas Robitscher Professor of Law and Ethics,
Director of the Law and Religion Program, and Director of the Center for
the Interdisciplinary Study of Religion at Emory University in Atlanta. A
specialist in legal history and religious liberty, he has published 100 professional articles and 12 books, including *From Sacrament to Contract: Marriage, Religion, and Law in the Western Tradition* (1997); *Proselytism and
Orthodoxy in Russia* (1999); *Religion and the American Constitutional Experiment* (2000); and *Law and Protestantism: The Legal Teachings of the
Lutheran Reformation* (2002).

EVAN WOLFSON, formerly the marriage project director for Lambda Legal Defense and Education Fund and cocounsel in the historic Hawaii marriage case *Baehr v. Anderson*, has been awarded a grant to launch a new
project to win the freedom to marry. Citing his national leadership on marriage and his appearance before the U.S. Supreme Court in *Boy Scouts of
America v. Dale*, the *National Law Journal* named Wolfson one of the 100
most influential lawyers in America.